Realityland

Realityland
True-Life Adventures at
Walt Disney World

by David Koenig

BONAVENTURE PRESS

Realityland: True-Life Adventures at Walt Disney World by David Koenig

Published by
BONAVENTURE PRESS
Post Office Box 51961
Irvine, CA 92619-1961
USA
www.BonaventurePress.com

Cover art and map art by Chas. Balun

Publisher's Cataloging in Publication Data
Koenig, David G.
    Realityland: True-Life Adventures at Walt Disney World / by David Koenig.
        p. cm.
    Includes annotated references and index.
        1. Walt Disney World (Florida) — History. 2. Amusement Parks (Florida). I. Koenig, David G., 1962- II. Title.

Library of Congress Control Number: 2007903089

ISBN 978-0-964060-52-4 (Hardcover)

Printed in the USA
10   9   8   7   6   5   4   3   2

For Princess Rebecca,
My own white-knuckle, true-life adventure

Use of the Term Disney: Within this text, "Disney" typically refers to the Disney company or its corporate decision-makers. For clarity's sake, members of the Disney family, including Walt Disney, Roy O. Disney, and Roy E. Disney, are referred to by their first name.

Use of the Term EPCOT: Walt Disney's proposed community is referred to as uppercase "EPCOT." The theme park is referred to as "EPCOT Center" (and occasionally, for brevity, simply "EPCOT") until 1994 and as lowercase "Epcot" thereafter.

Contents

acknowledgments

AS anyone who has been waiting for this book since the mid-1990s can deduce, this project's journey from idea to printed page has been a long, arduous one. Fortunately, the Lord Jesus placed just the right people in my life to assist and inspire and browbeat this book to completion.

Above all, I am indebted to my "home team," Laura, Zachary and Rebecca Koenig, who provided support and much-needed distractions. Laura assisted in every way imaginable. The children may have made the process longer at times, but also infinitely more enjoyable, and the final product is better for it. Support was also provided by Anne, Gerald, Joe, Paul and Maryanne Koenig; Larry, Sheryl, Garth and Mimi Hamlin; Michelle and Paul Roden; and my accommodating bosses, Alan Oakes and David Cutler.

I was blessed with not one but two extraordinary editors, Sara and Tom Graves. The superbly talented Chas. Balun created the cover and map art. For research assistance, I thank the staffs of the Orlando Public Library, the History Room of the Anaheim Public Library, the University of Central Florida Special Collections Department, and Sharon Wilcox (*Ultralight Flying*). For securing photographs, I thank Judy Alderman and Nancy Kunzman (*Orlando Sentinel*), Neal Adam Watson and Jody Norman (Florida State Archives), Barry Szulc, Al Lutz (MiceAge.com), and Frank Anzalone (Frank Anzalone Photography).

Most of these fascinating tales come from interviews with 100 present and former cast members who graciously shared with me their time, memories and fragments of their fascinating lives. While researching previous books, I was fortunate enough to have my own Jiminy Cricket as a guide—Van Arsdale France, the founder of the Disneyland University. Van understood why everything at Disney was just the way it was and taught me that people were more important in "making the magic" than contraptions or trinkets. A short ways into this project, Van departed for an even happier kingdom. Fortunately, I latched onto an able replacement, Disneyland Club '55er-turned-Disney World Club '71er Bill Hoelscher, who equally understands the Disney difference. No one has been more helpful—or fun to be around—than Bill. Also readily available for repeat interviews and ongoing consultation were Peter and Donna Clark, John and Valerie (Watson) Curry, Bob Gurr, Stephen Halpin, Gloria and Marvin Jacobs, Tom Nabbe, and Howard Roland.

Others who kindly consented to interviews include Rollie (Mrs. Robert) Allen, Steve Baker, Tony Baxter, Ed Beaver, Peter Bloustein, Chuck Boyajian, Dale Burner, Wayne Busch, Henry "Ray" Carter, Jim Christensen, Frank Cornelius, Spencer Craig, William Cullity, Thor Degelmann, Mike Demopoulos, Tom DeWolf, Clayne Dice, Mark Eades, Tom Elrod, Dorothy Eno, Robert Foster, Herb Gilliard, Tom Hamilton, Jim Haught, Gene Hawk, Dan and Rosemary Healy, Sam and Brenda Holland, Colonel Harvey "Tom" Jones, Wolf Kahn, Keith Kambak, Ted Kellogg, Chris Kraftchick, Frank Kubicki, Mike Lee, John Lehtonen, Krissy Lewis, Arnold Lindberg, Jack Lindquist, Kyle Madorin, Andy Manor, Amy Massenburg, Bob Mathieson, George McGinnis, Arlen Miller, Jim Moore, Richard Morrow, Bill Moss, Mike Munoz, Larry Nunez, Peggy Patrick, Bob Penfield, Larry Pontius, Jerry Pospisil, Harrison "Buzz" Price, Dave Pritchett, Sandy Quinn, Morris Raschy, Cicily Rigdon, Harris Rosen, Jason Rowland, Tyler Schwartz, Bill Skiles, Phil Smith, Dennis Snow, Tommy Sparks, Jeffrey Stoneking, Bill Sullivan, Dennis Swinburne, Michael Tangel, Jerry Van Dyke, Gwen Van Voorhis, Gerald T. "Pat" Vaughn, Bob Wacker, Robert Wilkins, Mary (Hopkins) Wood, Hobart Wooten, and Bob Ziegler.

Those who helped get me in touch with these folks include Disney World's Golden Ears Club, Mark Goldhaber (MousePlanet.com), and Wini Smith. Specific questions were answered by Phil Boyle, Pat Dyer, Anne McDeed, Jim Hill (JimHillMedia.com), Jim Korkis, Jim Passilla, Charlie Ridgway, Dave Smith (Walt Disney Archives), Art Tome, Leo Waldon, Card Walker, and Jean (Mrs. Bud) Washo.

Introduction

By the time I agreed to write a book about the inner workings of Walt Disney World, I thought I knew most of the "secrets" of the Disney theme parks. After all, I'd just spent seven years overturning every cobblestone of Disneyland, interviewing 250 cast members to create *Mouse Tales*, the first unauthorized, behind-the-scenes look at the Happiest Place on Earth. Collecting a few hundred more anecdotes and wacky tales for a sequel about "Disneyland East" should have been simple. I expected to encounter a similar assortment of current and former cast members—middle-aged, upper-middle-class professionals happy to wax nostalgic about the good old days while sipping iced teas during a return to the hangout of their college days, a comfortable lounge within earshot of magic wishing wells and singing pirates.

I was tipped off that an altogether-different experience awaited me the moment I arrived for my very first Disney World interview back in 1995. The on-again-off-again cast member I'd located asked me to meet him at an off-duty favorite, the Big Bamboo Lounge, in nearby Kissimmee. Unlike the choice hangouts for Disneyland employees, the "Boo" wasn't right across the street from the Magic Kingdom. It was several miles down a main drag that out-tackied even Anaheim's Harbor Boulevard. The "lounge's" site was so poorly lit, I drove past twice before spotting its dilapidated observation tower holding up what was left of a homemade wooden sign. A rusted-out MASH ambulance rested at the entrance to the dirt parking lot. The building itself looked like a rundown biker bar. Stepping inside, I felt as if I'd stumbled into a Goodwill store after an explosion. Every inch of wallspace was covered by business cards, newspaper clippings, animators' napkin sketches, theme park nametags, and discarded clothing.

Reassuringly, to my right I spotted a welcome reminder that I was in the backyard of the Magic Kingdom. At the bar sat two beautiful, wholesome-looking blonde 20-somethings, radiating the Disney Look. I imagined that just an hour before they must have clocked out after a day of posing as Cinderella and Alice in Wonderland. A second later, the girls began French kissing each other.

My host that evening shared a batch of humorous anecdotes. But what I soon discovered was that there was far more to this story. That while central Florida B.D. (Before Disney) started out considerably more rural than even Anahcim in its orange grove days, Disneyland would be the one that remained most provincial.

Disney World would draw visitors and employees from a much wider area, and its executives were, on the whole, a more daring bunch. "When we opened Disney World, those who stayed behind at Disneyland experienced a stilted maturation," theorized one transplant. "All the risk-takers and adventurers, everyone who was adaptable and willing to try new things, went to Florida. We hired outside people and learned from them. Those who stayed behind always looked through a tunnel."

At Disneyland, their sole preoccupation was operating an amusement park the "Disney Way." Those standards came from Walt Disney, whose idea as an animation studio chief was to create the medium's most enjoyable, memorable, emotional experience for the audience, so that they — and everyone in their circle of acquaintances — would become customers for life. He maintained the focus in later products — live-action movies, television shows, records, comic books. Yet Disney remained essentially a manufacturer, creating high-quality products that others would then distribute to the masses.

With Disneyland, Walt was now in the retail business, for the first time making direct contact with the audience. He now required his representatives to create enjoyable, memorable, emotional experiences one consumer at a time. Though intensive and expensive, the mission to exceed customers' expectations was contagious. Cast members by the thousands and customers by the millions bought in. Employees, in fact, became so dedicated to spoiling the customers, that Donn Tatum, the erudite chairman of the company during the 1970s, would occasionally note, "This is not an eleemosynary organization." Besides sending them scrambling for a dictionary, he was reminding his troops that Walt Disney Productions was not a charity—it was a business. And spoiling the customers wasn't done for altruistic motives; it was a calculated business strategy to generate long-term growth by convincing guests to reflexively buy Disney products. Creating an affinity between company, employees, and customers was great for business.

But as exhausting a proposition as that was with a theme park, Walt's plans for Florida were far more ambitious: to take the company's operating principles and apply them to all manner of conventional city operations—hotels, factories, offices, transportation systems, airports, schools, hospitals, and homes. He and his successors just had to figure out how to keep the real world from getting in the way.

– David Koenig
May 2007

1

Waltopia

OVER the years, Walt Disney had made hundreds of appearances exactly like this one—pitching potential corporate sponsors and government officials to gain funding or favors for his latest project. The only difference was this time he was dead.

It was a warm winter's afternoon in 1967, and close to 1,000 hand-picked VIPs and curious gatecrashers crowded into the Park East Theatre in Winter Haven, Florida, for the first showing of Walt's last film. Cancer had taken the showman's life seven weeks earlier. He had shot the film seven weeks before his death.

Now here he was up on the 20-foot-tall screen, in living color, speaking from beyond the grave. He had reappeared to reveal his plans for the 43 square miles of central Florida swampland he had secretly bought. Walt wanted to build an amusement park similar to Disneyland in California, but much larger, plus hotels and other recreational activities. But that was just the beginning. He also wanted an "airport of the future," a massive industrial park, and a high-speed monorail running the length of the property.

Then a twinkle came into Walt's eye as he began talking about "the most exciting, by far the most important part of our Florida project, in fact the heart of everything we'll be doing in Disney World." It was an entire city of the future. He called it "Ep-cot"—the "cot" hanging in the air with his slight Midwestern drawl. EPCOT, Walt explained, would be the Experimental Prototype Community of Tomorrow, a place that would bring together the latest systems and technologies to demonstrate the "ingenuity and imagination of American free enterprise." Visitors from around the world would come watch how people worked, lived and played at EPCOT, and then take what they had learned back home to help solve problems in their own cities.

Conceptual art showed an elaborate, multi-leveled city encased under a glass, climate-controlled dome. A network of monorails and continuously moving trams shuttled people from the city to the outlying residential neighborhoods and clusters of high-tech labs. The model city would be serviced from below, where conventional vehicles scurried about in underground tunnels, hidden like moles.

"That's the starting point for our Experimental Prototype Community of Tomorrow," Walt smiled. "And now where do we go from these preliminary plans and sketches? Well, a project like this is so vast in scope that no one company alone could make it a reality. But if we can bring together the technical know-how of American industry and the creative imagination of the Disney organization, I'm confident we can create— right here in Disney World—a showcase to the world of the American free enterprise system. I believe we can build a community that more people will talk about and come to look at than any other area in the world and, with your cooperation, that the Experimental Prototype Community of Tomorrow can influence the future of city living for generations to come. It's an exciting challenge, a once-in-a-lifetime opportunity for everyone who participates. Speaking for myself and the entire Disney organization, we're ready to go right now!"

With that, Walt faded away. The house lights came on. For a few moments the audience sat speechless, stunned. Finally, Walt's typically backstage brother, Roy, ambled to the podium. Walt, the infectious idea man, was always the one to sell the dream. It was left to soft-spoken Roy, the money man, to close the deal. "Our corporation is dedicated to making Walt Disney's dream a reality," Roy announced, "*but* it cannot be done without the help of you people here in Florida."

Then came the *but*. "We must have a solid legal foundation before we can proceed with Disney World," Roy continued. "This foundation can be assured by the legislative proposals we are presenting to the next session of the Florida legislature. If these requests are granted, I believe that we can make the new theme park a reality by 1971."

COMING ATTRACTIONS. Disney rented out a Winter Haven movie theater to present its *EPCOT Film* and sales pitch. (February 2, 1967) *Photo courtesy State Archives of Florida*

Walt Disney Productions wasn't anything like other big companies, looking for tax incentives to come to town; the company seemed happy to pay its fair share. It wanted more. If it were really going to undertake such a massive, ambitious project—and bring thousands of jobs and billions of dollars to the backwoods of Florida, it first had to be guaranteed more control than any company had ever been granted. Disney was asking for its own government, one devoted to high standards yet open to experimentation. A model city required a model government, free of the bureaucratic red tape that normally strangled innovation.

In the decades to follow, Disney's hometown government would help facilitate the creation and operation of four of the world's largest, most popular theme parks, dozens of exotic hotels, and countless other sup-

porting amusements. Ironically, the empire would grow to include most
every type of facility you would find in a conventional county—just not
Walt's City of Tomorrow, Disney's primary argument for needing the
government in the first place. Walt's successors, both the sincere and the
self-serving, would never figure out a way to pull it off. That doesn't
mean they didn't try.

2

The Undercover Expansion

W ALT Disney never set out to be a city planner. He was a story-teller. The folksy manner and products reflected his formative years spent growing up in Marceline, Missouri. In 1906, his family of seven—four boys and baby sister—had moved to a farm in the country to escape the dangers of big city Chicago. The youngest boy, precocious Walt enjoyed tagging along with practical-minded Roy, eight years his elder and adept at keeping his little brother out of trouble.

Into the 1920s, the Disney brothers launched their own animation studio. Walt oversaw the creative end, Roy the business side. Walt firmly believed that if he utilized the latest technology and best production talent to produce superior products, success would automatically follow. Yet the brothers were at the mercy of unscrupulous agents and distributors. Their first popular series, the Alice in Cartoonland comedies, placed a live-action girl in a cartoon environment. After 56 shorts over four years, Walt grew bored and moved on to his first entirely animated series, Oswald the Lucky Rabbit. In 1928, Disney's distributor, Charles Mintz, pulled the character from him and assigned it to animators who could crank the films out less expensively. The loss devastated the brothers' tiny studio. Roy was determined never to lose control again.

He made sure the studio owned all rights to Walt's next creation, a mouse named Mickey, and success came quicker and bigger than before. Yet Walt, the restless risk-taker, didn't make it easy for his conservative brother. He continually searched for ways to improve his work and to bring order to the disordered. Animation had been a thriving medium when Walt came along, but was dismissed as amateur entertainment for children. Common were bland, forgettable, poorly drawn characters going through nonsensical antics. Walt himself could barely draw a decent Mickey Mouse. Yet he created memorable characters, placed them in engaging storylines that retained the innocence of a bygone era, and employed the latest technological advancements. Disney infused animation with sound, color, dimensional layering, stereophonic sound, and feature-film length.

Still, respect came grudgingly from his Hollywood peers. They were filmmakers; Walt Disney ran a "Mickey Mouse operation." So, too, the medium frustrated him. Animation required years of painstaking labor to produce a film that, once released, could no longer be tinkered with.

Gradually, Walt's interests began to drift from movies to real estate. With a theme park, the results were more immediate. It could be continuously added to and subtracted from. Best of all, it was three-dimensional; Walt and his audience could step into it and participate. They wouldn't just watch Disneyland; they'd live it.

Permanent carnivals had been around for decades and suffered from the same ills as primitive animation. They were typically a random collection of thrills, dirty and of questionable safety. Good for a few screams, but quickly forgettable.

Walt intended to create a land of fantasies, isolated from the outside world by a twelve-foot earthen berm along its perimeter. Inside, each area, or "land," was themed as if a self-contained scene in a movie. The settings were more like storylines, whether in the Old West, an unexplored jungle, a turn-of-the-century Main Street, the world of the future, or the environments of his cartoon creations. The backdrops gave visitors a context, a story, something to engage them and make their visit more meaningful and more memorable. When Disneyland opened in 1955, few of the attractions were more than redressed carnival rides. Yet recognizing a character or storyline gave visitors an instant connection. Guests weren't just spinning in the air; they were riding a flying elephant!

Roy was instinctively wary of such risky ventures, but as usual, he raised the money to proceed with construction. But because the entire idea was so unusual, in 1952 Walt had to form his own private company, WED Enterprises, to design and develop the park and attractions. In time, having Walt, not Walt Disney Productions, own WED would become one of many sources of conflict between the brothers.

"I think there was a certain antagonism," recalled Dick Morrow, who as the company's general counsel often found himself in between the two sides. "Roy felt that he had to take care of little Walt, and little Walt didn't care for that. There was a lot of bickering, but it was all in love."

The staff at Walt Disney Productions naturally split into two well-defined camps—the creative-minded "Walt's Boys" and the financial-minded "Roy's boys." The most visible Walt's Boy was Card Walker, a tall, imposing figure, who began his career in the studio mailroom in 1938 and worked his way up to head of marketing, all the while swearing his allegiance to everything Walt said, did and believed in. The most favored of Roy's boys was Donn Tatum, who joined the company in 1956. The scholarly lawyer had worked for ABC when the network convinced Walt to produce *Disneyland*, the television show, in exchange for funds to build the park. Quiet and reserved, Tatum always dressed in coat and tie, making him look more the part of corporate executive than his more relaxed associates, who usually wore golf shirts.

The success of Disneyland—and the resultant boost to the economy of Anaheim, California—caught the attention of cities around the country. Everyone wanted Walt to come build a theme park in their town. At first, Walt had no interest. He wasn't one to repeat himself, and if there was ever anything he didn't like at Disneyland, he just pulled it out. If there was something new he wanted to add, he did. As long as Disneyland would never be completed, why would he need another one? Walt also found charm in Disneyland's uniqueness. A Disney theme park wouldn't be nearly as special if every big city had one.

Disneyland seemed to satisfy Walt's desires as the perfect playground—until he took a close look at the real world degenerating around it. Outside the gates, the rural landscape was fast transforming into disorganized, urban sprawl. Ugly neon signs, liquor stores, cheap motels, cheesy souvenir stands, and unsightly power lines began to dot the park's entry road, Harbor Boulevard. Traffic jams and exhaust fumes began to choke the once-pristine air. The Disneys, obsessed with control, felt helpless to control the circus breaking out in their front yard.

Walt must have suspected that, despite the company's influence at Anaheim city hall, he wouldn't be able to hold back high-rise growth forever. By 1960, Jack Wrather, owner of the neighboring Disneyland Hotel, had submitted plans to add a modern eleven-story tower, one that could prove a visual intrusion to Disneyland's Frontierland of the late 1800s. A few years later, Sheraton applied to build an eighteen- to 20-story hotel across the street from Disneyland.

So, too, all these roadside businesses collectively were making more money off Disneyland than Walt was. Before Disney came to town, Anaheim had 84 motel rooms. Within two years of the park opening, there were thousands—none of them owned by Disney. Reluctantly, Walt began listening to the siren calls beckoning him eastward.

The task of financially screening the various cities' proposals fell to Donn Tatum. To evaluate the viability of the markets themselves, Disney hired Economic Research Associates' Buzz Price, who had completed similar studies years before for Disneyland. In 1959, the numbers seemed to favor a joint venture with RCA in Palm Beach, Florida. The Disneys, however, were reluctant to share control. In the end, Walt blamed pulling out of Palm Beach on the city's beachside location. He wanted to avoid the coastal humidity, hurricane warnings, and competing with the beach. Walt pointed inland. "We'll create our own water," he said.

By 1960, a more intriguing opportunity developed in St. Louis. Local leaders, hoping to rejuvenate the city's aging downtown, offered to subsidize construction of an indoor Disney theme park along the riverfront.

Instead, in 1960, Walt convinced Art Linkletter, John Payne and a few other Hollywood cronies to open the Celebrity Sports Center in Denver. The center featured a massive 80-lane bowling alley, huge arcade, Olympic-sized swimming pool, and other amusements. Despite the glamorous name, the business never made anyone a fortune. To appease Walt's buddies, Walt Disney Productions bought out the partners in 1962. Still, they refused to promote the center's Disney connection. It couldn't quite match Disneyland standards. The company viewed it more as a place to train park management away from the bright spotlight of Disneyland.

Disney also began commissioning studies of mountain areas in the West to build a ski resort. Yet Walt's appetite had been whetted for something bigger, a "Disneyland East." As Economic Research Associates studies confirmed, only Florida appeared to have a climate that would permit year-round operation—a necessity for such a large investment. Yet such a park could never succeed if it relied too heavily on Florida's own population. It would need visitors from the Northeast. But would they be interested?

Walt was acutely aware that nearly two-thirds of Disneyland's visitors came from California; in fact, only eight percent came from east of the Mississippi River. When Disneyland first opened, the entertainment and financial press from the East Coast couldn't understand it. Why would Walt waste millions of dollars turning orange groves into a circus?

"The eastern media just totally pooh-poohed [Disneyland]," said the park's first marketing chief, Jack Lindquist. "It was the old Lalaland routine: 'We're too sophisticated. It'll never fly here.'"

So Walt devised an ingenious way to test how Disney entertainment would play to East Coast audiences. In 1960, he began soliciting top American corporations, offering to produce attractions for them at the 1964-1965 World's Fair in New York. His "Imagineers" at WED would design and build the attractions at the companies' expense. When the fair was over, the attractions would be shipped to Disneyland, where hopefully the companies would remain sponsors. Best of all, Walt could test his product in New York with someone else paying the bill.

Also, now that Walt had bigger pockets to write the checks, his Imagineering staff could escalate research and development of groundbreaking technologies both to entertain and to increase capacity. For the Ford Motor Company's pavilion, WED developed the WEDway PeopleMover, a continuously moving electric tramway. For General Electric, Disney created the Carousel of Progress, a circular theater that rotated around stationary stages. For Pepsi-Cola, the Imagineers came up with It's a Small World, featuring a boat system that could cycle through up to 5,400 people an hour. For the State of Illinois, WED quickened its progress in audio-animatronics by creating a robotic Abraham Lincoln that could deliver the Gettysburg Address. The technology would become a staple of Disney rides for decades to follow.

All four Disney attractions ranked among the five most popular exhibits at the fair, confirming to Walt that the East Coast did indeed appreciate his brand of entertainment.

Walt's rising confidence in the abilities of WED allowed his expansion plans to grow ever grander. His ambitions swelled again after hearing of a speech before the 1963 Urban Design Conference at Harvard University. Keynote speaker James W. Rouse, developer of the "new town" of Columbia, Maryland, said, "I may hold a view that may be somewhat shocking to an audience as sophisticated as this, that the greatest piece of urban design in the United States today is Disneyland... It took an area of activity—the amusement park—and lifted it to a standard so high in its performance, in its respect for people, in its functioning for people, that it really does become a brand new thing. It fulfills all its functions it set out to accomplish—unselfconsciously, usefully and profitably to its owners and developers. I find more to learn in the standards that have been set and in the goals that have been achieved in the development of Disneyland than in any other piece of physical development in the country."

The words would become the most famous non-Disney Disney quote ever, repeated endlessly in company publications and by executives, including Walt himself. For once, the "Mousetro" believed his own press clipping. The more the area around Disneyland deteriorated, and conditions in big cities across the nation worsened, the more Walt thought about what would he do with the miles of periphery he sought for Disneyland East. Sure, he could use it as just a giant buffer to push the inevitable big city as far away as possible. Or what if, instead, he devoted his surrounding property to a big city of his own creation? What if Walt brought his drive for order, control, quality and cutting-edge technology to real-life hotels, offices, manufacturing facilities, stores, restaurants, highways, skyways, public transportation, hospitals, schools, and residential neighborhoods? And, since Walt was at heart a showman and communicator, this idealized community could serve as a showplace for people to visit from around the world to find out how to make a city work, Exhibit A for building cities right. In a sense, he would be taking the Disneyland template of fantastic, idealized versions of America's past and future and imposing it upon America's present. People visited Disneyland to forget about their troubles for a day. Walt now wanted to eliminate their troubles at home, too. He would break down the berm and allow the pixie dust to flood into the outside world.

Certainly the need was there, but no one seemed to be making any

progress. When Walt introduced the first monorail in the western hemi-
sphere at Disneyland in 1959, he envisioned cities around the world taking note and adding their own fleets. That none did greatly frustrated
him.

As he did with animation and theme parks, Walt would texture his
city with familiar, reassuring components of the past while using modern
tools. To Walt, progress meant sharpening—not erasing—what came
before. It was like restoring color to a black-and-white photo—enhanc-
ing an image while retaining its essence.

His land search intensified in 1963 after Disney acquired a corporate
jet. Groups of executives began making regular scouting trips to Niagara
Falls, the Great Smokies, Washington, D.C., and anywhere else East
Coast tourists were drawn.

By November, Walt realized it was time to make a move. He gathered
onto the private plane Tatum, Walker, Price and the few other insiders he
had let in on his plans. The pilot charted a course for St. Louis, where
the city leaders still held out hope that Disney would change its mind.
No, St. Louis wouldn't work. Too little land, too much financial risk.
The plane continued on to Niagara Falls. Already the group could see
that the winter would be too cold and last too long. The plane flew to a
site between Washington, D.C., and Baltimore. The weather there, too,
could be harsh.

Their only option was to head south. Walt asked the pilot to fly along
the coast to make sure that he didn't want to build near the beach. The
pilot finally headed inland, toward central Florida. Walt asked him to fly
as low as possible, so he could get a good look at the expansive swamps
and woodlands near Orlando. Before heading back to California, the
plane stopped in town to refuel. There, the group heard the news—
President Kennedy had been shot.

During the flight home, every passenger sat in stunned silence. The
nation's young, optimistic leader had been mortally shot in the middle of
a Dallas city street. Was this the hopeful, productive America that Walt
and his Disneyland celebrated and held up to the world as a shining
example? Never before had the entire world so badly needed the promise
of Walt's City of Tomorrow. He had no more time to waste. He'd made
up his mind. Just before the plane touched down in Burbank, Walt broke
the silence. "Well," he said, "that's the place—central Florida."

If Walt Disney Productions were really going to buy enough property to contain all of Walt's increasingly ambitious dreams, it was going to need a lot of land—10,000 acres minimum. And it would have to be acquired in absolute secrecy. One word of what Disney was up to would drive prices out of reach, making the entire project unfeasible.

To serve as point man, Disney appointed Robert Foster, the unassuming secretary and general counsel of Disneyland, who specialized in real estate. He first analyzed central Florida survey maps, scoured the real estate ads in small-town newspapers, and kept track of circulars from real estate agents.

Foster needed help on the ground. Disney asked its New York law firm, Donovan, Leisure, Newton & Irvine, for a referral who could keep a secret. The firm' founder, General William J. Donovan, helped create and oversaw the espionage agency Office of Strategic Services (OSS) during World War II. Donovan's OSS chief in China, Colonel Paul Helliwell, later became a CIA operative, then set up his own law firm in Miami, from which he developed high-level connections throughout the state.

Late in 1963, Foster paid a visit to Helliwell's office. He wanted assistance in helping his unnamed client secure a large parcel of land primarily for recreational purposes. Helliwell's partner, Tom DeWolf recalled, "We closed the door. [Foster] explained who he was, what he was interested in. The main thing was secrecy. It had to be strictly confidential. We set up a lot of safeguards. We were told not to talk to him or anyone in California about this. We would use a special phone line through New York. We'd call Donovan, Leisure, Newton & Irvine in New York, and they would transfer the call to California."

Helliwell knew Foster would need an expert on Florida real estate, and suggested Roy Hawkins, a good old boy with 40 years experience in Florida who was retiring as property manager for the wealthy Phipps family of Saratoga, New York. Foster introduced himself as "Robert Price"—his first and middle names and what would become his ID with all future Florida contacts. Foster even had Robert Price business cards made up, using the address of Helliwell's law office.

Hawkins and Helliwell then went to William H. "Billy" Dial, chairman of First National Bank of Orlando and the man you went to "when you needed to get something done in central Florida." They explained their quest and how they could not afford a leak. So Dial took them to the region's main information stopgap, the last man Disney expected to share its secret with—Martin Anderson, owner and publisher of the *Orlando Sentinel*. To Disney's surprise, Anderson vowed to play along by not printing any wildly speculative stories, but cautioned that he wouldn't stop his reporters from doing their jobs.

Hawkins turned up several potential locations throughout Florida, but Walt pointed to the dead center of the state, at the strategic intersection of Interstate 4 and Florida's Turnpike. The vast majority of Florida's tourists traveled from the Northeast down I-4 southwest to Tampa or from the Northwest southeast down the Sunshine State Parkway. The two highways created a giant X through the center of the state. Walt wanted land where the two highways crossed.

The general area included three sizable properties separated by dozens of tiny ones. The largest tract, 12,400 acres, was held by the most moti-vated seller. Three years earlier, Orlando homebuilders Jack and Bill Demetree and Bill Jenkins had paid less than $100 an acre. Now they wanted out. In May 1964, Hawkins called Jack Demetree, saying he had a client who would like to see his land. Demetree, his real estate agent, Hawkins, DeWolf and Foster, as "Bob Price," hopped into a pair of Jeeps and drove along a dirt rut road that circled the property. The dense woods looked uninhabitable, save the occasional campsite cleared by a turkey or deer hunter. Even with the bugs and ungodly humidity, Foster liked what he saw. Demetree asked for $165 an acre. Foster sounded interested. After two weeks, though, he didn't submit an offer and Demetree panicked. He dropped his price to $145 an acre. When his calls weren't returned, Demetree grew even more impatient. He drove to the Miami address on Foster's business card and asked the receptionist to see Bob Price. The woman said she had never heard of such a person. Demetree turned, ready to storm out of the office, when Helliwell stepped out of a back room and tried to calm him down. Helliwell explained that "Price" was an alias used by an attorney representing a group of purchasers and, yes, they were still interested in his land.

After agreeing to buy the property, Disney quickly discovered why the Demetrees were so anxious to part with it. Early in the century, the primary industry in the area had been phosphorous mining for use in fer-tilizer, so the state separated the mineral rights from land ownership. When the mineral rights owner was ready to mine, he could build roads, towns, whatever he needed, right through the property, and there was nothing the owner of the actual land could do about it. The mineral rights for most of the Demetrees' land was owned by Tufts College in Boston, which refused to sell. Demetree and Helliwell flew to Boston. After marathon negotiations, Tufts' trustees agreed to sell the mineral rights for about $6 an acre.

Disney, recalled DeWolf, "started out with the idea that the 12,000 acres would be more than enough, but because of lakes and contours of the land, they would need more. Our engineers recommended another tract, a big cypress swamp, to be used for water control."

Walt was able to convince Roy to keep buying land by reminding him that, like at Disneyland, the surrounding acreage would shoot up in value as soon as they announced Disney was coming to town.

The second largest site was about 8,500 acres owned by State Senator Irlo Overstreet Bronson. He was a fourth generation cattle rancher and wealthy enough that he had no reason to sell. Hawkins, an old friend, visited the senator at his ranch and the two sat in rocking chairs on the veranda, talking about the history and the future of Florida. For hours, Hawkins rocked, and alluded to an historic opportunity Bronson possessed to change the face of Florida. The sun set, and Hawkins left. He returned the next day to rock some more. Bronson finally relented.

A third key chunk of land, about 1,800 acres running north from Bay Lake to County Road 535, was owned by a group of investors represented by the local Hall Brothers Realty. With the help of another real estate agency, Florida Ranch Lands, Foster and Hawkins secured an option on the Hall Brothers property.

With the three major properties under contract, now came the hard part: acquiring the "outages" that connected the larger pieces. There was no time to spare—speculation on the buyer's true identity, as well as land prices, would escalate the moment the three main deeds were recorded. The Bay Lake property had been subdivided in 1913 into about 48 five-acre lots. The small, inaccessible plots were then sold by the Munger Land Company through mail order catalogs to gullible Yankees. Owners of the then-worthless swampland were scattered around the world, most having never even seen what they owned. Some, having inherited their land from a long-gone generation, didn't even know what they owned. Florida Ranch Lands assembled a research staff to trace the descendants of the original buyers and offer by phone to buy their property. Agents manned the phones day and night for months, into

1965, into September. One night, a hurricane struck central Florida and knocked out the office's electricity; the tele-researchers continued calling by candlelight.

As leverage, Foster acquired another large piece of property miles west of the target site; it was higher and drier than the land Disney was after and had better access to 530. Foster then broke it up into five-acre parcels that he would use to trade.

Back in Burbank, Walt checked the progress in the top-secret "war room" on a daily basis. Inside, acquisitions were marked on a giant map of the target site, as if noting enemy territory captured during a battle.

In late 1964 and early 1965, Disney set up a half-dozen dummy corporations, all based in Miami, to take title on the land. Ayefour Corporation was listed as run by Foster; Bay Lake Properties and Tomahawk Properties, by Bob Price; Compass East and the Latin American Development & Management corporations, by Roy's alias, Roy Davis, and Reedy Creek Ranch Lands, by the mythical M.T. Lott. As expected, the instant the first deeds were recorded, rumors began to circulate as to the identity of "Mystery Industry X." With so much land, so close together, it had to be someone big. Some locals suspected it was large automaker or, because of the proximity to Cape Canaveral, an aerospace firm. Some mentioned Disney. After Roy Hawkins sent postcards to friends in Orlando during a trip to Seattle, some figured it was Boeing. When flight records showed Bob Price often flew to Kansas City, some were convinced it was Hallmark. Actually Foster stopped off in Kansas City to visit his mother and throw the press off his trail.

In mid-October 1965, Walt was entertaining a group of East Coast reporters visiting Anaheim to cover Disneyland's tenth anniversary celebration. One, the *Orlando Sentinel's* Emily Bavar, nonchalantly asked Walt if his company was buying land in central Florida. "Why we would want to locate way out in that area?" Walt replied. He then listed several reasons why Disney would not want property in the region. Curious, Bavar thought. First, Walt never directly answered her question. Second, he knew an awful lot about central Florida.

That night, Bavar secretly telegraphed a short story to her paper about Walt's evasiveness, which ran Sunday, October 17, 1965, below the tiny headline, "Disney Hedges Big Question." After Bavar returned to Orlando and sorted through the clues with her editors, they let her write a longer article with a larger headline: "Is Our 'Mystery' Industry

BREAKING NEWS. Project Florida is officially announced by Walt Disney, Governor Haydon Burns, and Roy Disney. (November 15, 1965) *Photo courtesy State Archives of Florida*

Disney? Girl Reporter Convinced by Disney." As the week went on, more pieces of the puzzle fell into place. All signs pointed to Disney. The "girl reporter" had convinced her editors.

That following Sunday, October 24, Bob Foster was in Orlando to tour the site, when a newsrack caught his eye. A banner headline blared: "We Say: 'Mystery' Industry Is Disney." Foster immediately called Burbank and had Card Walker pulled off the golf course, to break him the news. Fortunately, by this time Disney had acquired or optioned all but a handful of sites, totaling less than 300 acres. It was time to announce the Florida Project. Foster flew to Miami to brief Florida governor Haydon Burns. The governor was ecstatic. He was just ramping up his re-election campaign and insisted on making an official announcement the next day at a convention luncheon.

On November 15, Walt, Roy and Governor Burns held a press conference at Orlando's Cherry Plaza Hotel. Walt confirmed that Disney would be building another theme park, similar to yet bigger than Disneyland. Then, for the first time in public, Walt mentioned what he'd like to do with the rest of the property: he wanted to build "a city of tomorrow."

Instantly, the asking prices for the remaining parcels jumped from an average of $183 an acre to $1,000. Still, Disney had been able to acquire over 27,000 acres for just $5 million.

With its cover blown, Disney at least could operate in the open. A year before, Helliwell had hired a young lawyer with a real estate background who, after the announcement was made, could be switched to the Disney payroll—and informed whom he was working for. Phil Smith was not only an excellent business attorney, but he displayed that "can do" attitude Disney was looking for to help accomplish the impossible. "Phil knew how to get things done quickly," said DeWolf. "A lot of lawyers are purely negative, [saying] 'You can't do this, you can't do that.' Part of [Disney World] was using experimental materials, so Phil was very good at solving their problems."

In February 1966, Smith opened Disney's first office in downtown Orlando, a ramshackle suite in the old Metcalf Building. "Initially it was trying to get to know some people in town, getting to know the county commissioners, county attorney, and the people that we'd have to work with in order to get things going," Smith recalled. He put a sign reading "Reedy Creek Ranch Inc." on the door, and typically worked with just a secretary. Foster, Roy and others from California would also use the office when they were in town.

In addition to a business presence in the city, Disney also needed a security presence on the property. Several farm houses had been abandoned by the previous land owners, so Smith, his wife Gwen, and their two small children moved into the newest one—a three-bedroom bungalow built a few years earlier by Irlo Bronson's son. An adjacent airstrip had been used for the cropdusters that sprayed the citrus trees.

Smith was to keep an eye over the fifteen acres of groves near the house and 35 acres of groves to the north. Farther out were swamps to the west, cattle grazing land to the south, and to the north, Bay Lake, a favorite fishing and partying spot for the locals. Tall pines filled in the miles of dense forestland that surrounded the countless swamps. Smith got to know the property well, and was charged with driving Disney executives by Jeep on bumpy tours through the wild.

At night, the Smith homestead disappeared into the darkness. "At that time," Smith recalled, "you could get on I-4, drive into town, and you'd hardly see any cars until you got to the outskirts of Orlando. There was nothing out that way. At night, we could hear animals. We thought we heard panthers. A pond behind the house was loaded with water moccasins. We used to get water moccasins that would come up around the house and even into our garage. One day, as I was taking out the trash to burn on the side of the pond, I practically stepped on one. I ran inside, got a shotgun, and shot it. I took Tom DeWolf down to look at this moccasin, and it struck at us! It was dead, or practically dead, but it struck."

The local wildlife was actually more welcome than the visitors. Smith said, "People used to come in and try to get [construction] jobs. Gwen would be at home alone because our office was downtown, and they'd come by and ask for jobs. Some of them were kind of seedy looking, so she got a little frightened sometimes. The county had constables back then, and if Gwen needed anything she could call this constable and he'd come out. And once in a while, highway patrol would land at the airstrip."

About the same time that reporter Bavar was sniffing around Southern California, little did she know that back home in Florida, Disney had just begun initial ground clearing. Crews isolated 300 acres in the northwest corner of its property and began pulling out stumps, grading the soil, planting grass, and conducting drainage studies. To get things going, Walt had just recruited retired Army Major General William Everett "Joe" Potter. An MIT graduate and combat engineer in World War II, Potter specialized in overseeing public works for the Army Corps of Engineers and spent four years as governor of the Panama Canal Zone. He caught Walt's eye while serving as second-in-command to Robert Moses at the New York World's Fair, as liaison to the pavilions' corporate and government sponsors. Potter quickly noticed that Walt, like Moses, "was a beginner of things, not a finisher." That would be left for the general and others.

Their first task was getting the newly acquired land into some sort of commercially usable condition. Bob Foster explained, "We had to convert this bare, foul land into a reasonable piece of real estate, whether we went forward with Disney World or not. We had to make it a sound financial investment, to get our $5.2 million out of it."

WHAT HAVE I BOUGHT? Walt looks over his newly acquired property with Joe Potter. (c. 1966) *Photo courtesy Valerie Curry, from Marvin Davis*

Salvaging the vast swamplands would be the greatest challenge. Potter turned to a former military connection, Herb Gee, whose engineering company had formed a special "drainage district" to accommodate sugar operations 100 miles to the southeast in Okeechobee. Such districts allowed private landowners to design and self-regulate their own water control systems, and to sell tax-exempt bonds to finance it all. "What [Disney] really wanted to do," Smith explained, "was determine the destiny of the land they bought without being burdened by governmental controls and outdated building codes, and not to be a burden to the taxpayers or the county. An awful lot had to be done to set up the infrastructure for what was to become Walt Disney World, roads and drainage and sewage. It was obvious that you couldn't ask Orange County, which wasn't a big, prosperous county at that time. And the company wasn't wealthy, either. So what you needed to do was to be able to set up revenues, tax-exempt revenues, by selling bonds, with the proceeds used to put in the infrastructure."

Since a few outages remained, Disney was required to complete a costs/benefits survey and notify other affected landowners in the area. Roy flew in for the circuit court hearing to consider approval for the drainage district. During the proceedings, a local farmer with property bordering Disney's rose to speak. The man, fearful he would lose control and be unfairly taxed, wanted no part of Disney's drainage district. Roy didn't want to fight with him. He elbowed lawyer DeWolf in the ribs. DeWolf leaned over, and Roy whispered, "Let him win." DeWolf didn't contest the man's argument, and the judge excluded him from the district. In August 1966, Disney received approval for the Reedy Creek Drainage District, its first governmental entity.

Their challenge became draining numerous swamps, without upsetting the fragile water tables or causing flooding. Since central Florida basically sits on a body of freshwater, altering one area could damage the entire region. So instead of draining the land, Disney created an intricate system of canals and levees to control water levels while maintaining an overall reserve. As water rose in one section, gates would automatically float open to release water to the next section, then automatically close when the water level subsided. The 44 miles of winding canals followed the natural curves of the landscape, to blend in. A basin at the bottom of Reedy Creek could hold enough water to swallow a 50-year flood. Nineteen mechanical gates kept the water at identical levels throughout the canal system, preventing flooding on Disney's property and other owners' land to the south. Maintaining the water table also kept the surrounding grass perpetually green.

Disney viewed the drainage district as merely a first step. Privately, the company wanted absolute power over not just water control, but also all construction, eventual operation of facilities, and continuing expansion. Building an entire Vacation Kingdom from scratch—let alone a futuristic city—according to Bob Foster, "would have been difficult, in fact, near impossible under existing Florida and Orange County building codes, inspection requirements, zoning and land ordinances. And, had it been built, it would have been vulnerable to constant threats by Florida and Kissimmee counties."

Ideally, Disney wanted the autonomy of its drainage district applied to all other governmental functions. Setting up and maintaining a dozen separate districts, each governed by a separate board of supervisors, would have been untenable. As Disneyland's expert on real estate law, Foster knew that California allowed property to be consolidated into "community service districts," which could wield all manner of authority, from building sewers and streets and libraries to providing police protection. In one recent project, Foster City, a millionaire developer acquired a sorry collection of salt flats along the San Francisco Bay. He planned to dredge the marshes by forming a series of canals, then build custom homes and boat docks alongside them and market the tract as a "new world Venice." As the state's first "planned community," the development would also have an industrial park, town center, office buildings, shopping centers, apartments, parks, greenbelt walkways, and innovative schools. The developer received approval from the governor to roll multiple municipal functions into a single improvement district, which sold tax-exempt bonds to finance the extensive dredging as well as construction of roads, sewers, water mains, underground utility lines, and even advertising.

Foster had lawyer DeWolf investigate whether Florida allowed broadening the authority of its drainage district into a "super district." DeWolf found enabling statutes for a whole series of separate assessment districts, as well as instances where multiple functions were combined under a single board. But while an improvement district could oversee proprietary functions, such as utilities and zoning, civil authority—such as police powers—had to be granted to a municipality. If Walt wanted to control everything, he was going to have to get permission to found his own city.

3

Planning the Invasion

AS Project X morphed into "The Florida Project," activity in the war room switched from tracking territory captured to figuring out what to do with it. "It was a three-room office suite that was off limits," said Valerie Watson Curry, secretary to the master planner. "The conference room had huge, ceiling-to-floor blow-up maps of Orlando."

To develop the master plan, Walt called on architect Marvin Davis who, after devising the layout for Disneyland, had returned to his previous career as a motion picture art director. Walt knew that Davis, assisted by lead attraction planner Dick Irvine and other seasoned Imagineers, could turn his napkin scribblings into concrete drawings. They understood what made Disneyland successful and could faithfully recreate or, better, improve upon it at Disney World.

Whenever the design team asked for his opinion on some element of the new theme park, Walt invariably responded not to trouble him with questions that had been asked and answered years before. "You guys know that by now," Walt replied, impatiently. "I don't want to discuss what we learned in the past. I want to talk about the future." His mind was elsewhere, on elements of that master plan that he had never done before.

One new interest was hotels. While in Yosemite to research the proposed Mineral King ski resort, Disney executives learned that the Curry family was in the midst of selling the Curry Village lodging area. So, in

August 1966, Walt hired John Curry as his first hotel employee. As administrator of hotel planning, Curry would set up the main lodge in Mineral King and a series of hotels at Disney World. Davis and the Imagineering team would dream up the themes for the hotels and decide where to situate them. Architects at Welton Beckett & Associates— which had designed the buildings for the Disney exhibits at the New York World's Fair—would turn WED's concepts into functional buildings.

But more than just hotels, Walt was consumed with designing his futuristic city. He already had decided on a name, one afternoon at lunch with WED staff. "What we're talking about," Walt tutored them, "is an experimental prototype community of tomorrow. What does that spell? E-p-c-o-t. EPCOT. That's what we'll call it— EPCOT."

Walt immersed himself in reading books on city planning. Model cities became his favorite topic of conversation. As he would to flesh out other ideas, Walt had Imagineers begin work on a gigantic scale model, called "Progress City," representing many of the elements planned for EPCOT. Walt had letters of inquiry sent to 500 corporations seeking their participation. The goal was not just to sell, but to learn. Walt himself visited a few of the larger companies, but sent Joe Potter to tour 100 different factories, research laboratories, and think tanks, among them Westinghouse, General Electric, Bell, IBM, RCA, and Rockwell International. Walt commissioned fourteen different ERA studies for the Florida project, one specifically on the feasibility of a model city.

Even additions at Disneyland began to reflect Walt's ideas for EPCOT. The Anaheim park had always been an entertainment testing ground, regularly adding new rides and systems. Just as often, Walt would pull out attractions that weren't meeting their potential. He became fascinated with the idea of creating and operating a city the same way: continually institute new ideas, expand those that work, eliminate those that don't. Like Disneyland, EPCOT would never be completed, it would always be "in a state of becoming," a living, breathing, constantly changing showcase.

Gradually, his city began to take shape. EPCOT would copy Disneyland's radial "hub-and-spoke" layout, but with a 50-acre urban complex at the center. A climate-controlled dome would enclose the city, guaranteeing perfect weather day and night. Through the middle of the domed roof, a cosmopolitan hotel would soar 30 stories or more, featuring contemporary guest rooms, a convention center, and—for those seeking fresh air—a seven-acre recreation deck.

At the base of the hotel, Walt envisioned an international shopping area—years earlier proposed for Disneyland—with stores and streets recreating the character and adventure of exotic foreign countries. Restaurants, theaters and other nightlife would complement clusters of office buildings serving the needs of both EPCOT residents and major corporations nearby.

Directly underneath the hotel a transportation lobby would provide access to continuously moving WEDway trams for short hops and a high-speed monorail for longer distances. The trams, electrically powered by motors in the track, would run silently, pollution-free, and never cause a traffic jam, since no single car could ever break down.

Conventional transportation would be restricted to underground tunnels. The main highway would cut through the center of the property, so cars and buses could pass underneath the city, with no stoplights to slow the flow of traffic. Adjacent parking areas would be reserved for paying hotel guests only. Trucks would travel one level lower, where loading docks and service elevators would allow them to deliver the commercial goods required by the city.

The city would be circled by three concentric rings, interconnected by WEDway routes. The first ring would consist of high-density apartments for those who worked in the city. In the next ring, a broad greenbelt would contain a mixture of recreation facilities, parks, playgrounds, churches and progressive schools. The schools would welcome new ideas, so that every child raised in EPCOT would have the advanced skills required to keep pace with the fast-changing environment.

The outer ring would be low-density, single-family residential neighborhoods. The houses would be configured so that appliances and furnishings could constantly be replaced, tested and demonstrated. Each block would be grouped around a wide green petal, like collections of golf course view homes minus the golf. The interior paths would be reserved for pedestrians, electric carts, and bicycles. Children could walk or cycle to school or the playground without ever crossing paths with a car.

Motorists would reach their homes from the rear, along a separate, one-way road that circled EPCOT and connected to the main transportation corridor. Walt figured that most residents would drive their cars only on weekends, since they'd commute by public transportation. They

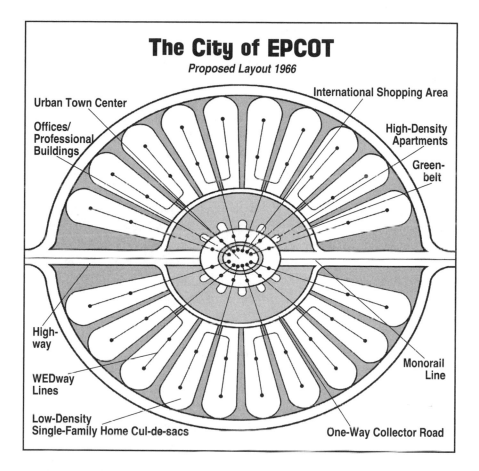

The City of EPCOT
Proposed Layout 1966

Urban Town Center

Offices/ Professional Buildings

International Shopping Area

High-Density Apartments

Green- belt

High- way

WEDway Lines

Low-Density Single-Family Home Cul-de-sacs

Monorail Line

One-Way Collector Road

could take the WEDway to the transportation lobby if they worked downtown or would transfer to the monorail for a job at the theme park to the south or at the 1,000-acre industrial park to the north. From the business park's monorail station, they could catch additional WEDway lines to the many industrial facilities. Out-of-towners could also visit the industrial complex, since each corporation would allow visitors to look behind the scenes at their experimental factories, research and development laboratories, and computer centers.

On the edge of the property, a jet airport would utilize new methods for quickly, efficiently handling baggage and cargo, loading and unloading passengers, and transporting them to the city.

Walt calculated room in EPCOT for 20,000 residents—all renters to protect Disney's land ownership rights. Everyone living at EPCOT would be required to work on property, to ensure that every resident had a stake in keeping the community an "exciting, living blueprint of the future." When they were ready to retire, they could relocate to and buy property in a second, more conventional city on the fringe of Disney World.

Walt knew that creating such a city would be impossible with current building codes and regulations, considering the routine he had to go through any time he wanted to make the slightest change at Disneyland. Now he'd be building not just a super-sized theme park, but an entire city of the future using experimental materials, systems and technologies, and constantly changing them out as new innovations emerged.

Convincing the titans of American business to help finance Walt's city would be difficult enough. Persuading the legislators of Florida to permit it would require Walt's shrewdest sales pitch yet. Yet a lifetime of smoking had taken a huge toll on his health. Walt knew he couldn't travel up and down the state continually making his case. He decided to commit the pitch to film. On October 27, 1966, Walt stepped before the cameras in the war room, its walls covered with charts, sixteen-foot-tall maps, and a series of romantic renderings depicting his still-evolving ideas about what an EPCOT might look like. The camera repeatedly zoomed in on Herb Ryman's three-foot-wide watercolor illustrating Walt's domed city with a 30-story hotel in the center.

At the same time, Florida was fast approaching a November 8 general election. Disney saw no need to waste its plea on legislators and a governor who might not be in office long enough to approve their requests. The presentation would be held off until early 1967, after the new state officials had been sworn into office.

Walt, as it turned out, would not be joining the delegation. On December 15, 1966, Walt Disney died of cancer. With his final breaths, he pointed at dots in the hospital's ceiling tiles, tracing the outlines of his dream city.

Disney management seemed to freeze, as if suddenly severed from their power source. A Walt-less Disney was inconceivable. The news devastated Roy in particular. The little brother he had devoted his life to taking care of was suddenly gone—not to mention 73-year-old Roy's long-anticipated plans for retirement. In Burbank, staff walked around dazed for a week. Roy then realized there was one last way he could look out for his brother, by protecting the thing that Walt cared more about than his health or his finances—his name. He called off retirement. Roy would stick around until the first phase of Walt's final dream was completed, with the new name of *Walt* Disney World, so people would always remember whose world this was.

Roy became president and chairman of the board of Walt Disney Productions. He named Tatum vice president and administrative assistant to the president, and Walker executive vice president of operations. With a paucity of creativity among the upper executive ranks, film production would be overseen by a committee of eight. Everyone was to forget, for now, about EPCOT. All efforts would focus on the vacation complex, which would begin attracting millions of tourists, which would help interest large corporations in the planned industrial park and other components of a future EPCOT.

Roy set the budget for phase one at $100 to $150 million. The lion's share—$75 million—would go into a Magic Kingdom five times the size of Disneyland. Another $10 to $15 million would be invested in the park during each of its first five years of operation for expansion. Ideally, the park would open by 1970 and attract six million visitors in its first year.

The timing appeared fortuitous. The company was just finishing up a $50 million overhaul of Disneyland, so they would have the staff and money available to take a "two-year interlude" from Anaheim to concentrate on Florida.

Meanwhile, back east, the natives were getting restless. After Walt's big announcement, the company had been silent for over a year. And now Walt was gone. Locals—the most vocal of them Paul Pickett, chairman of the Orange County Commission—began loudly criticizing the project. "Disney World would be a great thing," Pickett smirked, "if it were in Miami."

Disney, however, always worked on its own schedule. The company had reserved the Park East Theatre in Winter Haven for the afternoon of February 2, 1967. The night before, Disney executives had secretly wined and dined the local legislators and opinion leaders at Winter Haven's Villa Nova restaurant. The company wanted to give these very-VIP's a heads up of what it would be asking for the next day. Executives revealed that newly sworn-in governor Claude Kirk, a Republican fixated on economic development, was already on board.

Disney expected 550 invitees to attend the press conference. Exactly

908 showed up. Excited chatter filled the theater. As the lights dimmed, voices quickly hushed and the *EPCOT Film* began. Preserved on celluloid, Walt delivered one of his most stirring performances. The film mentioned the planned amusement park, but played up EPCOT; it, after all, was the truly extraordinary part of the proposal, and the part most in need of extraordinary measures by government.

As the film concluded, Roy took the stage. "Walt," he said, "did not want to travel the same route twice. He was a peculiar guy this way. He always told me, 'If you do something well, how are you going to top yourself?'" The new theme park, five times the size of Disneyland, was only a prelude to the City of Tomorrow.

Then, as delicately as he could, Roy stated that making the project a reality would require passage of several legislative proposals. He never implicitly said that if the company didn't get its way it would walk away, but definitely wanted the threat to be understood. Roy emphasized that the project would begin only after "our demands" have been met by the legislature. Catching himself, Roy smiled, looked over at the governor, and added, "In the presence of Governor Kirk, I use the word 'demand' softly."

Tatum then took the podium to provide the details. Walt Disney Productions wanted, foremost, creation of two bordering municipalities as well as a special improvement district encompassing its entire 27,400 acres. The legislation would enable Disney, Tatum explained, "to control the environment, planning and operation of the services and construction essential to the contemplated improvements and development of the property."

In addition, the company sought special legislation to protect its trademarks and trade names and to prevent unauthorized production of anything similar to the elements of Disney World. Disney wasn't asking the state for a nickel of tax money or any other tax concessions, other than for roads outside the property to accommodate the large increase in traffic. Tatum explained that the firm had sufficient capital and borrowing power to complete the project without subsidies.

Tatum then introduced the new governor. Kirk pledged his wholehearted support to the project and described the economic bonanza it would bring to Florida—50,000 new jobs and $6.6 billion over the next ten years. "Let's get the dirt moving, and get off the dime," Kirk implored.

The moment the hour-and-45-minute conference ended, Roy and the

SIGNED AND SEALED. Governor Claude Kirk signs legislation establishing the Reedy Creek Improvement District, as Roy Disney checks his work. (May 12, 1967) *Photo courtesy State Archives of Florida*

governor flew to Jacksonville to tape a half-hour report, to be televised that evening throughout the state. The program began with the *EPCOT Film*, then had Roy and the governor deliver pleas to the people of Florida. Roy reiterated the need for Disney World to not be hampered by "archaic laws" and outmoded building codes.

Disney's proposed legislation weighed in at 481 pages. Yet when the three bills came up in legislature in spring, all passed by overwhelming majorities. The legislators' quick acquiescence established the Reedy Creek Improvement District and the cities of Lake Buena Vista and Bay Lake. The bills were to be officially signed into law during a special ceremony at the governor's mansion. As the governor walked the Disney executives down the hallway to the garden for the signing, Kirk turned to Roy and said, "Mr. Disney, I've read and studied the Reedy Creek Improvement District. It's very comprehensive. I noticed only one omission." Roy looked puzzled. The governor explained, "You made no provision for the crown."

EPCOT may have been the main argument why Disney needed the enabling legislation, but behind closed doors in California everyone was pulled off of EPCOT-related research and development. "Walt's gone," Roy would explain—in other words, it was time, at least for now, to stop dreaming. Wherever possible, they would incorporate ideas and components of Walt's EPCOT into the entire resort. And, of course, they would continue to look for corporate partners, especially those that could offer something state-of-the-art to help justify the need for their special governmental status.

The only primary project associated with EPCOT that was allowed to

ON DECK. Disney executives prepare to board small boats for a tour of the property. Waiting on the ramshackle dock are *(left to right)* Card Walker, Roy Disney, Joe Potter, Jack Sayers, photographer, and Donn Tatum. (1967) *Photo courtesy State Archives of Florida*

proceed was construction of the Progress City model—since it had a sponsor, General Electric. The 115-foot-wide model incorporated numerous elements of Walt's EPCOT, including its radial design, transportation systems, and domed mall at the base of a massive tower. Ostensibly, Disney built it as the post-show for GE's Carousel of Progress when the attraction moved from the World's Fair to Disneyland. The tiny PeopleMovers and golf carts, for instance, were powered by GE engines. Yet the model also helped to keep Walt's idea alive and buy his successors time to figure out what to do about it.

Initially, innovation would be borrowed from the outside. Monsanto would develop new materials to be introduced and employed in the resorts. Aerojet-General Corporation would install underground vacuum tubes to carry away trash. RCA was working on "the first twenty-first century information-communication system" for guests and cast members, integrating computer, telephone, automatic monitoring and control, mobile communications, television and wideband into one system.

Another ready partner was U.S. Steel. A few years earlier, the manufacturing giant had been publicly vilified after being accused of price gouging by President Kennedy. A little pixie dust was seen as just the thing to polish its tarnished reputation. At the same time, U.S. Steel's construction subsidiary, American Bridge, was heavily promoting modular construction as the wave of the future. They proposed building structures by first assembling and furnishing individual rooms in a factory and then stacking them next to or on top of each other. In theory, the technique would increase energy and noise insulation, since each room had its own separate walls, floor and ceiling. And, prefabricating entire rooms should be quicker and less expensive. Disney agreed to partner with U.S. Steel on the first Disney World hotels. U.S. Steel would pay $50 to $60 million to build two hotels and own the buildings through its realty division. Disney would retain the land, lease the hotels from U.S. Steel, and operate them.

Within five years, Disney hoped demand and finances would allow a total of five hotels around a lake planned to front the theme park. Each would be heavily themed and positioned to complement the view from inside the park, such as a modernistic hotel that could be seen from Tomorrowland and a South Seas hotel beyond Adventureland. The flagship hotel was to be "contemporary" in design, inspired by the iconic high-rise Walt wanted in the middle of his EPCOT city. The design team fixated on carrying over from Walt's plans two architectural features: a large, open atrium with an "internal city" of shops and restaurants, and the ability to run a monorail through the middle of it. For inspiration on the atrium, designers looked to Atlanta's Portman Hotel, which became Hyatt's first upscale hotel, and the Brown Palace in Denver. There was no precedent, however, for incorporating a monorail. Yet, said John Curry, "The Palace Hotel in San Francisco used to have carriages come in. Walt was an ardent train lover. So the notion that the monorail would pierce this hotel was very enthusiastically received."

After U.S. Steel became involved, plans for the Contemporary Hotel evolved from a conventional skyscraper into an A-frame inspired by the Palacio del Rio, a Hilton in San Antonio. A supper club would occupy the glass-walled penthouse. At the base, a trio of three-story garden-annexes would increase capacity.

On the opposite side of the lagoon, U.S. Steel would build a hotel with a Polynesian theme. It was originally planned as a triangular high-rise with a flat top surrounded by smaller longhouses along streams, a pool fed by waterfalls, and a skin-diving lagoon. With U.S. Steel coming aboard, the entire resort was transformed into clusters of two-story buildings designed as individual "tropical isles" along the white sand beaches. Guests could also enjoy pools with cascading waterfalls, a putting green, tennis, an exotic restaurant and lounge, luaus, sailing and moonlight cruises on an authentic sidewheel steamer.

The third hotel, planned to be built between the Polynesian and the theme park, would be the Asian. Four hundred rooms in royal Thai décor would be laid out in a square that butted into the lagoon. Three sides would offer a view of the water, the back side a view of the gardens. All surrounded a massive recreation area. In the center, a 160-foot-tall tower would hold more than 200 additional guest rooms, convention facilities, and a penthouse Thai restaurant and lounge for dancing and stage shows.

The 500-room Venetian—located on the shores between the Polynesian and Contemporary—would be built around a small boat harbor carved into the shore. Guests could glide by gondola through an intricate network of canals that branched through the resort, under ornate bridges, and past a glass-atrium lobby and a shopping courtyard reminiscent of St. Mark's Square.

The fifth hotel would sit between the Contemporary and the park, but set farther back, making it a bit more mysterious. The Persian would simulate a Far East palace with a huge dome crowning the central lobby, from which balconies would look down from each of the 500 rooms. Outside, beyond the sheltered marina, jewel-like mosques and columns would rise above colorfully landscaped courtyards, and guests could enjoy sculptured swimming pools and "old Persian" dining facilities on the terraced sundecks.

All five hotels would be luxury level; for budget-minded folks, there would also be an Old West-themed campground off in the woods surrounding Bay Lake.

For Walt, the hotels and other city elements were the driving forces for undertaking the Florida project. He had already produced a theme park, so design of the Magic Kingdom was almost an afterthought. For exactly the same reason, Roy viewed the park as the centerpiece of the entire project—Walt had done it before, making it financially and creatively safer. Roy consequently insisted that the Magic Kingdom be as faithful as possible to the proven layout of Disneyland, incorporating only suggestions that Walt had earmarked for improvement in Anaheim or that would take better advantage of Disney World's unique climate and ample acreage.

Marvin Davis and Dick Irvine based the master layout of the Magic Kingdom on Disneyland, but made everything bigger—the streets, the walkways, the waterways, the buildings, and especially the castle. To preserve the uniqueness of Disneyland's Sleeping Beauty Castle, Florida's icon was reconfigured as Cinderella Castle instead of Sleeping Beauty's, with a moat large enough to accommodate boat traffic wrapped all the way around the central plaza. The castle was to be tall enough so that guests could see it beckoning in the distance as they left the parking lot and made their grand approach by monorail around the Seven Seas Lagoon.

Just as at Disneyland, guests would enter through a tunnel beneath railroad tracks that circled the entire park and step onto turn-of-the-century Main Street U.S.A. At the end of the street, a central plaza would branch off to other themed lands. Disneyland was originally crafted so each land was a self-contained dead end. The design may have been thematically correct, but created perpetual crowding, bottlenecks at the entrances, and undue wear and tear on the guests. Visitors would have to retrace their steps back to the plaza every time they wanted to visit a new land. Although, over time, trails would be carved between the lands of Disneyland, all areas in Disney World would be interconnected from the start. The worst bottleneck, Fantasyland, instead of being designed as a self-contained courtyard, became one long corridor.

Disneyland, after fifteen years of feverish expansion, had more rides than made financial sense to duplicate at Disney World, at least initially. Many lower capacity rides could be omitted or left for later. Inside Fantasyland, Dumbo the Flying Elephant and the Mad Tea Party were in; the Storybook Land Canal Boats, Casey Jr. Railroad, and Alice in Wonderland dark ride were out. WED proposed retheming the other dark rides to different movies, but Roy insisted they remain true to Walt's original thinking at Disneyland and retain Peter Pan Flight, Snow White's Adventures, and Mr. Toad's Wild Ride. The Imagineers did, however, make sure the actual rides were slightly different than the originals. Instead of a Fantasyland Theater to show Mickey Mouse cartoons, Disney World would receive the animatronic Mickey Mouse Revue. In Anaheim, It's a Small World was a late addition and had to be situated far from the heart of Disneyland's Fantasyland. In Florida, it became another standard dark ride.

Starting from a blank slate, Davis and Irvine had the advantage of placing attractions in more appropriate areas—unlike at Disneyland where years of additions had compromised the theming. The Submarine Voyage would be placed not in Tomorrowland, but in Fantasyland and given a *20,000 Leagues Under the Sea* makeover. The miniature California freeways of Disneyland's Autopia car ride were replaced with a Grand Prix Raceway track for cars representing different countries. A spot was also reserved in Fantasyland, not Tomorrowland, near the Skyway aerial tram station for later inclusion of a Matterhorn.

The designers thought that Central Florida was too close to the real New Orleans and the real Caribbean for there to be interest in a faux New Orleans Square or Pirates of the Caribbean. Instead, Disney World would have colonial Liberty Square, situated at the eastern edge of Frontierland. Walt had envisioned the area ten years earlier as an adjunct to Disneyland's Main Street, primarily as a showplace for a "One Nation Under God" presentation in a Hall of Presidents. At Disney World, there would be room for every animatronic president and Mr. Lincoln wouldn't be forced to deliver speeches in an awkward location near the park entrance. To pad out Liberty Square, the area would inherit the

Haunted Mansion from New Orleans Square and the Mike Fink Keel Boats and Golden Horseshoe Revue from Frontierland.

The heart of Frontierland, with a Mississippi riverboat and canoes circling Tom Sawyer Island, translated nicely across country. Disneyland's pesky pack mule ride and Indian Village were left behind. A new addition was the Country Bear Jamboree, a humorous hoedown with animatronic bears originally designed for Mineral King. At the far western end of Frontierland, Davis and Irvine reserved a nice plot for Disney World's first major expansion project, Thunder Mesa. The area was to feature hiking trails across a table-top mountain to a pueblo-style village, a runaway mine train-themed roller coaster, and an elaborate dark ride—the Western River Expedition—to replace Pirates of the Caribbean

Adventureland was to make the trip eastward intact, with the Jungle Cruise, Swiss Family Treehouse, and Enchanted Tiki Room.

Tomorrowland would mimic the plans being used for Disneyland's remodeling in 1967—a Skyway station, PeopleMover trams, a CircleVision theater showing the 360-degree movie *America the Beautiful*, the Flight to the Moon ride, the retractable Tomorrowland Terrace stage, an undetermined dark ride, and plenty of room for anything else Disney could convince a company to sponsor. And the monorail, as per Walt's wishes, would not whisk visitors through the park, but rather to it and, in time, to other corners of the property.

As land preparation work began to give way to physical construction, Disney realized it faced a tremendous obstacle to staying on schedule. Unlike California, Florida was a right-to-work state, where union membership was optional. The various building trades were all fragmented. Apart from loose associations in Miami, Tampa and Jacksonville, the state had no acknowledged labor organization. With no governmental union structure, Disney had no one to negotiate with between and within the trades. The company was particularly afraid of jurisdictional disputes. Deciding which trade had the right to perform certain types of work could be a gray area in a project as large and complicated as Disney World. For example, if a carpenter had to move a stack of water pipes out of his way to complete a job, did he have to wait for a plumber, or could he move them himself? Or if the plumber had to pound a nail to secure a hose, could he do it or did he have to call in a carpenter? Already, during the initial site preparation, dragline operators had stormed off the job due to a jurisdictional dispute and walked the property with pickets for several days. Under Florida law, there was nothing Disney could do.

"The labor unions were not organized, so they could not provide adequate discipline," attorney Bob Foster noted. "They would have wildcat strikes for no reason. That's the kind of thing that went on. We'd be at their mercy. So it necessitated putting together a project agreement."

The unions turned up the heat in January 1968. Several thousand union members marched outside Disney's construction fence to protest the use of non-union workers. After several reports of rock throwing, fistfights and tire slashings, governor Kirk ordered the nearby sheriff's departments to maintain peace on the picket line. The picketers' resistance to the authorities grew so bitter that a few days later a phalanx of sheriff's deputies and policemen had to shove the striking mob away from the fence "inch by inch."

Bonar Dyer, Disney's corporate head of industrial relations, had seen enough. He knew all too well how unions in Hollywood could bring a film production to its knees. In 1941, Dyer watched as the Disney Studio was torn in two by an animators strike. Although in Anaheim management worked with multiple construction unions, Disneyland negotiated simultaneously with all the trades at the table. So to ensure that Disney World was completed on time, Dyer demanded that all the unions in Florida be similarly pulled together. He sent a team of lawyers to Washington, D.C., to work out a special agreement with the AFL-CIO and the Teamsters guaranteeing unions-scale wages, benefits and working conditions. In exchange, the unions pledged that there would be no strikes or work stoppages, so long as the company was working to resolve any disputes through binding arbitration.

The job quickly mushroomed into the world's largest private construction project. To oversee it all, Disney hired J.B. Allen Company, a California construction management firm that had served as primary contractor on several large projects at Disneyland. Their first jobs had been simultaneously creating a monorail route, Submarine Lagoon, and Matterhorn mountain in 1959. After major construction began in Florida in the spring of 1969, J.B. Allen would be in charge of 10,000 workers from 87 different subcontractors. To oversee Allen, Disney turned to another mainstay, Admiral Joe Fowler, the former Navy man who helped get Disneyland built on time. Tall and relaxed, Fowler had no fear of the

Florida wilderness after serving two years in the jungles of the Philippines and five years in China.

The first big decision would be where to place the Magic Kingdom. Several of Roy's boys argued for building the park at the most visible location—near the intersection of two highways at the front of the property. The accountants' proposal would have saved Disney time and millions of dollars in the short term, since much of the wilderness could have been left as was. Walt, however, had wanted the park at the back of the property, enticing visitors slowly through the entire development. As well, installing infrastructure throughout the property from the get-go would save money in the long term. Roy chose Walt's way.

Next, Fowler had to decide whether to locate the park's service areas in backstage buildings like at Disneyland or underground, beneath the park, mimicking Walt's plans for EPCOT. If he opted for the mega-basement, the park would have to be elevated sixteen feet, because the area's shallow water table—just four feet below the surface—precluded digging down. The basement would have to be built at ground level, then buried, and the park built on top of it. Fowler chose Walt's way, even though it increased land preparation costs from $4 million to $9 million. A battery of earth-moving equipment scooped out eight million cubic yards of dirt to form a 200-acre lagoon, then an army of trucks, called in from everywhere inside and outside the state, redeposited the fill on top of the basement, raising the ground level sixteen feet.

Downstream, Disney set aside 7,500 acres for a wilderness preserve, intended to be left in its natural state indefinitely. The area would help purify the drainage, act as a buffer to protect neighboring farmlands from stormwater runoff, and provide natural habitat for indigenous plants, trees, birds and animals.

Nearby, landscaper Bill Evans established a 110-acre tree farm. There, he could experiment with trees and plants from all over world to determine which could grow in Florida. Some species refused to adapt to their new climate; those that thrived would be transplanted to the most appropriate part of the property.

Next to the park was Bay Lake, a 450-acre sinkhole, its murky waters stained brown with tannic acid from the cypress swamps that fed into it. No guests would enjoy looking at, boating across, or especially swimming in what looked like a massive pool of iced tea. So, Fowler spent five months draining its 3.5 billion gallons and having giant earthmovers scrape fourteen feet of root mass and muck off the bottom—right down to the fine white sugar sand underneath. It didn't help matters that several bulldozers got caught. The heavy equipment then shoved the pure sand up on the shore to form tapered white beaches. Workmen next began laboriously refilling the lake with ground water. The hole had to be filled to a foot-and-a-half higher than the previous ground level to ensure water would flow out of rather than into the now sanitized lake. Despite assistance from the constant rains that slowed other construction on the property, it took nine months to refill Bay Lake.

The Reedy Creek Improvement District sold tax-exempt bonds to fund construction of the property's water system and infrastructure, including its energy plant and electrical distribution system.

To pay for the commercial construction, Disney had to look elsewhere. Following Walt's death, a number of corporate suitors had stepped forward, hoping to merge with Disney. Roy refused to sell out and lose control of the company. Walt Disney Productions had a fair amount of cash on hand, but Roy detested debt. Instead, attorney Nolan Browning suggested Roy take advantage of his company's steadily rising stock price by looking into convertible debentures. Disney could sell bonds that would be converted into stock once the share price reached a predetermined level, instantly retiring the debt. In January 1968, the company issued $40 million in convertible debentures. They quickly sold out. Disney's stock price continued to climb, and the bonds hit their conversion level before the year was out. Disney promptly sold out a second bond issue for $50 million. Later, Disney issued an additional $72 million in stock and, just after the Magic Kingdom opened, offered a third set of convertible debentures for $100 million. Roy had found a way to get the resort open debt-free—although his and the rest of the Disney family's ownership interest in the company would be diluted. Still, while their ownership percentage slipped, what they owned doubled in value.

Just as crews began assembling to begin physical construction, Disney realized it was time to begin preparing Floridians for the enormous changes ahead. The company never believed in big expensive advertising campaigns. Instead, it concentrated on continually building up its image. Word of mouth, Disney calculated, was its most effective marketing tool. And Disney saw its own good name as so valuable that other companies would pay to include Disney's theme park, films, and characters in their own advertising. As well, Disney viewed itself as such a fascinating subject of study that it assumed newspapers should want to write endlessly about its latest productions in their news pages; paid ads would be a waste. Likewise, television commercials cost too much. Walt preferred to just plug his newest attraction on the *Wonderful World of Disney*—and the network would pay him for the privilege.

Radio? Too segmented. Billboards? Obnoxious. Disney's marketing philosophy was to connect the public with its product as personally and inexpensively as possible. Disneyland drummed up local publicity by organizing special events for cities, clubs and other groups. Nationally, the park would tour in small town parades and visit children's hospitals with a small band of costumed characters and the year's tour guide "ambassador."

Yet at the time most of Florida was even too "small town" for Disney. Residents subscribed to a traditional Deep South mentality, their lives firmly grounded no farther than their own tiny farming or ranching community. Most seemed content with their uncomplicated surroundings, reflexively resistant to change and distrustful of the smooth-talking newcomers from Hollywood. Even the more worldly of the citizenry—retirees who had spent their working lives in the big cities of the Northeast—wanted peace and quiet. They didn't move to Florida for a theme park.

In late 1967, Disney World hired its first director of marketing, fair-haired Sandy Quinn. Quinn was one of several recruits whom staunch Republican Card Walker hired from the Nixon campaign, which he viewed as an assurance of their sincerity and patriotism. "I was an early disciple of Disney and Americana," Quinn related. "And there was no bigger, better known, more respected symbol in the world than Mickey Mouse. Mickey's non-controversial. Even God is controversial."

Following several months of indoctrination in California, Quinn headed to Orlando to "establish a beachhead," joining Joe Potter, Phil Smith, Smith's secretary, and accountant Jim McManus. Gradually, Quinn was to organize the advertising, promotion, public relations, community affairs, photography, publicity and graphics staffs. Among his first tasks: sending pink "call-back" slips that gently broke the bad news to those who had left messages that their Uncle Walt, in his dying days, had promised them free trips to the new resort.

MARKETING PLANS. Disneyland Operations executives Dick Nunis *(left)* and Bob Mathieson *(right)* review Florida promotional literature with Milton Wier, chairman of the state Department of Commerce. (c. 1970) *Photo courtesy State Archives of Florida*

Most importantly, Quinn was charged with getting Florida ready for Disney, a mission that had some co-workers referring to him as "John the Baptist." Quinn traveled the state, speaking to small local business groups and attending Chamber of Commerce meetings to encourage members to begin formulating ways to capitalize on the coming tourism. He suggested they create package deals, offer special incentives, partner with transportation providers, and brainstorm other ideas to take advantage of the gold rush that would be pouring into Central Florida. During one early stop, Quinn visited Miami Beach to address a local hotel association. General managers from all the big hotels attended. Quinn presented a slideshow with beautiful concept drawings and photos of the early stages of construction. He then opened the floor to questions. An older hotel manager stood up: "Mr. Quinn, I don't think you understand why people come to Florida. They come to see our hotels and our beaches." His compatriots nodded. Your little park sounds nice, they agreed, but we don't need one.

"It was hard to comprehend what was going to happen," said Bob Mathieson, who was putting together impact studies of the Disneyland area. "At that time, the intersection of Harbor Boulevard and Ball Road had an average traffic count of 95,000 cars a day. Well, you can put that up on a chart, but you can't relate to that. It doesn't really register. So we hired a helicopter, took film of it, and showed that to the county commission. We said, 'Okay, this is what 95,000 cars a day through an intersection looks like.'"

Mathieson speculated that the populace's difficulty visualizing a Disney World was to be expected. "In the '20s, there was a big real estate scandal in Florida," he related. "Property was being sold to people in Iowa and Minnesota, and it was romantic to go to Florida and get a piece of land, which they never saw, until later. It was underwater, a swamp, a big scam. I think that mindset still lasted while we were developing. We didn't take tours on the property. We were building this huge thing, and nobody could really see what we were building. So to the day we opened there was still skepticism. 'Well, is this really going to come off?' 'Are they building Ferris wheels?' There was still skepticism about what this thing, Disney World, is going to be."

Clearly, the Marketing department had its work cut out for it. "A very small percentage of the population [in the East] had ever been to Disneyland," Quinn recalled. "The concept they knew about because of the Sunday TV show, but they hadn't experienced it. So we couldn't assume, come Opening Day, they'd know what it was."

The one big official update came in April 1969 when Disney hosted media and government officials from all over the state for three full days of hoopla. The company booked every room in a just-opened Ramada Inn in nearby Ocoee and set up a circus tent in the parking lot to display artwork and scale models. A caravan of buses took everyone to a nearby theater, where Roy and Governor Kirk introduced a new film showing exactly what Walt Disney World would be. Then buses took the group through miles of trees and swamps, to a man-made clearing populated with bulldozers and dumptrucks.

Despite the activity deep inside the forest, few signs of life could be seen from the outside. Along the northern boundary, Disney was assembling a growing collection of double-wide trailers to serve as manage-

ment offices. Down the street sat two businesses, Jock's Corner and a
Stuckey's family restaurant. Jock's was a sleepy convenience store that
early every morning and late every afternoon suddenly transformed into
a bustling madhouse as the bypassing construction workers dropped in
for hot cold sandwiches, cold hot sandwiches, and warm beer. Stuckey's
accommodated both tourists headed to or from the beach and local folk,
whose favorite topic of conversation was speculating on what Disney
might be up to in the woods.

"There was one guy, a Mr. Clemmons" recalled Disneylander Bill
Hoelscher, "and he would hold court at Stuckey's. Folks would come out
to see what we were up to, and 'Mr. Stuckey' would tell everybody a
bunch of misinformation. He was the tour guide for anybody who wanted to know what was going to happen. So at that time, the company
thought, 'Hey, it's a good idea. Why don't we build our own Preview
Center?'"

According to Hoelscher, who oversaw the operation, the Preview
Center was built to accomplish several objectives. First and foremost,
the company could tell the public "what was really happening out here."
Second, it could gain its first experience in hiring. From a pool of 400
lovely applicants, Valerie Watson selected fourteen women to staff the
Preview Center—the first full-timers hired into all-critical guest contact
positions.

"The employees in Florida were refreshingly wholesome, eager,
enthusiastic," she remembered. "Originally it was an agrarian area.
There wasn't a degree of sophistication. I found them delightful to work
with. Whereas Anaheim and Orange County is a worldly part of
Southern California, moving fast all the time, early on Disney World was
innocent, laid back. Some of those girls spent most of their time in their
bare feet. It was a very educational and heartwarming experience."

Third, the Preview Center's small souvenir stand allowed Disney to
begin testing the appeal of different types of merchandise. Visitors could
buy park tickets and make reservations to later stay at the Contemporary
or Polynesian hotels. In addition, marketing vice president Jack Lindquist had the Preview Center staff track the license plates in the parking
lot, so he knew where people were visiting from. Just as at Carefree
Corner at Disneyland, hostesses asked visitors to sign a guest book to
create a "Year One Club" to whom Disney could mail promotional literature. Finally, the Preview Center provided Sandy Quinn with a nicer

WELCOME. To promote the coming Kingdom, at the edge of its property Disney opened a Preview Center, headed by Bill Hoelscher *(front row, third from left)*, Valerie Watson *(seated)*, and merchandise manager Bob Welch *(far right)*. (January, 1970) *Photo courtesy Bill Hoelscher*

base of operations than a double wide trailer for meeting with potential sponsors and beginning tours of the property for stockholders and other interested VIPs.

Near the northern entrance to the property, Disney built a one-story white building—about 1,000 square feet—featuring a large square theater in the center. Here, visitors would watch a film on the coming attractions while standing around a huge model of the entire resort. Spotlights from the ceiling alternately highlighted the Magic Kingdom, Contemporary Hotel, and other key features of the model as they were discussed in the movie. A hallway ran around the perimeter of the building, its walls decorated with concept art, which led to Quinn's office, a conference room, snack bar, merchandise stand, and restrooms.

"The ladies were kept up to date and schooled every week on what was new and what had changed," said Hoelscher. "We'd take the pictures down, put new pictures up, change artist renderings. We kept it new and fresh, and the press would come out so we could yak to them about what was going on."

The snack bar served both Coca-Cola and Pepsi, since both companies would be non-exclusive sponsors inside the park. Coke, as the first one to sign up, installed its fountain equipment in the snack bar, infuriating Pepsi that its syrup had to be pumped through its rival's machinery.

As the first operational facility in Lake Buena Vista, opening January 10, 1970, the Preview Center was the first to use the over-sized water and sewage lines installed to eventually accommodate about a half-dozen high-rise hotels and other businesses. Hoelscher recalled, "About the second day that we were open, a lady went into our restrooms to use the facilities. She flushed the toilet, and a two-foot column of water blew her up off the seat. It was a mess—and it scared the daylights out of her. The pipes were too big. We had to reduce the pressure."

In 22 months of operation, the Preview Center would welcome more than one million visitors and, according to Lindquist, help pre-sell more than $11 million in tickets to the Magic Kingdom. The heavy interest it helped generate caused Disney to quickly change its first-year attendance forecast from six million to eight million guests and then again, by the summer of 1971, to ten million guests. Hotel reservations and inquiries were also pouring in at a rate of 300 a day. And months before the hotels opened, convention space was booked for a year solid.

4

Trouble Building

CONSTRUCTION was humming not just on property. In Glendale, Disney's ride designers at WED and ride builders at the manufacturing division, MAPO, were deluged with Disney World projects. Some entire rides were built in Southern California and then shipped, piece by piece, for reassembly at the Magic Kingdom. For other attractions, Disney craftsmen built individual components, such as the steam engines for the 200-passenger sidewheelers or the animatronics for the stage attractions. To save time, the Imagineers working on the Haunted Mansion for Disneyland built two of everything, putting the spare set off to the side for Disney World.

Other elements were shipped in from around the world—ski lift equipment for the Skyway from Switzerland, costume wigs from Guatemala, and monorail bellows from Germany.

Wherever possible, WED insisted on making period components as authentic as possible, even in areas where guests would never know the difference. "Most guests don't realize all of the things there that are of some significance," Bill Hoeslcher noted. "When you cross into Liberty Square, there are rocks on both sides of that bridge. Those rocks were quarried about six miles from where Washington crossed the Delaware, and they were bought at a lot of expense. We could have gotten rocks in Kissimmee. But we wanted some significance there. Some of the slate stoops of those buildings were actually bought in Philadelphia and were in place when our country was still going through its Revolutionary War and when they were signing the Declaration of Independence. All of the lights are of the period, too."

Disney purchased a giant 50-year-old carousel from a New Jersey amusement park, refurbished it in Northern California, and repainted it at its studio in Burbank. In San Jose, Arrow Development manufactured more than 700 ride vehicles, from miniature racing cars to Skyway gondolas. A shipyard in St. Petersburg, Florida, began assembling the submarines, while shipyards in Tampa put together the other 100-plus vessels.

Four forgotten Baldwin steam locomotives from the early 1900s were found rusting in the Yucatan Peninsula and hauled to Tampa for painstaking restoration. Martin-Marietta's aerospace plant in Orlando built next-generation Mark IV monorails.

Disney searched for but could not find anyone in Florida who could produce the beams for the monorail track. The closest source was in Tacoma, Washington—the same company that made the monorail beams for the Seattle World's Fair of 1962. To make shipping and installation easier, the manufacturer built the concrete beams with lightweight polystyrene cores. The 337 beams still weighed 55 tons apiece and measured from 85 to 110 feet long. Hauling each one across country required three flatcars, with swiveling pivots between each end so the trains could go around curves. En route, two trains ended up in a ditch. The freight bill came to $980,000.

The monorail track was to be installed atop a series of giant concrete pylons. Engineers conducted test drillings at each location where a pylon would be placed. They unearthed three sinkholes. In one spot, they drilled down 175 feet without hitting the bottom. Consequently, every pylon had to be designed differently and of a different length, forcing Disney to cast each one themselves, on site.

In addition to providing manpower and training, Disneyland itself became a testing ground for the Florida project. Anaheim's New Tomorrowland of 1967 featured the first WEDway PeopleMover and an underground tunnel that provided expedited, unseen travel between the park's backstage and the Tomorrowland Terrace food service and entertainment area. The subterranean corridor also provided easier access to the utility pipes that ran along its ceiling and walls. The same year, Disneyland completed New Orleans Square, with its own underground labyrinth and a central kitchen to serve multiple restaurants.

The central kitchen foreshadowed an idea of John Cardone, an executive chef hired by Disney to help set up the food facilities in Florida. In the late 1960s, Cardone was sent to Florida for two weeks to figure out what his division's needs would be. He was back in California in two days. He didn't need any more time; there was nothing to see and no local connections to be made. Unlike bustling Southern California, where food supplies were so close there was no need for considerable food storage, Central Florida lacked sources for fresh produce, meat, dairy products, and other food items. Cardone proposed that Disney build its own central plant to store and process food for all of Disney World's restaurants. Construction began on a 55,000-square foot Central Food Facility, a mile north of the Magic Kingdom. It would deal directly with vendors, many inevitably out of state, buying in bulk, freezing, storing, and handling all preparation work—forming hamburger patties, slicing meats and cheeses for sandwiches, baking bread and pastries, preparing soups, salads and pizza, all to be delivered to individual eateries ready to be cooked and served.

Staffing Disney World would be a little trickier than the typical annual hiring Disneyland conducted before each summer. There, tens of thousands of applicants vied for a predictable assortment of a few thousand temporary, hourly positions. "Outsiders" were rarely hired into salaried positions; for Disneyland, outside experience was a black mark on your résumé. Disneyland wanted recruits young, fresh, impressionable and smiling.

The top executives were all personally taught at the knee of Walt. They each endured years of indoctrination in the corporate culture and traditions before they qualified for promotion. They uniformly considered Disneyland not just a business, but a show, one in which every employee played an integral role. Their job wasn't sweeping or cleaning or cooking or ringing up a cash register—it was creating happiness. The focus encouraged every worker to buy into the concept that they were part of something bigger than themselves. It also resulted in hands-on management; supervisors weren't supposed to be in their offices studying spreadsheets, but walking the park, side by side with the hourlies and the guests, "on stage."

They also developed a sixth sense to instinctively detect if something was out of place. If out of the corner of one eye, they spotted a piece of litter across Main Street, they'd head straight over to pick it up.

They did—and spent—whatever was necessary to please the guest in hopes of creating customers for life, who would spread the word to all their friends. It was the Disney way, or the highway. At the end of the day, success could be better measured not by how many dollars you generated, but by how many smiles.

If recruits fared well in part-time positions during their college years, having fully absorbed the Disney philosophy of sacrificing all to please guests and maintain the artificial environment, they might earn a promotion into the underpaid ranks of lower management.

Once inside the cloistered boys' club of management, they became keepers of show standards, protectors of the ways of Walt, entrusted to continue perpetuating the guest-first, hire-from-within, show-is-everything style of management.

To accentuate the intertwining nature of how the park should be run, Walt organized the original Disneyland management team as a "Park Operating Committee," composed of the heads of each department. The team would meet weekly to brief other departments on what was new and what was coming, to share their challenges and successes, and to glean advice from the other heads.

Naturally, when Disney World opened, most every top management spot would be filled by a trusted insider, versed in the Disney ways and secret handshakes. A few outsiders would inevitably have to be hired to oversee unknown areas, particularly for the hotels to please U.S. Steel. Most of the middle managers would also be Disneyland transfers. In all, 250 Disneylanders relocated. But Florida required more entry-level management positions than could be filled just by raiding Disneyland.

Instead, in the spring of 1968, Disney began sending pairs of executives to visit colleges in the East. The idea was to offer summer internships at Disneyland to 30 or so select sophomores. Students who performed well would be invited back the following summers until permanent jobs arose as Disney World neared opening. Recruiters targeted juniors the following spring and seniors the next. As a result, new hires straight out of college might already have had several seasons to ingest the pixie dust.

Management recruits first learned about the corporate culture in Disney Way I, a refined version of its long-time indoctrination program. An additional five-day program, Disney Way II, focused specifically on

Disney World—how the resort was organized and what each division was responsible for, with the teaching led by an old-timer from each division. The program culminated with the management trainee suiting up in a character costume and being tossed into the middle of a crowd, to see first-hand what Disney's product was all about.

During one recruiting trip to Michigan State University, human resources manager Jim Passilla and director of foods Jim Armstrong met Gerald T. "Pat" Vaughn, who was on a recruiting trip of his own for Martin-Marietta aerospace firm. Upon hearing that Vaughn was based in Orlando, Passilla asked him if he could call occasionally to quiz about the local labor market. About a year later, in early 1969, Passilla hired Vaughn to head up hiring for Disney World.

Vaughn relocated to California and for two years moved throughout the personnel division at Disneyland trying to learn the business and devise how to replicate it on a larger scale. Vaughn returned to Florida in March 1971 and set up shop in a spare construction trailer.

Vaughn remembered, "We'd work out of temporary buildings. We'd be in one place for several months and when they needed that for something else, they'd move us into another. It was all the back part of the property. It was tough to get to then. It was really a wild, undeveloped area."

The first Disney hourly positions to fill, after the Preview Center hostesses, were security officers. The massive construction project required constant oversight and Disney was disappointed with the security service it had initially contracted with. Besides, an in-house security force would have to be hired and trained by the time the park opened anyways. According to Disney legend, one rent-a-guard prevented Donn Tatum from parking his car on the not-yet-paved Main Street. "I don't care who you are," the temp barked, "you can't park here." Incensed, Tatum ordered Disney-trained guards be hired immediately.

"We put a little notice in the newspaper," Vaughn said. "We figured that we'd get enough people. We'd set aside one evening in a couple of the temporary buildings out there to do interviews. For 30 or 40 openings, we had 800 applicants. There were cars parked in ditches. It was awesome. Because it was Disney, because it was the first time we'd gone to the newspaper, people were so excited."

In all, Disney World would need to open with about 5,500 hourly and 500 to 600 salaried workers. About 5,000 of the employees needed to staff the resort had to be hired close to opening, but with enough time left for training. Vaughn said, "We worked out schedules with the directors of different divisions. We determined what needed to be in place on October 1 and worked backwards, based on what kind of training they needed. In some cases it was a day, some cases two weeks, some cases a month, depending upon the nature of the job. We created huge boards by job classification—we needed 40 for this division on this date and 120 of these for this division on this date. Some people we needed to bring on considerably early, probably in the first quarter of 1971. We needed people to staff our telephone company. We had warehousing. We needed people to receive the stuff that we were getting from California. As for the resort area itself, [hiring] was pretty compressed to the last couple months. As I recall, we had 120,000 applicants. We interviewed 35,000. We hired 5,000. So we absolutely had the pick, the cream of the crop. With the number of people to choose from, we had the most outstanding 5,000 you could possibly have under almost any conditions."

Vaughn also called on his contacts in the placement offices at colleges throughout the state. "Some time in 1970," he said, "I took the placement directors from the major colleges and community colleges in Florida that we thought we would be drawing from, put them on the Walt Disney airplane, Mickey Mouse One, and took them to California for a week, all expenses paid. We had a whole week full of activities lined up for them—seminars, presentations, meeting the leaders of the company. We took them to WED, where they saw some of the shows in design. The whole idea was they, like most people, had no idea what a theme park was. Most people hadn't gone to Disneyland. They'd only seen pictures of it. Our whole intent was to get the colleges to totally understand what it was that we were doing and what kind of opportunities that we presented to their placement offices. And it was well worth the time."

Disney ran minimal advertising for job openings, since the local newspaper was already covering the company's every hiccup. Whenever Vaughn had positions to fill, he simply informed a reporter what he needed, and the next morning—voilà—instant news story.

"And of course," Vaughn added, "word of mouth got around pretty quickly. We had people driving in from all over the Southeast and beyond to inquire about jobs and Walt Disney World. That's how big it was in the minds of people at that time, because there really wasn't anything like it anywhere in the Southeast. People saw this as an opportunity to get in on something on the ground floor. So we didn't have any problem soliciting applicants."

To handle the onslaught, Disney kept its makeshift "casting center" open seven days a week. All day long, hundreds of hopeful applicants lined up across the dirt parking lot. Countless qualified candidates had to be turned down. There were a fair number of odd prospects, as well. One applicant submitted his résumé rolled up like a scroll, written in pirate language. A musician walked into the trailer one Saturday and asked if Disney was still hiring. He said he'd be right back with his accompanist—and returned a moment later with an accordion and his dancing monkey.

Dale Burner, who arrived from Anaheim to screen prospects for the Foods division, recalled, "Coming from California, we thought that everyone knew what Disneyland was. That was not the case. After fifteen years, people still thought Disneyland was and Disney World was going to be a carnival. In interviews, people would say, 'I want to work the Ferris wheel.' One fellow's job experience was a sod stacker. Another was a clacker pourer—he poured resin into molds to make toy clackers. They didn't know, didn't understand."

It didn't take construction workers long to realize they were working for a company unlike any they had seen before. Disney designers always insisted on perfection and didn't think twice about making post-deadline alterations. Workmen quickly learned that "close enough," perfectly acceptable on previous jobs, wasn't good enough for Disney. Subcontractors were furious when Disney insisted they tear apart and rebuild the framework for the carousel when they discovered it had been erected two inches off from their specs.

Tommy Sparks, who began his lengthy Disney career digging canals and building roads in 1967, recalled, "Down here we do roads in straight lines. Disney wanted curved roads, all except the World Drive. 'We don't work with straight lines,' they'd say. 'Anybody can make a straight line.' They did zig zags. We had to redo one service road near Turnpike 3 at the edge of Bay Lake. It was straight and now it's a big double ess curve where they changed it. Disney wanted it done right."

The construction crews also didn't seem to be in any hurry because they knew how desperate Disney was to finish by October 1, 1971. The slower they worked, the more lucrative overtime would be required in the final months. Making time-and-a-half, even the guy running the construction elevator was eventually taking home larger paychecks than the Disney executives on site.

In general, the crew was a surly bunch, difficult to manage and prone to starting fights. The men once grew so impatient that a portable outhouse in the main parking lot hadn't been serviced, they set the structure on fire. Construction workers outnumbered Disney's fresh-faced security force by about 50 to one. In the event of an extreme emergency, the guards were armed to the teeth—with the phone number to the sheriff's department.

"The construction people didn't like security at all," said Henry "Ray" Carter, who joined the Disney force about six months before the park opened. "They would purposely drive through mud puddles to splash us. They even hit us with their cars. They were mean and nasty. Some were just like animals. The girls in PBX (telephone exchange) worked in a suite on top of the castle, and whenever they had to go to lunch or to their car, there were catcalls. It wasn't safe. So we had to escort them."

Such laxness and unprofessionalism did not befit a Disney project. Project management needed the magic touch. The opportunity arose, with less than a year left before opening. J.B. Allen was growing increasingly frustrated with Disney's ever-changing blueprints. Allen complained that the work was multiplying and time was running out. Maybe the opening should be postponed. Allen's pessimism, however, did not come as particularly bad news. Disney would need an experienced staff to maintain the attractions once they were built; at some point it would have to form its own contracting company.

Bill Moss, a field engineer, recalled, "My understanding was that J.B. Allen said they didn't think the project would be completed on time. That wasn't acceptable." Disney needed someone in charge who did.

So, one Friday afternoon, early in 1971, Disney fired J.B. Allen. Over the weekend, it hurriedly formed its own company, Buena Vista Construction Company, as a Disney subsidiary headed by Fowler, and moved most of those under Allen—project managers, supervisors, office staff and thousands of construction workers—to the Disney payroll. Over night, they repainted all the "J.B. Allen" signs on the property with "Buena Vista Construction," in time to greet everyone arriving at work Monday morning.

Placing Disney managers in the field also exposed additional reasons why costs continued to skyrocket, while work lagged farther behind schedules. To pick up their paychecks, workers would now be required to show proof of identification. The first day Disney was in charge of passing out the checks, about 60 contractors didn't show up to get paid. Evidently, a prior manager had been submitting hours for imaginary workers, and then pocketing their checks.

Disney also discovered that entire truckloads of materials were disappearing. A truck filled with lumber, plywood or other building materials would check in as it entered the property through the North Gate—and then keep right on driving out the South Gate. One construction manager had been diverting supplies to his own housing project a few miles away.

Individual construction workers had equally sticky fingers. One worker stole enough material from the site to build a camper shell for his pickup truck.

Security officer Carter found watchman duty during the initial construction a most difficult assignment. "It was tougher at that time than after the Magic Kingdom opened," he explained, "because you had to deal with all the construction problems, all kinds of thievery. You couldn't lay a tool down before it would disappear. There was even stealing from the attractions. When they were building the Jungle Cruise, they'd insert glass eyes into the elephants. They were stealing the glass eyes! I don't know as souvenirs or what. They had to hold up putting on the finishing touches until after they put the water in the river."

Theft got especially out of control at the hotels, where the supplies and furnishings seemed to be disappearing almost as fast as they were installed. "When we'd buy showerheads for 1,056 rooms, we'd have to order 4,000," remembered John Curry.

The television sets in the guestrooms were linked to a master receiver so the hotels could offer their own programming such as Disney movies and listings of hotel activities, while limiting programs from the outside. The TVs would not work on their own. Curry recalled, "We placed a placard on each set that explained this so that construction crews would not steal them. I guess the thieves thought it was just a gimmick to stop them from being stolen, because TV shops in the area all reported sets being brought in by people complaining they didn't work."

In desperation, Disney built a fence around each hotel and had security check lunch pails, toolboxes, and packages as construction workers left for the day. The union, unfortunately, threatened to strike if such harassment continued. Disney reluctantly stopped the searches. Without fear of being checked, construction workers soon began arriving with huge Coleman coolers instead of lunch boxes—which grew noticeably heavier by quitting time.

In the early stages of planning, Disney first considered hiring an outside firm to manage its hotels, then take over after it got to know the business. The tactic had helped Disneyland learned the basics of security, custodial, food service, merchandise and other conventional operations. John Curry contacted every major U.S. hotel chain and met with their top executives. He decided on Western International to manage the Polynesian and Marriott to manage the Contemporary. But during negotiations, Disney struck the deal with U.S. Steel, and part of the deal was that Disney themselves would run the hotels and form the Walt Disney World Hotel Company to do it.

Western International executives, however, had become so intrigued with the Disney project that in 1969 they agreed to serve as consultants for a year and allow Disney to study up close its five-year-old showplace, the Century Plaza Hotel in Los Angeles. Century Plaza staff in all departments offered advice, critiqued plans, and helped Disney put together its first hotel manuals. In particular, Disney's computer expert, Ko Suzuki, was allowed to adapt the hotel's computerized reservation system to create Disney's.

Running the hotels Disney-style was one of Burbank's biggest worries, because it had never operated a hotel before. As the consulting contract with Western was winding down, Disney noticed a small hotel under construction about ten miles north of Disney World. The owner, Orlando attorney Finley Hamilton, had opened a Hilton Inn on Colonial Drive a few years earlier. For his second hotel, he acquired ten acres for cheap because at the time it was in the middle of nowhere, accessible only by a dirt road. He'd pave the road himself and hope to lend it some notoriety by calling it "International Drive." The two-story, U-shaped hotel had a covered pool area in the middle, 140 guestrooms, and several meeting rooms. Hamilton planned for his new location to catch the attention of Disney-bound visitors driving down Interstate 4.

Yet those tourists wouldn't be Disney-bound for another year and a half. So, Disney offered to manage Hamilton's hotel for him. They would charge Hamilton standard industry fees, but grossly overstaff his hotel and ensure above-average occupancy before the tourists started coming to town. And to ensure Hamilton wasn't left in the lurch, Disney personnel would stay and help manage the hotel for several months after the Magic Kingdom opened to train Hamilton's employees.

By this time, Curry had hired all of one employee—New York hotel veteran Howard Roland as manager of planning. But when it came time for Curry to thank Western and move on, about a half-dozen Century Plaza managers wanted to move on with him. At first, Curry declined. "I didn't think it was right since Western had been so gracious and helpful," he said. But days later, the group returned to Curry and announced, "We're unemployed. We just quit our jobs." Curry hired them all, including the Century Plaza's beverage manager Harold Brown, bell captain George Woo, general manager's administrative assistant Clayne Dice, and general manager's secretary Jayne Kerr, who became Curry's secretary.

The team quickly set up shop at Hamilton's Hilton Inn South. They viewed it as a hospitality laboratory where they could develop and test operational procedures, training manuals, and accounting systems, and line up suppliers and employees. The chefs would also have a place to develop their menus and regularly hold food and wine tastings. As executive chef of the Contemporary, Curry hired Joe Mannke away from Anthony's Pier Four in Boston. To head the Polynesian's kitchen, Curry wanted the famed Hungarian Garry Reich, who had been personal chef to President Lyndon B. Johnson. Reich agreed, on the condition that he be allowed to continue serving one of his customers. Every Wednesday, he had to fly to Las Vegas to prepare a week's worth of meals for Howard Hughes.

Dan Darrow was recruited from Sheraton and placed as general manager of the Hilton Inn South. Disneyland old-timer Bill Sullivan was appointed assistant general manager, he said, "to add a Disney touch to the hotel business, because they were all good hotel people, but had never worked at Disney."

The Hilton opened in May 1970 and quickly became the default destination to relax and enjoy a drink after a long day on the jobsite. Darrow and his team were always on their toes, since Roy and the other Burbank bigwigs visited the hotel often—and noticed any flaws.

As well, the hotel provided the company with ample housing for its

MOBILE HOMES: Prefabricated hotel rooms were trucked to the jobsite...

own needs. Although the Hilton was open to the public, Disney employees typically occupied a large percentage of the rooms. Some were temporary visitors from California, others transfers who hadn't had a chance to find a permanent home yet. When Card Walker, Donn Tatum and the other top executives were in town, they stayed at one of five cottages Disney had built along a man-made lagoon in Bay Hill. The nicest cottage was reserved for Roy and his wife, Edna. Joe Fowler moved in next door, so he could reach Roy quickly when problems arose.

The cottages also became a popular spot for morale-boosting cookouts and Disney World Operating Committee retreats. As Roy told his executives during one such Bay Hill barbecue, "I hope you guys are having fun, because for how hard you're working, you're going to kill yourselves if you're not enjoying it."

Near the Bay Hill cottages, U.S. Steel joined together the first four modular hotel rooms around a central living area to create a model home. Called the "U.S. Steel House," it provided U.S. Steel executives with their own retreat, as well as a place to critique the rooms' construction and furnishings away from the busy jobsite and to pitch other hotel developers on the joys of modular construction.

The farther away the Disney brass was, the better, figured U.S. Steel. Construction of the hotels had fallen drastically behind schedule. Yet U.S. Steel wasn't about to say anything. They had seen what had happened to J.B. Allen. They just continued sending rosy reports back to Burbank. WED designers didn't make their job any easier by constantly revising engineering plans. Worse, U.S. Steel's experiment with modular construction—designed to speed things along like an assembly line—created its own share of headaches.

U.S. Steel built a factory on property about three miles away, where they were able to assemble about 40 rooms a week. Each measured nine feet high, fifteen feet wide, and more than 30 feet long, many with attached balconies. By the time they left the factory, the rooms had walls, floor decking, ceilings, air conditioning units, piping, mechanical, electrical, lighting, and—in the bathrooms—mirrors, bath fixtures, and vinyl floor and wallcoverings.

As needed by the installers, rooms were trucked to the construction site, where they were lifted and inserted into the hotel's structural frames

...then lifted into the Contemporary Hotel's steel A-frame by massive cranes. (January 1971) *Photos courtesy John Curry*

by six massive cranes—each taller than the fourteen-story Contemporary. Ideally, the finished rooms were to be slid right into the slots, like shoeboxes on a store shelf. In practice, the cranes grappled with the 4.5-ton modules, which more often than not didn't fit into the exacting openings on the first try. For the Contemporary, on top of the four-story base they had erected thirteen pairs of 150-foot-high steel A-frames, clad in concrete and spaced 33 feet apart. So the cranes had to alternate installing rooms on opposite sides to prevent the frames from becoming off-balance.

Accommodating the monorail created additional problems. The structural engineers repeatedly reengineered the Contemporary to avoid vibration. They quickly realized that it would be impossible to run the monorail through the middle of the hotel, as was originally planned. Instead, the monorail track was placed at the edge of the hotel, and anchored to the ground, not the building.

With six months left until opening, even the name of the high-rise hotel hadn't been settled. During the years of development and now more than halfway through construction, everyone referred to it by its description and working title, the Contemporary Hotel—against the advice of WED wordsmith Marty Sklar. He had warned, "If you give it a nickname, it's going to stick." But the hotel designers always had something more important to worry about. Finally, in early spring 1971, they came up with a permanent name, the Tempo Bay Hotel. Very clever, the designers thought. *Tempo* was short for Contemporary and also meant pace. It was on the *bay*. Perfect. All drawings, press releases, signage, everything was changed to reflect the new name.

Not long after, Roy was having lunch in the dining room at the Hilton Inn South when he saw John Curry enter. Roy called him over to his table. "John," Roy asked, "what is this Tempo Bay Hotel?" Curry revealed that the Contemporary had always been just a working title and then explained how clever the new name was. "I don't like it," Roy answered.

"What don't you like?" Curry asked.

"I just don't like it. I like Contemporary. I like names that are simple and say what they are. The other name is phony and plastic."

Curry ran out of the dining room and called Card Walker. Within five days, all paperwork was revised to reflect the new old name, the Contemporary Resort Hotel.

The Vacationland campground behind Disneyland had done very well, and Walt wanted Disney World visitors to be able to stay in everything from "a suite to a sleeping bag." But with resort construction in its full throes, little thought had been given to its campground except where to put it. The overburdened hotel division was happy to let the campground fall under the jurisdiction of the theme park management. Late in 1969, Operations chief Dick Nunis called Keith Kambak, a Disneyland cast member whom he knew had a degree in recreation. "We need to open a campground at Disney World, and we've kind of forgotten about it," Nunis said. "Do you have any experience at campgrounds?" Kambak admitted he hadn't. That was exactly what Nunis wanted to hear. He instructed Kambak to spend the next six months touring the country in a motor home and borrow the best practices from the campgrounds he visited. Then Kambak was to work with WED designing Disney's version, then relocate to Florida to build and operate it.

The main thing Kambak learned on the road was that most places he visited encouraged him to build "pull-through" campsites. Having parallel roads cut through the grounds allowed campers to drive their RVs right on their campsite and then, when it was time to leave, drive straight off. But Kambak thought such a layout would require too much land to be ripped up; he wanted to preserve the area's natural state as much as possible. For the same reason, he also placed each site as far from each other as possible. He would start out with 131 campsites and, as soon as practical, expand into an entire western village.

When Kambak arrived in Florida in the spring of 1971, the south shore of Bay Lake remained untouched wilderness. He figured that if the forest was going to be visitors' home-away-from-home, he might as well make it his own. The one structure on the property was an old fishing lodge by the lake. But the building was so decrepit, Kambak decided to set up a trailer next door to live in until the project was completed.

The first step was clearing the land, which included a mix of huge cypresses. "We tried to work with the contractors to save all the big trees," Kambak said, taking a cue from the environmental classes Nunis had sent him to.

Hidden in the forest, the campground was easy to forget about and became low priority for management and construction. As Kambak slowly built up his staff, he found it difficult to get any supplies. He would have to get creative. If someone left the keys in a company pickup over night, "Kambak's Raiders," as his crew became known, would sneak off with the vehicle and hide it in their secluded spot in the woods. When the requisitioned vehicles needed fueling, the Raiders would venture out with five-gallon gasoline cans and return for secret fill-ups.

"We were on a shoestring budget," Kambak recalled. "So we went around the property and acquired equipment. We had no office furniture, so late one night I drove up to the legal department, because we knew Phil Smith could get whatever he needed. We took his desk, credenza, all his furniture, and loaded it onto a truck and took it back to our office. We took the stuff out of his cabinets and drawers and left it on the floor. I don't know if Phil ever found out what happened."

To hurry the construction process along, Kambak put his crew to work after the contractors left on Friday afternoons. One weekend, his quasi-builders erected a fifteen-foot-by-fifteen-foot building by the lake to store the campfire equipment. When the contractors returned to work Monday morning, they were livid and complained to the union. Yet even after Disney paid off the union, the building still came under budget.

By May 1971 it became increasingly clear to Walker and Tatum that maybe J.B. Allen was right—at the rate construction was crawling, very little would be completed by October 1. They turned to the man who got things done at Disneyland, Dick Nunis. Six-foot-one with a vicious bark, Nunis had been a Scholastic All American free safety at the University of Southern California in the early 1950s, playing alongside Walt's future-son-in-law Ron Miller. Nunis had planned on playing professional football and then becoming a coach—until he broke his neck in a game against UCLA. Instead, he went to work at Disneyland before it opened in 1955, assisting Van France with the Disneyland University. Here, Nunis didn't just help administer France's indoctrination program, he swallowed it whole himself, developing a hard-core allegiance to the Disney Way that would mark his quick ascent up the park's ladder of command.

With Nunis, there were never any loose ends. "He's a dynamo," recalled Dorothy Eno, Nunis's first secretary back at Disneyland. "He has a built-in computer. He knows the right decision to make at the right time. He never asks anyone to do anything he wouldn't do himself. He doesn't sit behind a desk and think it will happen. He knows." Those who didn't follow through were left to face "The Temper."

As top man in park operations, Nunis had been flying to Florida about once a month. If the Magic Kingdom was to open on time, a hard-driving, single-minded general was needed on site, day and night. Nunis agreed to step in—if all the resources of the company were at his disposal. Walker and Tatum agreed; do what you have to do, don't worry about budgets, just get the place open on October 1.

Before temporarily relocating to Florida, Nunis let his fellow managers at the studio, WED and the park know he would be counting on them as well. "When I call," he warned, "don't say when. It means yesterday." In the original plans, Main Street would be paved with aged red bricks. Coincidentally, old brick streets were being torn up in nearby Winter Park. Unfortunately, the city wanted so much for the bricks that Disney decided to purchase just enough to cover the side streets. The rest of Main Street could be paved with red cement. The nearest source of red cement was in New Jersey. Nunis called Jack Lindquist, corporate vice president of marketing. "Get it," Nunis instructed. Lindquist dropped everything, jumped on a plane to New Jersey, and delivered the red cement to Florida in time to meet the construction schedule.

Rare was the day Nunis didn't get his way. In mid-August, a photographer arrived to shoot a cover for *Life* magazine. He wanted to pose a cast of thousands in front of Cinderella Castle. Nunis was less than pleased with the distraction, but knew they needed the publicity. He strained to hold his tongue as the photographer individually positioned more than 1,000 uniformed employees, including all the costumed characters, ride operators, tour guides, cooks, custodians, musicians and a smattering of executives. Then the cameraman rolled out two cherry pickers and began setting up his lights and other equipment. He then started running tests. An hour went by. The temperature continued to climb, approaching 100 degrees. Watching everyone standing around, Nunis was growing just as heated. Another hour elapsed. Two characters fainted. Other employees grabbed their costumes and took their spots. After three hours of testing, the man finally snapped his perfect photo.

Nunis' main concern was getting every facility completed on time and smoothly transferred from builder to show installer to safety inspector and finally to those who would operate it. "When those forces collide," explained Bill Hoelscher, "it takes somebody to get in between the operating people and the construction people and say, 'You guys leave, and you guys get in there and make it work.' Dick did that. He was a little like the movie with old George Patton—not the most popular guy, but he got it done."

In fact, in his office, Nunis hung a caricature of himself as General Patton wearing a hardhat.

Nunis would walk through every corner of the property once a week with his entourage and a punch list to chart—and hasten—the progress of every element. In the middle of one week, Nunis asked an area manager when the asphalt would be poured in Adventureland. The work was all set for Monday, the manager replied. "Do it by Saturday," Nunis answered, then walked away, with no explanation how it was be done but fully expecting that it would be.

With Nunis breathing down their necks, contractors poured the cement for some areas before the ground could be properly graded. To make the surface level, the concrete ended up being several inches deep in one area and several feet deep in another—a fact not discovered by Disney until later when work by the Facilities department required drilling through the varying depths.

Nunis carried a tape recorder and dictated continuously as he toured the jobsite. Secretaries typed up his notes at night and distributed them as memos the next morning. Nunis left his family in California and moved into one of the Bay Hill cottages, but slept more often on a cot in his office. As soon as the first hotel rooms were ready, he caught his few hours of sleep a night there.

Every morning began in one of the construction trailers with a meeting of the Disney World Operating Committee (DWOC). Nunis kept scheduling the meetings earlier and earlier, until he set one for 6 a.m. The disgruntled DWOC'ers exchanged phone calls and, knowing Card Walker would be in town, decided this would be their chance to lodge a protest. When Nunis arrived at the meeting the next morning, he discovered everyone was there on time—in their pajamas. Merchandise v.p. Jack Olsen, razor and mug in hand, was shaving himself. Nunis got the message; from then on, all meetings would start at 7 a.m.

For maximum intimidation, Nunis surrounded himself with his "mafia," as onlookers referred to such stern-looking executives as former USC football teammate Orlando Ferrante; Nunis' top Operations man in Florida, the no-nonsense Bob Mathieson, and Operations' Jim Cora, an intense Disneyland executive who developed a reputation as Nunis's hatchet man.

EARLY RISERS. Management protested the increasingly early meeting times by arriving one morning in their pajamas. *(Clockwise around table from lower left)* Jim Passilla *(human resources)*, shaving-creamed Jack Olsen *(merchandise)*, John Curry *(hotels)*, Carl Bongirno *(finance)*, Phil Smith *(legal)*, Dick Nunis, Card Walker, Jack Lindquist *(marketing)*, Bob Mathieson *(operations)*, Ted Crowell *(facilities)*, Dean Penlick *(back corner, sitting in for Jim Armstrong, foods)*, and Bob Allen. (1971) *Photo courtesy John Curry*

But Nunis preferred to encourage rather than threaten. If he spotted a group of workers lagging, he might roll up his sleeves and start working alongside them, to set a pace. Or he might bribe them with the promise of a case of beer.

Fortunately, whenever morale seemed to hit a new low, some milestone would arrive to give everyone an extra push. The first came late one night early in the summer, during a trial run of the monorail. Imagineers filled the train for its inaugural run around the track. They first passed Cinderella Castle, illuminated the first time. They rode past the Polynesian Hotel and finally through the Contemporary which, recalled Imagineer Tony Baxter, "was ablaze with welding, because it was so far behind. As we went into the cavern, under the red flashing work lights, you saw welding cascading like fireworks down from all the different levels. Then you noticed the workers stopping to watch this thing out of the future, traveling through this canyon of scaffolding, under that weird lighting. It truly was an amazing thing. I think it did a lot of good for not just those of us who were expatriates of California, but for the workers to see something that incredible. It was as if you were dead tired and suddenly you think, 'This really is a neat thing that I'm working on.' The guys were bused in, bused out, and they didn't even know what a Disneyland was. They had no concept of how this all was going to work, or what a ride was that wasn't a Ferris wheel or a merry-go-round. And so to see this absolute image of the future, traveling through that hotel for the first time, in the middle of the night, was just an awesome moment."

Another emotional boost came a few weeks later when Nunis decided to pull the workmen off the campground, to help finish the park first and let the campground open a month or two late. For those building the park, the reinforcements' arrival was like a breath of fresh air. With the extra help, maybe—just maybe—they might finish on time after all.

When all the construction workers were diverted from the campground, Kambak put his hourly employees to work building a bridge for the nature trails. "The union guys didn't want to do it anyway, wading through the swamp with snakes," Kambak reasoned.

And then there was August 15, the day set aside to dedicate the castle and hold a banquet to honor John Hench, a longtime Imagineer and lead designer of the castle. Obviously, the feast had to be held at the restaurant inside the castle, which was the closest thing the park had to a formal dining room. The 166-seat King Stefan's Banquet Hall was designed to look elegant, complete with fine white tablecloths, but operate as a fast-service restaurant. As at the park's other restaurants, guests needed to be served within minutes; all the food—possibly a thousand different items—would be prepared in one central building, packaged and transported to the appropriate restaurant for heating and serving.

A few weeks before the party, Nunis informed the Foods division's Dale Burner. Burner explained that the restaurant wasn't done. "Get it done," replied Nunis. As they leaned on the contractors to give them an operable building in time, Burner and his team rushed madly to track down the necessary food and furnishings. All other Magic Kingdom restaurants would use generic dishes; King Stefan's was supposed to have specially designed silverware and pewter plates. Days before the party, the ornate utensils still hadn't arrived. Supervisor Dave Vermillion traced the shipment to Alabama, had it pulled off a truck, and loaded on a plane. He then hurried to the airport to pick up the airborne utensils.

All the company dignitaries from California were in town for the event. In the afternoon, Roy took a sobering tour of the property. As his escort through the hotels, he selected Howard Roland, the intense head of planning. Roy recognized him as a straight-shooter and a hard-driver—a co-worker always introduced Howard as "H'ard." Roland had been sending memos to Burbank saying U.S. Steel's rosy predictions were untrue; there was no way the Contemporary would open on time. As Roland led Roy through the Contemporary, they had to step around construction workers playing cards and taking naps. Roy was incensed, but thought it better to put on a good face for the banquet that evening.

After dinner, Card Walker dedicated the castle to Sir John of Hench with a champagne toast. Next, Roy rose to poignantly honor the one man who more than anyone would have wanted to be there—his little brother Walt. Again, champagne glasses were lifted. Then, to take the curse off of all the drinking at a Disney theme park, the executives headed downstairs to, half-tipsy, ride the carousel.

The following morning, the WED liaison to the hotels was relieved of his duties as on-property point man and replaced by Roland. He was to find a way to get the buildings finished. The studio was already breathing down Roland's neck to get inside the Contemporary to begin filming a TV special to coincide with the park opening. On August 16, Roland said film crews could use part of the fourth floor mezzanine to shoot Bob Hope getting off the monorail. No cameras would be allowed any higher. Cast members could pretend to be guests standing against the railings and waving from above.

Among Roland's biggest challenges was getting the Contemporary's 1.5 million square feet of floors carpeted. The carpenters had claimed jurisdiction over floorcoverings, but most of the available carpenters were framers; only a handful had any experience installing carpeting. Roland called the union agent, Bill Wilson, and said he needed to cut some sort of deal.

Roland recalled, "I flew in six carpetlayers from Las Vegas whom I would pay piecemeal. Wilson said okay, if I'd match their pay hourly

HOTEL CIRCLE. With the Polynesian *(lower left)* rising fast, plots had also been reserved for an Asian hotel *(rectangle protruding into lagoon at upper left)* and waterside Venetian resort *(center right)*. (1971) *Photo courtesy State Archives of Florida*

with his guys. I brought in six men who did every room—the whole south annex, the tower, corridors, public spaces. They lived in the rooms they'd done. They sometimes worked twelve, fourteen, sixteen hours a day. They'd be waiting on rooms to be ready to be carpeted, so they'd fly back to Vegas for seven, ten days to get a backlog." The union guys carried the carpet for them and napped a lot.

All went well until Wilson discovered that the Vegas carpetlayers didn't have union cards. Wilson "blew the whistle," and 4,000 construction workers stopped what they were doing and began streaming off the jobsite. Roland was incredulous. Getting union cards was never part of the deal. But he didn't have time to argue. Construction stopped for two hours, as Roland rushed to the local union hall and paid $300 in initiation fees and back dues.

Union members also claimed jurisdiction to install the glass frame on south side of tower. But the only practical solution was using the crane operators from American Bridge. "Howard knows what kind of deal I can make," Wilson informed them. Roland accepted the same conditions: matching pay for 20-some union workers. American Bridge, however, wanted the union guys out of the way. The workmen sat on the dock playing cards.

Marvin Jacobs, a furnishings buyer for the hotels, recalled, "There were a lot of union people who said you can't do this, you can't do that. Howard Roland said, 'Well, let's come back here about 5:00 after they go home.' So we came back and did work there. For the Polynesian Hotel, they had to bring the tile in for the floors. And the union guys said they didn't want to do that till much later, but we wanted to get it done right away. So we came back, got a forklift, and brought in all the tile and put it where we wanted it. The next day when the union guys came in, they wondered how it got there. But it was there, so they figured they might as well do the work. And they started doing the floors."

Roland's hands were not only tied, but full. "There were so many people on site, they couldn't be managed," he said. "We were getting no production out of people."

Disney tried to make up the difference in quantity. The contractors who had been working ten hours a day, were now expected to turn in at least twelve. For salaried managers, twelve hours was an easy day. Halfway through the summer, all days off were cancelled.

Anything offstage was left to be finished later. They didn't even bother putting up walls to divide the second-story offices over Main Street, leaving them looking like long bowling alleys. As late as two years after the park opened, workers would discover forgotten backrooms in the tunnels that still needed electrical wiring or other final touches.

Just as during the construction of Disneyland 26 years before, management allowed most of Tomorrowland to fall behind and open later, buying time in other areas. The land—and the tunnels beneath it—were put on the five-year plan. Imagineer George McGinnis speculated, "Adventureland, Frontierland and Fantasyland are warm, familiar and welcoming and have much for the guest to relate to. Tomorrowland contrasts with all the other lands by offering a promise of exciting, new environments. The mystery behind the Tomorrowland construction fence, decorated with Tomorrowland concept art, assured the guest's future visit. As a designer, I know that selecting subjects to design from the research library is easier than starting with a blank sheet to design something that says 'future.' One is an interpretation, the other a new composition."

As on all Disney projects, all-powerful art directors had to sign off on everything. Late in the summer, Imagineer John Hench was shocked to discover that paint throughout the park looked different than he had intended. Everything ran the wrong "temperature." Since the sun appeared brighter in California, colors that seemed right in Glendale looked either too "hot" or too "cool" in Florida. Hench quickly reformulated the color schemes and had workmen begin repainting everywhere.

As the calendar turned to September, signifying less than a month before opening, the park was filled with unfinished show buildings and mud puddles for walkways. Work schedules—and exhausted workers—began to lag.

Despite Disney's pleading, the contractors refused to work on Labor Day. Nunis had a better idea. He put his managers to work for the day, running as many attractions as were operable to entertain the construction workers. The tradesmen were invited to bring their families—some evidently large, since about 12,000 guests packed the park that day. All through the day, children were overheard asking their fathers, "Daddy, did you really build that?" The preview gave the men a glimpse of what they were helping to create, as well as an individual sense of accomplishment and pride in their work. "Help us, guys," the managers then stressed, "and we'll have your families back again."

Challenges remained. In relocating flora from the tree farm to the Magic Kingdom, Bill Evans discovered that the ground cover for the theme park had been deposited in reverse order when it moved from the lagoon site, hard clay on top, fertile topsoil on the bottom. Consequently, Evans' crews had to dig extra deep before planting to restore proper order. In areas with the basement roof mere feet beneath the theme park's tar-covered streets, trees had to be planted in tubs.

Time was also running short to get the area's pesky insect population under control. Disney had established an eleven-man pest control team, headed by entomologist Fred Harden and superintendent Stan Young, to figure out how to keep the mosquitoes, gnats and deerflies away from the guests. They started by trapping insects with vacuum cleaners and Stickum-covered balloons. Each type of captive was studied—how far it could travel, how long it lived, how often it bred. Then in the field they began testing environmentally friendly ways to get rid of the bugs. No restricted chemicals were allowed. They tested new, safer sprays applied from the ground and from an airplane. They monitored insect movement up to twelve miles outside of the resort; if a nice breeze began blowing toward the park from a nearby salt marsh, the bug brigade would be alerted. They discouraged pests from nesting in their favorite grasses, leaves and by water control on marshes. They stocked Bay Lake with bass, in part, to feed on the insects. And, to deter attracting bugs at night, the team installed special low-intensity lights at the Magic Kingdom. Then-popular electric bug zappers were deemed ineffective, even though the devices "put on a pretty good show."

The main lobby building at the Polynesian appeared to be falling apart. "Originally around the Great Ceremonial House," said Clayne Dice, "they had used bamboo from the Far East, six to eight inches in diameter. By the time we were getting close to opening, it had split, rot and come apart. They had to tear it all out and do a simulated fiberglass bamboo."

Worse, some attractions hadn't even arrived yet. The submarines, being built by Morgan Yacht Company of Clearwater, Florida, had fallen dangerously behind schedule. So Disney pulled the job from Morgan and hauled the half-finished hulls to Tampa Shipyard, which was building other watercraft for the park. WED sent vehicle specialist Bob Gurr to Tampa in July to make sure the first sub was delivered on time, on August 13. Gurr and the Tampa crew faced a daunting challenge. Each day, the electricians at MAPO sent them revised wiring drawings filled with inaccuracies that the Tampa builders had to correct on the spot. Some parts that were specified never arrived. Other equipment showed up that wasn't on any of the diagrams. When the intricate interior trim pieces began arriving, the assemblers discovered that Morgan Yacht hadn't built the hull to match the diagrams provided by WED's George McGinnis. There wasn't time to complain. The workmen took hacksaws and forced everything to fit.

The Tampa crew toiled seven days a week. On August 12, they deemed the first sub ready to roll. Now they just had to figure out how to get it from Tampa to Orlando. They hoisted the 61-foot-long, 58-ton vessel on the back of the biggest rented trailer they could find. The truck puttered uneasily along surface streets of small towns, searching for a route clear of overhead powerlines and other low clearances. The trailer was so overloaded, several tires blew out along the way. As darkness set, the truck finally pulled into the park's Central Shop, the trailer's four tires flat and a trail of black smoke billowing from the burning rubber.

Gurr arrived back at the Magic Kingdom just in time to learn of a new crisis, this one involving the parking lot trams. Arrow Development had built an entire fleet of trams to shuttle guests between the parking lot and the main ticket center. To pull the trams, WED hoped to build its own high-tech tractors, powered by environmentally friendly compressed natural gas. Sounded great—until the accountants got one look at the expected price tag of the custom vehicles. Disney decided to buy stock vehicles instead. They awarded the job to the lowest bidder, United Tractor—a Chesterton, Indiana, manufacturer that specialized in tractors to tow commercial aircraft. United would supply 20 off-the-shelf tractors, slightly modified with a cab and air-conditioning unit.

United delivered its tractors on time, in early September. The monorails, however, were taking longer. By Opening Day, only three monorails would be available to transport guests from the ticket center to the park's front gates. The last thing Nunis wanted was an hour-long line of grumpy guests waiting to board the monorail—before they'd even gotten to the park. Worse, departing guests might be stranded if a thunderstorm hit and the monorails had to be shut down. Nunis decided to use some of the parking lot trams to take guests all the way to the park entrance. The trams would have to travel a single-lane service road that passed under the canal connecting the Seven Seas Lagoon and Bay Lake, at a five-percent grade. Having to climb the hill, often on wet pavement, and expected to run continuously for fifteen to eighteen hours a day, the United tractors weren't up to the task—they blew engines, scattered oil and transmission parts along the road, and stalled out with gasoline vapor lock.

Nunis went ballistic. He ordered United Tractor's president and its chief engineer to catch the first flight out of Chesterton and find a way to keep the tractors running. United's engineer examined the problem, but couldn't offer a solution to Nunis' liking. So, Nunis ordered Gurr to come up with something, fast. Gurr suggested removing all engine-driven accessories from the overloaded motors and adding power packs. As a test, he strapped a makeshift power pack to the back of one tractor and stripped down its engine. Into the tram climbed Gurr, Nunis and the president of United, sweat streaming from his brow. Miraculously, the tractor made it up the incline—roaring along at two miles an hour at wide-open throttle. Close enough. Nunis told Gurr to design the power pack, have park machinists build seventeen units in twelve days, and send United Tractor the bill.

The last frantic days before the park opened for the first time sped by in a blur. So much remained to do. Everyone was put to work, doing everything. Bill Justice, an animator who had pulled double duty designing costumes for the walkaround characters, spent the final days hurriedly painting Disney characters on the walls of the baby care center.

Bob Mathieson recalled a delivery truck rolling into the service area behind Tomorrowland, with a storm not far behind. "We grabbed people and formed a line, like a bucket brigade, to get this truck unloaded," he said. "It was getting pretty dark, and you didn't even know the guy you're working alongside of. We got this truck unloaded and covered. I went down the line, thanking everyone for coming to help. And at the end of the line is Roy. I said, 'Roy! What are you doing here?' 'Well, I came by and saw you needed some help. So I thought I'd help out a bit.'"

Disney University's Thor Degelman recalled, "The afternoon before the opening of the Magic Kingdom, I was on the lawn in front of Cinderella Castle laying sod. Two hours later I was washing windows in the castle. An hour after that I was training kids how to jump Autopia cars. We couldn't get in [earlier] because of the construction, and they didn't have a chance to train on the cars."

That last day, agreed Ed Beaver, "everything wasn't done. We put up [temporary] wood walls, and had Tony Virginia landscape the walls. There were unfinished spots we just filled up with concrete, seven, eight feet deep."

Bill Hoelscher remembered that one spot in particular near the submarine lagoon must have been ten feet deep. "It would have taken twice as long to go get a dump truck with dirt to fill the hole as it would to take the other truck that was cement and just fill it and level it off," he explained.

Truckloads of materials, all prepaid for, would arrive that weren't needed, but there was no place to store them and no time to figure out what to do with them. Instead, said Ted Kellogg, "they took it out and buried it. Truckloads of brand new plumbing parts, giant valves. We had the world's most expensive, million-dollar dump site."

"The night before [opening], we were laying carpet," John Curry
remembered. "The unions had tried to scuttle us. Pallets of pool chemicals were dropped in front of the main entrance, under the monorail, so
we couldn't get in or out. I found a forklift with keys in it and went to
work."

That night, the Contemporary was still weeks away from completion.
Even if rooms weren't ready for guests, the building had to look presentable—at least from the outside. Without any landscaping, the hotel
looked like some strange alien craft that had crash-landed in the middle
of the desert. The team quickly planted a few palm trees. It didn't help.
With sixteen hours until the media was to begin arriving, Nunis made the
call to truck in an extra four-and-a-half acres of sod. He then recruited
anyone he could find, even executives in white shoes and white polyester suits, to lay down the slices of grass, repeating his only direction:
"Green side up! C'mon, you can do it! Green side up!" All through the
night, about 100 unskilled anyones carried sod from truck to lawn. As
some would leave, others would join in. By 6 a.m., the Contemporary
lawns were fully dressed. Over the next three weeks, much of the sod
could be torn out and replaced with formal landscaping in time for the
hotel's official opening.

5

a grand Opening

W ALT, the optimistic showman, had timed the opening of Disneyland in 1955 for maximum exposure—a Sunday, family day, in the height of summer—and set a live television camera on every corner. Not surprisingly, the heat was sweltering. The place was packed. The crowds got a little unruly. More attractions broke down than not, and ABC-TV was there to make sure millions of people around the country knew it. Disney executives would refer to the day as "Black Sunday."

Lesson learned. For Disney World, Disney purposely scheduled the first day of operation for Friday October 1, a school day, on the slowest day of the week during the slowest month of the year. They also set the actual grand opening festivities for three weeks later, spread them out over three days, and prerecorded most of the sequences for the telecast. They proclaimed all of October "preview month" and regularly sounded warnings that big crowds might develop, hoping the faint of heart might delay their trip a week or three. It wasn't so much that the executives hoped nobody would show up the first day; they just wanted to keep the crowds manageable to allow the staff and attractions to gradually become acclimated.

Disney's downplaying didn't stop news organizations and local officials from making wild predictions that tens—if not hundreds—of thousands would storm the gates. The state highway patrol stationed extra troopers along the roads to deal with the expected gridlock. The Red

Cross set up a dozen first aid tents along Interstate 4. Management, against its better judgment, couldn't help but feel some pressure for a big turnout.

Early that first morning, Dick Nunis and his executive team huddled around a radio receiver, listening to a helicopter pilot's traffic reports, so they would know when the first crush of guests was arriving. Suddenly the pilot exclaimed, "There are people out there! Thousands of them! They're coming this way!" After a short pause, he continued, "Wait! They're turning off on 535!" The first swarm of cars turned out to be cast members headed for the employee entrance.

Security officers had spent the predawn hours shooing away guests eager to be the first in line. But a couple of hours before the park opened, they allowed cars to begin queuing up at the parking toll booths. A thick fog rolled in and settled at the parking lot entrance, creating a wall of gray that masked just how many thousands might be lining up. As the fog finally lifted, attendants could see that each lane held about 20 cars—disappointing for such an anxiously-awaited event.

The first person to sprint to the turnstiles was a University of Florida student, who had one classmate park their car and another buy their tickets. Yet Disney wanted its first guests—and recipients of lifetime passes—to be a wholesome-looking family, not a group of college buddies. Marketing's Jack Lindquist chose a blonde-haired, blue-eyed family of four.

As the company expanded, Lindquist would perfect the selection process—and at least once be sued by guests who claimed they were really first and unfairly passed over. "First of all, you don't pick out [the first family] until five minutes before," he said. "There can really be no first person, because there are 20 gates. You'd go out a half-hour before time and just walk by the gates and look at people. Look for sort of a type. You didn't want to pick teenagers. You didn't want to pick an old couple. So you'd want to find a family and decide which gate would you open first. That gate opens. The first family walks in. Flash bulbs pop."

And did his technique ever leave other guests unhappy? "Sometimes," Lindquist admitted. "We never had any contact [beforehand]. There's a certain liability. So nobody should approach anybody."

With reporters scribbling in their notebooks and photographers clicking off shot after shot, Mickey Mouse and ambassador Debbie Dane took the Magic Kingdom's first family by the hand and led them to an antique fire truck. The vehicle carried them up Main Street, a battalion of tour guides walking alongside. The crowds followed behind, as hundreds of cast members stood on the curbs, waving, clapping, cheering, many with tears in their eyes. Wide-eyed, the small boy looked out from the fire truck and gushed, "This is better than Christmas!" The parade stopped at the front of the castle. Mickey led the first family to the plaza, as the Walt Disney World Band broke into "When You Wish Upon a Star." Suddenly, the castle doors swung open and out streamed every costumed Disney character imaginable, all dancing and waving.

After the initial hoopla, Card Walker and Donn Tatum grabbed their golf bags and headed for the Magnolia Golf Course. Burdened by the pressures of the day, both would record uncharacteristically high scores.

The rest of the staff quickly noticed that, once the mob dispersed from Main Street into all corners of the park, the place looked half-deserted. None of the attractions had long lines. This was no Black Sunday. More like a Gray Friday.

The entire staff had been so pumped up, running on sheer adrenaline after weeks without sufficient sleep. Wayne Busch remembered, "Thirteen people came from California in Merchandise, and they would tell us what it's going to be like when Opening Day comes. 'We'll throw open the gates, and the people will race down Main Street, and run for the attractions like a stampeding herd of cattle,' and we should just get out of the way. They'd tell us war stories from Disneyland. It really wasn't anything like that. On Opening Day, we threw open the gates, and a few people strolled in."

"What a brutal disappointment," Jerry Van Dyke remarked. "We got there, expecting road jams, traffic jams. We had a plan how we were going to close the parking lot. The day finally rolled up and we kept saying, 'Where are the guests?' 'Where are the guests?'"

Opening morning, remembered Steve Baker, "I had been working about 36 straight hours. I went home, showered and came back to wait for the guests to arrive—and they didn't. It was sort of ho-hum. I was disappointed, thinking we did all this work and nobody liked it."

VIP hostess Dianna Morgan recalled, "On Opening Day, I was standing out in the train station, in the dark, with a flashlight, waiting for the crowds to come. They never did."

"As we walked through the park, we were a little in shock," admitted marketing chief Sandy Quinn, remembering the empty walkways.

"Unlike Disneyland, you couldn't just run an ad and turn [the business] on. For the most part, you weren't attracting locals, but people from New York, Toronto, and so on. We kept asking ourselves, 'What should we do?' 'Maybe we ought to run ads.'"

The evening ended with a press party in the Polynesian's Papeete Bay Verandah dining room. On the surface, everything appeared festive—the luscious dinner, the popping champagne corks, the Tahitian drummers, the Polynesian dancers, the romantic view of torch-lit beaches. Still, the media saw nothing but failure. The reporters wanted to know what was wrong that there were only 10,400 visitors—heck, there was one cast member working for every one-and-a-half guests! No one seemed to be buying Card Walker's explanation that it was intentional.

Banner headlines the likes of "Florida Disney World Opens to Sparse Crowds" graced the morning papers.

The news did not slip past Wall Street. Disney's stock price had been climbing steadily since Walt's passing, as investors speculated that his heirs would make more aggressive use of all the treasures in the vault. It plummeted $9.38 in one day—coincidentally, the same amount to the penny that the share price had increased by the day after Walt died.

The stock price was further deflated with the revelation that, by the time Disney resolved an avalanche of construction claims, the cost of the Florida Project would surpass $400 million—nearly triple initial estimates.

Even though Disney executives intentionally planned to minimize crowds, subconsciously they got caught up in all the outside hype. Even Nunis admitted to his aides, "Okay, we blew Opening Day. But if we don't do well Thanksgiving, we're in trouble."

Management figured it had eight weeks to ramp up. The Admiral Joe Fowler Riverboat opened one day after the rest of the park, Peter Pan's Flight two. Gradually, scenery was added the along the Frontierland riverbanks so the riverboat's passengers would have something to look at.

Some of the kinks had already been worked out during a series of crowd-controlled previews held for employees' families during the weekends in September. On Main Street, recalled Michael Tangel, "the Harmony Barber Shop was done with the criteria of the 1920s, so there were no [electrical] plugs for clippers. We had a tryout day for families of employees and invited guests, so we could test everything: the period hand clippers, shaving with a brush. We gave a demonstration. We had to immediately ask the electricians to put in plugs. The employees couldn't handle it."

The resort's quiet opening—and glacially slow first weeks—did have a fortunate side effect. Disney could finish the loose ends and fine-tune the ragged ones without hordes of demanding guests in the way. Human Resources could offer extra training and adjust scheduling so each facility was properly staffed.

There would also be time to woo the media. Twice every week through October, the company flew in 250 reporters at a time for three days of fun, all on Disney's dime. A few years later, *60 Minutes* would interview Lindquist for a story on the use of lavish junkets to unethically manipulate the media. On camera, Lindquist responded that most of the reporters Disney flew to Orlando weren't from organizations like CBS. Most came from small markets, where they had two choices: they could run a canned press release or they could fly to Orlando and experience it for themselves. And, stressed Lindquist, Disney never pressured reporters or told them what to report.

Then, the interrogator asked, why was 90 percent of the coverage extremely favorable? "Because 90 percent of them must have had a good time," Lindquist answered. "We let them go home and report on their radio or TV or newspaper about what they saw, and what they saw, they liked."

Although the submarines arrived in time for Opening Day, the ride itself would not open for another three weeks. Due to construction delays, the lagoon wasn't ready to be filled with water until about three days before opening. Then came the tedious process of placing and timing the nearly 180 underwater figures. Imagineer Tony Baxter recalled, "There's a tremendous amount of work that can't be done until you've got water in there, such as placing all the fishes that are on little wires. There would be a guy with a radio in the boat, and divers in the lagoon. If the script said, 'Giant groupers,' you had to be looking at giant groupers; so either the tape had to be adjusted or the fish had to be moved until all those things were right. And once you installed one side, you'd switch over to the other side, because there were identical shows on each side. It took nearly a month to get in there and place all those things."

Even after the ride opened, the subs proved to be a maintenance nightmare. Since they were made of fiberglass instead of metal like the originals at Disneyland, Disney World's submarines required that their bottoms be loaded with lead ballast to ensure they didn't float too high, off the rail.

Worse, the subs leaked severely, at least the portions exposed above the surface of the lagoon. "During the day," explained Baxter, "the fiberglass would heat up and expand, and in the evening it would cool, so there were always cracks developing—not in the integrity of the thing leaking underneath, but on the hull above the water. When it went under the waterfall, cracks would open, and water would drip in from the waterfall. So we ended up having to dam off the waterfall, so it didn't fall on the boat. The intense heat of the sun would heat it and putting cold water on would chill it. Heat it, chill it, heat it, so the parts that were out of the water were always expanding and contracting."

Despite John Hench's rush repainting job, some areas of the park still needed help. The contractors who had painted the rockwork along the Jungle Cruise had copied Marc Davis's watercolor concept sketches a little too literally and ended up with bright blue and purple rocks. Surrounded by real foliage, moss, dirt and camouflage-green-dyed water, the rocks looked jarringly cartoonish. A team quickly moved in to perform "washes" on the rocks with various aging colors to make the scenery look more realistic.

Transporting guests from the parking lot to the theme park gates remained a challenge, even with the light crowds. Come Opening Day, only three monorails were in service, with a fourth on the way and two more still under construction. Guests crammed into the monorail stations, impatiently waiting for their trip around the lake. So, Nunis ordered anything that floated to help get people *across* the lake.

Six steam launches, designed as ferries for the hotels and campground, could each hold up to 40 guests. A handful of houseboats, planned for rental to hotels guests, could handle maybe a dozen. During one preview day, Disney even pressed one of the Frontierland keel boats into shuttle service on the Seven Seas Lagoon.

Most helpful were a pair of replica "Osceola class" steam ships, ornate sidewheelers originally intended to specialize in "honeymoon cruises" for up to 250 hotel guests. Disney had the boats specially built in Tampa to be historically accurate to the mid-1800s, from their large

HIGH DEMAND. Guests overwhelmed the monorails during the first months of the Magic Kingdom. (1971) *Photo courtesy State Archives of Florida*

wooden steering wheels to their teak decks and the replica "walking beam" engines below. Each craft had a crew of three—a pilot to steer, a deckhand to cast off from and secure to the dock, and an engineer to operate the unconventional engine and control the speed. The latter position required 80 hours of training. So, for the first few weeks, management struggled to find the time to get pilots and engineers trained. In the process, one boat ran aground onto a sandbar.

Nonetheless, watercraft took so much pressure off the monorails that Nunis rush-ordered three 600-passenger ferries to replace the smaller boats. As the large ferries began arriving, the Osceola steamers could finally be used as party boats. Still, overuse during their first year had taken a heavy toll. "The boats were under water when you came to work Monday morning," recalled Arnold Lindberg, head of maintenance and manufacturing. "One sunk in the dry dock area [during refurbishment]." The steamers received early retirements from the Disney waterways and were dismantled to reuse their parts.

Initially, half of the parking lot trams were used to haul guests from the parking lot to the ticket center. The other half carried visitors from the ticket center to the park. Even retrofitted with power packs, the tractors could barely pull the grade coming back up under the canal and kept overheating. Nunis told the operators to just keep removing cars until the tram was light enough to pull. "We've got to get these people in," he would say.

"We broke down under the water bridge more than once," said parking lot manager Jerry Van Dyke. "We had tow trucks just sitting there. We tried everything. We'd run them for two hours, then shut the tractor down, disconnect it [from the tram], and hook up a new tractor. It was a logistics nightmare."

Mornings would begin with 20 trams operating and, with any luck, by the end of the day eight might still be mobile.

The company recognized that the tractors were no long-term solution. Three days before the park opened, in-house design resumed on the original CNG tractor—although it would be six months before the first one arrived in Florida. It was worth the wait. These 24 trams would be built by MAPO, under Arnold Lindberg, the Swede who began building railroads for Walt in 1954 and believed if you're going to build something, build it to last. Forever. "Arnold was not going to build trams that wouldn't pull the hill," Bill Hoelscher said. "He was going to build trams that could pull any hill that may be developed by WED designers. His tractors had the biggest engines. They were geared so low; they were so overpowered and overbuilt. We could have pulled 20 airplanes if we were going over flat ground. They'd pull eight cars of people through sugar sand. You could pull the castle off its foundation. He built some great trams."

As the new tractors came on line, their overmatched predecessors were retired. A few found use as utility haulers at the Disney Studios in Burbank.

Yet even with a more reliable ride, Disney realized that guests forced to take the parking lot trams to the entrance were missing out on part of the show. While everyone else was gliding through a hotel on a futuristic monorail or sailing across the Seven Seas Lagoon on a vintage steam vessel, they were struck on a wheezing parking lot tram. So WED was asked to create a topiary garden that would be strung out along the route from the ticket center to the front gate.

"Of course we had no time to grow the topiaries, so we made all these phony topiaries," recalled Tony Baxter. "I was pretty good at painting, so I went to work burning them and ripping out foliage and painting it dead so that they looked real, not like the perfect green that you see in shops."

As they traveled past a topiary Mary Poppins, a train of elephants, a giraffe, and other leafy creations, tram riders felt for the first time that they weren't getting a raw deal.

Other problems could be remedied more quickly. During the first days of operation, a few guests complained that the carousel's music track included the Russian national anthem—a politically awkward choice for All-American Disney. Sure enough, the person who compiled the sound-track had heard the song on a record and liked the melody, but couldn't translate the title because it was written in French. Disney yanked the song within two weeks.

The official opening ceremonies went smoothly enough, with crowds still light and activities spread out over three days. Everything was orchestrated by Bob Jani, Disneyland's entertainment director, an ambi-tious believer in spectacle who would say, "If one finale is good, three finales will be three times better!"

A concert by the World Symphony Orchestra, with Arthur Fiedler leading 140 musicians from 60 countries, kicked off the festivities on Saturday, October 23. The next day, Bob Hope hosted a noon reception to officially open the Contemporary, which, he cracked, was "where the Goodyear blimps come during mating season." That evening, to cele-brate the official opening of the Polynesian, revelers enjoyed a luau and torchlight ceremony on the beach. After the show, music again enlivened the beach to herald the arrival of fourteen waterborne floats, covered with twinkling lights and themed to fanciful creatures of the deep. The Electrical Water Pageant was a cross between an electrical parade Jani was considering for Disneyland's Main Street and a water procession his predecessor had proposed for Disneyland's Rivers of America. High above the lagoon, a Goodyear blimp flashed its own animated lights in unison with the water pageant. After ten minutes of synchronized twinkling, all fourteen barges lit up completely, before simultaneously blacking out—just as the first shells exploded overhead for the Fantasy in the Sky fireworks show.

On Monday, the Magic Kingdom's opening ceremony began with the character-filled Walt Disney World on Parade and climaxed with the grand entry of the world's biggest marching band playing "76 Trombones." Only instead of 76 trombones, there were exactly 276— plus 64 piccolos, 144 clarinets, 72 tubas, 210 trumpets, 102 French horns, 72 baritones, 64 snares, sixteen tenor drums, 24 bass drums, and 32 cymbals.

Jim Christensen, the organizing and rehearsing conductor, had been concerned that the whole affair might end up as a jumbled cacophony of noise. He asked Jani, "If all these musicians are spread blocks apart, how can we all hear each other?"

Jani replied, "As long as they can play the same as those who are within their field of hearing, who cares what they're playing two blocks away." It came off without a hitch. The 1,076 red-uniformed musicians streamed into Town Square. Viewed from above by television cameras, their entrance looked like ketchup pouring out of the train station. They marched up Main Street and assembled around the Plaza, where "Music Man" Meredith Wilson conducted from a podium in front of the castle. A 1,500-voice choir followed by singing "When You Wish Upon a Star." As they hit their final note, thousands of colorful balloons were released to the heavens.

The only glitch arose shortly before the parade, when it came time to feed the thousand-plus high school musicians who had been practicing since morning. About 500 of their pre-ordered box lunches had disappeared. Half the band came close to storming out before parade aides could scrounge up replacement grub.

The most touching moment concerned 78-year-old Roy standing in for Walt at the official dedication ceremony in Town Square. Roy had pulled a costumed Mickey Mouse up to his side to divert the focus from himself to his brother's creation. He then talked about Walt and his brother's dreams, and read the dedication plaque as his brother had done at Disneyland 26 years before.

That evening, back in his Bay Hill cottage, Roy watched the TV spe-

cial uneasily. Every song, every skit, every dance number played flawlessly—because most everything had been filmed weeks before the park
opened and heavily edited. That left Julie Andrews, Glen Campbell, and

The Mad Tee Party

In addition to trying to convince people to visit an empty park,
marketing director Sandy Quinn also was scrambling to throw
together a world-class golf tournament. Shortly before the park
opened, Card Walker told Quinn to try to organize a PGA golf tournament with the likes of Arnold Palmer and Jack Nicklaus. Quinn
knew nothing about golf, but was able to set up an appointment
with PGA Tour commissioner Joe Dey. A distinguished older gen-
tleman, Dey was intrigued by the scrappy young man's vision. By
the end of the meeting, Walt Disney World had a date on the PGA
tour: the week after Thanksgiving. It just didn't have any golfers.

As luck would have it, when Quinn returned to Disney World he
heard that Arnold Palmer was just a few miles away, at a new
country club he helped build in Bay Hill. Quinn immediately headed for Bay Hill and convinced Palmer to stop by for a tour of
Disney's new courses. Quinn began rhapsodizing about the first
PGA event where the entire family could enjoy itself, as he and
Palmer climbed into a golf cart. But as they motored up and down
the gorgeous fairways, Palmer kept staring off into the distance,
seemingly oblivious to Quinn's sales pitch. Arnie, a private pilot,
was enamored with the monorail.

Quinn drove him to the roundhouse, where engineers were
preparing to take a monorail on a test run. "Can I have a ride?"
Palmer asked. The workmen consented. Palmer jumped in and rode
around the track for hours. As the golf legend finally climbed out
of the monorail, Quinn again mentioned the golf tournament idea.
"No problem," Palmer said. "Sign me up. I'll call a few friends."
Using Palmer's pull, Disney was able to attract a full roster of
name golfers—including Lee Trevino, Billy Casper, Chi Chi
Rodriguez, and first-year winner Nicklaus—and plenty of publicity
for Disney World and its inaugural Walt Disney World Classic.

friends cavorting in a Magic Kingdom unnaturally devoid of guests.

Yet, overall, Roy was satisfied. He had accomplished his mission—to make Walt's greatest dream a reality. He had already decided to do what was best for the company by looking past his fondness for Donn Tatum and appointing the more forceful executive, Card Walker, as president. Tatum would become chairman. Roy could now retire in peace. The place had cost a fortune to build, but Roy had done it debt-free. Eight weeks later, Roy died of a cerebral hemorrhage.

The holidays would indeed provide the true test of the resort's success. The day after Thanksgiving, traffic ground to a halt ten miles up International Drive. By 2:00 in the afternoon, with thousands of cars crammed in and around its parking lot and 56,000 guests squeezed inside the park, Disney was forced to close the access ramp leading off Interstate 4. All four lanes of traffic slowed to a crawl in both directions, creating a 30-mile stretch of confused, angry motorists. Inside the Magic Kingdom, guests had to wait two hours or more to ride the submarines, Country Bear Jamboree, and other top attractions. Service at the park's 30-some restaurants and snack bars wasn't much quicker. The young Florida cast was overwhelmed. The veterans from Disneyland, on the other hand, folded their arms and smiled, as if to say, "Ah, that's more like it."

Motorists who were turned away at the toll booths pulled to the side of the road to wait for the gates to reopen. "Whenever the park was filled to capacity, we'd have to have people park on the grass out front and wait," said security officer Ray Carter. "There wasn't room for any more cars, but they'd still be coming in solid. We'd get cursed at, but it was our job. They told us they'd come from so far away. We'd tell them to go listen to the radio and come back later in the day."

Bob Mathieson said, "People were parked off the side of the North-South road playing Frisbee, volleyball, picnicking. It was quite a scene. Guests kept asking, 'You ready yet? You ready yet? Well, you can let just one more in!' Well, no you can't. We had to wait until people left [the lot], and then we reopened it, and that's a challenge because we had to have a moving phalanx of cars in front of that or otherwise it would be the Daytona 500. So from a safety standpoint, we had to slowly allow cars back in."

The crowds remained heavy throughout Thanksgiving weekend, forc-

THOROUGH FAIR. Disney World designers created multiple entrances to Fantasyland, turning what at Disneyland had been a charming yet clogged courtyard into a bustling corridor. (1971) *Photo courtesy State Archives of Florida*

ing early closures Friday, Saturday and Sunday. The Florida Highway Patrol, overwhelmed by the traffic, demanded to know what Disney was going to do about the traffic. "Not a thing," management responded. "We're taking care of the traffic on our property. You need to take care of it on yours. And, get ready, because the crowds are going to be even bigger come Christmas."

Over the next few days, Disney restarted its hiring machine, this time looking for seasonal workers. The hourly workforce—which numbered 6,000 on Opening Day—had to be bulked up to 9,400.

After another four-week lull, crowds returned in even larger numbers beginning December 26. "We told [the Highway Patrol] it was going to happen again," said Bill Sullivan. "They believed us this time. We backed traffic up again, and we handled it better. We closed the park systematically. And we closed the park for five days after that. And we only had a 9,000-space parking lot. We parked them on the grass. We parked on a field, until we could enlarge the parking lot to 12,000 parking spaces by the next year. We rerouted them. We sent them back out and said, 'We're sorry. Come back tomorrow.' We had opened at 10:00, so the next day we opened an hour earlier. We were still backed up. We opened at 7:00 in the morning; we still had people backed up, waiting on the road to get it."

"Christmas we got killed," confirmed fellow Disneyland transplant Ed Beaver, remembering the sudden onslaught of tourists from the Northeast and how tired he was of calling in complaints over his radio. "The 1960s and '70s in California was a kinder, gentler time and place. We were not used to the New York/New Jersey mentality. New Yorkers were not shy. By the end of the week, we'd say, 'What do you want? Here, take my radio.' After work, some of us would go bowling and pretend the pins were people from New York."

Filling the park to capacity magnified its remaining flaws. The Florida-born staff was not accustomed to working at the frenetic pace needed to service such crowds. The Disneyland-steeled managers grew frustrated that the cast didn't seem to realize they had to work quickly, and the employees viewed their managers as too demanding.

The pressure was particularly intense in Foods, where some facilities were serving over one ton of hamburger and two tons of French fries a day—not to mention the countless special orders, impatient guests, and few of the emotional rewards offered by other departments. "It was difficult trying to teach the fast food environment to people in Florida," said fast food leader Jerry Pospisil. "They were not used to that. There were very few McDonald's. Everything was so small and slow. There were no Mexican restaurants, nothing with any theming to it. We taught them you had to hustle, especially when Christmas and Thanksgiving arrived. There were incidents with guests. We had guests jump over the counter and say, 'There's the hamburger right there! Put it in a bag!'"

An immediate casualty was the restaurant next to the Borden's Ice Cream Parlor at the end of Main Street that specialized in crepes, for breakfast, lunch and dinner. Guests would look dumbfounded at the menu and say, "No, we don't want these crepes things. We want something to eat."

"Crepes were a cutting edge thing in California," said Bob Ziegler. "Walt Disney World guests wanted hot dogs for breakfast."

Quickly, the restaurant's menu was expanded.

The food planning staff, which had calculated the food requirements based on Disneyland's, had not anticipated that breakfast would be such a popular meal at Disney World. But in Florida, Disney had two large-capacity hotels that emptied every morning into the Magic Kingdom. Yet they built only one breakfast facility—Main Street's Town Square Cafe, based on the compact Hills Brothers Coffee House at Disneyland. At Disney World, the cafe was continually blitzed. Disney had to shut down the restaurant for several days and institute a new, quicker system for guests to place their orders.

"We had serious capacity problems," said Ziegler. "Guests started looking for lunch at 11:00, and they wanted to be done by 1:00. We tried to get them to eat early, before 11 or after 1, but discovered you can't change people's eating habits. We had to change. We streamlined menus, instituted preorder systems, put people out in line taking orders. We discovered that the two things that took the most time were: one, people making up their mind and, two, cash transactions. So you'd take an order, rip the slip into three pieces, and hand one copy to drinks, one to food, and one to the cashier. We did it to speed up capacity."

The Ice Cream Parlor was equally overwhelmed. Dale Burner said, "We came up with a Lazy Susan to hold pre-scooped ice cream. We figured how much of each item we sold—say we sold chocolate two-to-one over vanilla—and had some people just scooping and other people just taking money. We had scoopers and servers isolated. They'd sell it before it would melt."

There also were not enough restaurants nor time to instantly build them. Instead, Disney set up temporary quick service stands throughout the park. In Fantasyland, a tent-like structure went up to sell hot dogs and hamburgers, and another sold pizza.

Later, as the weather began to heat up, so did the demand for cold beverages. Many of the food facilities added "drink only" lines. Disney converted a phone booth into a beverage stand. And they added more shade coverings outside and air-conditioning inside buildings to make the wait more tolerable.

Most urgently, the park woefully lacked attractions and, with tickets ten to 90 cents apiece, people standing in lines weren't spending any money. Management was terrified that first-time guests would be so angry at waiting in lines that they would never return—and relay their bad experiences to friends. Some relief came as Tomorrowland attractions already under construction were completed. The Circle-Vision 360 theater playing *America the Beautiful* opened on Thanksgiving Day. Flight to the Moon was finished Christmas Eve. If You Had Wings, a dark ride sponsored by Disney's official air carrier, Eastern Airlines, opened six months later. Four more monorails arrived soon after, bringing the fleet to ten. A year later, a tribute show, The Walt Disney Story, opened on Main Street and Frontierland's Rivers of America received a second Mississippi sternwheeler that could hold 400 passengers at a time and rafts ferrying to a new play area covering Tom Sawyer Island.

Card Walker personally championed another quick-fix, the Swan Boat ride. The moat in front of the castle had been built large enough that it encircled the park's central plaza. Yet all that space was home to only a flock of swans. So Walker had the Disney World staff shop build boats shaped like giant swans. The boats ran on a joystick-controlled jet propulsion system. Operators at times struggled to master the sensitive controls within the narrow canal—and bumped a few boats into the riverbanks. Guests were even less enamored by the plodding ride, because it offered nothing to view that couldn't already be seen just by walking around the plaza. And management disliked that the boats were low in capacity, accommodating just 26 guests per trip. So the ride was used only during the summer and removed as soon as the Magic Kingdom's overall capacity was built up.

What the park really needed was a ride that could handle thousands of people an hour, along the lines of Disneyland's celebrated Pirates of the Caribbean. Disney World's first E-ticket addition was supposed to be Thunder Mesa featuring Marc Davis' Western River Expedition. The ride had been fully developed, from creation of models and a few full-size animatronic animals to highlighting it as "coming soon" in brochures and postcards. Yet during the first months of Florida's Magic Kingdom, the biggest guest complaint was, "Where's Pirates of the Caribbean?" The corporate executives seemed oblivious that in five years, Pirates had become Disneyland's most popular and famous attraction. They decided to indefinitely shelf the Western River Expedition and immediately begin work reproducing Pirates.

Marc Davis was furious. To mollify the veteran artist, corporate allowed him to slightly change the original Pirates ride he had designed for California and add a few new scenes, such as a drunk pirate with a cat and a finale with soldiers tied up in an armory and the pirates getting the loot. The redo also gave Disney an opportunity to correct a "mistake" in the ride's original version: eliminating the protracted beginning through dark caverns. The caves had been built at Disneyland only to fill space in a smaller show building that the plans had outgrown.

Yet while Disneyland's Pirates of the Caribbean is commonly acknowledged as the world's greatest theme park attraction, Disney World's "improved" version would be viewed as just another ride, in great measure because it lacked the moonlit bayou and foreboding tunnels. Imagineer Baxter speculated, "The Pirate ride in Florida has never garnered the same mystique as the one in California. And I'm convinced that there's a level of removal that goes on as you descend deeper and deeper into this dreamlike state where finally at the last, lowest level it all comes to life. The characters are there, alive and so forth. In Florida you just put your packages away, you cast off, and—boom—you're in the city. Then, while you're still in there, struggling with the pirates and the prison, you hear the girl on the intercom saying, 'Ladies and gentlemen, please stand and exit to your right.' It's rather jarring to be asked to leave when there are people dying in the cell next to you. So I don't think it's ever connected. And the romance of the Blue Bayou is gone and all those things that really help to set this one up. I think the lesson learned in Florida was you can't race people into something, whether it's a queue line or it's a conditioning experience."

If nothing else, the ride—with a capacity of 4,300 guests an hour—at least helped occupy the growing crowds.

6

Room Change

IT took an extra couple of months, but the construction crews finally did complete the Contemporary Hotel's tower and garden annexes. That still didn't put Disney at rest. One loose end had been nagging at Roy: the deal with U.S. Steel. Through construction, the relationship between the two companies had been contentious; how would it be once the hotels actually opened? Their agreement was also fraught with potential conflicts, such as who profited from rentals at the U.S. Steel-owned hotels of boats that ran on the Disney-owned lake. Disputes would only grow more complicated as the resort added amenities. Plus, modular construction, touted as the wave of the future, resulted in more cost over-runs and headaches than benefits. U.S. Steel had forecast that each room would cost $17,000 to produce; actual cost turned out to be closer to $100,000 a room. They gained no cost savings by pre-enclosing the main open portion of a room. The only real advantage was in prefabricating specialty areas, such as bathrooms. The factory was used to produce prefab bathrooms for a couple of other local hotel projects before being shut down.

So, in early December 1971, as his final major business transaction, Roy arranged for Disney to pay U.S. Steel $50 million for its interest in the hotels as well as assume all remaining costs of completing the Contemporary. Disney had already invested $28.5 million designing, equipping, furnishing and helping to construct the hotels, and expected

BETTER LATE: The park may have opened on time, but the Contemporary Hotel required three additional weeks of finishing touches. (October 1971) *Photo courtesy John Curry*

to spend at least $12 million more to finish construction.

"Disney never was a very good partner with anybody," admitted company attorney Phil Smith. "Disney liked to do things its way. The deal with U.S. Steel was originally made as a matter of money. It was a convoluted deal. We leased the land to U.S. Steel to build the building, they were going to own the building, and we were going to manage it. We'd want to manage it our way, and the concern was that it might not have been the way they wanted to do it. We just felt that we'd be better off running it ourselves. It was an amicable [parting]. There was no litigation. They were willing. It was just decided that the relationship wasn't going to work that well."

For Disney, the purchase formally removed the necessity of having hotels managed by a separate division composed of outside hotel professionals. They could now run the hotels the Disney Way.

Certainly, the park old-timers mistrusted the "hotel people" from the start. Hotelier Clayne Dice remembered, "One of my assignments before we opened was to talk to all the park managers and tell them why Disney changed to serve alcohol [at the hotels]. It was a whole new thing. At Disneyland, they only served alcohol at [the private] Club 33. I explained that mother and father might like to have a martini before dinner or a glass of wine with dinner. We were resort hotels, and were going to compete with the best. Disney wanted to make sure everyone understood why. Some people were unhappy; they thought it was changing traditions."

Not long before opening, Operations also considered not allowing the hotels to have their own parking lots, since Walt had wanted cars segregated from show areas. John Curry was beside himself. He quickly located Clayne Dice and told him to compile a list of reasons why off-site parking would fail—guest services reasons, arguments that Operations could understand. What if little Suzie left her teddy bear in the car? What if guests needed to get to church on a Sunday morning? The hotels got their parking lots.

One morning in the Contemporary's lobby, Dick Nunis noticed a hotel industry-trained manager asking guests to walk around the freshly waxed tile floor. Nunis hated to see inconveniences placed on guests. He pulled the supervisor off to the side and chewed him out. "We don't treat our guests like that," Nunis barked.

Operationally, the Polynesian—with its more laid-back atmosphere and more manageable 492 guests rooms divided between eight two-story longhouses—ran relatively smoothly. Any problem was at most a two-minute golf cart-ride away. Most of the early bumps related to the entertainment—often a source of friction for the Operations department. "Operations is looking for a smooth operation, that's what makes them happy," said Entertainment director Peter Bloustein. "Everything every day should be the same. That's what makes them successful. But Entertainment is geared to go against the grain. Whenever we do anything special, we cause a ripple in the lake."

An obvious fit was a nightly luau. The format had already been devised for the opening ceremonies. Disney could have set up a stage in the Papeete Bay Verandah restaurant for a little show, but discovered that if they staged the luau on the beach, particularly for conventions and other private parties, they could maintain their dinner business and charge extra for the show. With no dedicated facility on the beach, set-up was a chore. Staff had to assemble and then dismantle power cords, banquet tables, and a temporary stage for every performance. Crews then had to work late every night raking rice out of the sand.

Rain caused even more trouble. Diners would either demand refunds or the staff would hurry to relocate everything and everyone inside, along the atrium lobby's second-story balcony. By 1973, a sheltered Luau Cove with its own portable kitchen was built to allow the show to go on year round. Outdoor heaters were installed a year later and wind screens three years after that.

Entertainment also experimented with various water skiing shows on the lagoon, but they never caught on. "I was not a strong supporter of it," Bloustein said. "We were not a water ski company. We were doing it mid-afternoon to late afternoon when people should be in the theme park, spending money. Why pull people out of shops, stop them from eating, to see some people water ski? Let Sea World do that, that's fine. I think the whole ski show phenomenon lasted at the most three months. A number of different shows were tried, a number of different concepts, but again the whole thing was that people were not there to see a water ski show. They were there to buy an ashtray, buy a T-shirt, have a hamburger and French fries, enjoy the Haunted Mansion, and listen to the Dapper Dans on Main Street. And a water ski show really didn't have an interest."

Nunis, the former jock, was more consumed with devising a way to bring surfing to the Polynesian. He found a fledgling company in San Diego that promised it could deliver a contraption capable of producing surfable waves of varying heights. In mid-1971, the hulking machinery was shipped to Florida and set up on an uninhabited island across from the Polynesian's West Beach, which Nunis hoped to rename "Surfrider Beach."

The technology amounted to eight gigantic, hydraulically-activated "paddle pushers" arranged in a semicircle on the island and, near the beach, an eight-foot-deep artificial reef made from river rock. The paddles churned sixteen feet into the water, creating ripples that turned into waves. Unfortunately, remembered test surfer Bill Hoelscher, "for every action, there is an opposite reaction. The water has to go back. So it started eating away at the island."

The machine could be cranked up to produce some beautiful waves, but the return current would be just as strong, sometimes knocking the wavemaker off its piling. Reedy Creek's Tom Jones recalled the equipment's "overriding problem was structural. It shook itself apart in operation, and attempts to strengthen the anchor system were not successful."

As well, others feared that if the device were run at its highest setting, the waves would swamp the Polynesian Hotel.

Nunis tenaciously defended his wave machine, well after the hotel had opened and everyone else had given up on the idea ever working. Nunis even invited engineers and designers from WED to watch him surf. In the middle of his demonstration, one Imagineer declared, "I think the island's moving! The surf is pushing back the island!"

Of course, the island wasn't actually moving, but it was beginning to get eaten away. Finally, after months of tinkering, Nunis reluctantly gave up. Some of the machinery was removed, other components left there to rust, to this day, as a reminder of "Nunis' folly."

Hotel division head John Curry had his own pet project, too. Not long after the park opened, he and Howard Roland tracked down an antique Chinese junk for sale. The agent told Curry it had been owned by NFL quarterback Joe Namath, a believable claim since the cabin featured a circular bed with a glass ceiling. On the outside at least, the 65-foot teak vessel fit perfectly with the theme of the Polynesian Hotel. They arranged for the ship to be sailed to Cape Canaveral, where it was to be hoisted on to a semi with a custom-built cradle and trucked to the Seven Seas Lagoon.

Unfortunately, recalled Curry, "what seemed like a simple thing got really complicated. It turned out that there were several bridges it could not go under and several power lines that had to be cut and spliced en route. It was a most expensive trip. Next, when it was rigged, the main mast was too tall to go under the monorail track to get to the Poly resort, so they cut the mast several feet, which caused significant change in the rigging. Next, once it was in the lake for a period of time, it began to rot below the waterline in fresh water. Salt water did not affect it. So they had to haul it out and put a copper bottom on it. The cost went crazy."

At most every DWOC meeting, Nunis would be sure to mention, "John, let's talk about your junk!"

The ship was originally intended for atmosphere, tethered dockside at the Polynesian's marina. But when the hotel found itself short on meeting space, the junk was turned into a floating conference facility. After the hotel added several meeting rooms, the vessel's name was changed from the Outrider to the Eastern Winds and it was converted into a cocktail lounge.

The jousting lightly masked the growing tension between Nunis and Curry. Nunis didn't care for divisions that didn't fold neatly into his operational flow chart; he'd spent years at Disneyland consolidating as many departments as possible under the Operations banner. At Disney World, the hotels had their own separate management and janitorial, food, and entertainment departments. Curry knew what Nunis was after and zealously guarded his turf.

What gave Nunis leverage was the rocky start the Contemporary got off to. Most of the problems had to do with the sheer size of the hotel: over 1,000 rooms in a vast, fourteen-story tower and three disconnected annexes. "We had a lot of service failures early on," admitted Curry. "Any hotel opening is difficult, [but] a new hotel usually doesn't have any business. You struggle to get the occupancy up. We hit the ground at 100 percent and never had a vacancy. If the plumbing broke and you had to move someone out of a room, there was nowhere to put them."

And every room wasn't just full—it was packed. Nationally, hotels averaged 1.5 guests per room. Because it catered to families, the Contemporary averaged 3.2. Plus, most guests were only staying for one, maybe two nights, meaning that the staff was emptying more than half the rooms every morning and filling them back up with new guests every afternoon.

The crush of guests overwhelmed the facilities. There were kids running down the hallways, sand being tracked in from the beach, food and drinks being spilled everywhere, even pets being sneaked into the rooms. Three teams of "shampoo men" worked five days a week battling to keep the carpeting presentable.

At top capacity, the Contemporary's dining rooms could accommodate 800-some customers. Yet every morning, 3,000-some hotel guests came looking for breakfast before jumping into the monorail and heading to the Magic Kingdom. Their waiting wasn't over once guests reached the breakfast table. The Imagineers had been so preoccupied with how everything looked onstage, that little thought or space were given to backstage areas, such the restaurants' kitchens—severely limiting their ability to serve large numbers of guests in a reasonable amount of time. Call to schedule room service for 7:00 the next morning, and the staff would offer to bring your scrambled eggs at 11:00, after the rush had died down.

The guests were not so understanding. They might smile and line up peaceably in a theme park environment, where hour-long waits were acceptable practice. But customers knew what to expect in a hotel environment—even an exotically themed one—and Disney wasn't delivering.

Part of the problem was Disney's desire to take risks and experiment—a dicier proposition at a hotel, where visitors were often looking for a place that felt like home. To achieve a sleeker, more modern look, the Contemporary and Polynesian were originally furnished with no table lamps or floor lamps. Traditional lamps, explained Clayne Dice, "got very dusty, the lampshades tilted and became crooked. You could see the seams in the lampshades. Instead, we had strip lighting over the headboards of the beds and down lights shining from the ceiling on strategic locations, such as the chair. We received too many complaints. It was too hard to read. People were just not used to it. It lasted several months, until we began remodeling."

The hotels were also bound by some Disney company restrictions. As at the theme parks, the hotels did not accept credit cards, to avoid paying a percentage to American Express or Mastercard. Likewise, Disney refused to grant commissions to travel agents, assuming they could fill up their rooms on their own.

When the hotels first opened, Disney—trying to make guests feel as unpressured as possible—forbid employees from accepting tips. Inevitably, many guests would try to force the tips on the staff, who would have to return them, occasionally offending the guest. Of course, the impoverished service staff didn't like the rule any better and felt less motivated. After a few months, Disney allowed the hotels to drop the no-tipping policy.

The hotels' streamlined check-in procedure overwhelmed the staff. As first set up, the two far right lanes at the parking toll booths were reserved for hotel guests. Attendants would ask the guest's name, place a number on their windshield, and radio ahead to their hotel, so a hostess and bellhop could be waiting to welcome them as their car pulled up to the curb. A valet would then take care of their car, and both hostess and bellhop would escort the family to their room. The call-ahead system and having two employees "room" each party were too labor intensive and soon dropped.

Some hotel guests got lost driving from the attendant, so lines had to be painted on the road from the toll booths to the two hotels.

The trials forced management to become more familiar with the typical Disney guest. Curry said, "We thought the Contemporary and Poly would be luxury hotels, and we planned them after industry standards, such as one seat per guest in the main dining room. These hotels were attractions unto themselves. It was not four-star clientele; the guests who stayed there would stay in a Motel 6 all the way to Orlando, saving up to stay at the Contemporary so they could say they stayed at Walt Disney World. There would be a line a mile long at the coffee shop and nobody at the dining room. We had to downgrade, to better learn the clientele."

There were plenty of individual mishaps along the way. Preparing for one big celebratory banquet, a smoke alarm went off in the Contemporary's main kitchen and sent white Ansul powder cascading down on the food. The staff had to rush around the hotel, rounding up any ingredients they could find to create a makeshift banquet. Another night, the sprinklers went off in several of the concourse stores and ruined all the clothes in the mens and ladies shops.

Oddly, the hotel's financial performance appeared to be the last thing on the executives' minds. In fact, the Contemporary's struggles to make money were, at least in the short term, more due to its striving to meet Disney expectations as opposed to hospitality industry standards. The rooms weren't inexpensive—a then-priccy $29 to $44 a night, depending on the room. But Disney gave guests as much as they got. It was Walt's philosophy of "plussing the show" to the nth power.

Merchandise was one of the few operations at the hotels that fell under park management's purview. Resort-wide, the department was led by Jack Olsen, a heavy-set old-timer, who usually dressed in shorts and a golf shirt and constantly preached that his stores were not factories. He wanted all of them operated first and foremost as part of the show, rather than designed and operated to maximize profit. Even though souvenirs imprinted with Mickey Mouse and other characters were the best selling merchandise in the park, none were sold in Adventureland, Frontierland or Liberty Square. Everything had to be themed to the period.

Main Street was filled with shops chosen primarily for atmosphere. A candle shop, flower stand, and tobacconist helped recreate the look and feel of the turn of the century, even if they didn't belong in an amusement park. The china shop carried top-of-the-line serving ware and delicate figurines by Lladro and Hummel—despite the average vacationer having little interest in buying fine china while at a theme park.

And then there was service to match. Wayne Busch said, "If the trolley horse stepped on someone's bobblehead doll, we'd replace it. If we saw someone with a balloon that was losing air, we'd run after them and give them a new one."

Disney didn't like messages or signs that made guests uncomfortable, such as "Don't touch" or "You break it, you buy it." Toy rifles were a big seller in Frontierland, to the chagrin of the screeners at the local airports. An airport representative finally called Disney World and asked them to put a sign over the rifles: "If you fly, don't buy." Disney, not one for negative messages, declined. The airports eventually instituted their own rules requiring travelers to check toy rifles in their luggage before they could fly.

Olsen's five shops in the Polynesian sold clothing and trinkets, primarily tied to the South Seas theme: Hawaiian print shirts, sarongs, plastic and real flowered leis, and "Polynesian perfume." Internally, the staff referred to it as "little old lady perfume," but the horrible-smelling concoctions sold by the truckload. The sign over the lobby's newsstand read "News from Civilization."

The Contemporary was designed as the property's flagship hotel, able to provide any service guests might need—a noble gesture considering how isolated its location was at the time. There were a drugstore, liquor store, jewelry store, florist, tennis pro shop, beach shop, salons, and separate clothing stores for men, women and children.

As manager of "personal services," Michael Tangel oversaw the resort's barber shops, beauty shops, and health clubs. Tangel said, "Jack Olsen would say, 'It's not important to make money in a service area. We're trying to get people into the hotel, not into a barbershop.' So I concentrated on giving the best service possible."

The Contemporary's beauty salon opened with 32 employees, including young female attendants to pick up towels and flash pretty smiles. Anyone visiting the men's salon received a complimentary shoeshine. The company even went to the money-losing expense of having Tangel create a Contemporary Hotel-themed line of health care products, including men's and women's shampoo, conditioner, cologne, sprays, creams and bars of soap packaged in miniature Contemporary A-frame-shaped boxes.

According to Wolf Kahn, who managed the Contemporary's Magic Kingdom Jewels, "Disney had very little business knowledge. Anything Jack Olsen wanted was okay. It didn't matter what it cost. It was so far-fetched from a business sense. Very idealistic. Everything was show. The antique shop in [the Magic Kingdom's] Liberty Square made about $100,000 a year—but spent $1 million! Money didn't mean a thing. They were movie people, there to put on a show."

Disney's greater concern was that everything looked nice. The illusion of a professional, successful business was more important than its actual prosperity. As is common custom in jewelry stores, Kahn had placed sales pads on each of his shop's glass counters. Disney made him remove them, saying they looked cluttered and too commercial.

The Contemporary's penthouse supper club was another unprofitable venture mostly there for prestige—and the fact that there was precious little else for guests to do after dark. The Top of the World Club presented two shows nightly with performers like Donald O'Connor, Rosemary Clooney, Barbara Eden, Lou Rawls, Mel Torme, Kay Starr, and Patti Page, plus dining and dancing to the music of the full Top of the World orchestra.

By early 1972, as problems mounted at the Contemporary, Nunis was promoted from head of Operations at Disneyland to executive vice president over both Disneyland and Walt Disney World. Now even Curry reported to him. Soon, hotel management and staff began questioning just who was in charge.

The confusion deepened in March 1972, when Nunis assigned Jim Cora and several theme park managers to the hotels. Nunis hoped that by mixing a few Disneylanders into management, some of the pixie dust might rub off on the hotel people. If not, at least Nunis's agents would be learning the business, so Operations could move in and take over. Naturally, the degreed hotel professionals resented being told how to do their jobs by 28-year-olds who had spent their entire, brief careers at Disneyland.

Thor Degelmann, a Disneyland University trainer, transferred to the

East Coast with Cora, as a front office supervisor at the Contemporary. "Their attitude," Degelmann said, "was, 'We're hotel people. We know hotels. You know theme parks. Let us run the hotels how hotels should be run. You stick to theme parks.' The problem was that without the theme park, there is no hotel. There's no reason to stay overnight."

Operations and, more importantly, guests saw the hotel as an extension of the Magic Kingdom. "We were a family hotel, and guests all came from the theme park, all tired, grouchy and wanting to eat at the same time," Degelmann said. "No hotel had had to deal with that; a theme park did. The demand was just incredible. It left the experienced hotel people scratching their heads. The theme park people dealt with it every day, so they could go with the flow. So we brought in theme park-experienced people to create one entity out of it. The guest experience had to be the same—one Disney product, fully integrated, seamless. We had no time or patience. We couldn't wait one, two, three years. Word of mouth would have killed the whole resort."

The hotel professionals, Degelmann continued, "had a different perception of quality, so the service started to falter, both the systems and interpersonally. A Disney hotel is a different kind of quality than the Ritz Carlton, the Four Seasons. That's what people had to come to grips with. We were never going to be the St. Regis. It's a different kind of quality. We had to take the traditionally trained hoteliers and change the context, make them realize we were not diminishing service. We were taking into account demand. You had to break the 'I've been in hotels 20 years. I've been taught...' The middle and bottom management was starting to make progress, but it was difficult at the top."

The first cut hit the very top. In May, Curry received his walking papers, replaced by Bob Allen, an original Disneylander with zero hotel experience. Allen, compassionate and accessible, was known as the "great soother," the one who would build cast members back up after they'd been torn down by Nunis. Allen would oversee hotels and general services, Bob Mathieson theme park operations.

A great communicator, Allen would be the perfect conduit for selling the hotel staff on the new vision: replacing industry standards with Disney quality standards and creating a "comfort zone" for families. That meant less fine dining and more family-friendly options. Adding babysitting services. And eliminating luxury hotel formalities, such as requiring that tennis whites be worn on the tennis courts. As Allen would argue, "Are you going to tell someone who's come all the way out here they can't play tennis because they don't have a little white skirt?"

With Curry gone, the hotel-bred survivors did their best to prove they cared about show. At the Polynesian, Central Reservations' Harris Rosen thought the incessant ringing of the phones at the front desk killed the atmosphere. He had the phone company switch the tone, so whenever a call came in, the phones chirped like birds. Alan Hubsch, the first general manager of the Contemporary, got the message that he wasn't supposed to be hanging out in his office; he restructured his routine to include walking the length of every hallway on all fourteen floors once a day. Not good enough. Soon, Hubsch found himself walking the entire hotel grounds—not just the rooms, but its beaches, pools, docks, tennis, croquet, shuffleboard and sand volleyball courts, and parking lots—twice a day, to make sure everything was in "good show condition."

Inevitably, many of the top hotel managers—Hubsch, Rosen, Clayne Dice—would be gone within two years.

"Early in, it was clear that Operations had abdicated operation of the hotels reluctantly," Rosen recalled. "The new guys got chewed up and spit out. Alan Hubsch had a hard time. Bob Allen terminated me, explaining it was clear that I would never become a true Disney person. It was a culture thing."

One Disney trainer reasoned that such hotel people may have attended the Disney University, "but they just tolerated it." They didn't buy in.

A few were able to weather the transition, such as Dan Darrow, who would spend the next 35 years and counting running Disney hotels. Howard Roland, the New Yorker, figured he was next on the chopping block. "I was never Disney," he said. "I was always an outsider." Privately, he even consulted with cherubic Van Arsdale France, the motivational Disney University founder, for tips on becoming "more Disney." It was hopeless. Yet Roland's experience extended beyond hotels, and his integrity, shrewdness and innate business sense—at a company where some top executives didn't have college degrees—made him an ideal tool for use elsewhere, away from running the hotels. His first reassignment would be taking over—and cleaning up—the company's purchasing organization, where a number of kickbacks, payoffs and other discrepancies had been uncovered.

After a few months, Bill Sullivan transferred from the Magic Kingdom to the hotels as Bob Allen's number two. Another show-obsessed Disneylander, he was known by most co-workers as "Sully." They also nicknamed him "Five-eighths," short for "Five-eighths Nunis," paying tribute to the intimate scale used to build the railroad and other park elements, Sully's short stature, and his reputation as a cuddlier version of Nunis. "The only thing I took to the hotels was the Disney philosophy," Sullivan said. "We had hired a bunch of good hotel people, but they didn't know Disney. That was my job: teach them Disney."

Sullivan was less concerned about getting through another day than with the long-term damage to the Disney name that might result from delivering unacceptable service. Particularly troubling to him was the stack of complaints from outgoing guests that would be waiting on his and Bob Allen's desk when they arrived for work every morning. Dealing with yesterday's guests had been a low priority for the hotel people. Sullivan and Allen decided to write letters of apology for each complaint. After a few days, Sullivan had a better idea. He suggested personally calling every dissatisfied guest, so the customers could restate their grievances, know they had been heard, and work together to make things right.

"We bent over backwards for all our guests," Sullivan said, "because we wanted to build the best hotel chain in the United States, for the top 10 percent of the guests in the world."

Sullivan remembered one guest who was checking out after a particularly horrid three-day stay. The guest told him, "I want you to know how bad you screwed up my vacation." The man then recounted one service disaster after another, from his family's unpleasant arrival at the front gate through their troublesome checkout from the Contemporary. "Sir," Sullivan finally replied, "you can't be lying to me, because no one could make up that much of a story."

"You're right," the man nodded, pleased to have someone listen to him.

"Do me a favor," Sullivan asked. "Would you ever come back here again?"

"Nope."

"Would you give me a second chance? If you do, I'll take care of your three-day stay."

"Bull, you wouldn't do that."

"Sir, I screwed up. We screwed up. Would you give us a second chance?"

"All right," the man capitulated. Sully handed him his business card. Three years later, the guest finally returned. Disney paid for his hotel room, park tickets, meals, everything. The family had the best vacation of their lives. It cost the company a pretty penny, but they figured they'd won a customer for life.

The emphasis became Service under a Spotlight. If someone noticed chipping paint, it was to be repaired immediately. When a trash can neared full, it was to be quickly removed from sight and emptied behind the scenes. Even cars with flat tires in the parking lot would be rolled backstage, so other guests wouldn't see the tire change. Special scaffolding and a long pole were kept at the ready, to retrieve any mouse-ear-shaped helium balloon that might escape from a child's grip and float to the Contemporary's ceiling 90 feet up.

With the staff brainwashing well underway, it was time to start repairing the hotels themselves. Those who designed and furnished the hotels, Degelmann said, "had been looking at traditional hotels and numbers. These types of materials could not withstand the demand. Carpets, everything had to be replaced."

In the fall of 1972, Disney began systematically refurbishing each room—no small feat considering demand exceeded capacity on a daily basis. A traditional hotel might tear down a floor at a time during off-season. The Contemporary had no off-season. Instead, Disney instituted a "rolling rehab," rotating workmen among eight rooms at a time, similar to the modular concept used to build the hotel in the first place. The system allowed refurbishment of 500 rooms a year, meaning that by 1975, the hotel had been completely overhauled, top to bottom.

Studio art director Emile Kuri designed new carpeting, drapes and color schemes, in blue, purple and green. A mural of the Magic Kingdom was placed in each room so guests could "get an idea of where everything is." The walls were redone in vinyl wallpaper so it would be easier to wipe off children's fingerprints. The sleek Walt Disney World logo, present on everything from the trash cans to the fire hydrants, was purposely left off the hotel linens and towels—making them less desirable targets for souvenir hunters.

In late 1972, every piece of exercise equipment in the Contemporary's health club was replaced with the latest Nautilus machinery. Next came a wall-to-wall refurbishment of the hotel's indoor recreation center, the Exhibitorium. Disney also considered adding elevator systems to connect the north and south annexes with the main tower, but eventually conceded that the idea was impractical.

Disney also thought it could relieve some of the pressure from the hotels by expanding. A lack of time and—after buying out U.S. Steel— money prevented proceeding with the original plan of next building the elaborate Asian hotel. Instead, they needed something that was faster and more affordable to construct, and more manageable in size. Card Walker, the avid golfer, commissioned a cozy, 153-room Golf Resort Hotel, so players could stay near the two courses. Disney also ordered another 225 spaces be added to the perpetually-sold-out Fort Wilderness campgrounds.

To appeal to vacationers looking for mid-level accommodations, the area around the Preview Center had been designed as Motor Inn Plaza. There, Disney would lease the land to seasoned hotel operators to build a new flagship for their chains. The company put its Participant Affairs department to work looking for corporate sponsors among the hotel chains. The companies were encouraged to spend more than usual on their Disney World hotel to create a lavish property that could be highlighted in advertising for all their locations. Yet, to stay in line with the Disney philosophy, room rates should be affordable. The chains could justify the expense by viewing the whole project as advertising and drawing the funds from their marketing budget instead of their operating budget.

Disney would provide the hotels with access to the resort's central computerized reservation system, transportation to the theme parks for their guests, and would market them along with their own hotels. But perhaps the most valuable perk was that the hotels could be advertised as being located on Disney property.

Two large chains—Howard Johnson's and Travelodge—signed on, as well as an independent businessman who operated a small number of Royal Inns in Pennsylvania. Against its better judgment, Disney also came to terms with two smooth-talking partners who operated a 50-room Holiday Inn in downtown Miami and promised they could raise $12 million to build a Dutch Inn. Combined, the four high-rise hotels would cost $35 million and add 1,600 rooms to the resort.

Beyond Disney World's property lines, hotels and motels were springing up even faster, anxious to snare a share of the Disney dollars. Within months of the Magic Kingdom opening, an estimated 20,000 rooms were under construction or on the drawing boards. Disney wasn't drawing near enough guests to fill those rooms, even with attendance at the park climbing steadily. Just imagine the consequences should attendance start to fall.

7

Power Plays

W HEN Disney first arrived in Florida, the company realized that it needed local support, to supply labor, expertise, supplies and patronage. But the resort's early success allowed Disney the luxury of arrogance and the opportunity to provide more services itself, reducing its reliance on the local population and businesses.

With the Magic Kingdom, they had already created a virtual city, albeit one devoted to producing magic. They maintained control by charging the public to get in and being able to tell them to leave at the end of a long day. After the Magic Kingdom closed for the night, hundreds of maintenance men took over, working around the clock to repair and maintain every inch of the park. Crews steam cleaned Main Street and vacuum-filtered the castle moat. Landscapers trimmed and pruned, planted and fertilized, mowed and watered. Mechanics checked and tightened and replaced. Craftsmen polished and painted and repaired.

Employees were committed to ensuring everything looked perfect and ran flawlessly by the time the guests arrived in the morning. Late one night, a storm snapped the top third off the gigantic Christmas tree in Town Square. Cast members toiled until daylight to reattach the treetop with a collar.

Plenty of support work took place during business hours, though typically sheltered from daylight. Most managers were based in the offices that made up the second stories of the Main Street buildings. Additional operations were housed beneath the streets, accessed by 30 different stairwells and elevators hidden throughout the park. Rather than one giant basement, the subterranean Utilidors—short for utility corridors—were a network of tunnels that connected a series of smaller basements. The eight-acre underground was so sprawling that for months after the park first opened, guides had to be stationed in the tunnels to redirect lost employees. Soon after, the tunnel walls were color-coded by land and maps were posted at each intersection to help newcomers find their way.

The tunnels were built high and wide enough to accommodate delivery and maintenance trucks, allowing workers to replenish supplies and make repairs without intruding on the show. To prevent air pollution, all supply vehicles were electric. Only two internal combustion vehicles were permitted underground: the ambulance and the Wells Fargo armored truck.

Electricity conduits, each marked for easy identification, ran along the ceiling and walls. One wall held various-sized pipes, carrying heating, cooling and drinking water, compressed air to power the attractions, natural gas for the restaurant ovens, and fiber optic cable for the telecommunications system. Outside cities soon began copying Disney by burying their utilities for aesthetic reasons. But the Magic Kingdom's system was practical, too. Although subterranean, each conduit remained easily accessible, eliminating the need to dig up on-stage areas to service the utilities.

Even the garbage seemed to vanish into thin air. Every trashcan was decorated to blend with its surroundings, such as being hand-painted to resemble bamboo in Adventureland or logs in Frontierland. Facilities manager Ted Kellogg estimated, "By the time you painted and sealed it, it cost $1,500 to do a trashcan. Then, if it got any nicks or scratches, Decorating would strip it down and repaint it."

As soon as a can became filled with trash, a custodian would wheel out a replacement and roll the full can backstage, where he emptied it into large canisters in one of eighteen concealed dump stations. The canisters were then whisked away at 60 miles an hour through an underground exhaust pipe to a remote central collection point. There, the trash was compacted and hauled by covered truck a mile-and-half to a high-tech incinerator, with a smokestack scrubbed so well it emitted no dirt or smoke—only steam.

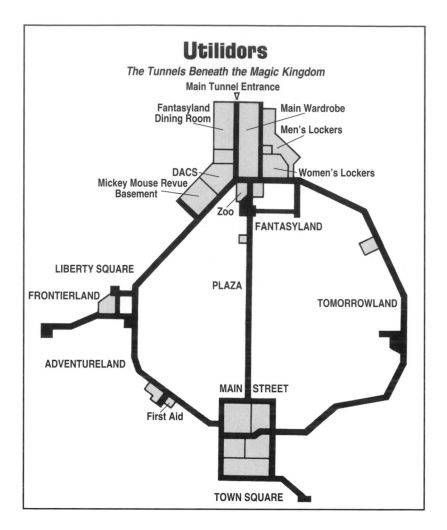

Utilidors

The Tunnels Beneath the Magic Kingdom

The below-park caverns led to a massive wardrobe room to store and hand out the costumes, separate locker rooms for men, women and costumed characters, break rooms, offices, meeting rooms, kitchens, an employee cafeteria, and a cast member barber shop with its own red-white-and-blue-striped barber pole. An underground engraving shop continually cranked out nametags. The musicians had a rehearsal room and two elevator stages that could lift entire orchestras at the touch of a button. Of course, the stages lowered just as easily, which came in handy for crowd control. During one Grad Nite in the 1970s, thousands of teenagers tried to swarm the Tomorrowland stage at the end of a concert by the Commodores. Security held the mob back as the stage lowered safely underground, removing the band from harm's way.

In a computer control center, technicians manned three separate systems that kept the resort running. The Digital Animation Control System (DACS) used 32-track magnetic tapes to control the sound and movement of theater shows, like the Haunted Mansion, Hall of Presidents, and Country Bear Jamboree. The Automatic Monitor & Control System (AM & CS) consisted of eight mini-computers that ran 24 hours a day to monitor 2,000 separate critical maintenance points across the property and send regular readouts to the Reedy Creek Fire Department, Security department, and energy plant. The third system supervised power switching, load sharing, and electricity distribution from the energy plant.

Other service and support facilities were located above ground, behind the Magic Kingdom. The technological marvel was the ultra-efficient Central Energy Plant. Built by Reedy Creek for $19 million, the facility could meet about a third of the resort's energy needs in a variety of forms. At its heart, clean-burning natural gas powered two 8,000-horsepower jet aircraft engines, driving a stream of 1,500-degree air through turbines to generate 12,000 watts of electricity. In addition, the turbine-cooling wastewater, instead of being discharged into a nearby stream, was channeled into boilers and heated to 400 degrees. Some of the superheated water was piped to the hot water faucets in the park, the rest to either building heaters or to absorption chillers to run the air conditioning throughout the resort.

The energy plant also generated compressed air for the attractions, pumped and stored up to one million gallons of potable water, and controlled natural gas distribution.

Reedy Creek also built its own $2.5-million sewage treatment plant. The facility cleaned the resort's waste water thoroughly enough to meet public drinking water standards—but Disney wisely used it to water plants and golf courses instead. Sludge removed was used as fertilizer.

The facilities, along with future additions like a state-of-the-art incinerator generated electricity as it liquefied garbage, were born of a quest to do something experimental in the hopes it would be more efficient, safer, stronger and more productive. Some, like the short-lived incinerator, might have the plug pulled on them when they'd had the usefulness sucked out of them, but the main idea was to try something new and let the outside world learn from Disney's successes as well as its failures.

For Reedy Creek Improvement District president Joe Potter, that "spirit of EPCOT" inspired everything he did. So he was particularly irked whenever someone asked when Disney was going to start work on EPCOT. He would explain that Disney began work on EPCOT on Day One. They put in the vacuum-powered trash system. "That's EPCOT," he'd say. They had the filtered tree farm and the clean energy plant. "That's EPCOT," he'd repeat. They were going to run the PeopleMover with linear motors, instead of the standard electric motors in use at Disneyland. "That's EPCOT."

Yet, except for the monorail, all of the experimental elements were behind the scenes, invisible to the public. Consequently, there began to rise a growing suspicion of the Reedy Creek Improvement District. As expansion continued at a frenetic pace across Disney property, critics saw a company-owned government that appeared to be rubber-stamping whatever the company wanted. Disney, of course, would argue that its relationship with Reedy Creek wasn't underhanded, merely more efficient. By eliminating burdensome red tape, everyone could focus on what was truly important—creating safe, sound structures—instead of rote fulfilling of obligations and completing of checklists. Building codes demanding the use of time-honored materials and techniques by definition outlawed innovation.

The inventor viewed code officials as people who told you what you couldn't do. Reedy Creek, instead, sought to help accomplish what had never been done before. They didn't want precedent; they wanted proof that plans were technically sound and safe, even if the construction technique had never been tried before.

Reedy Creek stressed flexibility, being open to consider that there might be a better way. No building code in the country allowed reinforced masonry buildings to be built higher than twelve stories. For the Travelodge at the Motor Inn Plaza, Disney engineers showed that they could increase strength by using epoxy rather than mortar to put the blocks together. At sixteen stories, the hotel became the tallest structure of its type in the U.S.

Still, for all practical purposes it was just a hotel. Sooner or later, Disney was going to have to build something that was unmistakably EPCOT. Yet the company was a long way from figuring out how to pull off a city of the future. The biggest quandary remained how to control the residents—and prevent them from gaining any sort of control over Disney World. Once the general public acquired property in Reedy Creek's domain, they would gain municipal voting rights. And they might not always see eye to eye with the company.

To ensure its power, Disney had groups of Reedy Creek employees live in trailers in each of its two cities, beginning before the park first opened. Seven furnished, two-bedroom, two-bath trailers, 60-foot-by-twelve-foot with ten-foot-by-20-foot screened porches, sat on the back shore of Bay Lake. Seven more were set up around Little Lake Bryan across Interstate 4 from Lake Buena Vista. One resident in each encampment was appointed mayor. As "permanent" residents—most for a stretch of a few years at a time—they would all have voting rights, dutifully opting for what was in the best interest of the property and the property owner, their boss.

Disney realized that it would need its lands much further developed before it could risk opening itself up to outside governance. To buy time and to take a small step toward a city of tomorrow, Disney decided to first build a more conventional city incorporating elements of EPCOT-like construction and design. In catering to vacation travelers, the city could be operated like the Magic Kingdom. And, it would give Disney a place to base non-entertainment operations, such as a market, a post office, and a hospital.

Years before, Walt had suggested such "conventional" services be located at the outskirts of the property, at the eastern edge where I-4 would funnel visitors to the Preview Center.

In January 1972, Disney unveiled plans for the first $50 million phase of the city of Lake Buena Vista. Subsidiary Buena Vista Land Company, which was planning and managing the project, had converted the Preview Center into its offices. Already they had started construction on the four motor inns, the city's first 27 townhouses, and an adjacent eighteen-hole golf course.

Between the townhomes, retail village, and support facilities, Disney would begin gaining experience in running a city. The best materials and systems could eventually be used in EPCOT.

Initially, Lake Buena Vista would be a recreational, "second home" community. Its 250 townhouses would be leased to national and local companies as "retreats for clients and productive employees" under one- or two-year contracts. The first units were one and two-bedroom townhouses with rents from $5,000 to $7,000 a year. Even before the first shovel of dirt was turned, 70 companies had expressed interest in leasing a residence. Encouraged, Disney expanded the options on the second batch of 53 townhouses. They would now offer four different models, ranging from an unfurnished one-bedroom, one-and-a-half bath unit on a wooded lot for $5,500 a year to a furnished three-bedroom, three-and-a-half bath townhome for $20,900 for two years. In the third batch of townhouses, they planned to build two of the units with solar energy cells.

As in EPCOT, cars would be banished to the fringes of Lake Buena Vista. Recreation would be family-oriented. All roads within the residential and recreational areas would be private. Residents could traverse the community via waterways, pathways and trails for boats, electric carts, horses, bikes or walking. Donn Tatum even insisted that Lake Buena Vista shouldn't be referred to as a city, "but rather as a park comprised of woods, waterways, trails and active recreation pursuits. We are creating a park-like setting and then making provision for people to live within the park."

If all went well, Disney envisioned that within three years, they would also be renting luxury apartments and selling condominiums and houses at Lake Buena Vista. In anticipation, WED designed and Disney constructed four single-family model homes—one three-bedroom and three two-bedroom units, both single and split level—to be priced from $40,000 to $75,000. For both condos and houses, purchasers would buy the building, but not the land.

Disney also selected a potential site for a school, but the executives secretly hoped there would never be a school-age population that would require them to actually build it.

In the meantime, they would build a cluster of art, handicraft and boutique shops and waterfront restaurants, patterned after the beachside villages that caught merchandise maven Jack Olsen's eye in Carmel and La Jolla, California. Down the road, Disney foresaw adding a suburban-style regional shopping center closer to I-4 and an urbanized office park.

Disney aimed to create a city of conventional services in an unconventional manner—preplanned and controlled down to the most minute detail. Lake Buena Vista was to serve as a stark contrast to the grubby blight that sat on Disneyland's doorstep in Anaheim. Yet building its own sanitized city at the edge of its boundaries didn't eliminate the existence of a seedy periphery. The seedy periphery merely moved from the theme park's gates to just outside Disney's city limits. Independent businesses were like moths drawn to light. They would find a way to place themselves between Disney World and the clamoring tourists.

The local population grumbled as International Drive to the north and the cow pastures of Kissimmee to the south quickly succumbed to the neon lights of tawdry motels and souvenir stands. And Disney's most vocal representative—Dick Nunis—did little to endear himself to the surrounding communities. The most visible squabble began shortly before the park opened. To minimize cast member impact on guest traffic, Disney had designated County Road 535 as its employees' access route to the resort. Orange County insisted that an eighteen-foot-wide, poorly lit back road snaking through orange groves could never accommodate the 10,000 to 12,000 cars a day Disney intended for it. The state had already spent $6.25 million to build a new highway out front, and was reluctant to spend any more. As soon as Nunis was put in charge of Disney World, he assembled the county officials and informed them—in their words—"what needed to be done and what time tomorrow are you going to start doing it?"

When local government continued resisting, Nunis turned to the Disney marketing machine. Their plan: play on residents' emotions by advertising the dangers of 535. In March 1972, Disney began giving presentations to county commissioners and the Department of Transportation (DOT). They charted how many hazards occurred on 535 and urged them to realign and upgrade the road, install warning and dangerous curve signs, and lower the speed limits. For its part, Disney donated road reflectors. The commissioners agreed to add signs, set a "more reasonable and realistic" speed limit, and install the reflectors to improve night-time driving conditions.

Disney wanted more. At a second meeting, the company again asked to straighten the road, widen the lanes, and repave and strengthen the shoulders.

A month later, Disney World launched a postage-paid "plea for protection." Cast members were requested to write personal letters to the DOT, state and county officials, and local newspaper editors, pleading that 535 be upgraded, maintained and reclassified as a state primary road rather than a county secondary road. The company would pay the postage. By this time, the road was handling 14,000 vehicles a day.

Disney began documenting every accident on 535 in employee bulletins. On May 26, 1972, for instance, it reported that a cast member rounded a curve on 535 and smashed head-on into a cement truck. Minutes later, another driver rounded a curve, skidded several hundred feet, and flipped over multiple times. Shortly afterwards, a car slowing for the first accident was rear-ended. Almost an hour later, two more cars collided near the Disney World turn-off.

One week later, the Florida Highway Patrol assigned two permanent motor units to cruise 535 and assist with traffic control.

Disney then took its plea to Tallahassee. It convinced the state to undertake a series of engineering and aerial surveys on the road. Legislators also agreed to search for state tax money to fund immediate improvements. Still, the government wasn't moving fast enough for Disney.

It was time for some marketing magic. The Captain Cook's Hideaway lounge at the Polynesian had become a popular after-hours hangout for hourly employees. So Disney had the lounge's resident singing duo write, perform and record a song called "Can You Arrive Alive on 535?" Disney submitted the song to local radio stations. It distributed thousands of "Arrive Alive on 535" bumper stickers and erected billboards on its property blaring, "Congratulations, You've Arrived Alive After Driving 535."

Finally, in autumn 1973, after two years and nearly 200 traffic accidents, workmen began clearing, grading and widening a 6.5-mile stretch of 535. In the coming months, they would completely resurface the road, install drainage, mark the pavement, and add shoulders—all on the government's dime.

Bitterness and resentment were already bubbling up in good times; the animosity would only get worse when outside forces began putting the squeeze on Central Florida.

Disney had tried to attract more out-of-state tourists by building a Short Take-Off and Landing airport near the Contemporary. Visitors could then fly into any of five Central Florida airports and connect to either of two commuter airlines contracted to fly to Disney's STOLport. Shawnee Airlines' nineteen-passenger Twin Otter turbo-props only ran for about a year; Executive Airlines' ran for just a few months. The short trips were expensive, and the airlines proved unreliable.

"The [airlines] did it to themselves," Jerry Van Dyke said of the quick demise of the STOLport. "They were really shaky. They'd do anything to make a buck. They might suddenly charter a flight to the Bahamas and strand [Disney-bound] passengers at the airport. We'd have to send a bus."

Most Disney World tourists arrived from out of state by car—an estimated 60 percent in the winter and 85 percent in the summer. The state's tourism industry lived off of gasoline. In the fall of 1973, war broke out in the Middle East. Western nations were hit with an oil embargo.

Three days after Thanksgiving, President Nixon announced that, to survive the energy crisis, service stations had to ration gas during the week and close on Sundays. During the two weeks following Nixon's speech, attendance at the Magic Kingdom fell twelve percent compared to the same period the year before. The biggest drop-off came the first gasless Sunday. Year-to-date attendance had been running 4.4 percent ahead of 1972. The gains were wiped out two weeks into December. Disney's stock price, which had reached $123 earlier in the year, sunk to $54 a share.

During the last two weeks of 1973, overall tourism to the region decreased fifteen percent. Nonetheless, Disney's hotels remained full. Everyone else's hotels were taking the hit—including the Lake Buena Vista Motor Inn Plaza. Occupancy at the Dutch Inn slipped to 75 percent, 50 percent at the Travelodge, 35 percent at the Royal Inn, and not much better at the Howard Johnson's.

In one month, the area's average occupancy rate fell from 64 percent to 37 percent. Total room count had ballooned to 24,000. Work stopped on hotels still under construction. A few hotels that had just been completed never opened. Recently opened hotels declared bankruptcy and shut their doors.

Disney, however, could not let the outside world see it blink. The resort proceeded with the already-promoted openings of Pirates of the Caribbean and the Golf Resort. They quietly delayed the completion of Space Mountain from June 1974 until the end of the year. And Card Walker, noting the growing discontentment among outside motel operators, decreed it would be a long while before Disney built another hotel.

Attendance at the Magic Kingdom was off 8.9 percent for the holiday season and looking worse for the new year. The executives realized they

had to adjust the business well beyond displaying fewer Christmas decorations. DWOC went into emergency sessions. Since tourists were less
inclined to drive in from out of state, Marketing was to refocus on
Florida residents. The resort had to reduce costs. The executives devised
charts outlining how their operations should be scaled back to meet various levels of decreased attendance. The park cut back on entertainment
and operating hours.

Now it was time to start laying people off. After the first of the year,
Disney trimmed its workforce by 1,700—although 1,000 of those dis-
missed were part-time, seasonal employees hired just for the holidays.
Part-timers who escaped the cut saw their hours drastically reduced.
Those terminated were told they were let go because of the energy crisis.
One fired cast member, however, told the press he "felt they used it as an
excuse to do a little housecleaning."

The downsizing appeared out of character for a company known for
nurturing employees from cradle to grave. Another terminated worker,
an accountant with Disney World since 1968, complained, "They used to
tell us it was one big happy family, but it's not a family and it's not
happy. It's just big."

Over the next month, attendance perked up slightly, thanks to repeat
visitors and the lure of new attractions. Occupancy held at 94 percent for
the Contemporary and Polynesian, 77 percent at The Golf Resort. But
Disney stock continued slipping, to $42 a share. For spring break,
Disney laid the groundwork to hire 500 seasonal workers, many of
whom had been laid off a month before.

Operations, however, would now be staffed based on precise forecasts
of daily attendance. Disney began monitoring the number of cars crossing the stateline into Florida, and used the traffic flow to determine how
many hours to schedule part-timers. Three months into 1974, park attendance was down more than seventeen percent, but profits were holding.
Disney's stock price fell another $3.25 anyways.

In Burbank, the executives were more concerned with making sure
the power stayed on at Disney World. Howard Roland, as head of purchasing, paid cash for one million gallons of jet fuel as emergency backup to keep the Central Energy Plant running. He had the 300-gallon storage tanks of fuel trucked to a holding facility in nearby Sanford, but
never had to use it. Still, Corporate was comforted knowing it was there.
They later sold the fuel to a utility company at a steep loss.

The gas crisis also energized exploration of alternative energy sources. At the time, the U.S. Energy Research & Development Administration was soliciting proposals for new solar energy concepts. Disney teamed with a Baltimore-area firm, Aircraft Armaments Inc., to propose building a 6,000-square foot office for the Reedy Creek Utilities Company that instead of placing a solar collector on the roof, used the solar collector *as* the roof. Disney already had a test unit operating on the roof of the Central Energy Plant. More than 300 companies submitted experimental proposals for Department of Energy funding. Disney's was one of 34 to be accepted. The Department of Energy paid $400,000 to help build the solar roof and operate it for five years; Disney picked up the difference. The second-story roof consisted of a series of parabolic mirror-covered troughs. Metal bars ran over each trough. As the sun reflected off the mirrors, the bars moved to where the heat was most intense, capturing the maximum heat. The system generated enough energy to power all of the building's heating needs and 60 percent of its air conditioning. As a demonstration unit, the set-up provided the government with invaluable data. Yet it also proved more expensive to operate than the ultra-efficient Central Energy Plant, so Disney switched off the solar power unit once the DOE funding expired.

A provision of the Reedy Creek Improvement District also allowed Disney to build and operate its own on-site nuclear power plant. Although the company never went that far, it did seriously consider investing in the Crystal River nuclear reactor that Florida Power Corporation was building on the state's west coast. Disney commissioned a feasibility study on the plant and was Donn Tatum's signature away from acquiring ten percent of the plant's capacity. In the end, Tatum decided the company had too many expensive projects in the works.

"The capital cost is what stopped it," explained Reedy Creek director of public works Tom Jones. "Maybe Donn was a little apprehensive of getting the company involved in that type of technology. It's perhaps a good thing because it's a Babcock & Wilcox plant, which is the same as the Three Mile Island plant in Pennsylvania that had problems about three years later."

Keeping the lights on at Disney World wouldn't be a problem. Now it was up to the Marketing department to convince out-of-towners to make the trip. In the summer of 1974, Sandy Quinn resigned. His replacement, Larry Pontius, had been a copywriter for the Leo Burnett ad agency, where he coined the famous jingle, "When you're out of Schlitz, you're out of beer." As an ad man, Pontius was astonished to learn he was expected to generate miracle results with a miniscule advertising budget.

The philosophy of not paying for publicity, he discovered, was chiseled in stone—because the chiseler was Walt. "There was an edict: no billboards," Pontius said. "Some time earlier, way back, Walt had said that he didn't like billboards, and it became ingrained in people. I fought it, but what could you do? Walt said it. They didn't have a problem with promoting things, just paying for it."

Instead, Pontius reorganized the Marketing department, so every person had training in all fields—promotion, advertising and creative. Everyone became a marketing rep. Next, he divided them into teams: local, regional and national. As long as the energy crisis lasted, they were to focus most intensely on the local market through special events. Pontius then sent his reps out on the streets, from Orlando to New York. They would meet with community organizations, sponsor promotions on radio stations, or strike deals with tour groups and convention planners. Taking along a few costumed characters usually got them extra attention.

The marketing team even met with gas station owners. "I can remember always strategizing about how can we assure people that they'll have enough gas to come down here and go back?" said marketing manager Tom Elrod. "The big thing was that was the mindset. You don't want to be stranded. So we brainstormed all kinds of ideas: having our own huge gas supplies on property where we could assure people that they'd get a full tank to go home. Along the interstates contracting with filling stations to assure Disney World guests that they'd be okay. Just a lot of some smart, some dumb ideas aimed at trying to relieve people's concerns."

The tactics were so successful that when a second gas shortage hit five years later, the marketing department created an entire "Chase" campaign to chase after the public to inform them that it was safe to come to Disney World. The company teamed with a network of radio stations to broadcast the status of gasoline availability along Interstates 75 and 95. In addition, its Central Reservations Office manned a toll-free hotline to report gas availability by city, off-ramp, and general proximity to the highways.

Attendance at Disney World gradually recovered. The day after Thanksgiving 1974, the Magic Kingdom broke its single-day attendance record of 73,168 four days in a row. For the weekend, regional motel occupancy hit 93 percent.

Although park attendance would be down 6.4 percent for the fiscal year, the recovery was picking up steam. Pontius noted, "The gas crisis was good for Disney, because suddenly they had to spend money, and they learned what good things can happen when you pay."

As well, Disney had found ways to increase revenue without breaking attendance records. "We saw [the gas crisis] coming," said Bill Sullivan.

Cashin' in on the Camp

Although the fallout from the energy crisis convinced Card Walker not to increase the number of Disney-owned hotel rooms in the near-term, he supported expanding the Fort Wilderness Campground, which wasn't viewed as competition by local businesses. Additions could serve not only campers, but also might convince hotel guests to spend an extra day or two on property. They had recently added a steam train to reduce automobile traffic in the campground.

Next, Disney hoped to build an entire western town with restaurants, stores and amusements. The town's first structure, Pioneer Hall, featured a buffeteria, arcade and dinner hall with a stage for yet-to-be-determined entertainment. "When it started," recalled Keith Kambak, "the entertainment was a long-haired country western band. At the time Disney had strict appearance guidelines. The very first night, Dick Nunis and Card Walker were there. They said it was 'terrible, a disaster. Have Entertainment design more appropriate entertainment.'"

The department created a corny dinner show, the Hoop De Doo Musical Revue, which would run for decades with minimal changes.

Across from the campground, the island in the middle of Bay Lake was renamed Treasure Island and opened up as a nature preserve. And plans for the rest of the western village were eventually shelved in favor of a "hard-ticket" attraction that would appeal to guests resort-wide — Disney's first water park, River Country.

"So we took some drastic steps. We realized we could really get hurt. We trimmed back. We got in there before it happened and took care of it. We managed our business on a proactive basis. We made more money that year than we did the year previous and the year after, because the year after we started building back up, so we could service our guests. We had to spend a lot of money on training, because we laid off a bunch of people. We had to make up for the deficiencies. But we had a good year. Everybody worked long hours, but we made it. We did that to keep the place afloat."

As the energy crisis began to fade, Disney was again in a mood to celebrate. The staff started organizing its most elaborate ceremonies in years to mark the opening of Space Mountain. Even community relations improved as Bob Allen, the great soother, took the lead role as "Mr. Outside," the public face of the company, and let Dick Nunis play "Mr. Inside."

Good times were here again. Well, mostly good times.

8

Crash Mountain

IN the dark ages before Space Mountain, common wisdom held that
there were few places on earth safer than inside the gates of the Magic
Kingdom. Disneyland's entire reputation hinged on preserving at least
the illusion that nothing ever went wrong. Guests were supposed to leave
behind the concerns of the real world.

Disney World was likewise designed and constructed for absolute
safety, albeit subtly. To reduce falls, non-slip materials were mixed into
the concrete as it was being poured to form walkways. Frontierland's
"wooden" handrails, which appeared to be freshly chopped from knotty
pine, were made of lookalike plastic to eliminate splinters. At the Jungle
Cruise loading dock, underwater hydraulic stabilizers were added to rise
up and steady the boats in place as guests boarded and departed.
Tastefully themed warning signs and audio recordings gently reminded
guests to remain seated with their hands and arms inside their vehicle at
all times. To make sure guests got the message, inconspicuous security
officers and hidden cameras were planted throughout the park to keep a
watchful eye.

Disneyland had also provided 20 years of practice perfecting safety
systems. At the time, major accidents at the California park had been
limited to a few incidents of overeager teenagers doing things they
shouldn't have been doing. Any problematic attractions—the tip-over-
prone stagecoaches of the 1950s, the ornery pack mules—were limited

in capacity, rudimentary in operation, and in time replaced.

Space Mountain was a different beast altogether—maximum capacity and maximum profile. And, as the world's first computer-controlled thrill ride, it was more difficult for the Disney engineers to wrap their hands around and apply proven safety procedures. The technology that ran the ride—a dedicated mini-computer with a logic system that monitored, controlled and spaced out the trains—went over the heads of most of the ride operators pushing the buttons.

More so, Space Mountain offered a strenuous trip that surprised many guests who were caught up in its rich theming. The idea for the ride came to Walt in the early 1960s as he marveled at the astronauts hurtling through space and back again in the Mercury and Gemini space programs.

"Seven astronauts—the Mercury Seven—used to get blasted into outer space, take a couple of tours around the world, and come back down in the Pacific Ocean," recalled Bill Hoelscher. "When they came back down, there was a blackout period where you couldn't communicate with them. The [capsule] was burning on the bottom and they were hitting heavy air, dense air. They splashed into the ocean. Helicopters went out and picked them up. They put them on the deck of an aircraft carrier, opened up the hatches on the capsule, and almost to a man the first thing they said was, 'Boy, what a ride! What... a... ride.' Disney said, 'Hey, not everybody is going to get to take that ride. Let's build something that simulates that.'"

In 1965, Walt assigned Imagineer John Hench to create such a trip through space as the centerpiece of an entirely remodeled Tomorrowland at Disneyland. He wanted something considerably more breathtaking than the sedate Flight to the Moon theater ride. The ride was eventually shelved for Anaheim, but resurrected several years later for the Magic Kingdom. Management thought it would be a more marketable climax to the Phase One expansion plans than the runaway western train coaster being designed as part of the aborted Thunder Mesa project.

To date, the Imagineers' entire experience with roller coasters had consisted of the Matterhorn Bobsleds at Disneyland. A realistic trip through space would have to be significantly more vigorous. The challenge became delivering genuine thrills without going too far over the top. Some ideas—such as Imagineer George McGinnis's proposal for a loop that could be seen from the inside queue and would be highlighted with a strobe light every other second—were deemed too violent for a family attraction.

To make sure the ride would please a Disney audience, the company didn't just test its limits on volunteering cast members. Matriarch Edna Disney, Roy's 83-year-old widow, was flown to Orlando to test it out. She loved it.

Like previous E-ticket rides, Space Mountain was elaborately themed—perhaps too themed. To maintain the illusion that passengers were really flying through the cosmos, cast members were forbidden from referring to Space Mountain as a roller coaster. Neither could warning signs outside the ride.

So, too, the true nature of the ride was cloaked by its massive, white-spired show building—a majestic cone soaring 183 feet skyward. Inside, guests followed a series of metallic corridors, past large windows that looked out on various space vignettes. Through unseen speakers echoed updates on the next flight departure. Continuing deeper into the space port, visitors approached the loading area, lit an eerie blue, just as a pair of rockets zoomed up on one of two intertwining tracks. A foursome climbed in. A moment later, they were launched into the darkness. Their rockets whipped through the black, faintly illuminated by whirling projections of asteroids, meteors, planets and galaxies.

Two and a half minutes later, rockets suddenly slowed as they entered a tunnel with rotating strobe lights intended to make passengers think that their craft was spinning as it reentered the earth's atmosphere. The riders then excitedly leapt or staggered—from their rockets and stepped onto a moving walkway that descended past RCA's Home of Future Living, scenes of an animatronic family of tomorrow enjoying space-age RCA products.

Although the journey felt fast, that, too, was an illusion. It reached a top speed of 28 miles per hour, but seemed quicker due to the relative smoothness of the trip and the constant changes in direction. Instead of the bumps and jerks of traditional roller coasters, Space Mountain used sharp curves and sudden drops to momentarily suspend passengers above their seats, as if weightless.

Space Mountain opened in time for the Christmas crowds of 1974. For the official media opening January 15, 1975, the Magic Kingdom staged its biggest celebration since Opening Day. Two thousand musicians formed ranks along the PeopleMover track. Donn Tatum acknowledged the contributions of sponsoring corporations, such as Coca-Cola, Eastern Airlines, Monsanto, General Electric and especially RCA, which helped fund the $23-million Space Mountain. RCA board chairman Robert Sarnoff then formally introduced the new attraction. As he finished, 50,000 balloons were released to the heavens, followed by a flurry of white doves. Astronauts Gordon Cooper, Jim Irwin and Scott Carpenter took the first ride and gushed about how thrilling it was.

Paying customers, however, had mixed reactions. Since the ride took place in the dark, guests had trouble anticipating and bracing for the dips and turns. Some staggered away with bruises, cuts, even broken bones.

Many victims claimed they didn't know Space Mountain was a roller coaster. One 67-year-old woman, who suffered a broken bone in her spine, said she was expecting a slow, panoramic ride past "all the beautiful pictures of outer space on the walls."

The attraction would require more than simply "working out the bugs," according to Imagineer McGinnis. "It was the guest not understanding the type of ride they were entering. Never before had a roller coaster been a dark ride. Therefore, some guests expected it to be like the Peter Pan ride."

Within two weeks of the opening, an audio-narration system was installed in the queue to warn guests that the attraction was "a thrill ride with high-speed turbulence."

In February, the words "roller coaster" were added to a sign at the entrance and in the audio narration. Cast members were also allowed to use the words "roller coaster." As well, since passengers were subjected to so much "air time," ride operators were trained to hit the ride's Emergency Stop button if a rocket returned to the station with an empty seat—just in case a guest had been thrown out.

Five weeks after Space Mountain's official opening, a computer failure allowed a rocket to crash into the back of a second vehicle. The next rocket then plowed into them, and then the next, and the next, and the next. In all, 41 passengers were injured. The ride remained closed for eight days.

In April, warnings were added directed specifically at guests with "weak backs." Mercury astronaut Gordon Cooper recorded a low-key video, played in the queue. He mentioned that the ride was "really exciting, super fast, and a real thrill," so guests with health issues might want to head for the exit ramp to the post-show. (Internally, ride operators referred to the escape route as the "chicken ramp.") To reinforce the message, a rocket carrying dummy astronauts was mounted to the tall RCA sign at the entrance in a steep diving position.

It wasn't enough. Beginning in late April, Disney started modifying the ride itself. The rockets received higher seat backs, thicker padding on the seats, inside handrails, and new seatbelts. Additional "Space Warning!" signs were posted outside, urging elderly people, pregnant women, small children and guests with health problems to stay away. Audio warnings were recorded in multiple languages. Company investigators had pinpointed the cause of the most serious injuries—spine fractures—to the abrupt shifts from negative to positive gravity. So, the track's sharpest turns were replaced to create "feathering" curves that generated lower G-forces. Disney had promoted the ride so heavily that it couldn't shut it down entirely. Instead, they overhauled the two separate tracks one at a time.

The media seemed to sense that all was still not quite right. Publicity man Bob Raymond, when asked by reporters about rumors of injuries and illnesses, would smile widely and respond, "People get scared to death more than they get sick. There's no time to get sick. Your stomach doesn't stay in one place long enough to get sick!"

As if a sign that the changes were insufficient, soon after the overhaul, a 70-year-old man suffered a fatal heart attack while riding Space Mountain. Now, in addition to weak backs, guests had to be warned not to ride if they had weak hearts. Cast members began patrolling the long line of customers out front, ferreting out anyone who looked too frail. Inside the ride, Disney installed television cameras to detect potential problems earlier.

By the end of the attraction's first year, 334 visitors had reported illnesses or injuries after riding Space Mountain—from scraped knees, nausea and fainting to broken bones, ruptured spinal discs, lacerations and the deadly heart attack; 73 made claims for compensation. Disney typically paid the medical bills of injured riders in exchange for a signed agreement that they wouldn't sue. The minority who did file, Disney aggressively tried to settle with before going to trial. They paid $40,000 to a woman who broke her spine and $2,500 to another woman with a fractured tailbone. The park felt particularly vulnerable in the earliest cases, after it had become aware that people were getting hurt, but before it altered the actual ride.

Disney was determined to continue making the ride safer. Company engineers speculated that the vehicles' cramped interiors may have been contributing to the banging of body parts. So, for its second summer, Space Mountain received new, wider rockets. The injuries kept coming.

Fed up, the park's insurance carrier sent a claims adjustor in March 1977 to test the attraction for himself. He rode five times in a row, sitting in a different seat each time. By the time the investigator hobbled away, the ride had tweaked his back.

Although the safety measures drastically reduced the frequency and severity of injuries, Space Mountain would continue to generate about 40 complaints from its average of seven million riders a year. Most would be of the general bump-and-bruise variety or be attributed to "overexertion"—code for reactions like panic attacks and fatigue from waiting too long in line.

One unforeseen danger initially seemed harmless enough—passengers losing personal belongings during their ride. Hats, car keys, souvenirs, anything that wasn't tied down might disappear into the darkness. Women in tank tops also discovered that the ride's G-forces could have an uplifting—or downlifting—effect on their blouses as they arrived at the unloading area fully exposed.

At first, Disney found it somewhat amusing. "We have a box over there with wigs, false teeth, glasses—everything but shoes and shorts," P.R. man Raymond pointed out to one reporter, chuckling. "They lose everything over there." Gordon Cooper's warning film even included a low-key reminder that "things float around in space, so be sure to hang on to anything that's not fastened down—eyeglasses, hearing aids, hats, and even wigs." Each night after closing an employee would be sent to the bottom of the ride to retrieve all the items that had flown from pockets, heads, faces, ears and necks.

Yet, unlike the single-track Space Mountains later built at other Disney parks around the world, Florida's had dual tracks that crisscrossed over each other—at heights of up to 100 feet above each other. Eventually, some of those airborne possessions were bound to hit a rider in a rocket passing below.

It didn't take long before a female rider was struck in the chest by a falling camera. In another case, heavy souvenir tumblers fell out of a guest's shopping bag and struck a second rocket, shattering. "It was a family from Italy," recalled cast member Kyle Madorin. The chards of glass "caused lacerations on their faces, red streaks going back. They were fine, a few stitches here and there. Disney took care of everything."

Most dramatically, during a 1998 ride on Space Mountain, a 37-year-old doctor from Venezuela was hit in the head by an unknown object and knocked unconscious. He was hospitalized for twelve days and suffered partial paralysis of his left arm, hand and leg and short-term memory loss, which prevented him from returning to his profession. Asked about falling objects in a pretrial hearing, a hostess admitted, "Every night we find something [such as] video cameras broken on the ground." The night of the accident, attendants found two bulky items on Space Mountain's concrete floor: a glass candlestick sold in Frontierland and a battery from a video camera.

With tens of thousands of guests and employees on the property at all times, injuries were inevitable. Most were minor and could be treated on site. Registered nurses and physicians staffed the multiple First Aid stations at the Magic Kingdom, the Contemporary Hotel, Fort Wilderness, and elsewhere as the resort expanded. "These people took care of predominantly employee injuries and also guest injuries," recalled Gloria Jacobs, who oversaw First Aid when it was organized under Human Resources in the 1970s. "They were usually quite busy because with that many employees, so many things could happen. Most of the time it was a minor thing, like headaches or the flu or someone cutting himself in the kitchen. Maybe they fell down, slipped on a wet floor or something."

She added, "If there was a person who became ill in the park, many times [nurses] would run out with wheelchairs and bring them into First Aid. We also had ambulances at the fire stations and at the big First Aid stations to take them to one of the local hospitals if they were in great need."

When attractions were involved, problems often stemmed from guests slipping as they climbed into or out of a vehicle. Countless visitors have been rattled—or worse—after collisions on the Grand Prix Raceway. Others have wiped out on the moving walkway at the end of the Haunted Mansion; one 66-year-old fell and broke both her wrists. Another woman injured her right leg when a metal comb at the end of the conveyor belt speared her shoe. Dozens of guests have been injured on separate occasions when the ferry boat they were riding slammed too hard into the pier while docking.

Some accidents were one of a kind. Five guests suffered minor cuts and bruises when they were hit by pieces of wood moulding that fell from the ceiling of the Haunted Mansion's "stretch room." On the Mad Tea Party, an eleven-year-old girl was struck by a giant teacup when it started spinning before she could climb in. She hurt her back, broke her leg, and cut her knees and abdomen.

The most serious attraction mishap would occur November 5, 2000. William Pollock, 37, a seasonal passholder from St. Petersburg, Florida, was gliding toward the 52-foot drop on Splash Mountain, when he became ill, possibly suffering a panic attack. He climbed out of his log-shaped boat and attempted to catch his breath while standing among the animatronic rabbits. Pollock soon noticed an exit sign on the other side of the canal. As he stepped onto a passing boat to climb over the flume, the vessel lurched forward. Pollock fell into the water and was hit in the chest by the next boat. He became caught between the left side of the boat and the canal wall. Several other boats smacked into the back of the boat, further wedging in the victim. Pollock died of blunt force trauma.

Disney would do its best to wine and dine injured guests and their party, hoping the hospitality would dissuade them from filing a lawsuit. Yet almost every day someone from somewhere would decide to sue Disney. Disney couldn't prevent a woman from suing who collided with the upraised arm of a cast member and dislocated a breast implant. Nor could they fast-talk a college student who was hit by the Main Street fire truck while posing for pictures in front of the castle. Nor could they dodge the legal wrath of a man who cut his foot when his canoe overturned, or of a woman who slid down a River Country water slide and knocked out her two front teeth.

When Disney knew it was at fault or, more importantly, sensed it would have difficulty in court, the company usually tried to settle quickly and quietly. Disney, for instance, paid $4,500 to a parade watcher who was accidentally kicked by Pluto. Disney also settled with six tourists who suffered minor injuries when the Disney World bus they were riding on was struck by a garbage truck.

In 1982, nineteen-year-old Victor Powell, a trombonist in a 450-piece band from around the country, was rehearsing for the grand opening ceremonies of Disney World's second theme park, EPCOT Center. The

Mississippi college student was on a lift being raised in the CommuniCore pavilion when a platform above him tipped over and came crashing down on his neck. The impact broke his neck and spinal cord, leaving him paralyzed from the shoulders down. Out of court, Disney agreed to pay Powell more than $1 million in cash plus annuities that could bring him another $41 million over 51 years.

The company got off cheap after a 62-year-old woman who, while searching for her car in the Magic Kingdom parking lot late at night, fell into a canal and drowned. Her family settled for $12,500.

Yet Disney successfully defended itself against a ten-year-old boy injured on Pirates of the Caribbean. Despite signs warning passengers to keep their arms inside their vehicles at all times, the lad had been hanging his right hand outside his boat when his vessel was rammed by a second boat. The side of his boat scraped against the side of the flume wall, tearing off the boy's right thumb. He later underwent surgery to have one of his big toes attached to his hand in place of the missing thumb. Disney claimed the boy was to blame because visitors are instructed to keep their hands inside the boat. Internally, Disney realized the ride's loading configuration—loading boats in two different lanes before merging them into a single channel—created a potential hazard. The company quietly reconfigured the loading area so the boats loaded single file.

Of the small percentage of cases that actually made it to trial, Disney would win about four out of five. Local juries were often predisposed to think kindly of the family-friendly company—not to mention it being the largest employer in the region. As well, the clean cut cast members made likable, believable witnesses. They were also trained to take copious notes at the scene of an accident and complete detailed internal accident reports.

Disney's attorneys defeated in court a fifteen-year-old who wanted to explore the Haunted Mansion on his own. He stepped out of his car into the dark, only to fall fifteen feet to the concrete below.

The company also won a jury trial against a fifteen-year-old from Brazil who dove into a three-foot section of a pool at the Contemporary Hotel and broke her neck. The girl, who spoke little English, thought the foot-marker "3" painted on the side of the pool wall stood for three meters. Although they won the trial, the company inconspicuously added the depth in meters to the sides of the pool.

Disney also bested in court a 55-year-old woman who broke her wrist after being pushed off a parking lot tram by fellow passengers she accused of acting "like a bunch of animals."

Often, Disney blamed guests for their own carelessness, such as the 34-year-old parking lot tram passenger who dropped a bag on the ground, reached down to retrieve it, fell, and struck her head on the pavement. An 83-year-old woman sued after falling down the stairs at the Top of the World restaurant and breaking her shoulder and pelvis. She blamed Disney for putting steps so close to a window. There, visitors would be "distracted by the panoramic view," because Disney "should have known that such an awe-inspiring vista would transfix the patron's vision."

Sometimes, the accusations were pure fiction, just someone trying to make a quick buck off the big corporation. One guest claimed she was injured by a brick that fell from Cinderella Castle. Impossible, Disney easily illustrated, since the castle has no bricks; it's a fiberglass façade. Another woman claimed the Hydrolator chambers at EPCOT Center's Living Seas pavilion descended so fast, they damaged her eardrums. Disney merely demonstrated that the pseudo-elevators only give the illusion of descending and actually let guests off at the same elevation as when they entered.

Still, the Mouse could be beat. One woman won in court who was rammed by a River Country parking lot tram and pinned against a fence. A jury awarded $841,535 to a man who suffered back injuries when his Grand Prix race car was rear-ended.

In 1979, ten high school friends decided to swim in Bay Lake after dark. During their swim, an employee in a motorboat sped across the lake and inadvertently struck one eighteen-year-old, a championship swimmer. The boat's propeller sliced the teen's left foot and ankle and cut the bottom of his right foot. A jury awarded him $170,000.

On August 11, 1977, four-year-old Joel Goode wandered off toward the castle after his family had staked out a spot to watch the Main Street Electrical Parade. The boy climbed over a short wall surrounding the castle to play in the grass behind it. At about 11 p.m., his parents noticed their son was missing. Following a three-hour search, divers found the boy's lifeless body under five feet of water in the castle moat.

In court, the Goodes' attorney blamed Disney for not putting a fence around the moat, arguing that the 31-inch-high wall was too low to prevent children for climbing over it. They also claimed Disney should have posted signs warning parents to keep their children away from the moat, which was twice as deep as the moat at Disneyland. Disney responded that the boy's mother was at fault for allowing him to climb the wall and wander on the grass around the moat while she was talking to some people at an ice cream stand. The jury awarded the family $1.5 million.

River Country had its share of mishaps, including three drownings. In 1982, fourteen-year-old Howard Pueppke visited the water park with a tour group. A poor swimmer, he nervously climbed onto a large slide. He was unaware that the water below was over his head—despite a sign that warned "Rapid Water—Strong Swimmers Only." Pueppke slid down the flume into a 6-foot deep pool and drowned. His family's attorney argued that the sign gave no indication of how deep the water was. He also got a Disney lifeguard to testify that on some days 50 to 75 people would need assistance after sliding and then discovering that they were in over their heads. In fact, five years earlier, a seventeen-year-old had drowned at River Country and a woman suffered head and brain injuries when her innertube got caught at the bottom of a pool. Seven years later, another boy, thirteen years old, would drown at the park. The jury awarded Pueppke's parents $500,000. The judge reduced the amount to $375,000.

Not just safety, but the mere appearance of safety has always been a top priority at Disney's theme parks. With his parks and even his proposed city, Walt was painting a picture, creating an idealistic environment as he had in his movies. He wanted to control every image that went into his "show" and edit out any that didn't fit. The theme parks produced manuals and training films on "good show" and "bad show." Wide smiles, courtesy, cleanliness, smooth operations—all good show. Frowns, rudeness, attraction breakdowns or, Walt forbid, injuries—definitely bad show. And few things could be more disruptive to the magic than blaring sirens or bloodshed.

Disney publicists were notoriously silent regarding any unsavory news seeping out of their Magic Kingdom. Second-hand stories became legend of park officials swooping onto the scene of a fresh accident and bribing victims to sign non-disclosure agreements in exchange for free park tickets. Or of security guards removing the film from witnesses' cameras, then handing them $5 and directions to the nearest souvenir stand to buy a replacement roll. Publicity director Charlie Ridgway did confess to the press that security would confiscate film from shutterbugs who wandered backstage, admitting the practice might appear hard-nosed, but explaining that the magic "is worth protecting."

Such ultra-secretiveness gave rise to many an urban legend, such as the unfounded insistence that no one ever died on Disney property. Whenever someone stopped breathing at a Disney theme park, according to one fanciful rumor, employees quickly sneaked the corpse off site before the victim could be officially declared dead.

Unlike the stricter state laws governing accident reporting in California, Florida companies reported to the federal Occupational Safety & Health Administration, which required it be notified only if a mishap resulted in a fatality or hospitalization of at least three people.

In the absence of readily available police reports, medical files, or comment from the company, the outside world was left to guess as to what Disney might be hiding. Even cast members were given to passing unsubstantiated stories among themselves, trading tales about countless unrecorded victims of the Haunted Mansion or a woman who supposed-ly was beheaded on the Pirates of the Caribbean. As the story went, her boat stalled at the bottom of the longest drop, automatically triggering a brake to hold the next boat at the top. A cast member, however, didn't see the boat below and manually released the brake. The second boat careened down the falls and up over the back of the first boat—and into the people sitting in the last row.

The most famous faux fatality was "George," the imaginary welder who was killed during the construction of Pirates of the Caribbean. Evidently, poor George was either electrocuted or crushed by a falling beam and continues to haunt the attraction to this day. Cast members still tell the ghost story to new hires, warning that they best say, "Good morning, George," when they prepare the ride for opening or they'll experience a day of breakdowns, evacuations or odd occurrences. "You'll see or hear something strange," warned one spooked ride opera-tor. "You'll see moving shadows on the [hidden camera] monitors or mysterious figures standing in the knee-deep water. You'll feel a sudden, icy cold breeze. You clean graffiti and it comes back."

The imaginary victim is most likely a Disneyfied amalgam of the some of the actual fatalities at Disney World, the first of which occurred about a year after Pirates of the Caribbean opened. In late 1974, two carpenters were working at a service bay near the maintenance shop behind the Magic Kingdom, inside a half-finished 66-foot aluminum boat they were helping to build for the Seven Seas Lagoon. The filament in their fluorescent light ignited fumes from their glue, causing an explosion that killed one carpenter, 49-year-old Robert M. Marshall, and injured the other.

"The investigation showed there had been some gases where he was working," confirmed Arnold Lindberg, head of the shops at the time. "There was more or less no action taken, except the safety people had to check the gas before they let anybody down there."

Weeks later, in early 1975, 39-year-old electrician Albert Cecil Johnson was electrocuted while working on an electrical panel in one of the Disney tunnels. He was rushed to Orange Vista Hospital, dead on arrival.

Unfortunately, construction accidents became more frequent as activity accelerated on property with the fast expansion that would begin with the building of EPCOT Center. In late 1981, 55-year-old Earl W. Meeker was working on a construction site near EPCOT's Germany pavilion. He had rigged together two six-foot-long steel beams, each weighing about 50 pounds, to be hoisted by a crane. As they were being lifted, the rigging unraveled. The bottom beam plummeted about 40 feet from the crane and fatally struck Meeker on the back of the head.

Unlike guest mishaps, construction or maintenance accidents typically occurred off stage and were "in the family." The same year, Bruce Anderson, also 55, was standing on a 20-foot-high scaffold performing welding on the EPCOT Center's telecommuncations building. A company pickup truck passing below caught his blowtorch's hose on its bumper and yanked the welder to the ground. His head struck a metal air compressor, killing him. In court, Anderson's family claimed that the supervisor in the pickup was driving too fast in an area he should not have been in. Disney argued that Anderson was to blame for laying his welding hoses where vehicles could pass over them. Midway through the trial, the parties settled for $350,000.

In 1988, construction worker Lawrence "Bud" Hefner, 59, was killed after being hit by a polyethylene pipe that burst while he was testing for leaks at the Typhoon Lagoon water park. Three co-workers were injured.

A year later, 30-year-old David O'Brien Lewis was helping to construct the Dolphin Hotel. While connecting scaffolding outside the twenty-third floor, he slipped. Since he wasn't wearing fall protection equipment, Lewis plummeted seventeen floors to the roof of the sixth floor.

In 1990, nineteen-year-old subcontractor Paul Morgan was working on an air-conditioning duct at a Disney-MGM Studios soundstage. He accidentally stepped off a scaffold and plummeted 33 feet to his death.

Inside the theme park gates, most employees who suffered serious injury were usually in the wrong place at the wrong time. In 1982, the Skyway had to be evacuated due to rain. Minutes later, the skies cleared and cast members prepared to restart the ride, unaware that 20-year-old hostess Jo Miranda was standing near the ledge of the station. She was struck by a moving gondola, grabbed hold, and suddenly found herself dangling in mid-air. The cabin traveled more than 100 feet before another cast member hit the Emergency-stop button. A few visiting sailors climbed on top of a nearby building, but couldn't reach her. She tried to swing the gondola in their direction, before her strength gave out. She fell fifteen feet to the roof below, slid and then dropped another 20 feet to the ground. Miranda injured her back, but survived.

The event, recalled Skyway operator Jeffrey Stoneking, "was spoken of as part of our training. It became taboo to venture beyond the dispatch area as the free-wheeling cabins accelerate to engage onto the moving cable."

Nonetheless, on February 14, 1999, custodian Raymond Barlow, 65, was sweeping the platform in the loading area of the Fantasyland Skyway Station when the ride was switched on for the park opening. A gondola rolled toward the part-time employee. Startled, Barlow had the same reaction as Miranda—he grabbed the cabin and was swept up into the air. He tried to pull himself inside the car, but didn't have the strength. He frantically looked for a place to land. Barlow let go over a flowerbed and plummeted 40 feet, snapping several tree branches on the way down to his death.

The accident resulted in a $4,500 OSHA fine for a "serious" violation of safety standards. Coincidentally, nine months later, the park permanently closed the Skyway.

On February 11, 2004, cast member Javier Cruz, 38, was dressed as Pluto, waiting backstage near Splash Mountain to bound onstage for the Share a Dream Come True Parade. As a three-part princess float rolled past him, Cruz's right foot caught between its second and third sections. He was pulled under the final 6,000-pound Little Mermaid section and crushed to death. OSHA's investigation revealed "serious safety viola-

HANG TIME. Cast member Jo Miranda dangles from the side of a Skyway gondola as visiting sailors climb atop a Fantasyland roof to help. Unable to hold on any longer, she fell and struck the roof before landing on the pavement 35 feet below. (May 24, 1982) *Photo by Barry Szulc*

tions," since employees were exposed to the hazard of being struck by motorized vehicles. The agency fined Disney $6,300 and ordered that barriers be added to floats with multiple sections to prevent people from walking between them.

Several cast members have also been injured by the monorail—ironic, since Walt envisioned his high-tech transportation system as eliminating traffic accidents. Ride operators had to train for 80 hours to drive the monorail, and the vehicles themselves were equipped with an artillery of safety mechanisms. Windows and windshields were made from shatter-proof glass. When a monorail pulled into the station, the doors could only be opened by pressing a button inside the cockpit. The train would not restart until all doors were closed—and the pilot would receive a signal identifying any hang ups. A two-way radio system kept the driver in contact with the maintenance barn. If a tire went flat, the vehicles were supposed to glide to a gentle stop. To prevent a runaway train, the pilot had to hold down on a "deadman's switch;" if the button was released, the monorail slowed to a stop.

Most importantly, an anti-collision system would stop the vehicles if they got too close to each other. Yet, not long after the Magic Kingdom opened, engineers deactivated the safety mechanism, so crews could film the front of one monorail from the back of a second. Unfortunately, monorails Blue and Yellow rolled into each other. The impact dented the vehicles' sheet metal exteriors, but caused no structural damage.

"You never let that big of machinery get that close together," said monorail designer Bob Gurr. "I requested the damaged sections be saved for me so I could trim both into an interlocking sculpture. I had these in my office for years, but they disappeared one night. Some folks did not like the reminders to please be careful."

Not everyone learned the lesson. In 1974, a 20-year-old ride operator drove his otherwise empty Monorail Blue into the Magic Kingdom station before Monorail Red, packed with 200 guests, had a chance to leave. Horrified guests looked on as his 40-ton train rolled into the back of theirs, crumpling the monorails' noses into a wad of aluminum and crumpling the driver in the cab into a fetal position.

Though Monorail Blue was traveling no more than fifteen miles an hour, the driver suffered severe lacerations and internal injuries, which required three-and-a-half hours of surgery. Two passengers in Red sustained minor injuries.

Publicly, the driver insisted the brakes failed. But, according to witnesses, in the hospital he confessed to his bosses of overriding the automatic braking system. "Since he was badly hurt, he was very cooperative," recalled an investigator. "He knew the locations of various switches and circuit breakers and how to gain access to normally locked electrical panels behind him. He also knew how the safety circuits were wired. The kid was termed 'brilliant but bored.' He put a toothpick into a control console button to jam it into a held position while holding two controls with his hands. He removed a sock and shoe, twisted his leg back behind him into the electrical panel, and physically held a relay switch closed, thus defeating the wayside anti-collision signal commanding the train to stop as he drove past a red light into the train-ahead zone. He was a contortionist. He didn't realize the outside of those monorails are made of Reynolds Wrap."

To minimize the press coverage, Disney immediately called in a battalion of maintenance workers. They detached the damaged ends from the two trains, then connected the undamaged ends and repainted the blue stripe red, creating a single, dent-free train. When the driver recovered, he was put back to work — in another department.

A third crash occurred in 1991, while filming a television commercial to advertise the monorail resorts. Two cast members were riding atop a maintenance rig, which they were using both as a camera platform and to tow Monorail Red. Over the parking lot just north of the Contemporary Hotel, the train and work tractor collided. The two cast members were slightly injured.

Then, in 2005, a work tractor went to tow in Monorail Yellow, which had broken down near the Magic Kingdom station. The rig smashed into the rear of the monorail, pinning a maintenance worker between the two vehicles. He suffered serious injuries and had to be airlifted to a nearby medical facility.

Guests, too, have encountered danger outside the theme park gates. In 1982, two-year-old Nichole Cotto was standing in line with her family outside the coffee shop at the Polynesian Hotel, when she and her twelve-year-old sister accidentally knocked over a large standing menu board. The 120-pound sign fell on the toddler's chest and knocked her to the concrete floor, killing her.

Two months later, a couple was riding near the front of a parking lot tram with their 20-month-old daughter in a stroller. As the tram made a turn toward the park, the stroller rolled out of the side of the vehicle. The baby was crushed beneath the tram's wheels.

One night in 2002, a New Hampshire woman got into a vocal argument with her intoxicated husband at the Grand Floridian Hotel. She stormed out and checked into another hotel. Hours later, she received a call that her husband's wallet and windbreaker had washed ashore at the Grand Floridian beach. Divers searched the Seven Seas Lagoon and located his lifeless body.

The highways and waterways outside the theme park's gates proved even more hazardous, because it was usually the guests themselves behind the wheel. In 1986, a 57-year-old woman and her 32-year-old son were driving near EPCOT Center's main entrance in a ferocious downpour. "The storm was so bad," recalled security officer Ray Carter, "that water was covering the roadway. You couldn't see where the road went." The motorists missed their bridge by about 40 feet. Their car hit a curb, went airborne, slid down an embankment, and ended up in a small retention pond containing runoff water from the parking lot. The pair struggled to escape, but the woman could not swim. It took five days before a tram hostess discovered their half-submerged car with two bodies sealed inside.

Four years later, a 33-year-old motorist drowned after accidentally driving his car into a canal near Lake Buena Vista Boulevard.

In 1989, Patricia Shenck, 33, rented a tiny speedboat from the Grand Floridian's marina and set out with her eight-year-old son to videotape family and friends water skiing. About halfway across the Seven Seas Lagoon, she inadvertently drove the Water Sprite into the path of a ferry boat. The ferry broadsided her. A crew member and a visitor jumped into the water to save the boy. It wasn't until three hours later that divers were able to recover the woman's body.

In 1990, four local teenagers were speeding through Lake Buena Vista at 85 miles an hour and smashed their car into the rear of a bus waiting in turn into the Caribbean Beach Hotel. All four teens were killed.

In 1984, a small private plane ran out of fuel while passing over EPCOT Center. The single-engine Piper Cherokee dipped over the parking lot, sweeping about fifteen feet over a tram. A pedestrian dove to the pavement. The plane struck a 50-foot light pole, which tore off one of its wings before toppling onto four parked cars. The craft then clipped several other vehicles and plowed into a car. The crash killed the pilot, his wife, and their one-year-old daughter. Their three-year-old daughter and five-year-old son sustained severe head injuries. The man had earned his pilot's license just four months earlier.

Three years later, EPCOT Center experienced another fatal plane crash, this time with a cast member at the controls. Pilot Rick Harper, 27, was flying behind the park, practicing maneuvers in a Buccaneer ultralight-type plane before the 2:00 performance of the Skyleidoscope lagoon show. Not long after takeoff, an overloaded shackle failed and caused the plane's right wing to fold back against the fuselage, sending the plane into a nosedive. Harper triggered the safety parachute, but it deployed into the folded-back wing. The plane plummeted more than 500 feet and crashed into a grassy knoll a few hundred yards from the runway, a mile-and-a-half from EPCOT. Harper was killed instantly. Disney immediately suspended the show.

The company responded to such accidents outside the theme parks— and inside them after the parks closed for the day—through its Reedy Creek Fire Department. In time, the RCFD staff would grow to more than 200—mostly firefighters and paramedics—operating about two dozen emergency and support vehicles from four on-property fire stations and responding to well over 20,000 911 calls annually.

When the department was formed, it was overwhelmingly preoccupied with fire prevention. Paul Pennington, who had recently retired as Orlando fire chief, became Reedy Creek's first fire chief August 1, 1968. For two months, he was a one-man outfit, with no staff or equipment. To begin his planning, he visited Disneyland. He quickly realized that unlike Disneyland, which was supported by the Anaheim Fire Department, his staff would be on its own. Back in Florida, he began assembling an initial crew of seven men and an antique tank truck. They created fire breaks throughout the property and regularly patrolled the vast compound. Pennington also reviewed the early construction planning and construction procedures for fire safety suggestions.

Reedy Creek mandated that every building be equipped with alarms, monitoring systems, automatic overhead sprinklers, and hand fire extinguishers. Theirs was the first building code to require smoke detectors in hotel lobbies and mandated elevators be prevented from stopping on a floor where an alarm was triggered. They were also the first to allow reduced fire protection where sprinkler systems were installed. Reedy Creek permitted areas in basements to be screened off instead of walled, making them easier to inspect. And they became the first to require door closers on hotel rooms.

By the time the park opened, the fire department had grown to 65 men, two engines, three forestry vehicles, a rescue vehicle, rescue boat, and ambulance. No aerial trucks were needed, due to the omnipresent sprinkler systems. During 1971, RCFD answered about 200 calls, none major. Most were automobile or brush fires outside of the park. Within a few years, the fire department would be responding to more than 500 calls a year and the paramedics to about 1,800. The majority of ambulance calls responded to the likes of exhaustion, breathing difficulties, and heart attacks.

Although Disney World insists it has never had a "major" fire, there have been a few memorable blazes. In 1985, Monorail Silver pulled into the EPCOT station with a flat tire. Since the vehicle had a backup tire and repairs are made at the monorail barn near the Magic Kingdom, the cast members decided to drive the vehicle back to the Ticket and Transportation Center—fully loaded with passengers. Moments into the trip, the backup tire went flat and the tire's metal mounting assembly began scraping against the concrete beam. Sparks generated from the friction ignited chunks of shredded rubber from the flat tires, and the flames quickly jumped to the monorail car above. Noticing a flashing warning light on her console, the pilot stopped the train about a half-mile south of the Magic Kingdom's main entrance. She calmly announced to the passengers that there was congestion ahead. She then radioed her lead to report smoke coming from the back of the train.

Flames were now licking the bottom of the rear car and noxious smoke began seeping into the cabin. Fortunately, two passengers—a 21-year-old and his father—took control. They kicked out windows and forced open a door, only to realize that they were 30 feet off the ground. The son began feeling around the roof for something to grab hold of.

Fire marshal William Cullity recalled, "I always thought the worst thing that could happen would be a fire that we couldn't access, so I designed a small D-ring, very inconspicuous, and put them on the centerlines of all the old trains. As one of the two heroes was running his hand on the roof, he found my D-ring." The son climbed on the roof and then began pulling his fellow passengers to safety. His father was the last

FIRED UP. Reedy Creek firefighters check the charred remains of Monorail Silver's car number six. (June 27, 1985) *Photo by Victor Junco; Reprinted courtesy Orlando Sentinel*

to climb out.

Like a scene from the *Poseidon Adventure*, the 35 evacuees walked unsteadily along the roof toward the front of the monorail. Along the way, they helped passengers in the other cars climb up with them. At the front of the monorail, they slid down the windshield and onto the two-foot-wide beam. By the time the Reedy Creek Fire Department arrived, about two-thirds of the 240 passengers had evacuated. Some were sitting on top of the monorail. Others were standing on the beam. Fire had damaged car five and incinerated car six. "When I got there," Cullity said, "one car was missing. It just dissolved. It was just a flat slab where the deck was."

Seven guests were treated for smoke inhalation. At least four groups of passengers filed suit, charging that Disney had no walkways, no ladders, no chutes, and no discernible evacuation plan.

The disaster was a wakeup call. Each Operations department formulated and began regularly practicing emergency response plans. Monorail cars were quickly retrofitted with intercoms, crude escape hatches, and fire extinguishers. Until the fleet could be entirely redesigned, a ride operator was stationed in the front and back of every train. Later monorails would be constructed of fire-resistant materials and have heat detection systems, pop-up evacuation hatches, sliding doors, rooftop handrails, non-slip-surfaced roofs, and, of course, plenty of D-rings.

Two years later, 60 guests were stranded when their monorail began smoking.

The same year, an electromagnetic coil running through the People-Mover track overheated inside a tunnel above a gift shop, setting fire to the plastic that covered the rail's electronic components. The fire burned for a few minutes before being extinguished by the sprinkler system.

In 1989, craftsmen in the backstage Central Shop were curing a model of a boat bumper in an oven when the sheet of plywood supporting the object caught fire. Thick smoke, tinged with the chemical used to make the model, spewed through the building, causing 800 employees to flee from the seven-acre complex. The fire eventually burned itself out. Fourteen employees had to be treated for difficulty breathing.

Six months later, hundreds were again forced to evacuate the Central Shop. In trying to create hard foam props, workers had mixed together two liquid resins, which instead generated billows of chemical smoke. Firefighters dumped the resins into two drums and transported them to a waste holding facility to allow the conflagration to burn itself out.

In 2002, an electrical substation behind EPCOT's Test Track ride caught fire while graveyard-shift electricians were performing routine maintenance on one of its switching gears. The RCFD extinguished the blaze, but in the process inflicted water damage on the backup system, leaving EPCOT without electricity. The theme park was unable to open for the day. It took repairman nearly fifteen hours to restore power.

End of the Line

Yes, people have died at Disney World. The majority of on-property deaths have been of natural causes—although sometimes attractions have hurried along the process by aggravating a pre-existing condition. In 1980, a ten-year-old Venezuelan girl, who suffered from a rare heart defect, collapsed after riding Space Mountain and died shortly after. In 1995, a four-year-old girl with a heart defect died after fainting on EPCOT's Body Wars motion simulator. And from April 2005 to July 2006, five guests collapsed at Disney World and died soon after—a 30-year old man with a heart condition on Animal Kingdom's Dinosaur attraction, a four-year-old boy with heart ailments and a 49-year-old woman with severely high blood pressure on EPCOT's Mission: Space, a twelve-year-old girl with a virus at the Typhoon Lagoon water park, and a twelve-year-old boy with heart defects on Disney-MGM's Rock 'n' Roller Coaster.

One stress victim, Dorothy O'Connor, became legend. As the story goes, this elderly woman from out of state took her two granddaughters to the Magic Kingdom. During their visit, one of the girls was caught shoplifting by an undercover security guard. In the security office, while pleading with the officers to release the girl, grandma Dorothy suffered a heart attack and dropped dead. Paramedics responded, but it was too late.

"So they called the girls' parents to tell them grandma was dead," related cast member Gwen Van Voorhis. "They flew to Florida to take grandma home. But when they found out how expensive it was to ship the body, they decided to cremate her in Florida and pack her in a suitcase. In their carry-on luggage, they had T-shirts, underwear, toothbrush, grandma. So every year in August we [cast members] toast Dorothy O'Connor."

9

Showcase for Sale

CLUES had slowly been leaking out of what was obvious behind closed doors in Burbank—that Walt's conservative heirs were terrified of the type of financial and creative risks Walt thrived on. His successors got along fine, so long as they had a ready supply of Walt-generated ideas to draw from—movies in production or development, Pirates and Haunted Mansion for Disneyland, a new Tomorrowland, the Vacation Kingdom in Florida. But once that reserve was depleted, Disney began to flounder. Management's natural inclination was to remake and repackage Walt's successes. The public was beginning to catch on.

Walt's one idea that the braintrust in Burbank would have loved to forget about was EPCOT—except that the public kept bringing the subject up. The idea was so different and underdeveloped that carrying it out would mean a lot more innovating than repeating. And, with Walt gone, it was difficult to get American industry behind such a daring proposition. Donn Tatum's role had become primarily administrative. Card Walker, the go-getter, had worked his way to the top through the sales ranks. His time in Disney's story department was spent polling audience reactions to proposed film ideas.

"I think Card saw the world as a place to sell movies and cartoons to," said one colleague. "I don't think he understood EPCOT." At a New York Society of Securities Analysts meeting, Card Walker was asked about EPCOT. After waffling for a few minutes about various components of Disney World that exemplified "the spirit of EPCOT," Walker finally admitted, "I'll be very honest to say that we don't have any definitive plan for EPCOT, nor did Walt."

For management in Florida, preoccupied with operating and expanding the Vacation Kingdom, EPCOT had begun to fade. "We always felt there would be an EPCOT, but everything we knew was from one TV show and the Progress City model at the end of the PeopleMover," said Dale Burner. "Nobody understood what it meant."

Still, the public and the press, their imaginations stimulated and memories seared by that famous picture of a domed city, refused to let the idea die. In interview after speech after press conference, Disney executives continued to be hounded by the question, "But what about EPCOT?" The company, in the words of Dick Nunis, was "haunted by a painting."

The final push to begin serious work on EPCOT came from an unlikely source—*Playboy*. Publisher Hugh Hefner had already tried to use Disney World to promote his magazine by visiting the Magic Kingdom with a bevy of centerfold stars, outfitted in skimpy Playboy bunny costumes. He and his entourage were stopped at the gate and the bunnies forced to don T-shirts and short skirts before they could enter the park.

Then, in *Playboy's* April 1973 issue, Disney was shocked to discover Disney Studio starlet Dayle Haddon, fresh from *The World's Greatest Athlete*, posing in the nude. Obviously, her Disney career ended immediately. Days after the issue hit the newsstands, an investigative reporter for *Playboy* landed in Orlando, sniffing around for any scent of discontent at the Magic Kingdom. Disney, naturally wary, offered the journalist access to some of the more polished in local management, such as Operations' Bill Hoelscher, Pat Vaughn in employee relations, and of course Charlie Ridgway, the press relations chief. Any information too deep or any executive too high up the food chain was off limits.

In December 1973, the article—an eleven-page exposé, picking apart everything about Disney World—hit the newsstands. How fake and out of touch the whole place was, how snookered the guests and the employees were, even how the Contemporary Hotel looked like a pop-up toaster on the outside and tiers of prison cells on the inside. The writer saved his most pointed—and insightful—criticism for Burbank. "Walt's dreaming has confounded the corporate dwarfs who inherited his sorcerer's robes," he wrote. He savaged Card Walker in particular, calling him arrogant, tyrannical, vacillating, gutless, unoriginal—all traits that would prevent him from ever fulfilling Walt's greatest dream, building the city of tomorrow. "EPCOT," he wrote, "died about three minutes after Walt stopped breathing." Walker and his minions were just keeping the acronym around for promotional value—"the only coming attraction that isn't Son of Disneyland, or sheer commercialism." Certainly they would never actually do anything about it. Walker was livid. *Playboy* was questioning the integrity of Disney!

Publicly, Disney dismissed the author as a twerp, a college kid who didn't know what he was talking about. But privately Walker knew the company was guilty as charged, and that the cries of "Where's EPCOT?" would not disappear. He had to do something.

Immediately, Walker assembled a "Wednesday Morning Club" at WED, with about 20 Imagineers from different disciplines, led by Marty Sklar. The meetings were free-for-all brainstorming sessions to figure out what could and what could not be included in an EPCOT. Sklar would then take the sometimes esoteric notes from the meetings and rewrite them in ways that made sense to Walker. "Card had the ability to not understand things well," one participant explained.

Walker preferred easy-to-digest ad slogans and mission statements. So, the group's task was formally boiled down to seven objectives:

• To encourage industry and the professions to introduce, test and demonstrate new ideas, materials and systems.

• To showcase and prove the usefulness of promising concepts, technology and specific prototype products.

• To provide an ongoing "meeting place" where creative people of science, industry and the arts, from around the world, may gather for days or weeks or months to discuss and develop specific solutions to the specific needs of mankind.

• To advance the excellence of environmental planning.

• To bring together, in a living, working, creative environment, people of varied interests, talents and backgrounds who will live together for days or weeks or months in a community and climate where experimentation is accepted and fundamental.

• To create an artful and efficient environment—a community fashioned in human terms and human scale that begins with the belief that the people who live and work and play in it are the heart of the city.

• To provide, for the first time anywhere, a practical basis for investigating and proving not only the "popularity," but also the economic feasibility of new ideas, materials and systems introduced and tested here.

The particulars would be negotiable, provided they supported these goals. The group then began pulling out smaller components of Walt's EPCOT to see if they could be expanded upon or tweaked into something both practical and profitable, such as the international shopping village from EPCOT's central tower or the always-on-display futuristic industrial park.

To keep the press hounds and critics at bay, during Walker's next big speech—in May 1974, while in Philadelphia to receive a marketing association award—he revealed that serious EPCOT planning was under way. The project would be built in phases, with the international village likely to break ground in 1977 or 1978, followed by the industrial park. The actual city was still some years away. They would work up to that.

In time, as the Wednesday Morning Club's efforts evolved into more concrete ideas, other designers and model makers joined the planning and began working on specific work projects. The Florida Room next door to Marvin Davis' office, reconfigured with giant sliding wall maps to focus on EPCOT, became the site of most of the planning meetings.

Initially, they decided to replace the domed downtown with a nonprofit "EPCOT Future World Theme Center." Displays would be grouped into three major pavilions—science and technology, community, and communications and the arts. The pavilions would be financed by participating companies, foundations and government agencies. Monorails would connect the center to the Magic Kingdom as well as to clusters of satellites. The satellites would house the research, testing and demonstration of prototype products and other exhibits, such as the international shopping mall, dubbed the Walt Disney World Showcase. Since the mall seemed to be the most marketable component, they would build it first.

For World Showcase, WED constructed a large-scale model of two semicircular buildings facing a broad plaza. The buildings were divided into pie-shaped pavilions, each an exhibit area for a different country. The entrances would be standardized in size and appearance, to promote harmony and fairness among the countries. But once inside, the recreated streets and bridges and shops and restaurants and monuments, icons and attractions could extend as far back as the countries' sponsors' money would allow.

Disney could partially address the city aspect of EPCOT, by building an International Village across the lagoon from World Showcase. The village would be home to the approximately 200 young adults from each country who staffed the international pavilions. World Showcase would charge about $5 a head for admission, and participating nations would pay to design, develop and build their pavilion and help fund the housing village. Disney would provide transportation, land, utilities, a central courtyard, and a central theater to stage performances by international celebrities and entertainment groups.

Disney timed the announcement for July 14, 1975, to coincide with the International Chamber of Commerce convention being held locally. The convention itself was a coup for Disney and Orlando since the prestigious group typically met only in world capitals. Reporters gathering for the press conference had little idea of what to expect. Disney World itself and later the Magic Kingdom had been unveiled at elaborate parties with hundreds of specially invited guests. This time, the occasion was more sedate, held in the Columbia Room on the second floor of the Contemporary Hotel and lacking the customary Disney hoopla.

This event, however, wasn't so much to rally the faithful as to silence the critics—to ensure the company still had the public's trust. A big party wasn't necessary this time, Card Walker would explain, because "we have credibility. People believe us when we say we're going to do something."

Tatum, in suit and tie, and Walker, in golf shirt, shared hosting duties. They explained that the Vacation Kingdom was merely Phase One. "We are now launching the second phase of Walt's ideas—the scientific, industrial, communication, world-cooperation aspects of EPCOT," Walker said. He tried to segue into World Showcase by explaining that Walt's concept was "truly international in scope" and stressing that every component of Disney World was considered "an eventual part of the master plan of EPCOT." Using diagrams, renderings and a giant model, the executives laid out the plans for World Showcase as, not a city of permanent residents, but as the first satellite to a Future World Theme Center. Like at a world's fair, participating nations would give visitors a taste of their native lands and show off their products and culture.

All that was left was figuring out which countries wanted to pay to be included. Plans showed room for a minimum of ten and a maximum of 30 nations; Disney estimated that they would open with between ten and seventeen. They hoped to begin construction later in the year, to open in 1979.

Sometime after opening World Showcase, they would begin construction on the Future World Theme Center, where U.S. and foreign companies would show off their latest innovations. Each group of pavilions would branch off into its own satellites for research and seminars. The entire set-up would be called "EPCOT Center," signifying it as the center of some future EPCOT. The combined projects might cost as much as the $650 million spent thus far on all of Walt Disney World.

Barely had the executives gotten the announcement out of their mouths, when newsmen began demanding to know why the plan had been changed. Walker tried to explain that the concept of a physical, "brick and mortar" city had become "obsolete." You couldn't achieve Walt's dream by building a place focused on serving the needs of a small group of permanent residents. The best way was instead to create a community dedicated to communicating to the world.

The reporters weren't buying. The barrage of questions continued.

Where's the domed city with the giant hotel in the middle? Where's the city with actual residents? Aren't you departing from Walt Disney's original idea?

No, Walker insisted, "we believe we are doing it just as Walt would have wanted it." In desperation, he turned to one of Walt's top idea men, Imagineer John Hench, seated in the front row. "Isn't that right, John?"

"Definitely," Hench nodded. "I'd say we are doing exactly what we talked about when Walt was alive. Walt introduced the ideas as, you might say, the title in Scene One. He knew better than to drop the big scene into people's minds at the beginning. We're engaged in Scene Two now."

Hench was trying to say, don't worry. This is only the start. There will be more to this picture than you see now. But to reporters, Disney had changed pictures after the first reel.

The questions ended. But most left the room unconvinced.

Disney gave themselves two years for a "worldwide marketing program." They'd already flown in representatives from fourteen different countries for the unveiling. All seemed impressed. None of them whipped out their checkbooks.

In theory, convincing countries to sponsor pavilions in World

Showcase, as they regularly did for world's fairs, should have been a cinch for Disney. The company had become a master at hooking "participants" since before the opening of Disneyland.

In Anaheim, the strategy actually began by targeting both participants and "lessees," an uncomfortable arrangement for control freaks like the Disneys. While building his first park, Walt had limited funds and no knowledge of operating shops, restaurants, a parking lot, or a security force. So he invited corporations and individuals to pay him to be a lessee (by running a mini-business at Disneyland) or a participant (by sponsoring an attraction without actually running it, to expose their company and products to a large, attentive audience). Walt also thought that inclusion of real companies made his fantasy world more believable.

Walt personally pitched the biggest corporations and convinced the first—Atchison, Topeka & Santa Fe Railroad Company—to sponsor the Disneyland Railroad. By the time the park opened in 1955, the team had enlisted several dozen participants, from titans of industry like TWA, Richfield Oil, and Coca-Cola to the wily entrepreneurs who ran most of the merchandise locations along Main Street.

The first proposals were a tougher sell, because no one had ever heard of Disneyland. In 1954, Walt attended a Richfield Oil board meeting to propose a kid-sized freeway be built at Disneyland dotted with miniature billboards for Richfield gas. The board wanted to know how much it would cost. "$25,000 a year for ten years," Walt replied. The board collectively grimaced at the price tag, then asked for an hour to discuss it. After an hour, they called Walt back into the boardroom. "Well," said top executive Leonard Firestone, "we decided we'll go for it. When is the first payment due?" Walt answered, "I'd like to take it with me." Firestone had a check written, and handed it to Walt. As soon as Walt left, Firestone turned to the board and asked, "Now you explain to me what in the hell we just bought."

The deals were instrumental in getting Disneyland open at all, let alone on time. In fact, by the time all of Tomorrowland belatedly opened, nearly every facility had a sponsor, many of them listless industrial exhibits like the Kaiser Hall of Aluminum Fame and the Crane Bathroom of Tomorrow. Walt was never happy with such marriages—where the advertising outweighed the entertainment. But worse was the loss of control to outsiders operating on the inside who appeared to represent Disneyland, but didn't do things the Disney way. Walt quickly replaced the outside security firm with his own men and, as leases expired and Disney's wealth and operational knowledge accumulated, took over most of the shops and restaurants, too.

Gradually, the lessee concept diminished, ceding control only to a handful of operators with special skills like glass blowers and portrait painters. More and more, instead of Carnation or Swift or Maxwell House running a restaurant, the companies would pay for their products to be used at Disneyland-operated restaurants.

Walt's eyes opened to greater possibilities at the New York World's Fair, where the largest companies spent millions of dollars to develop high-tech attractions. In addition, exhibitors included countries that paid to promote tourism or native products.

By the time the Magic Kingdom opened, Disney had the participant program down pat. For the first time, the company tried to push standard sponsorship contracts, instead of the unique, customized pacts at Disneyland, where every sponsor paid a different amount of money for different perks. The easiest sells were existing customers—those already participating at Disneyland. Now with Disney World, they could be offered a package deal, a "national ad buy" for both parks. Coca-Cola, GAF, Goodyear, Gulf Oil, Kal Kan, Monsanto, Pepsi/Frito Lay, and Welch's all signed to continue their relationships in Florida.

Others were seduced by the Disney name. One day Participant Affairs' Pete Clark heard a radio commercial for Smucker's Jams and Jellies and thought they fit perfectly with the image of Main Street. He called the company and set up an appointment to visit their company headquarters in tiny Orrville, Ohio. The chairman of Smucker's was impressed. "A lot of people call us, but few come down to Orrville," he said. Clark brought his own slide presentation, but when they couldn't get the boss' office dark enough to see the projections, the chairman decided to show it in the employee cafeteria. "The employees got so excited, he had to say yes [to co-sponsoring the Main Street Market House]," Clark recalled.

The chairman of Sara Lee visited Disneyland with his granddaughter, and as they walked down Main Street she noticed the real company names on the storefronts. "Grandpa," she asked, "where's Sara Lee?" The exchange led to Sara Lee sponsoring the Main Street Bakery at Disney World.

Roy proved invaluable filling Walt's role as celebrity CEO. About a year before the Magic Kingdom opened, a large group of potential sponsors was flown to Orlando and put up at the Hilton Inn South. They were shown the Preview Center and the construction site, where they could view the property from a raised platform. Roy stopped by to shake hands and agreed to make dedication speeches at little ceremonies to mark the opening of each sponsor's facility.

The most interested prospect was the promotional board representing the state's citrus growers. The group desperately wanted to sign up as the Magic Kingdom's first sponsor, but wasn't sure what it should sponsor. The best WED could offer was the Hawaiian-themed audio-animatronic bird show, the Enchanted Tiki Room. Disney offered to rename the show Tropical Serenade and build a juice bar to peddle Florida orange juice. They would call the combined structure the Sunshine Pavilion, as tribute to the commission's slogan, "Breakfast without orange juice is like a day without sunshine," and theme song, "The Sunshine Tree," sung by Anita Bryant.

On October 1, 1969, the group agreed to pay $1.5 million to underwrite the Sunshine Pavilion for ten years. As a final caveat, the commission wanted some sort of Disneyish identification for their participation. Yet, Disney had no intention of allowing one of its classic characters to become the official spokesperson for Florida oranges. Instead, Disney created the group its own mascot. A costumed "Orange Bird" would greet guests outside pavilion—as long as he didn't wander too far from his area and didn't mix with the other Disney characters. The bird could also appear at parades and other promotions, but since his likeness was created and owned by Disney, the commission would have to pay about $200 per appearance.

The sponsorship cost state citrus growers about $1 for every thousand crates of orange and grapefruits they produced. So Disney had to answer not only to the commission, but also to the small individual farmers who belonged to the group. The two sides wrangled constantly over every detail, from fees to signage to promotion. Their stormy relationship hit a low point in 1980 when Disney produced a classroom educational film, *Food & Fun: A Nutrition Adventure*. The movie prominently featured Orange Bird—but failed to mention the words "orange juice." Disney forced the commission to pay an additional $3,500 to slip the word "orange" in front of "juice" at one point in the film.

A year later, the sponsorship came up for renewal. Following contentious negotiations, the commission agreed to re-enlist for five more years—although their fees had jumped from $150,000 to $190,000 a year to sponsor the attraction, $135,000 for five years to open and sponsor a second juice bar in Fantasyland, and $52,000 for "creative development" and other remodeling work.

Needless to say, the juice bars never sold enough juice to cover the commission's sponsorship fee. In Disney's eyes, that was beside the point. In fact, the company would flat out tell prospective sponsors not to expect to break even on direct sales. They were to look at it as advertising. Sponsors were exposing their products to millions of potential customers. Even more important, Disney argued, was the "halo effect." The general public would reflexively feel better about sponsors and their products because they were associated with America's most beloved institution. To reinforce the connection, sponsorship deals regularly included the rights to use the image of Mickey Mouse or Cinderella Castle in the sponsor's own advertising and promotions.

Other corporations paid a fee for exclusive distribution of their products in the park. Kodak, for instance, paid for the right to be the sole supplier of film, batteries and cameras. Yet that didn't always sit well with overall Disney World Operations, headed by Dick Nunis, and specifically the purchasing department, led by Howard Roland.

"Operations versus Participant Affairs is like day and night," agreed Bob Ziegler, who worked both sides. "Foods didn't want to be told they had to use Coke not Pepsi."

Nunis saw participants as an inconvenience, a distraction from the Show. Nunis, according to Pete Clark, "never cared for the lessee situation. He always thought these people were damn lucky to be here. He always thought they didn't pay enough."

Roland thought that, by eliminating competitive bids, the participant contracts allowed suppliers to take advantage of Disney. "We constantly fought that battle," Roland said. "We could only use Coca-Cola, Oscar Mayer hot dogs, and Borden milk, so sometimes the sponsors made up their sponsor fee in overcharges."

Clark would regularly preach, "If a sponsor gives us $100,000, how many hot dogs do you have to sell to net $100,000?"

Roland, whose job was to find the best deal for the company, was not persuaded. At one point, convinced that he was being gouged by Coca-Cola, Roland found a small bottler in Cincinnati that would sell the soda at a significantly lower price and truck it to Orlando. When Coke corporate found out, they were incensed. Roland argued that the contract required Disney World to use Coke products; it didn't say where they had to buy them from. In the end, Clark appeased Coke by quietly working out a side deal between the sponsor and the Cincinnati bottler.

Selling World Showcase to foreign countries, Disney figured, shouldn't have been that much different. After all, they already had contacts in place around the world handling film distribution who should be able to show them the ins and outs of their markets. Teams of two, often a park executive paired with an Imagineer, were assigned specific countries to pursue. John Hench and Dick Nunis, for instance, were teamed up to go after Russia and Spain.

To help sell the idea, WED designed sample pavilion layouts and concept art for each targeted country, crafting rides, shows, shops and restaurants from romantic traditions and landmarks tourists might like to visit — Venetian canals, Bavarian forests, Oriental temples. Unfortunately most of the countries weren't interested in archaic stereotypes; they wanted to present a modern view of their largest industrial cities, filled with cloud-piercing skyscrapers and productive factories — certainly not the types of images that would pique the imaginations of Disney tourists. Morocco wanted rows of statues honoring its ancestors. Israel wanted to showcase its military's weaponry. Russia wanted to tell a political story.

Over the first two years, Disney made presentations to more than 50 different countries. At various points, six different African governments committed to EPCOT. Due to political turmoil, every deal collapsed. In Saudi Arabia, every time Disney talked to a "prince," he demanded to be paid to provide the names of proper government contacts. Several other countries verbally committed or signed preliminary agreements, but backed out when it came time to pay.

"A lot of time and money was spent on trips, but they didn't get us much," admitted Pete Clark. Foreign nations "could go into a world's fair because it was a sanctioned affair; Disney was not."

Disney opened a field office in Washington, D.C., to make government contacts, but the venture reaped few solid results. Attorney Phil Smith said, "We invited foreign ambassadors in for the weekend and wined and dined them, and tried to interest them in EPCOT Center. There was a lot of interest, but when it came to actually shelling out the money, it wasn't there. The countries didn't have the money, so we ended up dealing with companies within those countries."

Realizing they would never convince enough countries to pay enough money to get World Showcase built on its own, Disney changed its plan of attack. Rather than chasing foreign governments, Disney instead began targeting foreign companies, which were used to spending money on marketing and may have been looking for a quintessentially American venue for getting their products into the U.S. market. Imported beer manufacturers started to take notice, along with apparel producers and restaurant operators.

Even these deals, however, wouldn't add up fast enough. The project looked to be terminally stalled. Then, back at WED, came the "eureka moment." John Hench, the romantic, was still clinging to World Showcase. Marty Sklar, the forward-thinker, had been championing the Future World Theme Center. It took the more ethereal-minded John DeCuir, Jr., to take the models of the two proposed projects and shove them together. What if Disney combined both ideas into a single theme park? That way, the Showcase could lend the flash and flair and community angle to the project and Future World would provide access to the pocketbooks of large American corporations—a more comfortable target for Participant Affairs. It just might work. WED designed a series of presentation materials, including a beautiful boxed set of fancy brochures illustrating the various Future World themes: Transportation, Energy, The Land, The Seas, Space.

Committees began piecing together elements of each pavilion, bringing experts in the respective fields to lend credibility. Science fiction author Ray Bradbury was hired to write a story treatment for an iconic communications center, Spaceship Earth. Carl Hodges, head of the University of Arizona's Environmental Research Laboratory, spearheaded work on The Land pavilion. Power company executives consulted on the Energy pavilion. Many of the dozens of advisors worked for free, in hopes that EPCOT would provide real-life solutions for future generations.

The natural first targets for Participant Affairs were existing sponsors, but the corporate deals Disney proposed for EPCOT were in another league. By combining the two projects, the construction cost would likely exceed the $650 million already invested in the entire property.

The company was counting on six to ten mega-corporations contributing enough money to cover about half the expense. Disney figured it needed commitments for $3.5 million a year from primary sponsors, and contracts had to last at least ten years, as opposed to the earlier standard of five years.

"Companies were used to spending money on a single show," said Pete Clark. "The figure—$35 million for a ten-year contract—we just grabbed out of the air. They would all have a product area, which would be their cost to staff."

With the focus shifted to pursue both countries and companies—foreign and domestic, Disney decided to convert a radio recording facility it had rented from NBC in New York into an EPCOT corporate preview center. New York served as either a base of operations for many of the targeted companies or would be their point of entry from faraway countries. The office had room to display models of the proposed pavilions, show a pitch movie, and discuss the benefits of sponsorship.

Pete Clark, Pat Scanlon and Jim Murphy would alternate manning the office for a week at a time. A local temp answered the phone and made coffee. Disney also hired Langhorne Washburn, who had been President Nixon's assistant secretary of commerce for tourism, because he had political connections.

Participant Affairs operated the facility for about six months beginning in January 1978, and turned up several good prospects. Yet foreign governments, as Disney had seen, turned out to be tougher customers. "We brought a lot of foreign people through," said Pete Clark. "The [First Lady] of the Philippines, Imelda Marcos, came in and held court: 'If I had $8 million, I'd fix the sewers and do this and do that!' I didn't think we would get a lot of international exhibits."

As another strategy to try to open doors in corporate America, Disney hired fair-haired astronaut Gordon Cooper, who had assisted in developing and promoting Space Mountain. As vice president of research and development for EPCOT, Cooper ostensibly was supposed to provide creative leadership. Yet all his ideas sounded too far out—such as a hydrogen-fueled car and a "secret carburetor" that was going to revolutionize the world...until the government suggested otherwise. His wild storytelling of earlier mid-air dramatics was equally beyond belief. For Disney, he would serve primarily as "decoration."

Cooper was sent on countless EPCOT sales call, often teamed with fellow pilot and Imagineer Bob Gurr, who dreaded the endless boasting during long flight stopovers. "When Gordon gave you a tall tale, he became twinkly-eyed and excited, he knew he had the 'right stuff,'" recalled Gurr. "Gordon was so charming and upbeat at all times. Sort of a boy enthusiast. WED had no fear to send him off anywhere on a Disney sales mission. His fame preceded him. I saw him collect a crowd at every stop. Get him in a bunch of fly guys and you couldn't stop him. I don't think we ever got around to any serious selling, but we sure left a room full of folks eager to pursue further talks with Disney."

Cooper seemed to understand his role. He once admitted, "I know people. I can open doors. It only makes sense to use me that way."

He added, "It's interesting to talk to these old conservative companies. When you first tell them about EPCOT, they laugh. They think it's ridiculous. Before the end of the day, it blows their mind. They're totally converted."

Yet even the largest corporations were taken aback by the steep price tag of sponsoring an EPCOT pavilion—including those already used to dealing with Disney. No one wanted to be the first to jump in. To the press, Disney maintained that EPCOT was still a go. Behind closed doors, Card Walker revised the project's expected completion from 1979 to 1980, and stalled development work. His team, however, hoped that if they could land just one big corporation, it would create a "bandwagon effect" and others would follow. That brave first turned out to be General Motors.

GM's lead was unexpected given that fifteen years earlier it had opted out of becoming one of the first companies to hire Disney to design its pavilion at the New York World's Fair. GM instead suggested Walt pitch its top competitor, beginning a lengthy relationship between Disney and the Ford Motor Company. But in early 1976, while attending the dedication of the new campus at the Art Center College of Design in Los Angeles, Imagineer Gurr was introduced to Bill Mitchell, vice president of design at General Motors. Gurr lost no time in telling Mitchell about EPCOT. Gurr explained that EPCOT would feature exhibits along the lines of GM's old traveling car show, Motorama, and asked why they didn't stage them any longer. Mitchell's ears immediately perked up because, unbeknownst to Gurr, Mitchell planned to retire in a few years and wanted to open a Race Driver Hall of Fame in Florida. He thought

EPCOT might be just the place.

Gurr quickly phoned Marty Sklar and asked him to send the sponsor packet to GM. Sklar refused. "Dammit, Gurr, we can't do that," Sklar barked, furious that Gurr had approached GM, since EPCOT could accept only one sponsor from each industry. "All our studies show that because of our past relationship with Ford, Ford would be the right company to pursue." But the promise had been made. Reluctantly, Sklar sent the materials. Within days, GM responded with serious interest.

Over the next eighteen months, Disney and GM arranged countless meetings in Orlando, Southern California, and Detroit. GM executives received tours of Disney World and WED. In Michigan, Imagineers were shown GM's Test Track in Milford and Tech Center. By August 1977, Disney was itching for a commitment. They flew in a contingent of senior GM executives for a major presentation at the Contemporary Hotel. The GM brass smiled and nodded approvingly as Disney unveiled plans for EPCOT and the particulars for the Transportation pavilion. At last the presenters divulged the sponsorship cost. Anthony De Lorenzo, GM's vice president of marketing, pulled out a pocket calculator and punched in the numbers. "That's 53 cents a head," he noted. "What am I getting for that?" The room momentarily went silent. Fortunately, the discussion remained positive, and the meeting ended with the executives piling into Jeeps and heading into the woods to tour the proposed site of the pavilion.

Four months later, GM was ready. On the last business day of 1977, Card Walker and Pete Clark flew to Detroit so GM could sign EPCOT's first major letter of intent. The car manufacturer explained that they had to finalize the deal before the end of the year or it would be too late to budget it for 1978.

As expected, the first deal triggered more. Within weeks of GM's signing, Exxon agreed to sponsor the Energy pavilion. In fast succession came letters of intent from AT&T's Bell System, Kraft Foods, Coca-Cola, American Express and General Electric.

By the fall of 1978, Disney finally had the minimum number of sponsors it required to justify EPCOT. It also had a clearer picture of what would be in it. In the still-evolving plans, the park's entrance is dominated by a spectacular, 195-foot-tall geodesic sphere. Inside this Spaceship Earth, sponsored by AT&T, guests travel back in time, viewing historical milestones in communications and looking ahead to technological advances for processing ever-increasing amounts of information. The "time machine" journey also sets the template for all Future World pavilions: use an innovative ride system to show visitors how man historically faced a certain challenge, wind toward the present, and finally allude to the possible solutions that the future might hold.

Exiting Spaceship Earth, guests enter the Future World Mall, nicknamed the "Main Street of Tomorrow." The marketplace of ideas, systems and technologies gives the public a "hands-on" opportunity to sample products of the future. By early 1979, this "communications core" would be renamed "CommuniCore," allowing Disney to stress its own role as a premier communicator and bridge the gap to the ideas of others demonstrated in the remaining pavilions.

As at the Magic Kingdom, guests enter through the mall area and reach a central courtyard that branches off into various themed experiences. To the left, in the relative position of Adventureland, guests travel into a primeval forest in Exxon's Energy pavilion. The vehicles, however, are powered by solar collectors in the building's roof. At the end, the cars assemble into rows of theater seats for a movie on tomorrow's energy sources, while the cars recharge.

In the approximate position of Frontierland, Kraft's Land pavilion focuses on cultivating the earth as a garden for its own and man's greatest benefits. Inside its glass walls, a variety of shows stress nutrition, food production, and wise harvest. *Celebration*, a 3-D movie with in-theater effects, showcases the world's harvest festivals. The star attraction, a boat cruise, takes guests through authentic desert, tropical and marshland environments, experimental food production areas, and a biome on the farmland of today and tomorrow.

Next door, GM's Transportation pavilion humorously illustrates how man evolved in direct relation to his "freedom of mobility." The ride mimics various modes of modern transportation—including racing at high speed—and previews prototypes of futuristic vehicles.

On the "Tomorrowland side" of Future World, the Space pavilion beckons visitors to a twelve-story-high gantry. Here, guests board a massive "interstellar vehicle"—actually a 768-seat theater that uses flight simulator technology to create the sensations of hurtling through space and encountering zero gravity.

At The Seas, the mighty Poseidon challenges visitors to journey through the ocean depths from the Continental Shelf to the Great Coral Reef to his lair beneath the sea. Suddenly, their clamshell vehicles begin undulating to the sounds of Ravel's "Bolero," as they pass animated sealife projected on the walls around them. In time, they realize that they are in fact beneath real water, populated with real marine life. They disembark at Sea Base Alpha, where they can view a huge aquarium, oceanographic exhibits, and an underwater restaurant.

Finally, at the Life & Health pavilion, guests enjoy a number of exhibits celebrating good health and stressing its basis in personal responsibility and behavior. Featured are the film *The Joy of Life*, the thrilling "inner space" ride The Incredible Journey Within, and the whimsical amusements of the Great Midway of Life.

At the far end of Future World, in place of Cinderella Castle, stands the American Adventure, serving as the gateway to World Showcase. America's greatest philosophers—Benjamin Franklin, Mark Twain and Will Rogers—lead an all-animatronic cast tracing the story of the American people from the first step on Plymouth Rock to the first step on the moon.

Passing through the American Adventure, guests see a giant lagoon surrounded by ten other countries. In Mexico sits an ancient Indian pyramid, its face covered with a giant mural. The rest of its exterior appears to be polished gold, but is actually mirrored windows that reflect the sun's rays by day and reverse the effect at night, turning the pyramid into a shining beacon of light. Inside, a Mexican marketplace takes up the lower level, a Mexican dinner theater and lounge the upper level. They look down on a water cruise, loosely inspired by It's a Small World, sailing the "river of time" through the history of Mexico.

In Japan, guests traverse downtown Tokyo's famous Ginza nighttime shopping and entertainment district. Its central building includes a major department store on the first floor, a teppanyaki restaurant on the second floor, and a VIP tea garden on the third. Next door, a round Carousel of Progress-inspired theater rotates past four acts of "The Winds of Change," tracing the major influences on Japanese culture through film and audio-animatronics. The show concludes with a multiple-screen film depicting modern Japan's vast manufacturing output and its effect on the rest of the world.

Germany features its own Storybook Land-type ride—a simulated cruise down "Germany's most picturesque rivers," the Rhine, the Tauber, the Ruhr and the Isar. Vessels float past intricate miniatures of famous landmarks, including Neuschwanstein Castle, the Garmish Ski Area, Rothenburg and the Cologne Cathedral, scaled so they appear to be full-sized scenes viewed from a distance. In the faux night sky, animated lights recreate milestones in German history and culture. The boat ride debarks at an authentic biergarten, its upper level devoted to shops and displays. The pavilion also contains a wine cellar, tasting room, and Rathskellar restaurant.

Green lawns, ornamental gardens, gable roofs and spires evoke the romance of the United Kingdom. A two-story pub, with a tea room serving fast food downstairs and a public house serving a full dinner upstairs, sits at the shoreline, as if affording a scenic view of the Thames. A village lane leads to a gift shop, mustard shop, toy store, coat-of-arms store, and, at the far end, the distinct facade of the Selfridges Department Store. Its lobby branches into boutique areas and the concourse of a train station, dotted with newsstands and a travel agency. From there, visitors can walk through rail cars to view recreated scenes of the British Isles through the windows. Guests exit the train into a 200-seat theater for a travelogue of the U.K.

France recreates Paris around the river Seine—a promenade lined with bookstalls and poster kiosks, a boulevard winding past an outdoor cafe, with a more formal restaurant upstairs. Across the street, Montmarte, the artists' quarters, offers two floors of adventure into art, perfumes, shopping and culinary displays.

Entering the United Arab Emirates, guests pass two ancient Arabic sailing ships, before reaching a Bedouin encampment. At the center of the desert oasis, a cluster of black tents contains treasures of Arabian handcraftsmanship for display and purchase. Past the Arabian restaurants, an opulent royal marquis beckons visitors to experience a thrilling ride through the Arab World's most fascinating cultures, past and present. Once aboard a "magic carpet," guests seem to glide above the courtyard as a holographic genie appears before them to serve as narrator and guide. Leaving the black tents behind, the carpets actually pass through the genie's apparition into a starlit night where the narrator describes early Arabic contributions in the fields of astronomy, navigation and mathematics. The host later reappears to guide the approaching carpets into a showcase of medicine, chemistry, libraries and science, all of which had their earliest beginnings in the Arab World, before ending with a look at the region's current cultural contributions.

Italy emphasizes the romantic architecture of famous Renaissance era buildings. Passing several gondolas docked nearby, guests traverse a stone footbridge, modeled after Venice's pedestrian bridges. Shops and an Italian restaurant ring a central courtyard, marked by an obelisk in the middle. The main structure has three stories—an art museum on the first floor, an art gallery for sales on the second, and on the third VIP accommodations, including a lobby, reception room, banquet facility, and garden terraces.

To reach Canada, guests first pass through a Northwest village offering native Indian and Eskimo arts. From this log and timber setting, guests reach a fortress tower, leading to a suspension bridge spanning a "bottomless" river gorge. Once across, guests wind their way along a path blasted out of the steep mountainside. More timid travelers can opt for an alternate route to the warm, hospitable Chateau Frontenac Hotel. The final destination, a Canadian trading post, houses a nine-screen CircleVision theater showing *Canada, Country of the Future*. After the film, guests emerge through a mineshaft into a futuristic Canadian panorama highlighted by imaginative uses of one of Canada's leading energy stockpiles, before exiting through a quiet grove of maple trees with the vast wheatfields of the Central Provinces on the horizon.

Olive and cypress trees line the entrance to Israel, leading to a casual outdoor eating area and bazaar. The ruins of an ancient minaret serve as an information center. In a covered amphitheater modeled after the theater at Caesarea, Israeli musicians perform classical and traditional folk music.

Rustic paths dotted with exotic plants reminiscent of Hesperides Gardens then lead to the Kingdom of Morocco. A terrace refreshment bar sits amidst the jagged rock formations of Hercules grotto. An arcaded bridge, its ceilings painted to depict Morocco's five Great Dynasties, connects the upper level of the grotto with Jemaa Square. Here, the ancient city is recreated as a labyrinth of shops, populated with craftsmen and wandering street vendors. The marketplace opens into the Southern Morocco sector featuring a desert Kasbah. Inside, diners enjoy lunch as scenes of the Moroccan landscape pass along the walls. In the evening, the "Magic of Morocco" dinner show combines live action with the panoramic backgrounds. A storyteller appears on the stage and begins to relate tales of Morocco, as scenes from each story appear behind him. He turns and seems to step into the film itself. In the film, he guides guests through each setting until he comes upon a troupe of dancers and acrobats. They in turn step out of the film and onto the stage to complete their performance.

For Card Walker, the plans struck a comfortable balance between Disney-style attractions he was comfortable with and futuristic-sounding elements the public might associate with an Experimental Prototype Community of Tomorrow. Now he just had to get it built and paid for.

10

Constructing the Future

DISNEY had more than just its reputation riding on EPCOT Center. Overall, the company continued to notch record profits year in and year out. Yet Disney was no longer a Wall Street darling that investors bought merely on faith. Its stock, which once sold for an astronomical 82 times anticipated annual revenue, had sunk to a more reasonable 20 times earnings. After bottoming out just before Space Mountain opened, the price would waver around the $40 range for the next five years. The problem was the public used to think Disney had all the answers, that it could see the future, that it was so creative and resourceful, it could do what no one else could: it could work magic.

By the mid-1970s, Disney looked more like an anachronism than a forward thinker. In Walt's day, the company's optimism and vibrancy could be seen in attractions like the Carousel of Progress, at the time a technological tour de force with both a sentimental nod at the past and an optimistic look to the future. In 1974, the Carousel of Progress was pulled out of Disneyland and moved to Disney World, where sponsor General Electric figured it would get more attention. With the Bicentennial coming up, WED opted to fill Anaheim's vacated theater with America Sings, an animatronic revue celebrating different styles of American music. The show, while cute, had no place in Tomorrowland. Worse, its final scene, with long-haired geese singing bad rock and roll, proved just how out of touch the aging Imagineers were with contemporary tastes.

A more glaring target for ridicule was the company's motion picture division, which traditionally provided the characters, songs and storylines that inspired every other division. Within five years of losing Walt, the studio had become a joke in Hollywood. Card Walker and his braintrust, paranoid about producing anything that Walt would object to, basically refused to greenlight anything that didn't have the founder's everfainter fingerprints on them. Creativity was stifled, as the Disney Studio was left to release a decreasing number of pictures, typically sequels to or inadvertent remakes of *The Love Bug* or other pedestrian family comedies of the 1960s. Fully half of the film division's revenue came from theatrical reissues, once every seven years, of *Pinocchio*, *Bambi* and Walt's other animated classics.

At the same time, the theme park division—once Walt's diverting playtoy—had grown to provide 70 percent of the company's income. Yet, as the corporation relied more heavily on Disneyland and Disney World to keep the bills paid, the parks were maturing. Attendance at Disneyland had flattened at about ten million a year. The Magic Kingdom had risen from 10.7 million in its first year to 13.1 million in its fifth, but growth was beginning to slow. Disney desperately needed to expand the business. Since they were still spending a bundle to produce each movie, the executives blamed the studio's troubles at the box office not on quality, but on the public's waning interest in family entertainment. Maybe it was time to build something primarily for adults. Ideally, it would be something that increased the amount of time—and dollars— that guests spent at its most profitable money-making machine, Walt Disney World.

EPCOT Center sounded like the perfect solution. Yet such an ambitious undertaking could cost a fortune and place the entire empire at risk. In building EPCOT, it was essential that Disney avoid the mistakes made in creating the Magic Kingdom. Not only would runaway construction costs displease Wall Street, they also might frighten away potential participants. The onus to control spending fell on Howard Roland. Early in planning, Roland was promoted to a vice president of purchasing and contract administration. "Now we have someone to blame if something goes wrong on EPCOT," Donn Tatum explained.

Roland was convinced that there was no way Disney's own construction company could handle a project with the magnitude of EPCOT. He

would have to sell the board of directors on hiring a professional construction management firm, one that would be responsible for devising
the complicated construction schedule and manipulating the thousands
of workers so they got their jobs done without getting in each other's
way. Plus, a management company could act as a "restraining wall,"
aggressively dealing with combative contractors while Disney called the
shots from the shadows.

Walker deferred. "Do what you want," he told Roland, "but we can't
have the problems we had on Magic Kingdom."

Tatum, at first, was against the idea. "How can we do that?" Tatum
asked, the J.B. Allen fiasco running through his head. "We already tried
and failed."

"I'll find the best there is," Roland promised, and Tatum finally
relented. Lee Iacocca, president of Ford Motor Company, which had
been one of the primary targeted sponsors, suggested Tishman
Construction. Tishman essentially had invented the practice of construction management. Disney was particularly impressed with the company's work overseeing construction of the World Trade Center in New
York and Renaissance Plaza in Detroit. Roland was interested, provided
Tishman put in charge Milt Gerstman, the man who oversaw the Twin
Towers and the Renaissance. Tishman had already promised the hard-
driving Gerstman to Steve Wynn to manage construction of the Golden
Nugget in Atlantic City. But the scale of EPCOT was too exciting an
offer to pass up. Disney compromised; Gerstman could work part-time
for Wynn, at least until serious construction work began on EPCOT.

By 1977, after eighteen months of interviewing general contractors,
estimators and architects, Disney and Tishman came to terms.
Construction managers often set their fee as a percentage of the job's
final cost. Roland persuaded Tishman to accept a flat fee of $9 million
plus expenses. He had based the offer on two percent of an estimated
$450 million price tag, but knew the figure would likely increase. Yet no
construction plans or timetables could begin until the project found some
sponsors. To buy time, Card Walker offered Tishman $9.1 million to
manage a 144-room "Oahu" expansion of the Polynesian. Tishman had
plenty of reasons to turn down the offer. The firm rarely handled such
small jobs and was concerned that if it took the job and made minor
errors, it might be jeopardizing its chance to build EPCOT. Still, it didn't
want to tell Disney no. Tishman finished the job under budget and in

twelve months—30 days ahead of schedule.

By this time, participants were finally beginning to fall into place for EPCOT —with most having signed at least preliminary agreements. Inflation and rising interest rates, however, had pushed the estimated price tag to just under $800 million. In October 1978, Walker announced EPCOT Center would open at 9 a.m. Friday, October 1, 1982. It was not only the slowest month of the year and the eleventh anniversary of Walt Disney World, but also the first day of the company's fiscal year, so if they missed the deadline, they would forfeit about $60 million in investment tax credits. The same month, Disney officially signed the deal with Tishman. The construction manager calculated that it required, at minimum, three full years to build the place, so Disney had, at most, twelve months to come up with workable plans. Walker tried to make light of the deadline, telling John Tishman, "I'll tell you what. On the assumption that no contractor gets things done on time, we'll open the gates at 9:02 a.m. That will give you guys some extra time to finish up." But Walker knew that, at least initially, the pressure was on Disney to give the go-ahead to break ground.

Every pavilion had the same primary design consideration: did it have a sponsor? Several companies backed out along the way. Time Inc. changed its mind about having *USA Today* sponsor a CommuniCore exhibit. When funds promised by Israel and the United Arab Emirates failed to materialize, Disney pulled their pavilions from World Showcase and convinced Costa Rica to sign a preliminary sponsorship agreement. As a backup, WED designed other possible alternates—a rainforest and a cable car ride for Venezuela, an ice skating rink for Scandinavia and Denmark, a travelogue and waterside tapas restaurant for Spain. Although time was running out, the countries all looked like solid candidates for Phase Two.

Walker was most excited about an Equatorial Africa pavilion, after recruiting *Roots* author Alex Haley as a consultant. Prospects for getting sponsorship money out of African nations were slim; however, Walker knew that Haley's participation added prestige to the entire project that might draw interest to other pavilions. Africa's, in fact, was to be the most elaborate of all World Showcase pavilions. Guests would climb a giant treehouse to an observation deck, from which they would look down on realistic, 3-D animals gathering at a watering hole. Inside an amphitheater carved into the boulders, the Heartbeat of Africa show would feature tribal musical instruments coming to life, a la the Tiki Room. Guests could also enjoy a widescreen film, *Africa Rediscovered*, and a "sound safari trail," where infrared sensors triggered stereophonic jungle noises.

Late in 1979, the stack of signed contracts seemed sufficiently large enough to get started. As Gerstman required, EPCOT Center's official groundbreaking came October 1, 1979. Tishman had exactly three years to transform 600 acres of swamps and wilderness into a futuristic wonderland. Gerstman insisted that the first move be to prepare the entire site at once. He wanted all parking lots built immediately, so the thousands of construction workers could then park their cars close to the job site. They would also need temporary roads to provide access to the site for the people and materials, temporary electricity and water lines for the contractors, permanent utilities for the pavilions, foundations for the monorail, and excavation of the World Showcase lagoon. Gerstman argued that bundling all site prep work into a massive, $75- to $100-million package would be sure to catch the interest of the nation's largest heavy construction companies. The conservative Disney executives shuddered. Without final plans for any of the pavilions, how would they know exactly where to place the utilities? Gerstman contended that if utilities were put in later, installers and their equipment would get in the way of other contractors. Work would fall behind schedule. Construction claims would pile up. Workers in other areas might not have power. Laying all utilities at the start might result in too much pipe being installed, but at least it would be in the right general area and contractors would have all the power they might need.

Nervous about the size of the package, Disney was determined to trim out anything it could. One executive suggested that, with all the timber on the site, some logger might pay $25,000 to remove it. "What are you talking about?" Gerstman exploded. "This is an $800 million project!" The last thing he wanted to worry about was dodging logging operations for two weeks to save a few pennies. Gerstman didn't care if his men ground the trees into matchsticks so long as they got them out of the way fast. "If a job starts out behind," he warned, "you'll be playing catch-up all the way."

Roland, left to make the call, thought Gerstman was right about the trees. But he suspected that it was too early to lay all the utilities on the first go. As WED and the sponsors changed their ideas, the pavilions' dimensions and locations might change. The first site preparation package included storm drains, but no other permanent utilities. The winning bid was $48 million. Yet, Roland soon discovered the complications that came in trying to install utilities later. From then on, he trusted Gerstman's judgment.

The park's layout was too grand and expansive to seriously consider Walt's plan of placing EPCOT on top of a giant cellar like at the Magic Kingdom. Director of construction Bill Moss explained, "The difficult thing is ground water is awfully high in Florida, so we would need a special drainage system. The basement became a very expensive way to move people around. That's why it was never repeated; it wasn't financially feasible."

Instead, designers situated most pavilions along the park's perimeter, so they backed up to a massive backstage complex that ringed EPCOT like a horseshoe, hidden behind a grassy berm. A single, 8.5-acre basement was built for the park's computer station under Spaceship Earth and CommuniCore, the welcoming pavilions that couldn't be placed at the park's edge.

The construction crews also learned from earlier mistakes. On the Magic Kingdom, earthmovers were used to bulldoze out the lagoon and became mired in sludge. For EPCOT's lagoon, flatbed trucks hauled in an ocean-going dredge capable of removing muck up to fifteen feet deep. The job took three months instead of nine and cost $2 a yard instead of $4.50. Two massive tangles of roots and stumps that couldn't be dredged were buried under 27 feet of sand. Pumping in sand to line the lake bottom took another three months.

Meanwhile, soil engineers performed 730 borings around the lagoon to test below-ground conditions. The entire site, they discovered, was riddled with deep underground caverns that could collapse if subjected to sufficient weight. What the borings didn't find—but the dredge did— was one enormous sinkhole, 1,500 feet wide, northeast of the lagoon. Engineers modified the park layout to make the huge sinkhole part of the lagoon and relocated the World of Motion farther from the shoreline. For smaller caverns, contractors pumped out the swamp water and muck, and replaced it with more stable material. In all, site preparers would move 54 million tons of earth.

As crews broke ground, EPCOT was no longer a faraway dream, but a fast-approaching reality. Disney designers and engineers felt increasing pressure to crank out completed plans. Yet, like dominoes, small changes in one area of a complex attraction often caused a cascade of changes throughout the rest of the show and sometimes the building that housed it. And every decision had to be approved by both the executives and the sponsor, leading to thousands of revised drawings flying back and forth across the country.

In Future World, Disney was relying on participants to cover 80 to 90 percent of building and maintaining every show, so no construction could begin on any pavilion until someone promised to pay for it. It wasn't until 1979 that Kodak started showing serious interest in sponsoring a pavilion. Space, The Seas, and Life & Health still weren't spoken for. But Kodak executives wanted "something more imaginative." Using that as a directive, WED developed the characters of Dreamfinder, the level-headed guide, and his pint-sized purple dragon, Figment, the voice of wonder and curiosity. Their dark ride, Journey into Imagination, would anchor an Imagination pavilion on the site originally slated for Life & Health. Companion attractions included a 3-D movie shot in 70mm, *Magic Journeys*, and an interactive play center upstairs, The Image Works.

The Land pavilion had been changing composition and location, joining Imagination on the right side of Future World. The Land originally had been designed for Georgia-Pacific, the lumber and paper producer that performed logging on undeveloped portions of Disney property. From the outside, the pavilion's elaborate cluster of towering crystals resembled the Emerald City of Oz. Inside, guests would board "hot-air balloons" to fly through the seven crystals, each containing a different habitat of the earth, from a frozen mountaintop to a low-lying desert and swamp.

As The Land's primary consultant, Disney enlisted Dr. Carl Hodges of the University of Arizona. Hodges, recalled Imagineer Tony Baxter, "figured out how exhaust energy from a hot area could be used to make an area cold and conversely [how a cold area could heat itself], so everything was in balance. So when this was thrown out, he said, 'Don't worry. I'm going to do it anyway.' He actually built it. You can go visit it in Arizona. It's called BioSphere, and it's a self-perpetuating environment that people lived in for a year. He had done all the research for us."

Kraft Foods, however, wanted to emphasize harvesting and food production. The Land pavilion evolved into a stylized greenhouse containing an animatronic nutrition show, 70mm environmental movie, food court, revolving restaurant, and a boat ride through dark ride recreations of different climates as well as actual greenhouses, fish farms and laboratories showcasing futuristic farming techniques.

Disney was determined that computers—as the 1980s' most visual representation of the future—be everywhere in Future World. A network of WorldKey information kiosks allowed guests to use touch-screen television monitors to access park information, watch video previews of the attractions, arrange dining reservations, or ask questions of a live cast member on the screen.

Disney desperately wanted a computer company to sponsor the CommuniCorc. Years before, they almost signed a computer firm as a Magic Kingdom participant—RCA. John Hench had designed an Alice in Computerland show based on the time-worn "Peppers Ghost" effect used in the Haunted Mansion's ballroom scene (in which reflections on glass appear to be cavorting in the room behind them). But the idea fell dormant in 1971, when RCA sold its computer division to Sperry. For CommuniCorc, Disney got Sperry's attention by reviving the concept as the Astuter Computer Revue. Based in a theater that looked down into the giant room housing the park's computers, the show was to star a miniature Bert the chimney sweep from *Mary Poppins* singing and dancing on the computer consoles as he explained their role in EPCOT Center. When Dick Van Dyke declined the invitation, the star became another Cockney song-and-dance man teleported from the United Kingdom pavilion. Despite an insipid script, Sperry agreed to sponsor the attraction and other exhibits that comprised Epcot Computer Central, the heart of CommuniCore.

General Electric, which at the time had an aerospace division, initially considered sponsoring the Space pavilion. Yet GE's executive team, notorious for its superiority complex, decided it didn't want to fund just another pavilion. If GE put its name on it, it would have to be something grander that incorporated all the themes of EPCOT. GE would pull its sponsorship from the Carousel of Progress when its new attraction opened at EPCOT. So Disney suggested an update of the old carousel show. It already followed EPCOT's familiar pattern of retracing the history of one facet of life and suggesting possibilities for a great, big, beautiful tomorrow. But GE wanted all the emphasis on the future.

WED suggested, then, making the attraction a history of the future and calling it Century 3, referring to America's third century. Using animatronics and nine-story-high film projections, guests would be transported 100 years into the past to observe how H.G. Wells and Jules Verne looked at the future, then travel to the United States during its Tricentennial. For the finale, passengers would select the ride's ending, whether they preferred life in a space colony, an undersea city, or a desert farm run by robots.

WED eventually changed the attraction's working title to Future Probe, reasoning that the third century reference might escape international guests. But Future Probe sounded uncomfortably "medical." They finally renamed the attraction Horizons, but due to the late start and increasingly ambitious plans, there wouldn't be time to get the attraction finished by EPCOT's opening day. So they sold GE on opening Horizons one year after the rest of EPCOT, when GE wouldn't have to share the spotlight. Starting later also allowed WED's best designers and artists to finish their work on other EPCOT projects and devote themselves more fully to GE.

Each corporate sponsor was given input and veto power over everything that went into their attractions. Partly that was because they were paying an inordinate amount of money. In addition, explained participant affairs manager Steve Baker, "we didn't want it to be Disney's opinion of the future of anything. We wanted it to be GM's opinion of transportation, Exxon's opinion of energy, Kraft's opinion of food."

Primary participants would also receive their own private lounge to entertain clients and employees away from the maddening crowds. "The VIP lounges came out of the World's Fair," said Pete Clark, "a place where you could take your special guests, and serve them soda and coffee. It would have a special entrance and a back door into their ride. You usually entered through the exit, so the regular guests didn't see."

Walt had latched onto the idea during the New York World's Fair and made sure to include a single private lounge for all Disneyland sponsors in the revised plans for New Orleans Square. The facility opened months after Walt's death as the secret, members-only restaurant Club 33. Later that year, VIP lounges were included at some of the attractions in Disneyland's remodeled Tomorrowland, including General Electric's Carousel of Progress and Goodyear's PeopleMover.

At Disneyland, representatives of sponsoring companies were escorted to their lounges by tour guides, who held the keys at City Hall on Main Street. For EPCOT, sponsors would be responsible for continually staffing their private centers. The lounges could be as modest or elaborate as the corporations' budgets allowed. AT&T commissioned a sprawling second-story conference center on the back of Spaceship Earth that overlooked the Fountain of Nations. American Express paid for an upper-floor, colonial-style suite at the American Adventure. Kodak and Exxon wanted more modest, ground-level hospitality centers behind their attractions. Kraft's corporate hideaway had one-way mirrors to look down on The Land's boat ride, while GM built its facility over the entrance to World of Motion, so invited guests could view inside or outside the attraction.

Since foreign countries were providing at best token financial assistance, Disney left it to the Imagineers' discretion as to which nations to include in preliminary designs, and then tried to recruit companies from those countries to participate. The targeted countries, Clark explained, were based on which "WED felt had a real reason to be there. We needed Mexico, because it's so [geographically] close. Germany, France and Japan are all strong countries that have an interest in tourism. China is so mysterious."

The final say on what to build, however, would be up to Burbank. Six months after groundbreaking, the executive committee decided to pull Costa Rica and Morocco when the countries couldn't come up with the promised funds. In their place, they added China, which had agreed to sponsor a pavilion at the 1982 Knoxville World's Fair and promised Disney filmmakers access to previously forbidden regions of the country.

With Disney paying for most of World Showcase out of its own pocket, most proposed E-ticket attractions were cut. But the area did need some rides, so they proceeded with the simple boat ride for Mexico and filmed CircleVision travelogues for China, Canada and France. Optimistically, they also constructed hints of attractions they hoped finances would one day allow them to build. In Japan, Disney constructed a cavernous feudal castle with two towers, planning to eventually install the Meet the World carousel show in the main building and a Japanese tea garden in one tower. They built another huge show building in Germany to one day accommodate the boat ride past miniature castles.

Between China and Germany they lined the front of the lagoon with

large, sandy-colored boulders, as the eventual foreground of the African
pavilion. In the United Kingdom, Imagineers designed a little cul-de-sac
that curved behind the shops and opened into a little park with benches
and a bandstand, room enough to one day add a music hall. And between
Mexico and China they decorated a quaint little restroom in a
Scandinavian motif, as a placemaker for a Denmark pavilion.

World Showcase did get one major attraction—the extravagant animatronic retrospective the American Adventure—because both
American Express and Coca-Cola co-sponsored the pavilion. As host
country, the American pavilion had originally been envisioned as the
entrance to World Showcase. The positioning, however, left the pavilion
as much in Future World as in World Showcase and blocked views of the
lagoon, so it was moved directly across the water. From there, the set
designers decided where to place the other countries.

"It was a major concern we had: who would get the prominent spot?"
recalled Operations' Bill Sullivan. "We put the U.S. in the center,
because we were the host country. Mexico and Canada are our neighbors, so they were the entrance, as you walked in. Italy and Japan and
Germany are all close to us, because that's our American heritage. There
was no science to that. It was just, 'What do you think would look best?
Okay, that's where we'll put it.' It worked."

Early on, Disney realized that the Magic Kingdom's familiar A
through E admission tickets would not work well with EPCOT Center.
Few people would pay separate entrance fees for the international pavilions, since most were atmospheric shops and restaurants. Somehow the
cost of World Showcase had to be built into the price of admission. More
importantly, with so many big-money sponsors, Disney wanted to
encourage that every EPCOT guest visit as many exhibits as possible.
"We had to have a new system of ticketing," said Bob Mathieson,
"because how do you tell one pavilion that they're a B ticket and another
that they're an E ticket?"

Disney decided to begin selling at the Magic Kingdom alongside the
ticket books a single "unlimited use" passport that provided admission to
all attractions—a common practice at other theme parks and a system
used by Disney for special events. By the time EPCOT Center opened,
they would eliminate all ticket books.

Although the Magic Kingdom remained the company's cash cow, the

THUNDER CONSTRUCTION. The Magic Kingdom's addition of Big Thunder Mountain was designed to dissuade visitors from putting off their next trip to Disney World until after EPCOT opened. (1979) *Photo by Dale M. McDonald; Reprinted courtesy State Archives of Florida*

park was all but ignored once design work began on EPCOT. The Kingdom hadn't received a new attraction since Space Mountain opened in late 1974 — just inexpensive shows and parades. As construction began on EPCOT, management realized that its first park needed something big or tourists would delay their next trip to Orlando until the second gate opened. Construction hurriedly started on Big Thunder Mountain Railroad, the roller coaster designed a decade earlier as part of Thunder Mesa, which had just opened at Disneyland. After it opened in 1981, nothing new was slated at the Magic Kingdom for the foreseeable future. And as if to underscore the original park's suddenly second-class status, in late summer 1982, hundreds of the Kingdom's top cast members were transferred to EPCOT.

Disney's design and planning staffs were further distracted when, six

Tokyo Clones

WED used Disneyland as the design basis for the Magic Kingdom, but tweaked most elements to accommodate the climate and greater acreage in Florida. For Tokyo Disneyland, the Imagineers now had two parks to choose elements from.

In Tokyo, the arrival plaza, parking lot, main entrance, and overall park layout were based on Disneyland's. Main Street and Frontierland were renamed World Bazaar and Westernland, themes that conveyed the same meaning as their sister areas in the U.S., but which could be more easily understood by a Japanese audience.

The larger, more impressive castle was taken from the Magic Kingdom. The scale of the castle then, allowed for larger "full scale" buildings in the World Bazaar, a la Florida's Main Street.

Japan's Autopia used the plans for Disney World's Grand Prix raceway. The Jungle Cruise featured Florida's boat designs and show and animation elements, but was laid out in reverse.

The steam trains, Space Mountain, CircleVision 360 theater, and Golden Horseshoe facility and show copied Disneyland's. The Mark Twain steamboat was designed after Disneyland's, but modified to meet Japanese navigational requirements. Similarly, Pirates of the Caribbean was based on the original Disneyland design, but with structural considerations unique to Tokyo Disneyland because of the differential settlement considerations from building on land fill. The Skyway design was closer to Disneyland's, removing the Magic Kingdom's "dog leg" route because it was more difficult to evacuate, and Tokyo's windy, rainy climate would ensure frequent shutdowns. Japan's Fantasyland mimicked the new designs being produced to update Disneyland's Fantasyland.

WED also designed one original attraction—the Meet the World carousel show—that could also be replicated for the Japan pavilion of EPCOT Center.

months before breaking ground on EPCOT Center, Disney agreed to build another theme park, simultaneously, halfway around the world. Nineteen years before, the Mitsui Real Estate Development Company had obtained permission from the Japanese government to dredge ten square miles of Tokyo Bay. Their permit allowed them to build a shipyard, shopping centers, hotels and residences on the condition that one square mile be reserved for recreation. Mitsui formed the leisure-industry-centered Oriental Land Company to complete the task within 20 years. The government assumed they would build a park or a golf course. But OLC analyzed the recreation industry to find out who was making the most money and how. The answer was Disney. So OLC proposed paying Disney to help design, build and open a Disneyland-like theme park—and then keep paying handsome licensing fees and royalties on every dollar they collected. After Disney spent years begging foreign countries and companies to participate at EPCOT, now someone was begging to pay all the bills. Though swamped with work on EPCOT, Disney considered the offer too good to pass up. WED could recycle old, time-tested designs—the basic layout of Disneyland, the castle from the Magic Kingdom—and let the Japanese layer on their own details.

"Tokyo Disneyland was to be based on existing attractions with minimal new design work," said John McCoy, a member of the Tokyo planning team. "Card Walker was very specific that internally EPCOT was to have design priority over Tokyo Disneyland as EPCOT was a Disney investment."

Disney could also appoint a relatively small management team to help train the Japanese cast members and open the park six months after EPCOT Center. One of the few potential hangups was OLC insisted on including the expensive, time-consuming-to-build Mickey Mouse Revue. Burbank demanded the attraction be pulled out of the Magic Kingdom and shipped to Tokyo—much to the chagrin of Disney World management.

"It was a very big fight," Mathieson recalled. "We screamed like crazy on that one. It was a very popular attraction, and it was so much of our culture. It was what people really loved. But they didn't have time to build their own. They had to take it."

Disney had always been a company that grew gradually. It ramped up for each big project, then scaled back slightly by assigning as many employees as possible to the next big project. That way employees' immersion in the Disney culture could age and deepen, and rub off on the newcomers. But with EPCOT and Tokyo Disneyland underway, WED's design staff quickly ballooned from 450 to 2,500. More frightening, the company and its cast members were about to be spread around the globe. At the same time, Ron Miller was pushing to double the studio's capacity in animation, from one feature every four years to one every two years. Card Walker began to fear that the hiring spree would dilute what made Disney different.

"Some of these people think Walt and Roy are two faces on a cough-drop package," Walker grumbled. So he decided that the Disney University program that did so well brainwashing the theme park division recruits should be expanded to bring that culture to the studio and WED. Walker, now in his 60s, was consumed with keeping the Walt in Disney and ensuring that influence lasted even after he was gone. He had already succeeded Donn Tatum as CEO, and informed the board that before he retired he wanted the chance to be chairman. So in 1980, Tatum graciously stepped aside and Walker became chairman. The move also allowed Walker to promote his hand-picked successor, Walt's son-in-law Ron Miller, to president of Walt Disney Productions.

Into 1980, Disney had posted road signs all over the property publicizing EPCOT Center's impending opening. They used the marketing department's tag line: "The Twenty-first Century Begins October 1, 1982." Gerstman and his crew couldn't drive anywhere without constant reminders of just how firm their deadline was. It didn't help to have to constantly wait for drawings from WED. Gerstman considered the Imagineers a flighty breed, artists pretending to be engineers. To them, quality trumped deadlines. Like Walt, they would tinker endlessly with a project until achieving perfection. The Imagineers also felt more comfortable working in teams and committees, bouncing ideas off each other and reaching consensus. Gerstman grew increasingly impatient. He wanted decisions. Construction bosses overseeing as many as 4,600 men at one time can't constantly call "time out" for a huddle. Roland, for his part, had to keep reminding Gerstman that Disney was a creative company and "good ideas can't be cranked out like bricks."

Responsibility for ensuring that the Imagineers' drawings got properly engineered fell on WED vice president of engineering John Zovich, as it had a decade earlier on the Magic Kingdom. A husky chain-smoker,

Zovich oversaw a team of 260 engineers until he was sidelined by a heart attack in June 1981. Like the typical Disney old-timer, Zovich prided himself on loyalty, and his first instinct was to reward a job to a contractor whom he had worked with previously.

To form the 40,000 lineal feet of monorail track, Zovich wanted to hire Concrete Technologies, the Tacoma firm he used for the Magic Kingdom. Tishman admitted the manufacturer had produced quality pylons and beams, but there had been added expenses and delays because the company was located so far away. Disney had to assign three of its own people to keep track of the beams as they were shipped across country on railway flatcars. Tishman insisted that over the last ten years many other concrete manufacturers had improved to the point that they could meet EPCOT's needs. Zovich didn't think so. Over his objections, Disney selected Morrison-Knudsen, a Boise, Idaho, contractor that could fabricate the monorail track on the EPCOT jobsite and then have it installed by American Bridge. They completed the work on time, without a hitch, for about $4 million less than Zovich would have paid Concrete Technologies.

To spec out the pipes that delivered chilled water to EPCOT, Zovich hired the same civil engineer who worked on the Magic Kingdom. Late in the summer of 1982, the pipes were laid, buried and ready to be tested. "When we turned the water on, the pipes couldn't take the pressure and burst," Roland said, remembering the sight of the entire entrance plaza flooded just months before opening. "We immediately got backhoes and began ripping up the plaza. It was a one-man operation, and he didn't have the right insurance. Apparently, he had taken the plans for the Magic Kingdom and just copied them." The burst pipes had to be removed, and new pipes installed, anchored by massive, steel-reinforced concrete thrust blocks—eighteen feet long, eighteen feet wide, and four feet thick—to prevent the lines from becoming overstressed. Disney got stuck with the bill: $1.5 million.

Zovich also took the heat for errors in the drawings. Soon after construction began on the Land pavilion, contractors discovered that the structural steel didn't fit properly. All work stopped until the plans could be reworked.

Contractors installed three-quarters of the shell panels to the exterior of Spaceship Earth, before realizing they weren't going to fit. Zovich traced the problem to a geometry miscalculation by WED's engineers, an understandable error considering how few round buildings are built. "We offered the contractor several million dollars to take the problem over," recalled Roland. "They jumped at it. They thought they could do it for less. They couldn't. They eventually went bankrupt [getting the job completed]."

Part of the reason for the slow-going was that so many of the ride systems were prototypes. Every show was a development, engineering, installation and operation adventure. "The control systems in the shows and rides were a big step forward," said Bill Moss, director of construction. "Unlike the Magic Kingdom and Tokyo Disneyland, there weren't any duplications; they were all prototypical. The shows' actions, especially for American Adventure, you didn't know if they were going to work until you put them together."

Similarly, Journey into Imagination relied on a computerized system to move vehicles through the show building and engage them with a giant turntable, which they rotated around for four minutes experiencing a variety of complicated special effects.

On Universe of Energy, guests were to be rotated on a massive air-float turntable, 80 feet in diameter. Just three months before opening, workmen discovered that the concrete pad beneath the turntable began to flake under the intense air pressure. Contractors had to disassemble the entire mechanism, jackhammer away the concrete pad, pour in a new mix of concrete with a stronger, smoother finish, and reinstall the turntable. The pad still wouldn't hold up. Again, they removed the turntable, tore out the concrete, and replaced it with a new pad built from quarter-inch-thick steel. The third attempt worked, but put the job more than a month behind.

At the same time, the executive committee in Burbank was cutting elements from the evolving plans to keep the total budget beneath the magical $800-million mark. Most of the scaling back came in World Showcase, where Disney was footing most of the bill. They removed several water features from the Canada pavilion and specified less fancy paving. The Mexico pavilion was downsized, the show redone, and less expensive materials used to trim $5 million off the original $45-million budget.

Yet, even in Future World, the budget for the Universe of Energy was reworked seven times. The Land pavilion expanded and contracted multiple times. Spaceship Earth was downsized from 195 feet in diameter to

165 feet.

A gut check came September 8, 1981—when the executive committee met to review the project's progress with one year left. With a minimum four Future World pavilions and six World Showcase pavilions, Nunis said, "I can open a viable theme park. Spaceship Earth, of course, is a must."

Seven pavilions—the Land, World of Motion, World of Energy, the American Adventure, Canada, France and the United Kingdom—were on schedule, structures rising. Germany was a little behind. The rest of the pavilions were bare foundations—except China, which hadn't even broken ground yet. Unable to wait for final drawings, crews began building China in mid-November—less than eleven months before it had to be finished.

Every day brought another delay. Gerstman, however, found a way to keep the project moving. Relentless, harsh and volatile, he commonly badgered, threatened, reprimanded and cursed out subordinates. Dick Nunis shared a similarly ferocious temper, but unleashed it when someone let him down. During the job, he was an encourager. For the most part, Nunis was one of the guys, willing to roll up his own sleeves and work side by side with anyone to get anything done. Gerstman, on the other hand, was known on construction sites as "Emperor." He thrived off instilling fear and wanted subordinates to know he was in charge.

The construction boss believed that every time he trusted subcontractors to get something done, problems ensued. So he constantly patrolled the jobsite. If Gerstman noticed any shoddy work, such as a crooked curb, he demanded it be torn out on the spot and done properly. It might cost thousands of dollars to stop everything to rip out and repour a patch of concrete, but Gerstman knew it would only cost more later.

He split the most expansive job—creating 600,000 square feet of walkways—among several contractors. They preferred to finish paving one area, then load their equipment and hundreds of concrete forms into their trucks and move to the next area. Unfortunately, blocking off wide swaths would have inconvenienced countless other contractors since there was work going on at every pavilion. Instead, Gerstman demanded that they pave around the lagoon first, and then zigzag out as other areas became available. And they had to complete all the paving in a set number of days.

That meant the concrete pourers and finishers often had to work through the night, beginning as soon as an adjacent patch became available. To accommodate around-the-clock construction in areas where electricity had yet to be installed, Disney brought in a hook-and-ladder fire truck to shine enough light to allow more than 100 concrete finishers to keep working. Disney chefs also showed up in the middle of the night to grill hamburgers for the graveyard shift laborers. To maximize every second, the Disney World weather station sent weather reports to the EPCOT jobsite every ten minutes. Construction workers then had advance notice to protect their freshly-poured concrete from an approaching thunderstorm.

For EPCOT, Disney retained its previous labor agreement: workers would not strike so long as the company used only union labor and immediately worked to resolve any issues. But whereas the unions twisted the deal to their advantage on the Magic Kingdom by forcing Disney to employ unproductive laborers, Gerstman convinced contractors that they needed him more than he needed them.

Every time subcontractors demanded more pay because their tasks took longer than expected, Gerstman refused. The inconvenience of coordinating with other contractors, he explained, was inevitable on a job as big as EPCOT. One carpenter threatened to withhold $775,000 in ornate woodwork for the China pavilion unless he received a bonus. The construction boss called his bluff; he told him to keep the trim and they'd just have Disney's own shop do the work. Panicking that he might be stuck with the material, the contractor begged Gerstman to take the material at the original price.

Another time, a plumbing and heating subcontractor tried to bully an extra $1 million out of Gerstman because he said he was losing money on the job. With final deadlines bearing down, the sub had his sheet metal installers slow work on Mexico and the East Restaurant complex. Gerstman tore up his construction claim and demanded the subcontractor be thrown off the property. The contractor pleaded for a second chance.

A year before Opening Day, drywallers at the Japan and France pavilions suddenly called a strike. They claimed that the subcontractor who hired them had fled the country with their work records and $50,000 payroll. The men refused to work or clock out until they were paid. Gerstman and Roland promised to spend the next day reconstructing their time sheets and would pay them everything they were owed. Since it was a good-faith offer, the laborers headed home.

Into the final months, Gerstman turned to other psychological tricks. CommuniCore had fallen critically behind schedule, because the designs had arrived seven months late. Gerstman assigned two shifts to the pavilion, and had them compete against each other to see which could get more done.

In May 1982, Gerstman informed the crew building the Italy pavilion that the top Disney executives had been invited to a special celebration on August 15 for Howard Roland's forty-eighth birthday. If their pavilion were finished, the dinner would be in Italy. If not, they'd dine in France. Gerstman made the same promise to the workers at the France pavilion. Come August 15, both pavilions were completed and signed off on by the health inspectors. The executives feasted at Alfredo's in Italy, then headed for several more courses of fine dining at Les Chefs de France. The ploy worked so well, Gerstman began planning more executive parties to motivate the contractors on other pavilions.

As he had done on the Magic Kingdom, Nunis invited the construction workers to bring their families to the jobsite on Sundays and on Labor Day. Trams transported the guests around the property, where they could view unfinished attractions as well as models and films depicting what they would look like when they finally were finished.

By this time, every Saturday morning at 7:00, Gerstman would escort Nunis and his senior team across the jobsite, from end to end. Workers on schedule received a pat on the back. Anyone falling behind was grilled: "Why isn't your work done?" "How are you going to catch up?" "How much can you make up by next Saturday?"

One Saturday, the executives discovered the Imagination pavilion cluttered with scaffolding and other equipment that prevented the Imagineers from testing the show elements. Gerstman tore into the general contractor and all his subcontractors and demanded they drop what they were doing and clean the place up. The contractors blamed WED and their last-minute changes. Gerstman refused to listen to excuses. He cursed them some more, told them to do it his way, and stormed out. Privately, even Nunis questioned whether the Emperor had been too hard on his minions. No matter, that was the last mess ever left at the Imagination pavilion.

Before anything was officially considered completed, finicky Imagineer John Hench had to make sure every show element was perfect. Every pavilion was filled with authentic props, such as the blown glass windows and cast-iron phone booths in the United Kingdom, or historically accurate knock-offs, such as the Sistine Chapel ceiling in Spaceship Earth. Hench was obsessed that everything looked like it did it real life or—better yet—as it would in a dream. He ordered the French marketplace repainted a darker green to better resemble the Les Halles in Paris. He demanded that the woodwork in Canada's Le Cellier restaurant be stripped and refinished with a lighter stain. He had 30-some gargoyles torn off the side of the Mexican pyramid and moved up two feet, at a cost of $15,000. He had workmen in the United Kingdom beat timbers with chains to achieve a weathered look. Later, a well-intentioned foreman noticed all the scarred woodwork and had the nicks and scratches filled in with caulk. The Imagineers were furious. From then on, once WED approved something, no one was allowed in the area without special permission.

Redoing their work was a daily activity for the landscapers. Construction crews kept tramping over flowers or, while sandblasting curbs, spewing sand over nearby shrubs and lawns. The culprits would have to pay for new plants, but Disney crews still had to do the work. The day before EPCOT opened, film crews used a helicopter to get overhead footage of the entrance. The downdraft decimated the garden below. In one night, landscapers had to procure and plant 10,000 flowers. In all, a third of the EPCOT's landscaping had been replanted before the park ever opened.

In the meantime, the Entertainment and Merchandise departments had been scrambling to develop an entirely new strain of Disney offerings. For the first time, the divisions were forbidden from using traditional Disney characters—especially Mickey Mouse. " I didn't ever want Disney characters in EPCOT," said Jack Lindquist, who as vice president of marketing sold the idea to Card Walker. "The Magic Kingdom and EPCOT are two separate places. I thought characters should only be in the Magic Kingdom. My feeling was each park had to stand on its own, and if you could see Mickey Mouse in EPCOT, why would you go to the Magic Kingdom? I think, more importantly, you should create new icons for new parks."

Walker agreed, since he viewed EPCOT as serious, educational and adult-oriented. "EPCOT is a new era in Disney entertainment, a forum for future technology," one Disney spokesperson explained. "Mickey just doesn't fit in here."

They knew, however, that EPCOT needed some sort of characters to mollify the youngsters and to put on T-shirts. Walker figured his artists could simply invent dozens of marketable characters that tied into the industrial aspects of Future World or represented the nations of World Showcase. What he perhaps failed to realize was that audiences loved and identified with the characters at the Magic Kingdom because they were already old friends. They had already shared countless adventures together in movies and on television. Theme park attractions, on the other hand, were more successful at transporting visitors to new environments, rather than bonding them with new personalities. Guests rarely felt as if they knew a character after a three-minute ride or standing in line to hug its furry, five-foot-tall likeness.

Fortunately, the late addition of the Imagination pavilion brought with it the introduction of Figment and a ride system expressly designed for riders to lock onto a turntable for four minutes to get to know the impish dragon. Merchandising, hoping they'd found a marketable mascot, dreamed up Figment T-shirts, keychains, mugs, and adventure books.

In World Showcase, some stores had primary sponsors that took care of supplying their products, such as Pringle's sweaters in the U.K. and Hummel collectibles in Germany. For the rest, Disney wanted authentic merchandise imported from the respective countries. Merchandise executives spent much of their time traveling the world to track down jewelry, crystal, clothing and other goods that evoked their homeland. Some small foreign factories, Disney's buyers discovered, were not motivated sellers. They might reluctantly part with a fraction of their limited production. "I'm going to sell you the merchandise," one Norwegian glass vendor would say, "but I hope you don't sell it. I already employ everybody in town, and I don't want to work any harder." One music box purchased for a shop in the Germany pavilion was so difficult to find, Disney priced it at $15,000 and hoped no one would buy it, so they wouldn't have to find a replacement.

EPCOT's general manager of merchandise, Wayne Busch, traveled so much that his boss, Bob Mathieson, would ask, "Do we still pay you? You're never around." Mathieson was perturbed that Busch missed most of his weekly meetings. Busch wasn't exactly living it up. During one flight from England to Morocco, the airline lost his luggage. Once in Morocco, Busch was pickpocketed. After being forced to wear the same shirt for three days, Busch agreed to attend a lunch meeting wearing a flowing garment provided by his Moroccan guide. During lunch, he discovered that his hamburger had been made with goat meat. Busch unobtrusively slipped the rest of his patty into a planter. Oh, how he wished he were at Mathieson's meeting instead. He immediately left his boss a phone message: "Wallet stolen. Lost luggage. Wearing dress. Fed me a goat. Wish you were here."

Making EPCOT Center a Disney character-free zone also handcuffed Entertainment. "It hurt us," said Peter Bloustein. "It would have been easier if we had a recognizable look that people could feel comfortable with. Whatever we did there, no one was immediately comfortable, because where was Mickey? Is this Disney? Because what says Disney? But that was the order, and we had to deal with that."

For characters in World Showcase, the Entertainment division remembered the oversized doll costumes that Bob Jani had created for the Bicentennial's America on Parade. Although the 8-foot-tall characters looked intimidating marching down a scaled-down Main Street, they would be more in proportion along the huge promenades of EPCOT, with the sky as their backdrop. So they created some new dolls and replaced the old characters' colonial outfits with everything from kimonos to cowboy duds.

As permanent entertainment, Future World received a giant centerpiece fountain that every fifteen minutes burst into a synchronized water ballet. There were also a Future World Band and Future Corps drum and bugle troupe.

Finding World Showcase entertainment was trickier because management insisted that it all be authentic. Talent agencies in China and Japan had experience arranging visas and shipping their acrobats and musicians to the States for limited engagements. Other countries were more difficult to navigate.

"I went to Germany to look for German musicians—and they were the pits," Bloustein said. "They were the worst musicians. There was no such thing as a young musician in Germany. They were a bunch of old farts sitting in beirgartens. And they only played for fifteen marks—20 marks if you want to conduct them. It was just terrible. I thought, 'I can't do this.'"

Upon returning home, Bloustein ran audition notices in Pittsburgh, Philadelphia, Chicago and Buffalo, which had a large number of

German-American and Polish-American clubs. And he held his auditions in upstate New York, in the city of Hamburg. Although most of the applicants were of German descent, they had spent their entire lives in the United States. "There comes a time when you can't argue with silly dictums," he said. "The only way around it for me to put on a good show in the German pavilion was to get good musicians. I could not find any in Germany. One or two, but they wouldn't leave. So the only way out of it was Hamburg, New York. That's how we got our German musicians. In fact, I think I told them, 'Now if you can, for the first six or seven months, you must always say you're from Hamburg. And try to put on a perfect German accent. You know, [as if] you've only been in the States for six, seven years.' As far as the company knew, the musicians came from Hamburg. I never said Hamburg, Germany. I never said Hamburg, anything."

Mexico, being closer, was easier. Disney arranged to fly a mariachi group into Tucson, where a talent booker auditioned them at the airport and hired them on the spot to play on the steps of the Mexico pavilion. To play inside the restaurant, Disney hired four fellows who played giant marimbas.

At the American pavilion, Bloustein assembled an a capella singing group, the Voices of Liberty. He also wanted women playing musical water glasses in the American Adventure lobby, explaining that Benjamin Franklin had created a similar instrument called the "glass armonica." He couldn't fit it in his budget.

For Italy, Bloustein wanted an improvisational commedia dell'arte group. Several months before opening, he recruited an authentic repertory company, complete with period costumes and masks, and gave them a trial run at the Lake Buena Vista Village shopping center. Passersby would stop for a moment and then continue walking. In the meantime, while attending a Renaissance faire, Bloustein discovered a trio of irreverent street performers called SAK Theater. "I brought up these three people from Minneapolis, and they were hilarious," Bloustein recalled. "Within five minutes they had 150 people standing there—and sitting on the ground, and doing all sorts of terrible things. They just knew how to deal with a crowd. So I hired them and put them in Italy."

Although the African pavilion had been delayed, Bloustein hoped to feature authentic African performers on the American Gardens stage. Unfortunately, some of the musicians he hired insisted on cooking their native meals on a roaring open fire—in their hotels rooms. One day, Bloustein received an urgent call from the owner of the hotel, pleading, "I swear they're going to butcher a goat here soon!"

Worse, Bloustein had hired a group of Mexican acrobats, who swung around a maypole. What he didn't realize was that before their act, for good luck, they would sacrifice a chicken. At the last moment, a manager persuaded the troupe that this part of their act would be "bad show" and unbecoming of a Disney cast member.

11

Starring in the Show

THROUGH the 1970s, Disney World gradually increased its ranks of employees as it added new attractions and facilities. The resort's opening day workforce of 6,500 had grown to 14,000 by 1980. Yet operating EPCOT Center would mean adding roughly 3,500 employees to the payrolls in one fell swoop—and hoping the new hires would meet the same lofty standards.

Disney recruiters' jobs would be a lot more difficult than when they hired 5,000 hourlies during the summer of 1971. Back then, they received eight to ten applications for every opening, allowing them to be extraordinarily selective. Prospects with any conceivable shortcoming were weeded out. Ideally, Disney wanted the workers "green," before they had been "corrupted" by outside experience or special training.

A framed quotation hung at the entrance of its first temporary employment center, declaring, "You can dream, design and build the most wonderful place in the world, but it requires people to make the dream a reality."

In the early days, Disney made clear it was casting for a show. "Individuals," stressed one recruiter, "must look and act like the roles they are cast for. A monorail operator, for example, would be a person whose appearance would lend itself to the sleek, lean lines of the futuristic monorail train. A Main Street fire engine operator, however, would reflect the mature, experienced appearance one would expect of such an individual."

Disney's official rationale for not hiring anyone "too wide" was that the limited number of costumes could not accommodate them. They made sure men's pants started at size 28 and only went up to size 44. "If they hire you, they know where they're going to put you," said ride operator Chris Kraftchick. "They compartmentalize you by looks. The largest size [women's costume] in Attractions was like a 3 waist. Fat people were put in the kitchen. The custodians were more homely."

Custodians at least had the freedom to roam the park, thereby placing them one peg above the lowly Foods department workers. The top choices were tour guide and ride operator. "The biggest difference between the typical Foods and Op[eration]s cast member was psychological," theorized Mike Lee. "Within the context of the park, you were either 'stuck' in Foods or you talked yourself into believing you preferred being there. Only a handful of people could have really liked it—those earning tips as servers or those who enjoyed what they did in the kitchen because either they really liked to cook or they dreaded interaction with the guests in the park."

Fortunately for Lee, he quickly transferred out of Foods. "I fit the physical mold of an Ops cast member," he explained. "Appearance-wise, I was the right height, not too hideous in the face, and could present myself with a measure of poise and decorum."

He instantly discovered that Operations "was probably the most fun you could have earning that little money. And there was that prestige thing, of course. The pay wasn't much better, but in terms of the park's 'caste system,' it was like moving from the rabble to the nobility. For example, I had gone to high school with a prima donna who played Cinderella. When I walked down the tunnel in my Liberty Square stable boy costume from Harbour House, she wouldn't even notice me. I'll never forget coming out of the locker room in my Haunted Mansion suit a couple months later, and she was standing in the tunnel talking to a couple guys. She went out of her way to say, 'Hi, Mike! How are you?,' as if we were friends, presumably because knowing people who worked at the Haunted Mansion was cool. It was pretty comical, the extent to which people constructed a microcosm of society in the confines of an amusement park."

Every new hire had to pass multiple interviews, followed by from two days to two weeks of training. On the first day of indoctrination, they arrived at the Disney University building, where on the front lobby wall was painted Mickey Mouse in cap and gown hoisting a diploma. They were ushered into a large waiting room decorated with Disney movie posters. Disney tunes, some dressed up in jazz versions, played over the speakers. Recruits then marched into a classroom, referred to as a "stage," where they sat on canvas-backed directors chairs, reinforcing the image that they were now "actors and actresses in the Walt Disney World cast."

Here, everybody introduced themselves by first name only, a practice insisted on by Walt to promote friendliness. They also learned that, to maintain the illusion that this was all a show, they were to use the terminology of show business. They were cast members, not employees, wearing costumes, not uniforms, serving guests, not customers. The audience, not crowd, enjoyed attractions and adventures, not rides.

The first all-day class, "Traditions," covered the history of the company, so students understood the magnitude of what they were becoming a part of. Then came an overview of the Disney Way, the company's unique brand of personalized service. You were to become both an "information expert" as well as a "people expert." Remember every guest is a VIP. Constantly remind guests that you're glad they're here, so they feel they belong in Disney World. You work while others play. If guests are happier when they leave, you've played your role correctly. Never mention to guests your personal problems, social adventures, or operating difficulties. Keep the magic in Disney.

"A friendly smile from your heart is a magic mirror which works miracles in your relationship with your guests," the employee handbook explained. "It's an essential discipline of show business that we smile... in spite of our own problems." In fact, the manual continued, "Each employee when he starts to work will be given a personal locker. If you have any personal problems, when you come to work, put them in your locker. Then when you go home at night, you can put them on again."

Occasionally Disney tried to sound hip, but it usually rang false. "If you tune out the outside world, turn on to Walt Disney World, and get with it, you'll find that you'll be helping to create a very important thing in life," read one 1972 personnel brochure.

Next came classes specifically on Disney World operations, followed by job-specific training at one's work station. Of primary importance was the rigid dress code. As the "Disney Look" grooming handbook stated, "Into each life some conformity must fall, and quite a bit falls into yours when it comes to your 'stage appearance.'" The dress code had remained relatively unchanged since it was first designed for Disneyland in the 1950s. The company said it mandated the clean-cut look to separate the original Disneyland "theme show" from the traditional amusement parks of the day—generally "dirty, hazardous places run by sloppy, rude employees." Employees sporting the Disney Look appeared safe, approachable, and professional. "You look as if you know the answers," said one Appearance Coordinator. "It gives you credibility."

The standards were strict and inflexible: women's hair was not to exceed two inches in height; men's one inch. Men's hair was not to touch their ears or collar. Sideburns were not permitted below the middle of the ear. No beards, mustaches, or toupees. For women: no wigs, frosted or streaked hair, eye shadow, eyeliner, false eyelashes, or fingernails longer than a quarter-inch. No perfume. No earrings or more than one ring per hand. No visible tattoos. And absolutely, positively, undergarments were to be worn at all times.

"People expect an image when they come to Walt Disney World," said one manager. "We're just playing along with their dreams."

When the Magic Kingdom opened, Disney relaxed the standards slightly; women could now wear quarter-inch plain stud earrings. It would take another sixteen years before hostesses could wear earrings the size of a penny and seven more years before they could wear eyeliner, eye shadow, earrings as big as a quarter, flat shoes, hairpieces, and colored fingernail polish. Underwear remained mandatory.

Primary responsibility for upholding the standards fell to Greta Heminger, who earned the nickname "Greta Groom" for her harping on employees to abide by the Disney Look, her constant surprise inspections of the troops, and accusations that she was always spying on them.

But the Disney Look wasn't just about neat and clean dress; even more it was about behavior and attitude. Square was beautiful. There was to be no smoking, gum chewing, eating or drinking on the job. Disney preferred to hire friendly people and hope they could operate a monorail, rather than hiring people to operate the monorail and hoping they were friendly. They figured they couldn't train workers to be happy or issue memos mandating them to smile. In fact, early employment ads encouraged, "Bring your smile to Walt Disney World!"

TEAMWORK. An annual softball game of the executives against the all-stars from the hourlies' softball league reinforced the concept that all cast members were really on the same team. The "Execs" included *(front row, left to right)* Keith Kambak, Larry Slocum, Tom Eastman, Eddy Carpenter, Jack Lindquist, Bill Sullivan, Bill Hoelscher, Bob Allen. *(Back row)* Bill Ward, Chuck Luthin, Pat Vaughn, Ralph Kent, Jim Passilla, Bob Billingsly, Ed Moriarty, Card Walker, Ted Crowell, Jud Perkins, Tom Garrison. (Late summer 1982) *Photo courtesy Bill Hoelscher*

For its part, Disney was committed to creating an atmosphere in which workers wanted to smile. Not an overly wealthy company, it couldn't afford to lavish its thousands of workers with huge paychecks. Instead, all full-timers received a two-week paid vacation, sick leave, regular merit raises, an insurance plan, and possible educational aid.

Disney, too, tried to reward employees with perks that built up camaraderie among the ranks and allegiance to the company. Everyone received access to all employee activities, such as photography, scuba diving or rafting clubs, softball and bowling leagues, and free access to Little Lake Bryan, a secluded lake at the northeast tip of the property. Reserved exclusively for employees and their families, the lake had a beach, swimming pool, clubhouse, tennis and volleyball courts, softball fields, fishing, boating and picnic area. Each month, cast members were invited to preview upcoming Disney movies. They received a 20-percent discount at all stores on property. Prices were kept low in the employee cafeterias. Disney didn't charge for uniforms and laundered them daily. A weekly cast newspaper tried to make cast members feel that they were part of a special community. The company staffed a career planning and placement office to help young employees with their future goals, even if those goals didn't include Disney. Still, "promoting from within" was one of Disney's many traditions; in just the first eight months of operation at the Magic Kingdom, 306 employees were promoted from hourly to salaried positions.

Disney's philosophy was that no matter what your position, you were an integral component in "making the magic," which was the purpose of your job, not operating rides, or taking tickets, or cleaning urinals.

In busy periods, the salaried folks would fill shifts stocking store shelves or flipping hamburgers alongside the regular hourlies. In addition to providing much-needed manpower, such "cross-utilization" reminded everyone that they were all part of the same team, and that every role was equally valuable in creating magic for guests. Cast members would also be regularly transferred to different attractions or departments to keep things fresh.

To underline the importance of each and every employee, Gloria Jacobs in the Employee Relations department developed a Golden Ears Club to benefit retirees. Those who retired were presented a pewter Mickey Mouse statue and a picture of themselves surrounded by dozens of Disney characters that read, "Now you are in the Disney Hall of Fame"—personalized touches that old-timers seemed to appreciate more than the standard gold watch.

Working at Disney World could also be plenty of fun. You were surrounded by thousands of attractive, personable co-workers and tens of thousands of visitors looking for a good time. "We met so many women. It was easy," recalled ride operator Chris Kraftchick. "They were on vacation, looking to meet guys. You worked with thousands of people, half of them women. It was just a big party. I heard that Sundays were always the biggest day for calling in sick."

Some of the wilder, college-aged cast would take the party to work with them. On slower days, to relieve the monotony, they might commit small—or not so small—pranks. One morning, a Jungle Cruise skipper poured a box of detergent in the hippo pool to make it look like the hippos were foaming at the mouth.

Say What?

Cast members joke that guests "check their brains at the gate" when they visit the Magic Kingdom. They're so caught up in the illusions, and so conditioned to let Disney do the thinking for them, that normally intelligent humans do and say ridiculous things.

Here are a few of the doozies tourists have asked park employees over the years:

- "Where is the train that goes all around the zoo?"
- "Are you part of the scenery or do you work here?"
- "When will they tear down the Temporary Hotel and build a permanent one?"
- "This place cost over 400 million? Do you have any idea what that is in dollars and cents?"
- "Is this bus going to the Polyester Hotel?"
- "Where is the Jungle Serenade?"
- "Where is the Hall of Fame with wax people?"
- "Is this the way to Fancyland?"
- (At the Main Street Cinema) "Do the films start in the middle?"
- "Where are the whispering flowers?"
- "Where is the Human House of Horror?"
- "Which way to the World's Fair?"
- "Is that the Fairy Godfather's Castle?"
- (To a Main Street vehicle operator) "Tell me, feller, has this car been resurrected?"
- "Which way to E Land?"
- "Can you show me the way to Toilet Land?"
- "Where is the flight to the molecules at?"
- "Just look at the water on that lake!"
- "These must be free—there's no price tag!"
- "Are those curtains above the door for sale?"
- (To a submarine pilot) "How deep do we go?"
- "Where's the Back to the Future ride?"
- "Does the Skyway go to EPCOT?"
- "Where's that EPCOT ride?"
- (Noticing the "Skyway to Tomorrowland" had shut down) "Does that mean Tomorrowland is closed?"

On Space Mountain, loaders asked gullible-looking riders to remove their shoes before boarding, explaining that they had just installed new carpeting in all the rockets. Some guests left their footwear behind, only to discover that the ride ended on the floor above the loading area.

More than once a prankish pilot has sounded the monorail's deafening bullhorn while the train passed through the Contemporary Hotel.

During late nights, to entertain themselves, submarine pilots held their throttles at full bore and raced through the ride to see who could get around the track in the shortest time. To prevent the trip from ending only minutes into the prerecorded narration, pilots set the tape far in advance, resulting in none of the narration matching up with what the confused passengers viewed through their portholes.

A pair of devious 20,000 Leagues under the Sea pilots enjoyed smacking their submarines together. They would wait until their boats were both in the darkest area of the cave, then the front skipper would throw his boat into reverse at the exact moment the rear skipper hit full-throttle forward. Both subs shuddered violently from the impact. Often, the lights flickered momentarily from the force, and guests were thrown from their seats. Both pilots would pretend they had no idea what happened, and none of their guests ever formally complained. "A possible explanation," one co-conspirator suggested, "is that people had no idea what caused the 'bang' and were glad to get out of the ride unscathed. There's also that old adage about people thinking *everything* at the park is scripted, and they may have just thought it was part of the show."

Still, while it is often unskilled labor, working at Disney World can be grueling. Cast members work hardest when everyone else is relaxing—weekends and holidays. All the rules, the monotony, the low pay, humorless supervisors, and demanding guests take their toll.

Daily, the front-line employees incur the wrath of unhappy guests, some with legitimate complaints, others merely frazzled after spending hours waiting in endless lines under the hot sun. Some think Disney World exists to make them happy and decide to see how far they can push it. One dissatisfied customer wanted to file a formal complaint because he couldn't make out all the lyrics to "It's a Small World."

No matter what a guest does or says, cast members are to remain courteous. One man spat in the face of a Grand Prix Raceway hostess when she asked him to stand on a numbered circle to wait for his car.

Other operators have been cursed at, shoved or punched by irate guests.

One submarine pilot was terminated after he was spit on from above by a Skyway rider. The host abandoned his post on the dock to chase down the guest and reprimand him at the Skyway station.

As ride operator Kraftchick explained, "Some guests would push your buttons, because they knew there was nothing we could do."

Visitors are usually on their worst behavior during the private Grad Nites for graduating high school seniors. The teens are searched before being allowed into the park, to keep out as many illicit substances as possible. The grads often try to inflict damage on the park far beyond the mild destruction of the unwitting day guests who might bump into each other on the Grand Prix Raceway.

During Grad Nites, cast members are assigned to "lookout positions" inside the dark rides that have no security cameras. They lurk in shadowy corners to detect guests causing mischief. One night a group of muscle-bound high school football players climbed outside of the It's a Small World canal and tried to overturn their boat. The lookout walked up and asked casually, "Excuse me, boys. If you flip your boat over, how are you going to get back to port? You'll have to listen to this music all night." The students sheepishly explained that they weren't trying to cause any trouble; the boat's seats were wet and they were trying to dump the water off.

Invariably, even many well-intentioned cast members burn out after a year or three. "It got to where I didn't want to be around people," said former Jungle Cruise skipper John Lehtonen. "They tell you that you may have done that spiel 20 times, but for the guest, it's their first time. You try going through the motions in a professional manner." Even 25 years later, Lehtonen still recalled the stunned look he received from tourists with whom he grew impatient. "I still feel bad that I gave someone a negative impression of Disney World."

Lehtonen knew when to quit. "It's like a cocoon—nice, safe," he said. "It paid adequately. I outgrew the place. I went to college. It was time to move on. It's a fantasy world. Some people get caught up in that; 20 years can go just like that, and they think, 'What the hell am I doing here?'"

Another free-spirited Jungle Cruise captain had no qualms about offending the guests by the time he decided he'd had enough of working for Disney. He wanted to go out in a blaze of glory, hopefully embarrass-

Between the Ears
What Cast Members Are Really Thinking

After a few summers—or even days—of abuse, many cast members develop a low opinion of Disney World guests. Yet they also learn that, in Disney-speak, "every guest is a VIP" and there are no problems at the Magic Kingdom. Everything's just fine, all the time.

In the late 1980s, a group of anonymous cast members started an underground newsletter to counter the happy talk of the official *Eyes & Ears* publication. They called it *The Nose & The Throat*.

Another anonymous employee, interning in the 1990s in the Magic Kingdom's College Program, disseminated this list of common phrases used by cast members—followed by what was really going through their minds. "As you know," he wrote, "Disney loves to sugarcoat anything and everything it says to the public, and therefore they encourage us as cast members to do the same when we speak to park guests. Here is some Disney Cast Member Lingo and their unofficial translations."

- "We are experiencing technical difficulties."
  Something bad just happened.
- "At this time, we will need to evacuate the line."
  Something really bad just happened.
- "We should be operating again in about an hour."
  I have no idea how long it will be.
- "Thank you."
  Go away.
- "How many in your party?"
  Are they with you? Eeeewww!
- "How many in your party?"
  I realize that there is absolutely no way that you know how many people are in your group, but have no fear. Mickey pays me $6 an hour to figure that out for you!
- "These 3-D glasses will impair your normal vision."
  They look goofy if you wear them outside, and we get in trouble if anyone sees you with them.
- "Excuse us, please."
  If you don't move, a one-ton cart will run you over.

- "No flash photography, please."

  It's not worth taking pictures of.
- "Rows 1 and 2."

  Go stand over there.
- "We will have to hold our position here for a few more minutes."

  The tram in front of ours is on fire, and if we move forward, we will be too.
- "Everything is fine. There is nothing to worry about."

  Everything is not fine. There is plenty to worry about.
- "This is a walkway only. I need you to keep moving."

  Beat it before I hit you with my flashlight.
- "I need you to step out of the planter, please."

  What the @%#& are you doing in there?!?!*
- "Yes, I do work here."

  What tipped you off, genius? The nametag or the dorky costume?
- "No, I'm sorry, the Tazmanian Devil is not a Disney character and, therefore, is not available for pictures in our park."

  You're an idiot.
- "I'm sorry the attraction did not meet with your expectations."

  Bite me.
- "My, that's an... interesting shirt."

  How did Security let you through the gate wearing that filth?
- "Actually, the giant golf ball is currently located at EPCOT."

  Castle = Magic Kingdom, moron.
- "Please remain calm."

  It's time to panic. You are all going to die!
- "You can purchase an E-ride ticket in the store across the street for $12 if you are staying at a Disney resort hotel."

  Magic's over, go back to your hotel room and let us go home!
- "The nearest restrooms are right there."

  See that big sign right in front of your face that says "RESTROOMS" in bold letters? It's right under that.
- "The attraction is not open yet."

  What did you think all those green and blue construction walls were up for? Decoration?
- "I'm very sorry, but because your child does not meet the height requirement for this attraction, it would be unsafe for him to ride."

  As much as I'd like to see your little brat paralyzed, I would get in trouble if it happened. Now go bother somebody else.

ing a fellow skipper who had turned him in for not following the ride's pre-approved spiel. The prankster took out a boat directly in front of his intended victim, coasted to a stop near Schweitzer Falls, and backed up into a pre-selected position. Sure enough, the second boat sped around a corner to escape the animatronic native attack and, unable to stop in time, crashed into the back of the first boat. The first skipper, pretending that his engine had failed, began shouting obscenities at his co-worker through his boat's microphone for plowing into his rudder. Guests in both boats were mortified. Our hero then grabbed his gun and ran to the back of the boat, still shouting profanities, and opened fire on the second driver. After firing his last shot, he threw his gun at the other boat, returned to his helm, and completed his ride. Needless to say, the large number of guest complaints ensured that he would never again lead a trip down the tropic waterways of the world.

The roughest—yet most rewarding—jobs are playing Mickey Mouse and the rest of the costumed characters. Nicknamed the Zoo Crew, they're primarily outgoing college students who find themselves on the receiving end of constant affection and abuse. They wear hot, heavy costumes in the Florida sun, often with poor visibility. Over the years, Disney has tried to provide them with some sort of relief, from making them work shorter "sets" to altering the costumes, including experiments to add in-costume air conditioning systems. One system consisted of plastic tubing that carried ice water throughout the costume; unfortunately, there was no way to keep the water cold. Another, using a battery-operated fan, didn't work out either.

The characters alternate between relishing the love of the adoring public and being roughed up by strangers who mistake them for their indestructible cartoon counterparts.

One six-year-old went down the line of Seven Dwarfs, kicking each one in the shin, much to the amusement of his mother.

"Children three to ten years old at the most don't think they can hurt these characters," said costumer Gene Hawk. "On television, they're run over by a steamroller. But a teenager knows there's somebody in there."

One teen kicked Mickey Mouse, so Mickey kicked him back. "Within five minutes, he was off the property," Hawk recalled. "He was one of our best Mickeys, but everyone understood. You don't do that."

The actors are constantly being watched so they remain on their best behavior and had better not fall out of character, even unintentionally. Disney paid out big settlements to a woman who was accidentally kicked in the ankle by Pluto and to a teenage girl who was humiliated when Brer Rabbit began playing with her orthopedic shoe. The company, however, fought back against parents who demanded $3 million after their four-year-old son was allegedly brutalized by a drunken Mickey Mouse. The plaintiffs claimed the young autograph-seeker had tried to get the mouse's attention by pulling on his tail, and Mickey went berserk. The mouse supposedly picked the boy up and threw him repeatedly against an iron railing near the castle. Although there was no record of the family filing a complaint, their lawyer claimed that the lad was treated at the park for a small cut on his back and that six witnesses said they smelled alcohol on the rodent's breath. Allegedly, another guest videotaped a "replacement Mickey" later apologizing to the boy. Worst of all, the family had already spent a fortune on the boy's psychological therapy, since he had "idolized Mickey Mouse, and the incident gave him feelings of mistrust, fear and anxiety that will last the rest of his life." The suit was eventually dismissed.

The costumed characters also aren't allowed to speak on stage, since they can't match exactly the characters' distinctive, commonly recognizable voices.

They're muzzled off stage, as well. To protect the illusion that those five-foot-tall creatures aren't costumed performers but real, live Disney cartoon characters, the actors must refer to themselves not as characters, but as "pageant hosts and hostesses," even to family and friends. And, talking to the press? Strictly forbidden.

Yet, in the early-to-mid-1970s, with no union representation, the characters were starting to break down under the workload. They had a particularly difficult time during the Magic Kingdom's parade to celebrate the Bicentennial. America on Parade featured 150 larger-than-life, doll-like characters dressed in period costumes—Pilgrims, Christopher Columbus, cowboys—riding floats to famous American tunes.

The costumes—eight feet tall with gigantic fiberglass heads supported by a back brace—were considerably hotter, taller and more straining than the regular character suits. The floats, consisting of oversized furniture and props, were equally awkward.

Mishaps seemed to occur on a daily basis. During one performance on a 90-degree day, five dancers on the showboat float fainted. An astronaut strapped to a rocket passed out midway through another parade. No one discovered his condition until the parade had ended and attendants began detaching his limp body from the rocket. Attendants had to be stationed at the end of the route, armed with cold, wet rags and vomit pans.

Conditions were even more dangerous in a downpour. The characters were paranoid that their giant metal back braces turned them into lightning rods. Dancing on his rain-soaked raft float, Huck Finn slipped doing a kick, fell and dislocated his shoulder.

Betsy Ross was seatbelted to a giant rocking chair. But when the float hit a bump, the rocker tipped over, taking down Betsy with it. The tricycle in a Sunday in the Park vignette was even more unstable, regularly toppling over.

Characters peered through camouflaged screens measuring just four inches tall by six inches wide. During one parade, a suffragette was dancing along Main Street, struggling to see—and smashed into a motorized gazebo.

Few conditions improved. The characters reached their boiling points after Disney switched the department's 112 full-timers from "permanent status" to two-year contracts, after which they would have to reaudition. At that point, they might be rehired for a new one-year contract, transferred into another department, or terminated.

In late summer 1981, an angry group of performers approached the *Orlando Sentinel*. They knew they weren't supposed to speak to the media. They also knew that bad press was about the only thing that seemed to get Disney's attention. Nearly two dozen past and present characters—including nine Mickeys—spoke to the reporter, two by phone, the rest in secret meetings. The writer chatted with some over coffee and smokes at a local diner. He lunched with Goofy at a pizza parlor. He unobtrusively questioned two of the Seven Dwarfs near Cinderella Castle.

The actors stressed that, on the whole, they loved their jobs. They couldn't imagine a greater joy than seeing all the smiles, sharing hugs, and knowing that each day—through family photos—they were "going home" with hundreds of visitors. Yet, sooner or later, they admitted, "The pixie dust wears off."

First, the characters wanted better pay. Stage performers like the Kids of the Kingdom, they noted, were making nearly twice as much—without any day-to-day hazards.

Second, they wanted better working conditions. The costumes could be excruciating, displacing their weight uncomfortably on their necks and backs. In fact, Disney had begun giving applicants back x-rays before hiring them as characters. The bulkier costumes, such as the bears, appeared to be intentionally designed as torture devices; if performers got on a supervisor's bad side, they might find themselves banished to work as Baloo or Brer Bear.

The outfits could also get disgusting, despite the company's promise to launder the exteriors at least once a week and the interiors more frequently. Considering the high volume of sweat generated, the cleanings weren't often enough.

As well, some guests used the characters as punching bags. Parents would tell kids to go kick the characters or pull their tails, so they could snap a hilarious photo. Adults would blow cigarette smoke into the costumes' ventilation holes. Other guests tried to trip characters or pull their heads off. Mickey was stabbed in the hand with a pencil. A drunk tourist dragged Goofy across Fantasyland. Teenagers tossed Brer Bear in the Jungle Cruise river. A man shoved Winnie the Pooh in the face until he broke her nose. Someone shot Dumbo with a pellet gun. At least one Pluto wore a protective cup in case he was kicked between the legs.

The characters told the reporter about the day Mickey Mouse fell from the top of a parade float onto the blacktop of Main Street. She badly cut her head, but managers refused to allow her to take off her head until she could be carried backstage, out of sight of guests. It took four months to recover from her lacerations and bruises. When she finally returned to work, she was reassigned to a different department.

When the article appeared, management was livid. Del Schilling, director of the Entertainment division, wrote a letter to be distributed to the characters. He cautioned them that they were not to speak to the press without company permission. "Walt Disney World has a professional publicity department and insists that all interviews go through that area," Schilling wrote. He didn't want them going around spoiling children's illusions—or anyone else's—"by telling them regular folks are inside the furry costumes."

The characters sneered at the letter. To the public, Disney preached that its cast members were the heart of the company. In training, Disney told characters that they were entrusted with the most important, magical roles imaginable. Yet, privately, it referred to them as "regular folks."

The same day, the *New York Times* came calling. Nine characters agreed to meet the journalist at a motel they had selected, following a late night of rehearsals. As they arrived for the midnight meeting, they showed their Disney employee identification cards and, as further proof of position, photos of themselves half in costume, half out.

They repeated their litany of woes. Eeyore complained of the rigors of wearing a 35-pound donkey head. Brer Bear said he stuck a thermometer inside his pelt one day and got a reading of 130 degrees. Pluto, outfitted with steel taps and other metal parts, was concerned he'd be struck by lightning. Several said they were regularly groped by young men trying to discover if there was a woman inside the costume.

Basically, they were tired of being treated like animals. They felt they should be paid like entertainers, and given better job security and a little respect from management.

For Disney's side of the story, *The Times* quoted publicity director Charlie Ridgway, who after decades of experience that began in the early days of Disneyland, should have been able to choose his words more sensitively. Ridgway defended the two-year contract as "fairly routine in show business." He stressed that characters shouldn't consider their positions permanent, since "after a while they lose their verve. They get burned out, it becomes old hat to them."

Then in explaining their low pay, Ridgway said that playing a character "is a non-professional job. The Kids of the Kingdom are singers and dancers, professional performers, and they are paid for it. But the characters, you can take almost any person, someone with only the ability to move, and train them to be a character in a short period."

As soon as *The Times* article appeared, television stations, newspapers, everyone from the BBC to *People Magazine*, jumped on the story. Disney had had enough. Management consented to improve working conditions and increase pay the following year, but the interviews had to stop. Any more would trigger a witch hunt, with terminations to follow. The vice president of entertainment called a meeting of the characters and warned, "About the articles, I don't care who spoke. Everything that's done is already past. But let me give you some advice. Cut the interviews because things could get nasty. You're not complying with Disney policy. And someone could get fired."

The furor died down. The next summer, the characters voted to unionize, joining the host and hostess category of the Services Trades Council

Contract of Teamsters.

At Disney World, membership in a union does not guarantee discernible perks. Employees who don't pay dues are entitled to the same pay and benefits as those who do, since Florida is a "right-to-work" state—or "right-to-freeload," as union members charge.

In the early days of Disney World, many employees—trusting that daddy Disney in management would take care of them—saw no need for a union at all. But, due to corporate's fear of the damage unions could inflict on the company's image, they decided in the late 1960s not to fight any attempts to unionize by the hourly workers.

"Some of us who had been [in Florida] a while realized that we didn't need to have unions," said Pat Vaughn, head of Employee Relations. "But we were overruled by decisions made in California. They were afraid that if we took positions away from the Teamsters or the electrical workers down here, that this would reverberate out there. And they didn't want any problems. So they just said don't resist them. The decision was made that we would not *freely* open up our workforce to union organization. But we would allow [organizers] to come on our property in certain areas and solicit cards, and if they could get a certain number of cards of the workforce, a certain percentage, then they could petition to come to negotiate a contract."

The union solicitors would collect a large number of cards, but—due to the park's notoriously high turnover—by the time they turned them in to Disney, too many of the signers had quit.

Another obstacle to recruitment was the organizers themselves. "A bunch of thugs would hang around in our parking lot, at the employee entrance in the back," Vaughn recalled. "We wouldn't allow any of them on our property where the guests were. They didn't understand that we were dealing with bright-eyed, young, energetic people at their first job. And the unions sent out their typical union-organizing thugs—older people, skuzzy looking people—to try to sign up our kids, and it wasn't working. They finally got smarter and started sending out younger people."

By 1972, the organizers finally gathered enough cards, and Disney agreed to negotiate, with the provision that—to avoid dealing with as many as two dozen individual unions—groups of unions form coalitions to be bound by master contracts.

As the contracts neared the end of their terms, union representatives would attempt to negotiate improved deals for their members. Typically employees voted to reject Disney's first or second offer before acquiescing to a final proposal that wasn't much better. Cast members seemed generally displeased with whatever they ended up with, but figured they didn't have much of a choice. Fewer than half of all employees belonged to a union and a large percentage of those who did join did not bother to vote. Worse, the unions dealt from an inherently weak position. Disney appeared to receive an endless supply of job applications and tolerated the unions more for public relations than anything else. More importantly, Disney owned thousands of acres of property surrounding its theme park and hotels, so any strike would be confined to surface streets miles away from the target of the protest.

"Picketing would be difficult due to the size of the property and the use of highways as entrances to the property," confirmed shop steward Frank Kubicki. "Walt Disney World has strike contingency plans to use managers and non-union office and technical workers to staff the resort. Despite these obstacles, Disney negotiates with the labor unions due to its fear that a strike could cause a massive impact on its profits and seriously disrupt the Central Florida economy. Most importantly, Disney knows that a contract obligates the labor union to have the workers use grievances and collective bargaining to get what they want from the company instead of engaging in disruptive activity, such as character employees removing their heads in the presence of customers."

Most cast members deduced it would do no good to walk out. One group did try. In late October 1981, 109 Disney World musicians went on strike after their contract expired and negotiations broke down. They had voted 78 to 25 to reject a three-year contract offering an eight to nine percent annual cost-of-living raise. The performers wanted a three-year pact with wage increases in line with the government's cost-of-living index. They peacefully walked the corner of S.R. 535 and Apopka-Vineland Road, carrying signs and playing their instruments.

The next day, about 750 construction workers walked off the EPCOT Center jobsite to support the picketing union musicians. Nearly 300 of them joined the musicians on the picket line. EPCOT construction came to a standstill. Disney, however, could play hardball. Company attorneys convinced the contractors to return to work by reminding them that their own labor agreement prohibited strikes and sympathy walkouts. Then, to discourage others from following suit, Disney filed a $100,000 lawsuit against the musicians' union in federal court, accusing them of fostering an illegal secondary boycott by the construction workers.

The strike did affect guests, minimally. Disney cancelled most live music at the park and in the hotel lounges. The name entertainers scheduled to perform at the Top of the World Club—Frankie Laine, the Spinners, and Peaches and Herb—bowed out to honor the picket lines. They were replaced by non-union musical acts.

Park attendance was unaffected. Most vacationers didn't even know there was a strike. Eight days later, the musicians reluctantly accepted a contract similar to the one they had rejected. The 30-month deal provided an 8.5-percent increase in base pay, as well as bonuses for musicians who played more than one instrument during a performance or who played for more than an hour without a break. In addition, Disney agreed to drop its lawsuit against the union and form a communications committee to discuss employee complaints. Employees' frustration would only increase.

Into the mid-1970s, the employee turnover rate began accelerating. With so much training invested in every cast member, the revolving door was costing the company a fortune. Management, accustomed to a never-ending stream of applications, had no answers. Personnel decided to interview employees to figure out what was making them flee in such significant numbers. Most of them blamed "The Hassle Factor."

Pat Vaughn explained, "The Hassle Factor included a lot of things, like driving all the way from east Orlando, maybe 20 miles to go to work. Then having to park in a parking lot, get on a bus, go to the back of the Magic Kingdom to Wardrobe, go to your locker, turn in your costume from the day before, get a new costume, get in your costume, walk in a tunnel the length of the Magic Kingdom, go up to your work assignment. When you think about the time and the effort it took to get from east Orlando to that work assignment, it was big. The whole thing was a hassle. The distance, the cost of gasoline, the bus ride, the way they were treated at Wardrobe, and having to walk all that way." Disney did pay employees for an additional fifteen minutes to cover "walking time," but it was little consolation.

Adding EPCOT Center could only worsen the problem. Human Resources had to make Burbank aware of the situation. Vaughn was cho-

sen to brief the board of directors during a meeting that had been intended as a cheery, optimistic planning session for EPCOT. "Gentlemen," he
announced, "I wish I had better news, but the news I have for you is
unless we can stem this turnover problem, there is no way we can open
EPCOT. We're spending the first three days of every week just replacing
the people who are leaving the Magic Kingdom. And we're spending the
last couple days of the week adding people to the Magic Kingdom. Now
to think about supporting another [3,500] people at EPCOT Center with
this condition, it can't be done." He then reviewed the numbers to prove
his point. To his surprise, the executives agreed and told him he had their
backing to do what he had to do, so long as he solved the problem.

Change had to start at the top. Many supervisors, unaware that the
labor pipeline was drying up, were placing unreasonable demands on
employees. Their attitude was, "It's my way, or the highway. I-4 runs
both ways. You took it coming in here; you can take it going out."

Human Resources launched an intensive "reorientation" program to
sensitize top management of the operating divisions, who in turn made
their supervisors and lower-level managers aware of the Hassle Factor.
Each of them then had to identify which parts of the problem they had
some control over. H.R. met weekly with key people from each division
to review the number of employees lost during the week prior. The
updates revealed not only how many workers they were losing, but
where they were being lost. "So," Vaughn said, "if someone from a particular division was exceeding his trend lines, all the other guys said,
'Hey, you're the one who's hurting us.' So there was a lot of peer pressure brought to bear. Everyone got serious about it. We slowly turned it
around to the point where the first three days of the week we weren't
replacing turnover, then the first two days. We got down to one day, and
then we could do the additions to the Magic Kingdom and the big push
for EPCOT."

Recruitment hit a snag in 1979, when a second energy crisis hit. So
Disney built a cast-members-only gas station behind the Magic Kingdom. The company contracted with Gulf, which operated the Car Care
Center in front of the park, to supply the gasoline. Disney ran the station
itself, selling the gas to employees at cost. Cast members, said Vaughn,
"could buy their gas cheaper there than they could at other places in the
county. I'm not sure that the gas made the employees' lives all that easier, but it was a symbol that this company recognized the problem and

did something about it. It sent a message to employees that we really cared and wanted to work with them to help stem this turnover problem."

As the rate of turnover became more manageable, Disney now needed to identify new sources of future labor. It had basically exhausted the local market for front-line service jobs. The focus turned to universities. Since before opening the Magic Kingdom, the company had worked with colleges to locate small numbers of choice workers. It started by forming relationships with local college placement offices. In 1970, Disney launched a cooperative program in which students could alternate between a semester at school and a semester at work that qualified for college credit if the duties related to their studies. Later, the program expanded to formal internships.

With EPCOT Center on the horizon, it needed a larger program that kept the bodies coming. But since most hourly positions at Disney World provided little educational value, they instead would offer weekly seminars on Disney-style management. Full-time students could then fill positions in attractions, fast foods, custodial, guest relations, ticket sales, merchandise, hotels and as lifeguards. In return, they received college credits, work experience, and the golden stamp of "Disney" on their résumés.

In the spring of 1980, Disney recruiters visited the University of Alabama, University of Georgia, and University of North Carolina-Chapel Hill to gauge interest for summer internships among students as well as the colleges that they hoped would grant participants academic credit. According to Vaughn, "The way we convinced the colleges was we said, 'Look, the student has already paid for a seat in your classroom. Now if you send them down to us, you can fill that seat with another student.' They saw that financially to their advantage. And they also saw the opportunity of the combination of work and study."

Students clamored for the opportunity. During the initial trips, recruiters selected 250 students to work at the Magic Kingdom for the summer and live off-property.

The program was so well received, recruiters took their first official trips the following spring—to 43 different schools. They hired 248 students. Now they had to figure out where to put them. The company leased an abandoned trailer park in nearby Kissimmee and moved the ramshackle homes off the property. They then contacted the Fleetwood trailer distributor who had supplied temporary housing for the athletes at the Squaw Valley Olympics. He specially designed 32 trailers for Disney. Each unit had a central kitchen and relaxation area, and four bedroom wings, two students to a bedroom. The trailer park already featured a swimming pool, recreation center, and full-time security guard. Disney called the place "Snow White Village."

The village, like the apartment complexes that would later replace it, took on a fraternity row atmosphere. "They got so many complaints from the [neighboring] KOA. The loud music, the screaming," said early College Programmer Gwen Van Voorhis. "One night we lined up on the Snow White boundary and were mooning the sheriff's deputies."

The furnishings were relatively primitive, never intended for many years of use. "We thought trailers were cheap for a billion-dollar company," Van Voorhis said. "There were no phones in the trailers. You had to stand outside [at the pay phone] and be eaten by mosquitoes. You'd stand forever in line to do your laundry. You'd see armadillos and different creatures. Someone cut a hole in the fence from a farm next door and about once a week there'd be cows walking through the campground."

Yet most College Programmers didn't seem to mind the accommodations. The program was a hit. More students and colleges began showing an interest. So, recruiters headed out again in the fall, this time to hire students for the spring. By now, 63 schools wanted to participate—with openings for just 345 jobs. From a particular college, Disney might hire five out of 300 prospects. The demand allowed Disney to expand the College Program over the next ten years to several hundred colleges from which they would hire 1,200 students three times a year—for ten-week terms every spring, summer, and fall.

Ideally, Disney hoped to staff the World Showcase pavilions at EPCOT Center using an international version of the College Program. They thought that having guests walk into an elaborate recreation of Japan only to be greeted by a blonde-haired teen with a Southern accent would spoil the entire show. Plus, the program could help promote the rationale behind the cultural exchange of World Showcase—foreign nationals could bring a little bit of their home countries to the U.S., and then return to their homeland with a little bit of the U.S. Planners envisioned the program as the "greatest U.N. ever created," which would promote world peace. Imagine the leader of an Arab country allying himself with a leader of Israel because of their days working side by side at EPCOT.

Tracking down international students would require more effort than delivering recruitment speeches at local colleges. At first, Human Resources suggested advertising in major areas of the country, such as Philadelphia, that had heavy ethnic populations. Perhaps they could find first-, second-, or third-generation immigrants willing to relocate to Central Florida.

When that didn't pan out, Disney realized it was going to have to actually go to the countries and find the employees—a daunting proposition considering how fruitless the search for international sponsors had been. Fortunately, organizations such as the American Field Service had been helping to arrange cultural exchanges for decades. AFS typically used "work-study" J visas to bring international students into the U.S., where they would attend school and be placed with a host family for up to a year. The J visa had been established by Congress in 1948 to encourage temporary swapping of citizens from various countries, build up international relationships, and help the participants build up knowledge and skills. Participants visited for a preset length of time, had to retain a permanent residence abroad, and had to return home when their visa expired, typically after one semester, one year, or two years at most. As intended, the J visa would allow the likes of foreign medical school graduates, teachers, scholars and camp counselors to broaden their expertise and experiences in America and then return to share what they had learned with their home country.

Disney field-tested the idea in the summer of 1980 by having eight students—one each from the United Kingdom, France, Mexico, Japan, Italy, Canada, Costa Rica, and Germany—who were finishing up the AFS program, delay their return home to work at the Magic Kingdom for the summer. For seven weeks, the youths lived with the families of Disney employees, and attended courses in Disney management philosophy when they weren't working at It's a Small World, the Plaza Pavilion restaurant, or the shops along Main Street.

Disney repeated the experiment the following summer, importing fifteen foreign students to work at the Magic Kingdom and live for ten weeks with the College Program kids at Snow White Village.

Next, Disney needed to find about 100 qualified youths willing to give them a whole year—and the legal means to do so. Working with the state department and immigration control, Disney lobbyists in Washington, D.C., received permission to issue J visas.

For the first year's recruits, Disney enlisted the aid of the International Association of Students in Economic and Commercial Sciences in Brussels, Belgium. The association provided a list of nominees, 20 to 30 names per country, from which Disney would choose about half. In January 1982, company representatives traveled to Europe to interview the applicants. To open EPCOT Center, they hired 85 foreign students to fill a portion of the 400 on-stage World Showcase positions. The inaugural class arrived in Orlando one month before the park opened.

In later years, Disney recruiters would take four-week recruiting trips every spring and fall. They would travel from city to city throughout North America, Europe, Asia and Africa, screening a two-hour film and a slide show presentation. Following interviews, they provided the choice applicants with J visa applications to complete and submit to the U.S. Embassy in their country. The embassy would forward the documents to Disney, which would authorize the kids to come to the U.S. for one year and then return home.

For the most part, the government left it up to Disney to perform necessary background checks. "They knew we were going to select the cream of the crop, and we did," Vaughn said. "They knew that we would be mobbed with applicants who wanted to come over for a year and be at Disney. You can imagine if some kid from Podunk College in Ohio wanted to come here, how much some kid in France or Morocco or Italy would want to come."

Participants were required to be college students, with good academic records, fluent in English, unmarried, friendly, outgoing, and agreeable to a full year's commitment.

To promote better understanding of different cultures, four international students—each from a different country—were assigned to a three-bedroom apartment with two American students. They would spend four days a week working in their respective World Showcase pavilion in a key "guest contact" position. A fifth day would be devoted to seminars on business management or cultural studies.

They were paid a stipend "large enough to cover living expenses," though much of it went right back to Disney to pay for the living quarters and bus transportation. In most cases, Disney paid for the students' roundtrip airfares. Some were sponsored by World Showcase participants, such as Dos Equis to staff the Mexico pavilion or Tokyo's Mitsukoshi department store to work in EPCOT's Japan.

Certainly, a number of students experienced culture shock. Disney learned that it had to walk newcomers through the apartment to demonstrate how the dishwasher, garbage disposal and other appliances worked. One student from China puzzled over a toaster. "What does it do?" he asked.

"You put bread in it," the cultural office representative replied.

"What's bread?" the man asked.

One German student wondered why he had been assigned to wear leather pants and sell cuckoo clocks. During his entire life in Germany, he'd never before worn lederhosen or even seen a cuckoo clock.

Some students were surprised to learn that deodorant, while optional in their home country, was mandatory at EPCOT. Girls from Paris discovered that their elaborate makeup was forbidden, while several from London were prevented from wearing multiple earrings in each ear.

The rules caused several students to contact the French Embassy in Washington, D.C., to report that they were being horribly mistreated. They implored the ambassador for help. He immediately called Pat Vaughn. "What's going on down there?" the ambassador demanded. Vaughn explained how the International Program worked and said that no other groups of students had complained, but promised to look into the problem. "I arranged to meet with the French students," Vaughn later related, "We had all 25 or 30 of them gather, and, as the French can be, they were just irate. They were hollering and screaming. We could hardly make any sense out of it. They were complaining about Snow White Village. 'You bring us over here, and you put us in trailers!' We had buses running to the park to Snow White Village all the time. I tried to answer their questions. Finally I said, 'You know, we have this many Moroccans. We have this many Germans. We have this many Italians. We have this many Japanese. This many Chinese. And we're not hearing these problems from them. What is it that we're doing or not doing for the French that's different from everybody else?' And the answer was, 'But we are French.' That was it. And I said, 'Well, there's nothing I can do about it. You're French. That's your problem. Here's what we have available for you.' Finally they calmed down. I think all they needed to hear was, 'We're not treating you any differently than we are anyone else,' and 'We're not having problems elsewhere.'"

Yet, almost from the start, the company could tell that the over-whelmed, crumbling trailer park couldn't accommodate both the International and College programs for long. It soon began laying the groundwork to build the first of several apartment complexes to house its fast-growing student worker population.

Near the end of their year of duty, International Programmers were sent off with an emotional graduation ceremony. Once free of Disney's protective custody, participants were expected to return promptly to their native country. Many would be homesick and head straight for the airport. Some students might do a little sightseeing through America first. Others might never catch a return flight.

"It was not our responsibility to see that they got home," said Vaughn. "Immigration had their names and [knew] that they were here for a year. At the end of the year, they were counseled by us and by the manager of their pavilion that they were to return home. That was the deal. But it was not our responsibility to see that they did. There were no opportunities for young people to work in Morocco. They had this year over here [at Disney World], and they would just sort of meld into the community. And there was nothing we could do about it, and Immigration didn't do anything about it. They could still be here, working in restaurants and such."

Minor problems aside, with the International and College programs Disney had uncovered a near-limitless, continually-replenishing source of labor, college kids who worked hard—and really cheap.

Graduation Day

By Tyler Schwartz, Canada International Program participant, 2000

One of the biggest highlights for Walt Disney World International students is Graduation Day. Around eleven months into your twelve-month contract, each "IP" receives an engraved invitation to their graduation ceremony. The ceremony takes place in the early morning on the last Thursday of every month inside the Germany pavilion, although for years it was held in the American Gardens Theatre.

Generally, graduates wake up at about 5 a.m. or, as is more often the case, they just don't go to bed the night before. There are usually many small early-morning get-togethers on that day for orange juice/champagne toasts. The girls get together to do each other's hair, and so on. Around 6 a.m., the participants board their shuttle buses to EPCOT. On any given Graduation Day, I would estimate that there are 150 to 200 people graduating.

Once arriving backstage at EPCOT, the graduates are assigned their graduation gowns and given a corsage, a unique "graduate Mickey" pin, and—best of all—their own pair of mouse ears, complete with a graduation tassel and their name embroidered on the back. They then load onto the double-decker buses that used to travel around World Showcase and are driven to the Germany pavilion.

Outside of the pavilion, there is a large reception area set up with coffee, juices, doughnuts and muffins, all very nicely displayed. The graduates mingle here as they are arranged in order to enter the building. This is a really nice time because you graduate with people that you arrived with. Often they drift apart through the year as everyone befriends their roommates and workmates. Graduation Day is a great time to reacquaint with the friends you arrived in Florida with a year earlier and reminisce about the early days.

Before the graduates enter the biergarten, their friends, managers and sometimes family members who have come a long way to see the event are already seated inside waiting for the grand entrance. Once everyone is organized, the processional music plays—often the processional theme to *Star Wars!*—and the IPs enter grouped in their country of origin. There is always lots of applause, flag-waving, and chanting from the crowd assembled inside as the graduates enter.

Once the graduates are seated, the ceremony gets started. It's quite a classy affair. They are usually welcomed by the manager of the International Program, who makes a nice speech touching on the importance of the IPs and the number of guest comments that management receives complimenting them. Then there is a guest speaker, usually of upper management such as the vice president of EPCOT. The World Showcase entertainment groups take turns entertaining; one month it might be Off Kilter, the next might be Voices of Liberty, or the instrumental group from Norway. Graduates often get up and dance.

After the speeches and entertainment, the diplomas are awarded. Unlike the College Program, the International Participants aren't required to take an educational component during their time in Florida, so these diplomas are really just certificates commemorating the year. Still very nice.

A special guest appears to hand out diplomas—Mickey Mouse dressed in a graduation gown and hat! A huge cheer goes up when he appears. Each participant is called on stage by name and handed the diploma by one of his managers from the pavilion. Everyone cheers for their friends and workmates as each name is called.

After everyone has received their diploma, each nationality group gathers on stage to have their group picture taken with Mickey. These photos are complimentary and available for pick-up a few days later. Then everyone exits the biergarten to the reception area outside. People congregate and linger here for about an hour while everyone takes pictures in their gowns.

But the best is yet to come—because Graduation Day is traditionally Drinking around the World Day! After the ceremony, groups of friends gather to eat lunch at a World Showcase restaurant. Usually, the graduates and other friends who have the day off will go eat lunch in their own pavilion. After lunch, the drinking starts! Drinking around the World involves stopping in each pavilion and having a drink or two before moving on to the next stop.

Some groups start on the Mexican side of the lagoon and work toward Canada, while others go in the other direction. Usually by the time they reach the American Adventure, everyone is feeling really good—until the realization that they are only halfway through!

Unfortunately, some people get a little too silly, and there are many stories of people being terminated on their Graduation Day for getting out of hand. Most common are people getting caught drinking under age in their own pavilion or working cast members giving away free drinks to their off-duty friends (in which case both get terminated). In fact, things have been known to get so out of hand that security cast members often go undercover on Graduation Days in order to monitor the graduation parties. This is often how the "free drink providers" are caught and terminated.

After they have finished their journey around the World Showcase, graduates gather for one last viewing of Illuminations. Somehow, even though they've seen it countless times, the graduates always get emotional at this moment. (It may have something to do with all that alcohol!)

Those left standing after EPCOT closes then head for a night of partying at Pleasure Island. Thursday nights are cast member nights at PI, so it's always a great party—Graduation Day or not.

12

EPTPOT

OPERATIONALLY, the park's layout and sheer size forced Disney to do things a little differently at EPCOT Center. Without Utilidors, employees reached their work stations by riding a bus around the berm. Because it would take the first guests a while to trek from the front gate to the far end of the lagoon, management decided to open World Showcase several hours after Future World—a departure from Walt's insistence that, since guests disliked being teased by closed facilities, every available operation should be running whenever his park was open. During peak season, Future World was planned to open at 8 or 9 a.m., depending on demand, and World Showcase at 11 a.m., and they would both close at midnight. During the slow season, Future World would open at 9 a.m. and Showcase as late as 2 p.m. Both would close at 10 p.m.

As the October 1 deadline neared, much of the park looked ready to go—at least on the surface. The show elements had been installed in most of the attractions, and ride operators were undergoing intensive training. So Disney, as it regularly did with new attractions at the Magic Kingdom, held low-key "soft openings" of EPCOT during the two weeks before its official unveiling. There was no advertising; cast members spread the word to family, friends and guests at the Magic Kingdom and on-property hotels that they could preview portions of the new park at no charge. Hopefully, Disney figured, guests who got in for free would better tolerate the inevitable malfunctions and breakdowns.

The testing revealed that the more complicated ride systems had more bugs than could be worked out by opening day. The biggest culprit was Exxon's Universe of Energy, which was controlled by three computer systems. During the ride, individual cars joined together to form one massive, 540-person vehicle. They sat on a turntable that floated on air and could be commanded to stop within an eighth of an inch of a designated spot. The seats were pulled together by one-eighth-inch cable, and if they didn't piece together perfectly, everything shut down. The theater walls retracted into the floor and ceiling and if they weren't exactly flush, they would be struck by the seats, also shutting down the ride. A master computer communicated with two computers onboard each car. If the computers lost contact with each other, the ride stopped. The onboard computers also responded to a wire buried in the floor to do the steering. The cars were partially powered by solar collectors on the building's roof. There were sensors in the doors and in the show computer. And everything could be thrown out of whack by an unexpected charge of static electricity—as Disney discovered on dry days when guests shuffled across the carpeting and then slid onto the long seats. By opening day, the Energy pavilion had an "Operational Readiness Index" of 54 percent, about the same as Space Mountain when it first opened, but meaning it ran properly barely half the time.

Spaceship Earth employed WED's time-tested Omnimover ride system. But whereas the systems on rides like the Haunted Mansion pulled long trains of vehicles over a series of tiny hills, Spaceship Earth pulled its loads up one giant hill—90 feet up and then 90 feet back down again, causing vastly fluctuating pressures and strains. The designers did what they could to try to balance the loads and stresses, so the cars were able to climb the incline, but not come down the other side too fast. As much as they thought they had perfected it, they discovered the pressures varied wildly once they were carrying live passengers, wiggling in their seats.

To achieve a more adult feel at the park, Disney had top-loaded EPCOT's roster of attractions with movies. Film crews were given two years to produce eleven major film projects to be shown on 121 projectors, including three CircleVision epics, dozens of film loops to support attractions, and the 70mm, 3-D movie *Magic Journeys*, which wasn't completed until five days before opening day. They were all on time.

MAJESTIC ENTRY. Thousands of colorful flowers filled the courtyard entry leading to EPCOT Center's iconic Spaceship Earth. (1983) *Photo by Dale M. McDonald; Reprinted courtesy State Archives of Florida*

Yet even the film attractions had problems in previews, since most of the audio and video controls were linked to EPCOT Computer Central. If a single wire became crimped, the projector could not read the directions it was being sent. The computers were also sensitive to temperature and humidity, so their performance suffered whenever their environment grew too hot, humid, dry or dusty. The actual repairs were usually quick and easy, but the show still had to be evacuated, tested and reset to the beginning.

Kodak's Journey into Imagination dark ride had an equally innovative ride system tied to a series of intricate special effects, and designers were working with a sponsor that signed on late. The show's creators had solved the problem of how to introduce new characters and tell a story in a dark ride by engaging the vehicles with a gear mechanism and for four minutes rotating them around a turntable of scenes. "Hopefully, at the end of the four minutes, you've fallen in love with little Figment and you understand who the Dreamfinder is, and now you travel out on an adventure with them as they imagine things for art and literature and science," said co-creator Tony Baxter. "So you had a very complicated ride interfacing with this giant gear. And, you had all these special effects."

Weeks before opening day, management decided to postpone Journey into Imagination until Christmas. "The show was ready to go, everything was running, and they made the call that the show was not perfected enough to guarantee the reliability they wanted," Baxter said. "You get it up, there are all these people in it, it breaks down, and then they're all mad and everybody in line is mad. Disney doesn't like that. Especially when you're under the gun, with the press there. It's an awful way to see something."

Disney would have loved more time to test every attraction, but ready or not came October 1. The night before, construction crews frantically worked around the clock, walling off unfinished exhibits and using bulldozers to shove mountains of dirt behind colorful barricades.

Since the media-directed ceremonies were scheduled for three weeks later, the first day's agenda was more limited. Card Walker delivered a brief dedication speech, reminiscent of those delivered years before by Walt at Disneyland and Roy at the Magic Kingdom. As Walt and Roy had seemingly willed open those parks, Walker seemed satisfied that he similarly had completed phase one of Walt's final dream. That evening he would inform the board of directors that he was ready to retire. After Walker's speech, Governor Bob Graham and the president of AT&T added their own remarks. Marching bands and dance troupes performed, accompanied by fog and smoke machines and the release of 15,000 balloons and 1,000 pigeons.

At the same time, fireworks were starting to brew about 100 yards away. Due to space limitations, only press, special guests, and a hand-selected "first family" had been allowed inside the park to witness the dedication ceremony. The thousands of real guests were left in the sweltering parking lot. Some booed through the front gates. Many complained. They thought that Disney should at least have set up a big television screen and loudspeakers. Instead, they would have to watch the festivities on the evening news.

Ninety minutes after the gates opened, a wheel in one of the cars on Spaceship Earth missed a cam and shut the attraction down. About 200 guests were evacuated and the vehicle had to be "jogged back into the system" before the ride could restart. The park's signature attraction was closed for two hours, then broke down again a few hours later.

Later in the morning, about 2,000 people were emptied from the Universe of Energy when a car suddenly stopped. The car was repaired, but the show halted again moments later when one of the attraction's twelve movie projectors broke down. Shortly afterward, the CircleVision movie in Canada also went down.

Then came the "lunch rush." Crowds swarmed every eatery. Several restaurants ran out of food. Lines grew to 30 minutes for an ale at the English pub, 45 minutes for a pastry at the French bakery. The sit-down restaurants filled up so fast, they stopped taking reservations.

Into the afternoon, the problems mounted. The down escalator quit working at the Imagination pavilion. In the World of Motion, the cars kept stopping and restarting. The sound equipment performed just as poorly. Sometimes, the narration was garbled; other times it played too fast or was totally inaudible. By this time, cast members were permanently positioned in front of the Energy pavilion to inform guests that the ride would reopen in some time between ten minutes and two hours. Every performance at the American Adventure was different, because its computer system was not yet fully integrated, forcing engineers to stand under the stage and physically operate parts of the show. Sometimes the animatronic Ben Franklin felt like standing up and climbing the stairs to speak with Thomas Jefferson, and sometimes he preferred to remain seated. Curiously, the Mexico boat ride, which wasn't even expected to even be completed by opening day because it required so much electrical work, was one of the few attractions that didn't break down.

As the afternoon sun grew hotter, so did the guests. Visitors could be overheard grumbling about the constant breakdowns, the long lines, and of "boycotting EPCOT" to get their $15 admission refunded. They thought it was outrageous that they had to, in essence, pay a cover charge to spend the day doing nothing but standing in endless lines.

Guests were also physically exhausted. EPCOT Center had a fraction of the attractions of the Magic Kingdom yet twice the acreage, and therefore required an inordinate amount of walking. A stroll just around the lake was well over a mile long.

Disney didn't release official attendance figures, but the outside estimate was upwards of 25,000 — nearly twice the number of guests expected. The tally did not include one gate-crasher, who soared down into Future World in a motor-powered hang-glider. Seconds after his feet hit the ground, security pounced on the trespasser and escorted him backstage. Disney quietly released the man without pressing charges, merely warning him of the "dangers" he presented to others. Disney hoped their quiet handling would keep the stunt out of the press, explaining that the man escaped arrest because he had been a construction worker on Spaceship Earth.

Management immediately began making adjustments. For EPCOT's second day, they pulled about 50 food service workers from the Magic Kingdom to join the 80 last-minute transfers already working at EPCOT. Henceforth, the Magic Kingdom would become a "feeder pool" for EPCOT, sending cast members over whenever it looked like EPCOT would be egregiously short-handed.

Disney also added two beverage carts in Future World, four carts in World Showcase, a picnic lunch facility in front of the American Adventure, and a snack counter in Germany. "We were the cold wrap sandwich king of the world, just so we could feed our guests," said Bill Sullivan, EPCOT's director of operations.

However, at World Showcase restaurants, wait times would remain long, and Disney was okay with that. The restaurants were never designed to handle capacity crowds. "We feel very strongly that we want people to be able to sit down and feel as though they are in France in a French restaurant, to have that kind of feeling," Nunis rationalized. "You're not talking about handling a lot of people in one day."

Nunis anticipated that the lines would get shorter during the peak seasons, when the mix of guests would include more tourists, who seemed to prefer fast food. The off-season drew a larger percentage of Florida residents, who were more likely to opt for specialty dining experiences.

Tourists, in actuality, were more easily confused. They usually spent a good deal of time waiting in long lines in front of the restaurants before learning that they weren't waiting to eat; they were waiting to make a reservation to return later in the day—if they were lucky. By mid-morning, seating times at almost every restaurant had filled up for both lunch and dinner. Upon learning this news, guests inevitably groaned and headed for the next country, only to encounter even long lines.

To work the World Showcase pavilions, Disney decided to immediately hire 500 more employees. Ideally, they would speak both English and the language of their host pavilion—or at least be vaguely familiar with the country's culture and customs.

To ease the walking problem, Disney ordered 186 more benches to add to the 272 benches already in the park. They also planned to spread the word that many of the planters had been designed for seating. Disney considered running a PeopleMover through Future World, but thought its money would be better spent on transportation through the more exhausting World Showcase. Two double-decker buses, each holding about 30 passengers, were currently in operation. Three more were under construction and ready to be completed by the end of October. After that, they planned to build two more. Two 100-seat boats already circled the 40-acre lagoon from Canada, past Japan, to Germany. Disney vowed to add two more boats and a fourth dock near Mexico, so boats could travel back and forth from the front to the back of World Showcase, either between Mexico and Germany or between Canada and Japan.

The attraction breakdowns, unfortunately, were a fact of life for the time being. "I don't like any downtime, but the shows are so sophisticated that it just takes some shake-down time," Nunis admitted. He noted that some rides, including Spaceship Earth, had been running only a few days. He even divulged that when Big Thunder Railroad opened at the Magic Kingdom the previous year, it broke down multiple times every day for months. Nunis promised that EPCOT's attractions would run smoother once operators gained more experience—and rest, after having worked 70 to 80 hours a week to get the park opened.

Sure enough, on day two, similarly large crowds packed EPCOT Center. Spaceship Earth and the Universe of Energy were down most of the morning and for long stretches in the afternoon. Wait times conse-

DOUBLE UP. EPCOT Center rush-ordered additional doubledecker buses to relieve foot-weary visitors. (1983) *Photo by Dale M. McDonald; Reprinted courtesy State Archives of Florida*

quently grew to over an hour at the operable attractions, including high-capacity, low-expectation rides like The Land boat ride.

"If we didn't have the Magic Kingdom as an example, maybe we wouldn't be as disappointed," complained one New Jersey tourist. "But we've come to expect perfection from Disney, and this is a fiasco." She said that, except for World of Motion, every ride she visited broke down while she was waiting in line.

To add to the frustration, even cash registers at some restaurants, drinking fountains, and a bank of pay phones would not work. One sun-scorched tourist sighed, "With all the high technology, you'd expect that they would have water fountains that would work."

Crowds remained about twice as large as originally forecast throughout the first week. Attractions and even the park's centrally controlled air conditioning system continued to go on the fritz.

Management held out hope that enough attractions would be operable to make a good first impression for the official opening weekend. Yet reporters were omnipresent during EPCOT's entire first month. Since the corporate sponsors were so integral to the park, Participant Affairs didn't want anyone to get lost in the frenzy of a single grand opening. Consequently, the opening of EPCOT, said Steve Baker, "overall was easier [than the Magic Kingdom] because we spread it out over [24] days of October. We had a grand opening of a pavilion almost every day. We managed each one from client relations' point of view. We had partners in every pavilion, so we'd do something special for a different one every day."

On October 13, executives of the LaBatt Brewing Co. were in town for the dedication of the Canada pavilion, which they co-sponsored. During the ceremony, the executives noticed that the Imagineers had named the pavilion's make-believe mineshaft "Moosehcad Mine" — unaware that LaBatt's chief competitor was Moosehead Beer. Immediately, workmen removed the offensive sign, and Imagineers began brainstorming for a less controversial name.

In fact, just selling alcohol inside a theme park was an education for Disney. Every facility serving beer and wine required its own liquor license. Management also needed to prevent guests from ambling away with open drink containers in hand, turning World Showcase into a mobile Happy Hour.

"We had problems," Sullivan said. "We'd never sold booze in our parks before. We didn't know what to expect. When we designed the park, we did not design it with the restrictions we had to have to make it really work well. Like we built a patio in Mexico and a patio in England, so we could serve beer outside, but had to say, 'Okay, guest, you can't take beer down the promenade.' We had a soft opening, and we had all the construction workers out there. We had a few of them get drunk, so we learned from that."

Through October, Disney relaxed its refund policy to hand out readmissions more liberally. Guest Relations refunded about two dozen admissions a day. Most of the disgruntled guests settled for, rather than cash, tickets for the Magic Kingdom or to return to EPCOT at a later date when the attractions might be running more reliably.

To celebrate the opening of the France and U.K. pavilions, a marketing rep suggested flying in European journalists on two Concordes and landing them in Orlando simultaneously. "Those two Concordes—one took off from Paris, one took off from London—landed on two adjacent runways at Orlando eighteen seconds apart," said marketing director Jack Lindquist. To tie the landing to EPCOT, "we built a whole school study program around it and brought out about 12,000 school kids from Orlando to see it happen. It had never happened anywhere else in the world, and it didn't cost us a nickel. British Airways and Air France picked up the tab. They were delighted to have 90 press people on board."

The media presence increased tremendously for the start of the official grand opening celebration weekend Friday, October 22. More than 5,000 invited guests, many in black tie or evening gown, gathered under Spaceship Earth and black rain clouds for music, dancing and hors d'oeuvres. The videotaped highlights would be incorporated into a television special airing the next day hosted by Danny Kaye, with appearances by Marie Osmond, Roy Clark, Eric Severeid, and Drew Barrymore, fresh from *E.T.*

The rain continued through the next day for the official opening of World Showcase, featuring groups of musicians and dancers from around the world and the All-American College Marching Band, composed of musicians from colleges across the U.S. In the evening, a reception and dinner was held in the courtyards of all the World Showcase pavilions. During dinner, the People of the World dolls paraded around the promenade, representing all the countries in World Showcase, in what was supposed to become a daily attraction. Then, the lagoon show Le Carnival de Lumiere combined colorful international scenes with music and dancing fountains, followed by a grand finale of fireworks.

Finally, on Sunday, 10,000 people associated with EPCOT Center's existence were invited for a parkwide dedication ceremony.

During the park's first two months, Disney paid all the expenses to fly in and care for 5,000 media representatives—more than twice the number they had brought in for the Magic Kingdom's opening. A bigger difference, however, was that more than 100 of them were television reporters, since Lindquist was able to convince Card Walker to spend $18,000 on a satellite uplink.

"Now we could bring people from smaller markets, like Winston-Salem, North Carolina, and they could do a 'stand-up' in front of Spaceship Earth," Lindquist recalled. "For most of the markets, this was the first satellite transmission that they had done. We never really broke it down, but that $18,000 bought us probably over $20 million in publicity. And these were local newsmen. These were guys [the public] knew, guys they watched on television, and here they were standing in front of Spaceship Earth, saying, 'And tomorrow I'm going to talk to you from the Kraft Pavilion....'"

Newspapers across the country, on the whole, gave the new park high marks, typically in their Travel sections. Television and radio shows, most of *The Today Show* variety, were positively fawning.

Surprisingly, the best reviews went to the Imagination pavilion's 3-D movie, *Magic Journeys*. Audiences were so enthralled by the movie that they spontaneously broke into applause at the end. The crowds were also entranced by the fountains out front, with jumping jets of water and a waterfall that appeared to run uphill. The interactive Image Works area was an instant hit, even though many of its gadgets weren't working yet. Guests appeared oblivious that the pavilion's main attraction, Journey into Imagination, was inoperable and hidden behind barricades. Ironically, Disney executives had always acted embarrassed about having an EPCOT pavilion devoted to a lightweight, non-scientific topic like imagination and starring a cartoon dragon. So, in publicity for Future World, Disney had always touted pavilions on "energy, transportation, communication and other topics for tomorrow." Imagination, the park's surprise sensation, was always "other topics."

Certainly EPCOT Center didn't escape criticism. As expected, countless commentators bemoaned that Walt's city of tomorrow had devolved into another theme park. One wag called it "EPTPOT," the Experimental Prototype Theme Park of Tomorrow.

Social critics writing in more serious publications or quoted within news coverage—presumably those who weren't sent an engraved invitation to EPCOT's opening ceremonies—were disturbed by the park's rosy optimism. Instead of complaining that Disney wasn't ambitious enough to confront the problems of tomorrow, some seemed incredulous that an entertainment company would even try. "How seriously can you take the view of the future proffered by the same organization responsible for Disco Mickey Mouse?" asked one critic.

They accused Disney of sanitizing reality and glossing over history, such as in making no mention of Vietnam in the American Adventure. Indeed, the executives had no appetite for controversy, nor did they think the typical theme park guest wanted to spend his vacation touring recreations of polluted rivers or toxic dumpsites or body-strewn battlefields. Disney preferred its history nice and neat, devoid of uncomfortable tangents and unanswered questions. Asked about the show's predominantly Caucasian cast, one designer explained, "You can't get into the minorities. Once you get started with minorities, there's no end to it."

Publicly, Disney responded that it was focusing on the promise of the future, not dwelling on the mistakes of the past; its job was to suggest ways to solve those problems. Its message was that it wasn't too late, that "the future can be whatever we choose to make it." Senior vice president of EPCOT development Pat Scanlon likened EPCOT to "a lightbulb in the night." The night was humanity's despair over environmental pollution, nuclear proliferation, world hunger, inflation. The light was hopeful suggestions of what could be done.

Other analysts found certain attractions, such as GM's World of Motion and Kodak's Imagination, to be marred by commercial messages promoting sponsors' products, even though Disney had gone out of its way to prevent the advertising from overshadowing or compromising the integrity of the pavilions. The companies' inclusion, Disney insisted, was designed to highlight solutions from experts, so an entertainment company didn't have to be making predictions about the future of transportation or energy.

Critics also found fault with The Land, with its rotating, space-age plants, grains raised on saltwater, and tomatoes—grown without soil— moving around on conveyor belts. While interesting, such techniques appeared to be wholly impractical in an age of high-yield, low-cost farming. Disney reluctantly admitted that it was putting on a show and trying to encourage discussion of possible solutions, rather than showcasing actual answers for eliminating world hunger.

Others were disappointed to learn that none of the crops harvested in The Land were being used at the pavilion's The Good Turn restaurant, as had originally been intended. Disney vowed that eventually it would serve some homegrown fruits and vegetables. A few malcontents even complained that there were no orange or grapefruit trees at The Land, despite EPCOT being located in heart of the country's citrus belt. Disney explained that it chose bananas instead because they were more vital from a global perspective.

The stings hurt. Disney made a small concession by adding a brief clip of Vietnam to a film montage in the American Adventure. But the company knew that its real responsibility lie in garnering the approval not of the media, but of its visitors. To that end, management paid more attention to individual guest complaints, even the ones it could do little about.

A number of guests groused that they had to repeat questions several times to be understood by the exchange students working at the shops in World Showcase. Others complained that the only things to do at World Showcase were eat and shop. "There's too much educational junk over at EPCOT," whined one sixteen-year-old. "If I want that, I can get it at school."

While most guests appeared to be impressed by the grandeur of EPCOT as a whole, many found Future World too sterile, too austere. It lacked the cheerful atmosphere of the Magic Kingdom.

The most common complaint was, "Where's Mickey?" Aside from a walk-around Dreamfinder—a complete stranger with Journey into Imagination not yet open—the only characters were the oversized People of the World dolls. Children did not find them suitable substitutes for Mickey and the gang. "The dolls did not go over that well," remembered Bill Hoelscher. "Children were frightened of them. They thought they were monsters. You can understand a kid thinking, 'I like Mickey Mouse. He's a little bit bigger than I am, but—my God!—what is this thing coming here?' That was probably their demise; they scared the kids." The characters did not last long.

Ironically, World Showcase's least authentic entertainers—the comic street artists in Italy—were its most popular. "Our financial records showed that they were the best value for the money," Peter Bloustein said. "More people saw them and it cost us less to operate than anything else in the park. They were so good [in Italy], and sometimes they had so many people around them, that back rows couldn't even see. So I said, 'I'll put them in the United Kingdom, too.' It was a little off the nationality, but we did English things, like some Shakespeare using the audience to participate. I had them bring in and train more performers. And then I put another group in Future World, because Future World was devoid of characters, devoid of personality, devoid of humor."

The worst received attraction was CommuniCore's Astuter Computer Revue. The show was not only of questionable entertainment value, but—with computers changing so fast—instantly obsolete. Its poor reviews bothered both Disney and sponsor Sperry. "We had to redo the computer show," admitted Imagineer Mark Eades. "Sperry wouldn't pay for it." Disney pulled the plug after just fifteen months, and created a less cheesy show, one Eades termed "a make good." Backstage Magic would run for nearly ten years.

Despite the ongoing glitches and grumbling, EPCOT Center seemed a clear success based on attendance. A month after the park opened, Disney's stock price broke $70 a share for the first time since before the 1973 gas crisis. Now, with two giant theme parks, Disney executives figured they'd never have to close the parking lots again. They were wrong. On December 28, 1982, Disney turnstiles counted more than 100,000 guests between the two parks. EPCOT's lot, consisting of 8,000 marked spaces plus grassy areas, closed at 10:30 a.m. The Magic Kingdom closed its 12,000-space lot at 11:15 a.m. Later in the day, the Lake Buena Vista shopping village even had to close its parking lot.

By Christmas, engineers had raised the Operational Readiness Index at EPCOT's least reliable performer, the Universe of Energy, to 75 percent. Installing grounding strips throughout the attraction helped discharge the static electricity that threw off the sensors in its guidance system. Yet the attraction, according to attendant Jeffrey Stoneking, required "several years worth of fine-tune adjustments. It got to the point where we would tell guests, 'Welcome to EPCOT, where we built rides for the future so they won't operate today.'"

Even with everything running smoothly, EPCOT would need more ride and restaurant capacity. During the winter, Disney unveiled additional exhibits at CommuniCore, as well as three new soda stands. At the French restaurant, a second dining room with a separate menu was opened upstairs. The outdoor patio received 60 additional seats and a protective awning. The adjacent pastry shop was tripled in size, since it found itself selling not 500 pastries a day, as anticipated, but 5,000. The U.K.'s Rose and Crown added a fish-and-chips outlet, expanded its patio, and considered building an upstairs dining room.

For the future, Disney unveiled plans for both fine dining and fast food eateries in China, an underwater restaurant in the Living Seas, two restaurants in a proposed Spain pavilion, and a Moroccan restaurant featuring exotic "Arabian dancers" — Disneyspeak for belly dancers.

After a second delay at Christmas, Journey into Imagination finally opened in March, as ready as it would ever be. The vehicles were supposed to travel at different speeds throughout the attraction, particularly as they whipped over the top of and down into a huge "monster book," mimicking the modest thrill plunging over the waterfalls in Pirates of the Caribbean. Yet the dark ride's main computer, which ensured proper spacing between the cars, reflexively inhibited such quick bursts of speed — and slowed down other cars as well.

Journey into Imagination would never run as smoothly as designed, said designer Tony Baxter, "because the ride was so darn smart. It was constantly monitoring all of the other vehicles, and if one of the cars decided there wasn't time and didn't get on the turntable, then all the other cars would slow down. So the ride was constantly adjusting itself, which made guests wonder, 'We just sort of stopped. Is it breaking down? Is there something wrong with the car?' It was like bad editing in a movie, where you were too long in one scene and didn't get enough time to see something else. We had no control over that because safety was number one and if that vehicle said it needed to go or needed to stop, that's what it did."

So, too, the overworked drive system on Spaceship Earth would permanently lurch and wheeze up its incline, sounding and feeling more like a ride on a dying automobile than a smooth trip into the future. And certainly passengers on World of Motion failed to associate General Motors with reliable performance whenever their car suddenly stopped before sluggishly restarting moments later.

The park also emptied of guests well before closing, as the crowds filed out from exhaustion or to ride the monorail to watch the evening parade at the Magic Kingdom. Less appealing was EPCOT's nightly Le Carnival de Lumiere. It employed rear-screen projectors on floating barges that could be viewed only from the entrance to World Showcase. The show was updated for EPCOT's first summer by expanding the viewing area and adding automated, synchronized spotlights. It would take another summer, however, to add lasers and a synthesized soundtrack and create Laserphonic Fantasy, which successfully retained the majority of the day's visitors late into the night, to the relief of World Showcase's restaurant operators.

On EPCOT Center's first anniversary, GE's Horizons opened. The next day, ground was broken on two new pavilions: the Living Seas, sponsored by United Technologies, and Morocco, funded by the Kingdom of Morocco. On paper, the new park appeared to have done its job: guests were staying on property longer (from an average 1.6 days to 2.4) and spending more money. In one year, Disney World's attendance nearly doubled, from 12.56 million to 22.7 million. Management had originally predicted eighteen million.

EPCOT's more adult clientele was also staying in the park longer—an average 7.7 hours compared to 6.9 hours at the Magic Kingdom—and arriving with fewer people per car—resulting in constantly closing the parking lot. On the plus side, EPCOT guests were less likely to throw trash on the ground.

Since guests' primary expenditure—theme park tickets—was typically purchased at the Ticket and Transportation Center, Disney encouraged guests to lengthen their stays by promoting "multi-day media," said Dan Healy. There were two parks, but no two-day tickets were sold. The options were one-park, one-day admissions and slightly discounted "hopper" tickets that could be used at both parks for three or more days. Unused days didn't expire, so guests didn't have to worry about buying too many days and had an incentive to make a return trip. "The strategy was to force them into a three-day ticket. Disney felt people would decide at the ticket booths."

As well, Disney refused to sell single-day hopper passes. If guests wanted to see both parks, they had to buy at least two days worth of tickets.

With the opening of EPCOT Center, Disney World could no longer be viewed as a day trip; it was now a "destination resort." Whereas just four years before, the resort was generating roughly twice the revenue of Disneyland, in EPCOT's first year, Florida made six times as much money as Anaheim. In deference to Disneyland, marketing of Disney World had traditionally been restricted to east of the Mississippi. It would now be national.

Yet Walt Street, fixated on the bigger picture, was not impressed. The studio's diminishing slate of new films continued to fare poorly. Only half the number of cable subscribers as expected had signed up for its new Disney Channel. Attendance at EPCOT, before its first year was over, had already begun to slow. Surveys showed that first-time visitors were far less likely to return to EPCOT than they were to the Magic

Kingdom. Worse, the huge expense of building EPCOT Center had cut into the company's short-term profitability. Earnings fell for a second straight year. Roy's son, board member Roy E. Disney, was so disgusted with EPCOT's cost over-runs, he refused to attend its grand opening. Although the company was able to settle all construction claims for 12 to 14 cents on the dollar, EPCOT's final price tag still weighed in at $1.4 billion. For the next ten years, whenever the company began contemplating another big construction project, the accountants repeated a familiar refrain: "Don't let this be another EPCOT."

Vice president of contract administration and purchasing Howard Roland, to this day, adamantly defends his work against those who say costs spiraled "over budget." "What budget?" he asked. "There was no budget! Where does it say, '$400 million?' We budgeted as we went along. [Initially Disney] said $400 million, but $400 million for what?"

Yet Disney felt that creating an experimental world's fair involving mega-sponsors necessitated the incredible risks. Monumental prototypes are expensive, especially when you have to thoroughly impress the largest corporations in America to gain funding. "I remember decisions that were made, such as to go or not go on the Energy pavilion concept, which was extraordinary and was going to cost a fortune," explained Imagineer Tony Baxter. "The thing was, if we lost Exxon, we lost EPCOT. It was that simple. There was no margin for losing anything. It was like the more you got out of a sponsor, the more colossal or stupendous [their pavilion] could be. Card Walker was bringing Walt Disney's dream to life, and he didn't want to risk it not being a dream. There were a lot of things out there, like the New York World's Fair in 1964, that cost as much as EPCOT in 1982. So were we going to do a worse version of that? We were participants in it. So, the Ford Pavilion, the General Electric Carousel, those were all benchmarks of what a pavilion was. That's what the expectation levels were. So when you look at the Energy pavilion, it's a dead ringer for the Ford show. When you look at Horizons, it's in the same ballpark as everything that was originally in Carousel of Progress [at the World's Fair]. So there was a lot of equating of the value everyone would be expecting to be about what it would be for a fair pavilion."

But Card Walker was gone now, retired to the golf courses and satisfied with his seat on the board. His successors, president and chief executive Ron Miller and chairman Ray Watson, were left holding the bill.

13

Upheaval

W ALL Street's approval did not last long. Disney stock peaked at $84 in April 1983 and then began slipping. Before Thanksgiving, it fell below $50. The declining share price, especially in light of the company's constantly rising net worth, had a two-fold negative impact. First, it angered loyal shareholders. Second, it caught the attention of "unfriendly" investors, those who might try to snatch up undervalued shares, wrest control of the company, and then begin selling it off, piece by piece, for a quick profit.

Disney retained accountants, lawyers and investment bankers to advise on its options. Certainly, they could borrow money and try to acquire shares themselves in a leveraged buyout. Yet such a move would likely spark a bidding war with hostile outsiders, whose pockets were considerably deeper than management's. And, even if management did succeed in buying out the company, servicing the $2 billion of debt would probably force them to sell off significant assets—exactly what they were trying to avoid in fighting against an outside takeover.

Even theme park attendance had begun to lag. During the last four months of 1983, attendance at Disney World fell eight percent below the previous autumn—despite the largest advertising campaign the resort had ever undertaken, featuring local television commercials in every major market in Florida. They also tried discounts—another unnatural tactic for Disney. By mail, Florida residents could buy a $40 seasonal pass that would admit them to both parks through January, May and September, historically the slowest months for tourists.

Next, it was time for some serious belt-tightening. With the opening of EPCOT Center, top management was no longer a small, cohesive group. Dick Nunis, who had been splitting time between both coasts while being based in California, relocated to Florida. In January 1984, just as the holiday rush subsided, Nunis reorganized the entire executive flowchart. It was like a game of musical chairs, although by the time the music stopped, several players found themselves holding multiple chairs and others none at all. Twenty senior managers, including vice presidents, lost their jobs, along with 180 other employees. Many full-timers who escaped the layoff had their hours cut.

"They were putting their house in order," explained Steve Baker, who found himself suddenly promoted to head of Participant Affairs, overseeing eleven smaller departments.

Spencer Craig said he, on the other hand, "went from being the training guru of the whole property to an assistant manager under Operations. It was like starting all over."

Since Foods operated on tighter budgets and margins, that department's managers were known for having more business savvy. Several were transferred to pollinate other departments. Bob Ziegler said, "They took a few of us with 'profitable' experiences and moved us to Operations, where they were more concerned with capacity and show."

The turmoil was even more ferocious on the outside. In February, at Disney's annual meeting held in a ballroom at the Contemporary, chief executive Ron Miller was peppered with questions from upset shareholders, complaining about declining profits and stock price and wondering about rumors of a corporate takeover.

The following week, Walt's nephew, Roy E. Disney, resigned from the board of directors, legally and ethically freeing him to pursue a change in management. Roy himself was among those speculators aggressively accumulating Disney stock. One corporate raider, Saul Steinberg, quickly amassed more than twelve percent of Disney's shares, intent on breaking up the company. Terrified, Disney paid Steinberg $52 million in "greenmail" to sell back his shares to the company and promise to leave them alone. The deal, however, made the company even more vulnerable, encouraging other vultures to try the same. The executives needed a better defense than paying ransom. Instead, they desperately began seeking acquisitions, hoping that increasing the size of Disney would make it harder to consume by an outsider. They settled on Arvida Corporation, a Florida land development firm specializing in planned communities like Boca Raton. Ideally, Arvida could help better develop Disney's own real estate in Florida. For the sale, Arvida received $200 million in Disney stock, instantly making Arvida's primary stockholders, the Bass brothers of Texas, among Disney's largest stockholders. The Basses now owned 5.9 percent of the company and, percentage-wise, everyone else's share—including Roy's—was reduced. The outsiders were furious, even as management continued seeking additional acquisitions. Rumors swirled about Disney's possible fates.

Out in Florida, the staff of Disney World knew that something drastic was underway, but not sure exactly what. Operations supervisor Dennis Snow recalled, "1984 was really scary. It was a strange time. During the takeover attempt, my wife was expecting our first child. We had just bought a house. We were afraid to go to work and find it closed or owned by somebody else. Guests were asking about it, and we didn't know ourselves. Everything we knew we read in the newspaper. We'd ask our managers, and they'd say, 'We'd love to be able to tell you, but we don't know ourselves.' Everybody wanted answers. Nobody had any."

The same day that Roy resigned, *Splash*, Miller's PG-rated mermaid movie designed to rejuvenate the studio, was released. Audiences and critics reacted favorably. Long-time Disney employees were more apprehensive. "They screened *Splash* in the theater at the Walt Disney Story, as a free cast member preview," recalled Snow. "In one scene, when [Daryl Hannah] rises naked out of the ocean, you see her bare backside. It was the first nudity in a Disney movie. There was a collective intake of breath, like, 'Here we go....'"

Through the summer, Disney's stock price lurched up and down like a roller coaster depending on the latest moves by the company and its pursuers. Roy was able to rally the larger shareholders—including the Basses—into a sizable voting bloc against current management. In the end, the only way to save the company was to bring Roy back into the company, along with two allies on the board. Miller was ousted and replaced by a new management team backed by the largest shareholders. Michael Eisner, an imaginative young executive from Paramount Pictures and, before that, ABC television, would serve as chairman and CEO. Frank Wells, a former vice chairman of Warner Brothers, would provide greater corporate experience as president and chief operating officer. Together, they provided a nice counterbalance between creative and business, just as Walt and his brother had years before.

As the new regime was coronated in Burbank in September, the finishing touches were being placed on a Morocco pavilion at EPCOT. The African nation had not only provided much of the funding, but also had sent native craftsmen to Florida to create all the tile work, carvings and paintings. The meandering alleyways and corners and hidden shops were so realistic that one International Program student got a strange look on his face and started fidgeting during his tour of the pavilion. "What's the matter?" his trainer asked. "I live down that street!" he replied.

Disney World management and staffers, while relieved that the company had avoided a cataclysmic implosion, were nonetheless suspicious of outsiders Eisner and Wells taking the helm of the family business.

"We didn't know who they were," Snow said. "There was a lot of skepticism, a 'let's-wait-and-see' attitude."

Fortuitously, Eisner and Wells' backgrounds were in movies and television, Disney's division in most dire need of resuscitation. Consequently, the most severe management and operational changes were made at the studio. They also wanted to get more mileage out of the venerable film library, which previous management limited to theatrical re-releases of the animated features every seven years. New management began saturating the market with the classics, releasing them on videotape and showing them on the *Wonderful World of Disney*, the Disney Channel, and other pay television stations.

Theme parks, however, were a business neither Eisner nor Wells knew the first thing about. Bill Sullivan, who accompanied the new executives on their first tour of EPCOT Center, recalled, "We blew them away. They didn't know what we had. I heard Frank say to Michael, 'We've been under-advertised and undersold. We have a hell of a product here.' I took them down in the tunnel [at the Magic Kingdom], and as we walked out the back door of cash control, we had to step over these huge mailbags. Michael looked at Frank: 'What the hell is that?' Frank looked at [the attendant]: 'What the hell is that?' 'Money.' We'd had a great weekend, and we had bags of money down there getting ready for the armored car pickup. Michael said, 'This is a hell of a business to be in.'"

Since Disney World was providing the bulk of Disney's profits and

Eisner didn't want to offend Dick Nunis, who sat on the company's board of directors, he left theme park management comparatively intact. Wells, however, did go to great lengths to quickly learn the business. He walked the parks with a critical eye, pored over every report he could find, and grilled the old-timers on every aspect of park operations. Wells reviewed the budgets for every department at Disney World. "The first year I went to Frank with my budget, I was nervous," recalled Sullivan, then heading the Magic Kingdom. "I had 139 items and I was looking for something like $600 million. He sat and reviewed each and every one of them and made me justify them."

Sullivan's budget requested $150,000 for new costumes for the monorail operators. Wells was incredulous, his background as a lawyer demanding to see proof. "Show me," Wells said. So Sully took him downstairs to Wardrobe. Wells agreed that the costumes looked terrible. "Yeah," admitted Sullivan, "I got an extra year out of them." Wells said to leave the new monorail uniforms in the budget, but to try to find something else they could get an extra year out of.

Sully also sought to replace several sump pumps that had deteriorated. So Wells donned overalls and climbed into the attics to check. Although Wells would analyze and approve future budgets with fewer inspections and more trust, he wanted to stress the importance of keeping costs tightly under control and eliminating waste.

So, too, the new executives quickly devised elementary changes designed to wring more dollars out of the guests. Eisner, Wells and their new corporate hires had no allegiance to—and in fact outright disagreement with—many of Walt's time-honored philosophies. Walt's focus had always been building up long-term value in the company. It was time to cash in some of that value.

Previous management intentionally kept prices affordable to draw from the largest possible pool of guests, who in turn would think fondly of Disney for giving them such good value. Immediately, prices began rising on food, merchandise, parking and particularly admission. During the eleven years of A through E ticket books, previous management had never increased the price of individual ride tickets, instead once a year nominally raising the park's admission price. New management began by raising admission prices about every four months, so their cost doubled within four years.

They also noted that, considering how convenient, visible and inexpensive they were to operate, outdoor vending carts were more profitable than many of the in-park stores and restaurants. Yet, to avoid intruding on the show, the only regular carts at Disney World sold popcorn and ice cream. Within months, the parks began rolling out pretzel wagons, churro wagons, baked potato wagons, silhouette carts, anything they could think of to peddle on wheels. They clogged the streets with as many sales opportunities as they could.

At the same time, the specialty stores that provided a diversity of merchandise and atmosphere began to wither away in favor of more souvenir shops. Merlin's Magic Shop in Fantasyland, the New Century Clock Shop, Greenhouse flower shop, and Cup 'n' Saucer on Main Street, and others were replaced by generic stores offering better-selling product lines like Christmas trinkets, character clothing, and plush animals.

EPCOT Center had been missing a merchandising and entertainment bonanza by keeping Disney characters out of the park. Soon, Mickey and the gang began appearing in Future World dressed as spacemen and in World Showcase dressed in kimonos, sombreros and other international garb.

New management also realized that the parks needed fresh new attractions to attract new visitors and ensure they kept coming back. Wells and the other financial types thought that the Imagineering division had grown bloated and oblivious to budgets. Certainly, they argued, the entire business of ride development could be dismantled and outsourced. Such talk evaporated after Eisner's first visit to WED. Marty Sklar regaled the new boss with stories of Walt and showed him the original models for Disneyland and Disney World, as well as mock-ups for possible future projects. Eisner was enthralled by the creative atmosphere. He was particularly impressed by the model for a proposed log flume ride themed to *Song of the South*. Instead of firing the designers, Eisner encouraged them to think bigger, fresher, to break out of the formula of cartoon-themed dark rides. They needed more Hollywood.

"When Michael Eisner came in, there was a lot of trepidation because he didn't know what to do with Imagineering," said Mark Eades. "He came in and gave us the chance to do bigger things. He brought in some outside creative blood that Imagineering seriously needed."

Prior management believed that if Walt or his creative heirs didn't invent a character or storyline, then it shouldn't be used—forgetting, of course, that Walt himself had co-opted ages-old fairy tales for his animated movies and the worlds of Davy Crockett, Mark Twain and Zorro for Disneyland. Eisner didn't care who invented a character or storyline, so long as it was an engaging one with a marketable hook. Just as the studio began striking deals with established stars and directors, the newly renamed Imagineering division was given the green light to work with George Lucas on fusing his *Star Wars* mythology with the flight simulator technology that it had been exploring, and pop singer Michael Jackson and director Francis Ford Coppola on a 3-D musical adventure film.

As well, the new executives had no qualms about upsetting the local hospitality industry by building more hotels. Corporate management felt it needed to get more hospitality experience into the hotels, and began negotiating on a partnership in which Disney would retain ownership of its hotels, but Marriott would build and operate them. The main stumbling block was a contract that previous Disney management had signed with Tishman. In exchange for quick cash to fight the then-raging corporate takeover, Disney would allow Tishman to build and own two on-property convention hotels.

Eisner demanded the contract with Tishman be broken. Tishman promptly filed a $300 million lawsuit charging breach of contract and demanding another $1 billion in punitive damages. Disney, realizing that it was clearly violating the terms of its agreement, convinced Tishman to sign a complicated deal in which it would still own the next two on-property hotels, could build them on a prime location next to EPCOT Center, and could use "Disney" in the name. Tishman could also set the construction budget, but Disney would determine the design.

While Eisner argued publicly that Disney's retaining design control would help prevent Tishman from building something like the plain high-rises they had originally planned, the new deal also gave Disney some measure over costs. Initially, Eisner figured he could use the design provision to punish Tishman by forcing them to go wildly overboard with post-modern touches. Fortunately, Frank Wells and other wiser heads were able to point out that ugly hotels would in fact punish Eisner more since people would view the hotels as Eisner's first accomplishment on Disney World property. The final results, the eclectic Swan and Dolphin hotels, would end up somewhere between, depending upon one's taste in architecture and tolerance for roofs topped by oversized concrete animals.

In 1986, construction began on the Grand Floridian, a swanky hotel that had been slotted into the Asian Hotel's site on the Seven Seas Lagoon during the construction of EPCOT Center.

Disney realized the Golf Resort was underperforming, since guests were under the mistaken impression that the hotel catered only to golfers. The resort was remodeled with a Snow White theme, expanded by 150 rooms, and renamed the Disney Inn. Business perked up immediately.

Eisner and Wells eventually decided against having Marriott build and operate its hotels, and decided to do it themselves. They hired a longtime Marriott executive, Robert Small, who at the time was overseeing hotels, restaurants and other businesses for the Bass brothers. Small quickly discovered that, "You run this company like it's an entertainment company, not a hotel."

Small began reintroducing hospitality industry practices to Disney's hotels, including a more variable rate structure between seasons. He also did away with anything that was there more for show than to make money. Plants and flowers inside the hotels were replaced by artificial greenery. Specialty shops were replaced by larger souvenir stores.

He also oversaw the construction of Disney's first non-luxury-level hotel, the Caribbean Beach Resort, with 2,112 rooms—more than twice as many as any other Disney property. "Instead of saying budget hotel, we called it a 'moderately priced resort,'" said hospitality manager Tom Hamilton. "We didn't do a good job conveying that to the guests. They were surprised to see the sparse accommodations. They complained it was not as roomy as the Contemporary. In the beginning, we transferred a lot of guests over to the Contemporary or the Poly[nesian], space permitting, at no extra charge. That didn't last long."

Situated down the road from EPCOT Center, Caribbean Beach was Disney's first hotel that wasn't a monorail-ride away from the Magic Kingdom. Instead, guests had to wait for a bus, once an hour. "The buses at Caribbean Beach were always full," Hamilton recalled. "I called for more buses and was told, 'Sorry, you're only budgeted for two buses per hour.' You'd think there would be team spirit at Disney, but each [business] unit was looking out for itself. The business was no longer being viewed as a whole."

A few of the old guard, disgusted by the new profit-obsessive mentality, disintegrating teamwork, and disregard for Walt's show-centric philosophies, quit. A number were terminated, including 100 full-timers during a reorganization in November. Others were reinvigorated by the new energy.

"We changed from an internally focused operation—'if it wasn't invented at Disney, it wasn't any good'—to 'there's a lot of good stuff out there.' There was more and more bringing in outside best practices," recalled Dennis Snow. "You had a percentage of folks who left or were unhappy because it wasn't what it used to be. It wasn't the same. In my opinion, it was better. There were so many opportunities for anyone who wanted to do anything. The world was their oyster."

Disney once again felt that it could do the impossible. The Entertainment department at the Magic Kingdom had spent a decade trying to figure out how to fly Tinker Bell by the castle to start the nightly fireworks show. Disneyland achieved the stunt by having a performer in a harness slide down a cable from the top of the Matterhorn, past the castle, to a raised platform hidden in the pine trees at the edge of Frontierland. But the Magic Kingdom had no Matterhorn to slide down from; the only massive structure in the area was the castle itself.

At a Christmas party in 1984, three tipsy old-timers who had helped launch the first Tinker Bell at Disneyland vowed to bring Tinker Bell to Disney World—by launching her from the top of the castle. First, to support the weight, the top spire of the castle had to be rebuilt from the inside, replacing flimsy chicken wire with six-inch I-beams. Next, they cut a hole in the top of the castle for Tinker Bell to access the outside ledge. Then, Hank Dains, who hung the original cable at Disneyland, ran a line from the castle down to several points around the Plaza. He experimented by sliding down sandbags and mannequins to determine which direction had the proper incline for a controlled descent and would be visible during the performance, yet unobtrusive during the day. The best route seemed to be sloping a 600-foot-long line nearly 100 feet down and anchoring the end at a catch tower on the roof of Tomorrowland's If You Had Wings show building. Dains then duplicated the harness and Arnold Lindberg the trolley system they had created for Disneyland.

Bill Sullivan, as head of the Magic Kingdom, was in charge of finding the money to fund the project. He was able to put aside $25,000 to get the project started. He had to go to his direct boss, Bob Mathieson, to get another $50,000. When it looked like they could finally make it work,

Sullivan needed another $250,000. Mathieson sent him to Nunis. Nunis agreed, if they could do it within budget.

To perform as Tinker Bell, Sullivan tried to hire a few aerialists who worked at nearby Circus World, but the competing theme park was furious that Disney was trying to steal its performers. So Sullivan went straight to the acrobats and offered to pay them $125 a night in cash, no paperwork. Sullivan knew Eisner and Wells would be in town for the Fourth of July, so he scheduled the first unadvertised performance for that night, to introduce the holiday fireworks show. Just as the show was about to begin, spotlights circled the sky, then converged on a tiny figure in sparkling green, 165 feet up, at the top of the castle. The crowd gasped as the pixie swooped down from the golden spire, smiling and waving as she sailed over the Plaza, before disappearing into the darkness. Eisner and Wells' jaws dropped.

The new corporate leadership rejected the traditional Disney marketing tact of soft-selling its product and pursuing free publicity in lieu of paid advertising. They authorized a multi-million-dollar, national television ad campaign. "Eisner and Wells came in with an aggressive attitude. There were no preconceived notions about what we should or shouldn't do," said Tom Elrod, vice president of marketing. "It was 'we got to get out there and take a kind of a motion picture approach to marketing,' which is hype."

Promotional special events grew even bigger, even when there wasn't a whole lot to promote. A thirtieth anniversary promotion at Disneyland was so successful in 1985, Marketing organized a fifteenth anniversary extravaganza the following year for Disney World. Whereas Disney World previously rotated in several hundred media personnel to wine and dine, it kicked off the fifteenth anniversary by flying in the world's largest press contingent — 10,000 media representatives and their guests — all at one time.

The promotion cost $7.5 million and caused a firestorm in the media. Newspapers across the country ran articles and editorials questioning the ethics of accepting all-expenses-paid trips to Disney World to cover such a non-event. As proof that the three-day junket had little newsworthiness, some of the press events were attended by as few as 20 reporters. Despite the controversy, Marketing had done its job. "All the commotion generated a record-attendance year," Elrod smiled.

Eisner and Wells realized that they had to start utilizing more of their vast Florida real estate. Only a fraction of their 27,000 acres had been developed, including nothing in the southern Osceola County portion of their property. They formed a separate subsidiary, the Disney Development Company, to complement Arvida in land-use planning.

In February 1985, Disney had ERA's Buzz Price organize a "super charrette." The high-powered brainstorming session would help identify the best uses of the land, and whether to sell it or develop it. In addition to Price, Eisner, Wells and existing Disney World management, there would also be a range of top experts from the outside—architect Michael Graves, developer James W. Rouse, *Megatrends* author/consumer survey guru John Naisbitt, and other noted planners, forecasters and scientists. Price called the summit "a quest to see if we could put the remaining acreage to use. The emphasis was peripheral, a general overview of big chunks of ground, what to do with the large acreage. I made a strong recommendation for low-cost venues. There was discussion on housing and a shopping area like Lake Buena Vista."

The consensus was that Disney should develop the property in line with what it did best: entertainment. Pent-up demand would support additional entertainment venues, and existing operations could use new attractions. Specifically, the property lacked night-time entertainment and sufficient lodging, especially in the lower price range. The "little course-directing conference," Wells announced, left "very little question about what to do next."

And, questioned one reporter, where did Walt's city of tomorrow fit into the revised plans? It didn't, admitted Wells. "Essentially, EPCOT is complete."

But wasn't it called EPCOT *Center* because it was supposed to be the center of an entire grand dream called EPCOT? "No," Wells corrected, "that's not my view."

Nunis, probably biting his lip, backed him up. He confirmed that Disney had named the park EPCOT Center not because it was the centerpiece of an EPCOT to come, but as "a marketing tool." Nunis justified the gimmick by saying that EPCOT was located in the physical center of the property and that the original idea was more a spirit that weaved through everything they did throughout the resort.

"You can't live in the past," explained Nunis, a warrior behind the scenes, but always the good soldier in public. "I think those of us that knew Walt Disney would say, 'Well, I wonder what Walt would do in this case?' But we don't consciously now get up and voice that openly."

Indeed, 20 years after his passing, his successors were finally, reluctantly admitting that Walt was dead.

14

reel Competition

"**O**LD Disney" held a curious view of competition. They didn't dislike upstart rivals so much as they dismissed them. They figured, arrogantly and probably accurately, that no one could do what they did as well as them, so there was no one to fear. Outside attractions were viewed not as *competing* amusements but as *supporting* amusements that, since Disney couldn't build everything, served to draw more tourists to its markets, prolong their vacations, and underscore just how superior its products were.

Walt himself invited Walter Knott, proprietor of Southern California's Knott's Berry Farm, to the opening of Disneyland in 1955, assuring the nervous berry farmer that their two parks would benefit, not suffer, from their close proximity. In fact, Walt's decidedly unconventional view of competition manifested itself as an inherent flaw in his plans for EPCOT the city. He completely overlooked the competitive nature of major corporations. "We don't presume to know all the answers," Walt admitted in the *EPCOT Film*. "In fact, we're counting on the cooperation of American industry to provide their very best thinking during the planning and the creation of our Experimental Prototype Community of Tomorrow." He hoped companies would fill his city with factories and research laboratories where visitors could learn about emerging technologies and inventions, and employ them in their own home, business or country.

But big business doesn't work that way. And Disney, of all companies, with its doors always locked and shades always drawn, should have known better. There are few competitive advantages more valuable to a company than proprietary products and systems, and little financial incentive to letting the world in on every stage of development and advertising it not as something to buy, but to borrow and profit from on your own.

With his movies, TV shows and Disneyland, Walt presumably didn't dwell on the competition because his products were so unique and not easily replicated. And, even those that tried—the cartoon knock-offs of the 1930s or the imitation Disneylands that began sprouting up in the late 1950s—suffered immediately because they lacked the main selling point: the Disney name.

After Disney announced it was coming to Florida, Cypress Gardens ran a full-page ad in the *Orlando Sentinel* welcoming their new neighbor and gushing that Disney was the best thing to happen to them since sunshine. Likewise, for the grand opening of the Magic Kingdom, Dick Pope, operator of Cypress Gardens, was one of the first on the guest list. "We appreciated Dick Pope, who was Mr. Florida when we went there," recalled the park's first marketing director, Sandy Quinn. "Before we arrived, Cypress Gardens had been the number one attraction of Florida. They had a ski show, lovely gardens, a tour in boats. We worked hard not to have an adversarial position. Our stance was that we were supportive of things that brought more people to Florida. We didn't worry about them. We were focused on us. We had a whole different product unlike anyone else."

Similarly, when Sea World broke ground ten miles to the north months after the opening of the Magic Kingdom, Disney appeared unfazed. "Nobody panicked over it," confirmed Bob Mathieson, head of Operations. "We have never been afraid of competition. We think it's good for us, because it keeps us sharp. [Sea World] was good for business. It promoted Florida more as a destination place, and we were confident enough that we would get our share of the audience. So, sure, bring it on. The more the merrier."

Although Disney declined to participate in formal cross-promotions, Bob Allen regularly invited Dick Pope and Sea World executives to preview new attractions before opening them to the public. The more and varied draws to central Florida, the better for everyone.

As well, having received unprecedented governmental favors, the company was committed to making Disney World a positive economic force for all of Florida. It intentionally underbuilt hotels and companion attractions such as miniature golf courses, leaving the moderate and low-end business for the locals. The strategy helped Disney ensure that its hotels were always considered top-of-the-line and were always full. Supply purposely was kept below demand.

After the corporate leadership changed in 1984, the mood shifted drastically. A Disney product didn't have to be different, so long as someone would buy it. New management saw little value in trying to reinvent the wheel. Because the majority of guests at Boardwalk and Baseballs, Sea World, and other International Drive diversions had spent the day before at the Magic Kingdom or EPCOT, Disney knew exactly what types of businesses their clientele would support. Disney could analyze competing attractions and improve upon the most successful. The company had already made a half-hearted attempt at competing with Sea World by opening the Living Seas pavilion at EPCOT Center in January 1986. That year, Sea World enjoyed its highest attendance ever.

Yet if Disney could offer the same type entertainment of a higher quality, guests would have little reason to travel off property. Most obviously, Disney World was deficient in after-dark entertainment. Every evening, on-property guests by the hundreds drove to downtown Orlando to visit the nightclub district Church Street Station. Eisner quickly gave the go-ahead for Pleasure Island, a late-night-oriented extension of the Walt Disney World Village shopping area.

Disney's water park, River Country, was smaller, more secluded, and more sedate than the competing Wet 'n' Wild water park. So Imagineers began work on their first water thrill park, Typhoon Lagoon, including a wavemaking machine light years beyond the contraption Dick Nunis tried to get working in the Seven Seas Lagoon fifteen years earlier.

A few miles north of Sea World, more formidable competition was in the works. In 1981, Universal Studios had acquired 400 acres of land to build an eastern version of the backlot tour it operated at its movie studio in Hollywood. Universal, however, planned its new theme park to be every bit as elaborate as Disney's. Parent company MCA was determined to find an investment partner and, after four years of pitching the idea to entertainment conglomerates and high-stakes investors, still had nothing to show.

Disney, meanwhile, had been toying with the idea of basing a theme park at its Burbank movie studio even before it built Disneyland. Imagineers even proposed an entertainment-centered pavilion for EPCOT Center. Eisner suggested expanding the idea into a separate movie studio park. Beating Universal to the punch shouldn't be difficult, since Disney World had ample land and, thanks to Reedy Creek, was guaranteed an expedited approval and construction process.

The numbers were clear. Everyone had seen how opening EPCOT Center had doubled the amount of time the average guest spent on property to nearly three days. They just had to avoid the EPCOT drawbacks—spending too much to build it, spreading it out over too much land, and employing too many innovative, unproven ride systems. The new plan was to add a "half-day park," more modest in scope and affordable to build than the other two, but flashy enough to persuade the average vacationer to extend his or her stay by an extra day. They could spend their rest of their third-gate day at the Magic Kingdom or EPCOT.

Yet Disney realized that, unlike Universal, its own studio was saddled with a spotty reputation and lacked the range of movie classics needed to create a well-rounded movie park. So it signed a licensing deal with MGM, the studio synonymous with classic Hollywood. The agreement allowed Disney to use "MGM" in the name of its park and to include a specified amount of footage from its classic pictures, including *The Wizard of Oz, Gone with the Wind,* and *Singin' in the Rain.*

During Eisner's first shareholders meeting in February 1985, he announced plans for Disney-MGM Studios. In the original 1985 layout, the $300-million park would include a Great Moments at the Movies ride-through adventure, adapted from EPCOT's entertainment pavilion; a Video Theater, where guests help create a TV show; Audio Adventure sound effects show; two stunt theaters, the Epic and the Slapstick; Disney Archives gallery and film theater; and the Video Playground, a backlot area with costumes guests pose in for photo and video setups. The star attraction would be a Studio Tour past an animation building, four soundstages, backlot streets and sets, administration offices, post-production facilities, craft and specialty shops—all operable. Having a fully functioning movie studio would take pressure off Disney's four soundstages in Burbank, since Eisner planned to increase feature film production from two to six per year up to fifteen, in addition to at least fifteen movies for the revived *Wonderful World of Disney* television

THIRD GATE. Mickey Mouse poses with ear-grabbing Governor Bob Graham behind a model of the proposed Disney-MGM Studios. (1985) *Photo courtesy State Archives of Florida*

series, six Disney Channel movies, and additional animated features. In Orlando, he anticipated building up to twelve soundstages.

His plans for a theme park/studio in Florida bore more than a passing resemblance to Universal's own theme park/studio in Hollywood. In fact, they looked even more like the plans for Universal's proposed park in Florida, down to the California architecture from the Golden Era of Hollywood. Universal executives were convinced that Disney had copied their ideas. MCA president Sid Sheinberg claimed that Eisner saw their plans during a July 1981 meeting when he was president of Paramount Pictures, MCA's first choice as a financial partner for its proposed park in Florida. The two-hour presentation included a slide show that moved street by street through Universal's planned attractions, supplemented by blueprints, color renderings and a live pitch covering the projected financials.

A few weeks later, Paramount decided to pass. MCA delivered the same presentation to other entertainment industry and financial powers, including RCA, Taft Entertainment, Lorimar and the Bass brothers—the billionaires who had become Disney's largest shareholders and whom Universal claimed failed to return several key documents about its tour.

As more details of Disney's plans leaked out, Sheinberg and MCA became even more incensed. The highlight of Disney's tram tour would be Catastrophe Canyon, in which an earthquake rattles the tram, brings down a power pole and a bridge, and causes fires, explosions at a nearby oil tank, and a flash flood. Amazingly, the most sensational effect on MCA's proposed tour was the "Hollywood Canyon" disaster. Their slideshow pictured a tram rolling onto a bridge in view of the picturesque Hollywood Hills. Suddenly, a massive earthquake causes the tram to shake. The ground rumbles. Power lines snap. A dam in the Hollywood Hills cracks, sending forth a wall of water. The torrent causes the bridge to collapse. The tram escapes just in time—but pulls into an oil field, where a semi slides across the slippery pavement, crashes into an oil tank, and explodes into flames.

Sheinberg knew that suing Disney was a no-win option. Instead, he took his case to the press. He stirred up "Tour Wars" stories at news outlets across the country, including the *Wall Street Journal, Washington Post*, and *Chicago Tribune*. One source quoted Sheinberg as saying, "The Mouse has become a ravenous rat." He even sent a ten-car caravan of Universal-licensed characters— Woody Woodpecker, Dracula, the Phantom of the Opera, Conan the Barbarian, Red Sonja, Charlie Chaplin, Groucho Marx, Laurel and Hardy, and W.C. Fields—and a mob of reporters and publicists on a trip to the Magic Kingdom. Disney refused to let the group in, explaining that the company prohibited people from visiting its parks in costume, but politely allowed them ten minutes to mug with Mickey and Minnie in front of the ticket booths.

In December 1986, Universal finally found an investment partner, the Canadian-based theater chain Cineplex-Odeon, selling a 50-percent stake in Universal Studios Florida for just $92 million. Seven months later, as a last ditch effort, Sheinberg and Eisner met to discuss combining their new attractions. MCA offered to pull the plug on its project in exchange for a half-share in Disney's new park. Disney was willing to pay MCA a small royalty, similar to the deals it was making to rent movie clips and characters from MGM and other studios. MCA walked away. Sheinberg was now even more motivated than before. In *Manhattan inc.* magazine, he called Eisner an "egomaniac" with "a failure of character."

Old Disney probably would have ignored Sheinberg's bleating. They let their products speak for themselves. Eisner, however, held an inflated view not of the Disney name, but of himself. In reviving *The Wonderful World of Disney* TV series, he cast himself as host, reprising Walt's role as fatherly emcee. Hourly cast members liken many of Eisner's theme park visits to the arrival of royalty. He might demand that the entire staff of a Disney World hotel line up for his entrance. Or, rather than slip in through a back door, he might evacuate a new attraction, queue and all, so he and his party could enjoy the entire experience, without consideration for guests' wait times. In comparison, Walt tried to disappear into the crowd at Disneyland, so he could experience the park exactly as a guest would.

Naturally, Eisner turned his rivalry with Sheinberg into a personal clash of titans. He called out Universal in a Disney profile in *Business Week*. "They invaded our turf," Eisner said, "and we're not going to take that without a fight." Weeks after the story appeared, Disney announced plans to build a retail/entertainment complex near its Burbank headquarters. A few miles away, Universal Studios Hollywood had just begun a $120-million expansion. MCA secretly funded a local group, Friends of Burbank, to campaign against Disney's project. It sent out flyers and riled up the locals at public meetings with dire warnings of the coming traffic jams. The group filed two lawsuits against the city, accusing officials of giving the company a sweetheart deal by offering Disney an exclusive one-year option to buy all 40 acres for $1 million. A year later, Disney later dropped the project, calling it financially unfeasible.

At the same time, Disney increased the budget for its studio park, from $300 million to $550 million. They planned live musicals in a scaled-down Hollywood Bowl. SAK Theater street players would perform interactive skits throughout the park, playing autograph hound, gossip columnist, and other Hollywood types. Star Tours, the *Star Wars*-themed flight simulator being built at Disneyland, seemed like another perfect addition. Yet Disney would have to delay Star Tours' opening at least six months after Disney-MGM opened as a concession to Metropolitan Life, which insisted on opening its sponsored simulator attraction, EPCOT's Body Wars, first.

Encouraged by the success of *Who Framed Roger Rabbit*, Disney expanded the animation studio into its own exhibit. Max Howard, general manager for the filming of *Roger Rabbit*, was hired to lead a staff of 71. Initially, the animators would work on Roger Rabbit shorts, a 22-minute featurette, and provide backup for *The Little Mermaid* and other features underway in California. Guests could then walk along glass-lined hallways to watch real animators working on real movies, drawing, laying out, cleaning up, creating backgrounds, inking and painting, and performing camera and Xerox work.

Universal Studios Hollywood's star attraction was a tram tour past streets, sets and soundstages that had been used in classic movies for 60 years. In Florida, Disney had no moviemaking history. So it decided to make it up in quantity, by recreating the steps of moviemaking, from start to finish. Guests begin by boarding a 70-seat Studio Shuttle to travel past the craft and wardrobe shops, where craftsmen can be seen hard at work. On Residential Street, one of the suburban shells was built expressly to film exterior shots for Disney's hit TV show *The Golden Girls*. At another home, when the tram rolls over a metal plate in the ground, Herbie the Love Bug rolls down the driveway, flips open its hood, and activates its windshield wipers, as if waving to the tourists. The tram continues into Catastrophe Canyon, then past facades of a New York City street set. Guests disembark at an outdoor eatery for a snack break before beginning the walking portion of the tour at the Looney Bin, a recreation of the warehouse scene from *Who Framed Roger Rabbit*. After viewing a special-effects demonstration in the Miss Fortune water-effects tank, visitors follow a plate-glass-lined corridor through the three soundstages, where they can peek in on actual productions, including *The New Mickey Mouse Club*. After watching a short film, *The Lottery* starring Bette Midler, guests tour a soundstage filled with *Lottery* sets and props that demonstrate the wide range of action that can be filmed indoors. Next, guests pass the post-production studios and finally end by watching previews for upcoming Disney movies at the Walt Disney Theatre.

Because Disney had been first to unveil its layout and would be first to open its park, Universal was forced to drastically alter its plans or visitors would think that it was the one that copied Disney. The budget was increased from $200 million to $500 million. They scrapped the legendary tram tour. Privately, Universal operators were relieved. They knew that having a headline, "must-ride" attraction that kept guests in line for an hour or more and then captive on a tram for another hour equaled two-plus hours that visitors couldn't be out spending money in shops and restaurants. Instead, Universal took the major effects from its Hollywood tram tour, such as attacks by Jaws and King Kong, and expanded them into shorter, self-contained rides. In all, they targeted opening with fifteen total attractions—three times as many as Disney-MGM on three times as much land.

Both companies built their soundstages first, so that by the time the parks opened, their facilities could have a year of making movies and television shows under their belts. Certainly, Florida loved the idea of turning Orlando into "Hollywood East." The state already had an aggressive film commission to court Hollywood studios and advertised that its unions-optional status allowed films to be produced for up to 30 percent less than in California or New York.

Disney announced plans to initially build three sound stages—one 15,000 square feet, two 7,500 square feet each. Universal countered that it would build four. Disney claimed its stages had the advantage of allowing visitors to view through darkened, soundproof glass. Universal scoffed that the gimmick would actually scare away big-name actors or producers, other than those working on a Disney production. Both planned to rent their stages to outside production companies, but Disney boasted that it could meet a film crew's every conceivable need—catering, lodging, golf and other entertainment, the whole package.

Universal reported that Nickelodeon agreed to produce more than 450 hours of television programming a year at their studios. With their 35 California soundstages already jammed with production, MCA's Jay Stein predicted that his Florida stages would have shooting every day of the year, ten hours a day. That way, he could advertise that every visitor would be able to see live production. Disney's publicity director Charlie Ridgway vowed that Disney-MGM would match and exceed those numbers. Universal bragged that it had Steven Spielberg as a consultant. Disney had George Lucas. Universal vowed to price admission for its park $2 lower. Disney was happy to let them have that distinction.

So, too, the fight outgrew Florida. As Disney acquired 5,000 acres of farmland near Paris to build a Magic Kingdom park, hotels and possibly a studio tour, MCA started looking for a joint venture partner to build a studio tour in Spain—the country Disney had passed over for France. MCA also divulged plans to build a studio tour in Japan, prompting Disney to begin discussing a possible studio tour next to Tokyo Disneyland.

Pleasure Island was planned to open one year before Disney-MGM. Operations management conceded that they needed some sort of adult entertainment to stem the nightly exodus of guests. And, numbed by the success of serving alcohol at the hotels and EPCOT Center, they trusted the Imagineers would temper the late-night district with a thick coat of pixie dust. The ambitious plan was to dredge a canal across the western end of the Walt Disney World Village's parking lot, creating a six-acre island. Imagineers then concocted an elaborate backstory about Merriweather Pleasure, the island's fictional former owner whose warehouses were turned into nightclubs and restaurants. The result was grown-up fun presented in a fanciful, family-friendly package.

To promote the nightclubs, guests would be allowed to stroll through the area for free, dining, shopping and enjoying the street theater performers, artisans, fireworks and water shows. By then, hopefully they would be sufficiently intrigued to pay a cover charge providing access to all six nightclubs. Originally planned were a jazz club; a comedy club featuring SAK Theater performers; the Adventurers Club, where guest could interact with SAK characters as well as the stuffed animals mounted on the walls; the Mannequins high-tech lounge and dance club; the Zephyr RockinRolladrome, combining rock and roll with rollerskating; and the Videopolis Cafe, an indoor version of Disneyland's popular under-21 dance area.

The subject matter was so foreign to the Imagineers that they could not resist tinkering with the designs. Nightclubs got bigger, smaller, and changed places. A country western bar was added. The continual changes pushed the project farther and farther behind schedule and over budget, much to the displeasure of the general contractor, the Carlson Companies of Atlanta. Frustrated, Carlson wanted off the job. Midway through construction, J.E. Merrit Constructors took over.

Pleasure Island ended up opening the same day as Disney-MGM Studios, May 1, 1989—its cost more than triple the original estimate of $30 million. All the attention of the press and public, however, went to

Disney-MGM. Most guests who did discover Pleasure Island either didn't quite understand or didn't care to pay for what the area had to offer. Its walkways filled with families and teens—the same demographic as the theme parks. This unfortunately was not an audience willing to pay a nightclub cover charge ($6 for one club, $10 for three clubs, or $14.95—the same price as Church Street Station—for six clubs). For them, it was just another backdrop for family photos.

The company's biggest asset—its squeaky clean image—was working against Pleasure Island. Disney reluctantly decided it had to more clearly define its target audience—eighteen-to-34-year-olds—and repackage Pleasure Island as a strictly adult attraction.

Most of the clubs changed. At the Neon Armadillo, the bar was torn out and moved to a more accessible location. Instead of subcontracting SAK Theater performers to perform at the Comedy Warehouse and The Adventurer's Club, when the SAK Theater contract ended before Pleasure Island opened, Disney decided to hire away SAK members to start its own group. While they worked perfectly interacting in The Adventurer's Club and as "Streetmosphere" performers in Disney-MGM, the reaction was a little shakier at the comedy club, although an irreverent "Forbidden Disney" show went over well. So Disney decided to supplement the improv with edgier, experienced stand-up comics.

Just as at Disneyland's Videopolis, Pleasure Island's Videopolis East was attracting the wrong crowd—local, sometimes troubled teens who used the nightspot as a hangout. One night, about 25 youths began arguing at the club. A full-scale brawl erupted. One nineteen-year-old pulled out a hunting knife and stabbed a sixteen-year-old. As the victim crumpled to the floor, an eighteen-year-old friend bent over to help and was stabbed in the lower back.

Unsupervised teens were not among Disney's target markets. Videopolis East, with its fog, strobe lights and corrugated metal pipes, transformed into The Cage, which retained the dark, misty atmosphere and video monitors, but would not admit unaccompanied minors. More seating was added to the once-primarily-standing-room club, to encourage staying a while and buying a drink. Black chain-link fencing was installed indoors to give the place a more adult, "lower Manhattan" feel. The revamped club proved so successful, Disney began laying out plans to add an outdoor dance area and a bank of TV monitors so those outside could watch those dancing inside.

Guests were in even greater danger at the XZFR Rockin'
Rollerdrome. Inside, an oval-shaped roller rink wrapped around the
dance floor on the second of the club's three tiers. But rollerskating,
Disney discovered, didn't mix well with drinking. Bumps and bruises
were commonplace. One woman collided with another skater, fell, and
broke her arm in three places. Disney pulled out the roller rink and
canned the Time Pilots, the corny, spacesuit-clad house band. The venue
switched to live classic rock and roll and was renamed the Rock 'n' Roll
Beach Club, with a Southern California beachfront theme. Officially, the
remodeling had nothing to do with safety; it was to increase capacity for
adults, who weren't interested in skating.

Disney also remerchandised the shops, realizing they would now be
frequented by active, young adults. They eliminated some of the higher
priced clothing lines, brought in younger, hipper styles, and redesigned
all the Pleasure Island-branded merchandise and logos with a more up-
to-date look.

Most importantly, an admission gate was placed in front of Pleasure
Island. As of April 1990, anyone who wanted to get onto the island after
7 p.m. had to pay $9.95, which included access to all six clubs. No one
under eighteen would be admitted without an adult. Instantly, the area
felt more mature and exclusive. The gate cut down on the hassle of
wristband checks outside every club and made it easier to market the
area for private events and convention functions.

Marketing now needed a hook to stress the district's uniqueness. One
staffer suggested having a spaceship land in the middle of Pleasure
Island to celebrate Christmas every day of the year. Although absurd, the
idea did lead to an inspired suggestion: throwing a New Year's Eve party
every night of the year, complete with countdown, party favors, and fireworks. On weekdays, they could even move the big countdown up to 11
p.m. instead of midnight.

At first, cast members drove visitors to distraction by constantly wishing them "Happy New Year." Still, the nightly promotion caught on
quickly as guests were handed party favors and hats and heard a band
begin playing at the end of the street. After fireworks, explosions and
showers of confetti, professional dancers appeared on the rooftops to
encourage revelers to dance in the streets. The entire island seemed to
turn into a live music video.

The new and improved Pleasure Island was relaunched with a mas-

sive television and print ad campaign to stress that it had grown up and
gotten hip. The changes worked. Soon, large crowds were packing the
place, at least on weekends when there would be a 45-minute wait just to
enter Mannequins or The Cage.

Previews for Typhoon Lagoon coincided with Pleasure Island's,
although the water park officially opened a month later. The 56-acre
venue featured a variety of extreme slides, kids' areas, a salt-water, coral
reef diving pool, and a signature wave pond, where a new surge rolled in
every 90 seconds. Waves could be generated as large as eight feet, but
for safety reasons Disney determined to cap their height at four feet. The
waves would still be large enough to surf, but a few weeks before the
opening, Disney invited a group of professional surfers and bodyboard-
ers to preview the pool. Watching the flotation equipment fly in relatively tight quarters, management realized they had to outlaw surfing and
bodyboarding—even though they had just invested in hundreds of rental
bodyboards.

The weekend before its grand opening Monday, May 1, Disney-
MGM held three days of invitation-only previews, portions of which
were filmed and then televised Sunday evening. Unfortunately, torrential
rain struck just in time for the second night's World Premiere gala, when
stars were supposed to "make their marks" in cement in front of the
Chinese Theater and pose for photos with Eisner. After an interminable
delay, celebrities in black tie and black umbrella began to wade down a
soggy red carpet along Hollywood Boulevard. In the stunt show theater,
Willie Nelson and the Pointer Sisters both cut their concerts short, and
comedian George Burns performed one half-hour set instead of two.
Thanks to slick editing, everything would run seamlessly on TV.

Guests received a more realistic picture when the park opened to the
public. On Day One, cars quickly overwhelmed the 4,500-space parking
lot. Not long after, the park itself reached its maximum of 25,000 guests.
The next morning, the park opened 90 minutes earlier, and the parking
lot was again packed by 9 a.m. Sell-out crowds returned nearly every
day during the park's first summer. What visitors discovered was that
Disney-MGM offered all of five attractions—the 22-minute Great Movie
Ride, 30-minute SuperStar Television, twelve-minute Monster Sound
Show, 25-minute Magic of Disney Animation, and two-plus-hour
Backlot Studio Tour.

Shortly after the park opened each morning, wait times surpassed an hour at every attraction. Makeshift queue lines snaked along the park's sidewalks and streets, increasing congestion in already tight quarters and forcing guests to wait unprotected beneath the scorching sun or rain clouds. Three of the largest capacity shows—the Indiana Jones stunt show, SuperStar Television, and Monster Sound Show—were also designed to exit into the same general area. When performances ended at the same time, 4,000 people poured into one thoroughfare, bringing the entire east side of the park to a standstill.

Since most of the ride systems were based on established technologies, breakdowns were less common. Occasionally, Catastrophe Canyon malfunctioned, and trams would take a detour around the area. The Great Movie Ride's 100-plus figures performed fairly reliably, though sometimes off-cue. During previews, however, Disney had been forced to place a plastic bag over the head of Clint Eastwood. The Imagineers had assumed that, because Eastwood and Frank Wells were close friends, they would gain all necessary permissions to use the actor's likeness. But the lawyers insisted the figure remain shrouded until the paperwork was finalized.

The ride's most problematic scene was its first, an extravagant set piece from Busby Berkeley's musical *Footlight Parade*, featuring dozens of 1930s bathing beauties rotating on a gigantic, five-tiered cake, as fountains of water shot forth and bubbles filled the room. Rarely could Imagineering get all the effects working simultaneously. As the years went on, they would gradually give up on the scene, first by covering the cake with a partially-see-through scrim, then by removing the art deco details and showgirls on diving boards that led up to the cake, and by turning off the fanciful lighting, fountains, bubble machine, and the cake's rotation mechanism.

More often, early guests complained that there was little evidence of actual filming at Disney-MGM. *The New Mickey Mouse Club* was the studio's only ongoing production. Most visitors peering through the glass walls into the soundstages saw a half-built set for a TV commercial, a rehearsal by college musicians, or an empty room.

Ironically, when New York Street was being used for real film production, the area had to be cleared of guests. To fake it, Disney had a group of cast members dress up as a production crew and each morning pretend they were doing actual shooting.

"The biggest concern about the studio, I felt, was this: how legitimate and how real was it?" said marketing head Tom Elrod. "So we were concerned about having production go on within the facility—shows being filmed, movies being filmed, having celebrities there all the time. We created a thing called Star a Day where a celebrity would be paraded down Main Street, sign autographs, and answer questions, so it differentiated it and made it an exciting part of what Hollywood was."

The tram tour, originally intended as the park's centerpiece, was the biggest letdown. Covering so little acreage and offering so little to see, the attraction seemed little more than an excuse to drive through Catastrophe Canyon. Disney tried to fill the tour's empty spaces with props like a trolley and the Dipmobile from *Who Framed Roger Rabbit*. Children usually perked up when Herbie the Love Bug came rolling down the driveway—though the Volkswagen's best reception occurred during one performance when the car shorted out and caught fire. The tram passengers, impressed by the pyrotechnics, burst into applause.

Disney-MGM's shortcomings were magnified when compared to its sister parks. Since the third gate was intentionally designed to be significantly smaller in size and to offer significantly less to do, executives initially considered pricing its admission significantly less than for the Magic Kingdom and EPCOT Center. Marketing's Jack Lindquist was among those who fought for—and won—identical pricing for all three parks. "The key in Florida is selling multiple-day admissions, three-, four-day tickets," Lindquist said. "So, the value—real or perceived—has to look the same. Disney-MGM just barely met that. My feeling was if you had separate prices, separate tickets, you would force people to choose between parks and they wouldn't buy three-day admissions. It's economics."

With the opening of Disney-MGM, the resort eliminated the two- and three-day park passes in favor of four- and five-day tickets. For the majority of guests, who purchased multi-park tickets, the shortcomings of the half-day park were quickly forgotten amidst the multitude of other activities during their stay. Using multi-day hopper tickets, guests could move on to the other parks once they had seen all of Disney-MGM. The single-park ticket buyers were not as fortunate. A number of them headed for Guest Relations to register their displeasure.

"We got complaints," admitted Jim Moore, recalling guest reaction to pricing, congestion and limited attractions during the park's first months.

"We had been told [to inform guests] that quality wasn't measured in size. But guests were paying the same price as Magic Kingdom and EPCOT for a park that was one-third the size. I remember giving full refunds. We were told to use our discretion."

Despite the grumbling customers inside the gates, from the outside everything looked perfect. In addition to the 8,000 reporters Disney flew in for the premiere, the company spent tens of millions of dollars on glitzy advertising to ensure a positive message went forth. They also reversed Old Disney's policy of refusing travel agents commissions on ticket packages, trading in a tiny percentage of the sale for ground-level public relations. Travel agents, in return, would pass along Disney-friendly advice, such as advising their clients that renting a car "usually" wasn't necessary, since there was an entire vacation's worth of activities just on Disney property.

The company left nothing to chance. For all the public knew, the park was an unadulterated smash. "There are a lot of people coming through and seemingly enjoying it very much," a park publicist confirmed vaguely.

Advance reservations continued pouring in for Disney's hotels.

In the meantime, Disney knew it had to act quickly before word of mouth drowned out the paid publicity. They planted shade trees in some of the waiting areas. To create more walking room, they deannexed New York Street from the tram tour and opened up the Ewok Village in front of Star Tours. To provide greater flexibility in viewing the park, they began offering the option of an abridged version of the two-hour backlot tour. By cutting the tour into two halves, Disney also created the illusion that it was actually two attractions instead of one.

Indeed, the lack of rides was by far the most acute problem. It took three months to get all the effects working in the Indiana Jones stunt show. The park absolutely could not begin a second summer season without more attractions. They furiously began courting television shows built around live audience participation—such as a revival of *Let's Make a Deal* and a *Disney Channel Auditions* talent contest—so they could double as attractions. They commissioned a new Dick Tracy musical for the compact Theater of the Stars, to replace a generic show-biz revue, and drew up plans to eventually replace the venue itself with a 3,000-seat amphitheater. Work started on a Honey, I Shrunk the Kids

Thrills and Spills

Training the actors to perform the elaborate stunts delayed the first performances of the Indiana Jones Stunt Spectacular until late May. Even then, technical difficulties prevented the entire show from being presented until August, when all major effects were fully functional.

Even with the huge rolling boulder and troublesome earthquake effect finally working, every performance did not run smoothly. In one scene, Indiana Jones was supposed to be slugging it out with a German mechanic near a spinning airplane. The villain was to lift Indiana just as the plane's wing passed over his shoulder. During one performance, the hero was standing just off his mark and, as he was picked up by his co-star, the wing hit him in the face. He lost one tooth and required seven stitches in his chin and dental surgery to wire in three other teeth. During another show, a stuntman's restraining cable malfunctioned, and he fell nearly 30 feet to the pavement below. In another stunt, Indiana was to balance himself on a ladder as it swayed back and forth three times. One actor fell 25 feet when the ladder gave way. In September, another Indy lost his grip on the ladder, fell and suffered cuts and bruises. Producers changed the stunt so the ladder swayed only once. Yet, the rash of accidents finally caught the attention of the Occupational Safety & Health Administration.

Midway through OSHA's five-month investigation, the German mechanic, who was supposed to drop through an escape hatch just as a pretend airplane propeller swung toward him, had the trap door close on him. Again, the script was rewritten so instead of being chewed up by a propeller, the mechanic is simply shot to death.

On March 1, 1990, OSHA submitted its report. Disney was fined $1,000 for unsafe conditions, including exposing actors to drops of 28 feet onto concrete. They were instructed to add padding and guardrails. Disney also revised its highest stunt. Instead of jumping off the top of a building facade, performers would hold a loop in a rope and slide to the ground, landing on newly installed mats. One month after the report was issued, an actress rehearsing the new stunt lost her grip on the rope, fell 20 feet, and broke her hip.

Adventure Zone to open by Christmas 1990.

Disney also agreed to acquire the Muppets from Jim Henson, with plans to open an entire new land at Disney-MGM called The Muppet Studios. The area would feature a MuppetVision 3-D movie theater, Muppet stage show, Muppet parade, and Muppets' Movie Ride, taking guests on "a misguided tour through movie history." Before the deal could close, Henson died. Disney negotiators nonetheless aggressively pushed forward, alienating Henson's heirs. His children canceled the sale and agreed only to license the characters for individual attractions, allowing the 3-D movie, Here Come the Muppets show, and Magnificent Muppets All-Star Parade to proceed.

With Disney-MGM open and a financial success, both Disney and Universal began to play down their feud—Disney hoping that Universal got as little press as possible, Universal hoping to generate its own identity and publicity. In a special supplement in the *Orlando Sentinel* to commemorate Universal's grand opening, Disney ran a full-page ad on the back cover declaring, "What's good for tourism and entertainment is good for Central Florida."

Universal unveiled its park thirteen months after Disney-MGM, at a cost of $630 million. Even then, it wasn't quite ready. Hours before the park opened for the first time, a power outage knocked out the software that ran the Earthquake attraction. Similarly, problems with the master software program on Kongfrontation forced technicians to trigger the 37-foot-tall primate's movements manually. That afternoon, thunderstorms shut down the Jaws boat ride. The three had been the most heavily promoted attractions at the park. Attractions that were operable, such as the E.T. Adventure dark ride and Ghostbusters special effects show, malfunctioned sporadically. Lines elsewhere grew interminably long.

Some vacationers, drawn to Orlando by the family friendliness of the Magic Kingdom, were shocked to witness the scarier edge of Universal, which celebrated monsters, disasters and the shower scene from *Psycho*. Finally, drained by the sweltering summer heat and angered by the closed attractions, visitors swarmed Guest Relations. One thousand guests—ten percent of the crowd—demanded refunds. News cameras, which one year before had captured the thousands of smiling faces at Disney-MGM's grand opening, now recorded the disgruntled hordes at Universal's.

To counter the bad publicity, Universal pulled all advertising that mentioned Kong and Earthquake, so the public wouldn't get the mistaken impression that the rides were working. Tickets takers at the front gate also warned visitors as they were entering that the slightly more reliable Jaws wasn't working either, even if it happened to be. Better to have guests pleasantly surprised than disappointed. And, through the summer, every customer who paid for admission was given a second free ticket to return a different day when all key rides were operable.

The bad news spread quickly. After three straight weeks of low attendance, Universal began reducing employees' hours. At the same time, they increased the park's first-year publicity budget to $150 million. It took the rest of the summer to get Jaws working more than part-time and to get Kong and Earthquake working at all.

Despite a coming recession, Universal Studios Florida eventually reached respectable attendance levels by establishing its own identity through tireless, extreme marketing and for one day prying tourists away from Disney.

Disney-MGM still needed its own signature, E-ticket-caliber attraction to establish itself as a legitimate full-day park. Eisner's preference was to beat Universal at its own game. Even though a segment of Universal Studios visitors complained that the park was too extreme, Eisner rationalized that folding a few thrills into Disney-MGM could expand its appeal to teenagers. Imagineers submitted a litany of proposals—a Roger Rabbit roller coaster, a horror film neighborhood, an interactive show about a mystery writer. One staffer suggested adapting the Freefall drop ride from Southern California's Six Flags Magic Mountain. In theory, the project would be affordable, since the ride technology already existed and could be combined with earlier plans for a walk-through haunted hotel.

For the storyline, Imagineers created a silent film director who, embittered after his career is destroyed by the advent of talkies, haunts the guests of a Hollywood hotel, ultimately cutting the elevator cables and sending visitors plunging to their doom. The unwieldy plot, however, centered on the silent film era—defeating the purpose of designing something hip for teens. Later, someone suggested theming the attraction to *The Twilight Zone* television series, which remained popular through reruns. By re-editing old footage of Rod Serling and dubbing in new dialogue by an impersonator, Serling could tell the tale of a stormy Halloween 1939, when during a swank party at the Hollywood Tower Hotel, an elevator carrying five guests disappeared into another dimension. The hotel has sat abandoned every since. Now, Serling invites theme park guests to step into the service elevator to re-enact the fateful journey. Once strapped into the elevator car, riders cross into a special effects-laden fifth dimension and finally plummet from the thirteenth floor.

Everyone loved the idea, except Operations management, which noted that riders regularly complained about being caught off guard by the sudden drop on Splash Mountain. On Tower of Terror, they insisted, guests should be able to see what they're getting into. Imagineers designed a hole in the front of the building, as if torn open by lightning, so the falling elevators were visible from outside. The array of changes and elaborations, particularly the prototype ride system required to transport vehicles through the fifth dimension, pushed the cost to an estimated $150 million. But when the ride opened in July 1994, the Twilight Zone Tower of Terror established Disney-MGM as a park that could stand on its own—with an edgy thrill ride that looked less like a typical Disney attraction than something to be found at Universal Studios.

15

It's a Jungle in Here

FOLLOWING five years of record-setting revenues, Michael Eisner brashly proclaimed that the 1990s would be "The Disney Decade." Internally, that meant continuing the seemingly unsustainable rates of growth. Eisner demanded that every division year in, year out, increase sales and profit by 20 percent.

To the public, he promised Disney cruise ships, more hotels, dozens of additional attractions, and entire new theme parks—a Magic Kingdom-style park in France and a fourth park at Disney World. The bulk of the building was earmarked for Florida, where the company's largest shareholders, the Bass brothers, encouraged Eisner to quickly develop as much land as possible. Disney's holdings stretched across both Orange and Osceola counties; yet by 1990, all commercial development had been restricted to Orange County. Situating operations closer together made them more accessible and convenient. In addition, by leaving its acreage in Osceola County as timberlands and cow pastures, Disney could lease portions to cattle farmers and loggers, and thereby pay the county taxes at an agricultural rate instead of the significantly higher commercial rate. Secretly, Disney Development Company land experts began researching possible residential and otherwise conventional uses for the Osceola land, since there seemed to be ample acreage in

Orange County for their amusement needs.

At the same time, neither county was happy with the arrangement. Heavy development of Disney's northern property upset Orange County. For years, the county had been trying to get the company to help pay for nearby roads, schools and other services required by the influx of workers and visitors drawn by Disney. Worse, the company had started building more hotels, convention facilities, and a Crossroads shopping center just off Interstate 4, all competing against businesses that were paying into county coffers. Disney executives also reneged on a previous offer to provide an EPCOT station for a high-speed "Mag-Lev" train from the airport, once they learned the train might stop at Universal Studios or other businesses along the way. Increasingly, citizens and civic leaders began urging city attorneys to challenge the Reedy Creek Improvement District's exemption from impact fees. In 1989, Disney reluctantly agreed to pay Orange County about $18 million for road improvements over the next six years. In return, the county would hold off on any legal action threatening Reedy Creek's charter.

Beforehand, Disney had been concerned primarily with its national corporate image. Now, for the first time, it could see the downside of a poor local identity. In 1990, Dianna Morgan, former Guest Relations hostess-turned-community outreach manager, was rehired as vice president of government relations. Conveniently, Morgan was also a close friend of Linda Chapin, Orange County chairman, and Glenda Hood, Orlando's next mayor.

"In the early days," Morgan said, "*anything* we did [for charity] was appreciated. In time, we became more strategic. We thought about what we should be [serving] with our dollars—issues with children, education. We began placing and encouraging our leaders to lead non-profit organizations, one as chairman of the Chamber of Commerce, one as head of a United Way chapter. As the area's largest employer, we needed to be recognized as providing positive value in the communities. We worked with schools. The company awarded grants and worked closely with many different children's organizations, such as Give Kids the World. Later, we created a very large employee volunteer program, realizing the executives on their own couldn't be the faces of Disney in the community."

While Orange County received more Disney development than it might have liked, more rural Osceola County received less. Osceola did inherit cheap motels with gaudy neon signs, tacky T-shirt shops, and other Harbor Boulevard-type tourist traps. County commissioners yearned for quality Disney investments—and the taxes they would generate. Despite years of vague promises by Bob Allen, nothing ever happened. In 1987, Allen died of a heart attack at age 55. Dick Nunis was forced to resume the community relations mantel. Subtlety was never his virtue. After Nunis let slip that development in Osceola County was pending, the county tried to impose the higher commercial tax rate on Disney's land. A nasty fight erupted that culminated in Disney conceding to pay the commercial rate on just a fraction of its land in Osceola, and each year pay the higher rate on a larger percentage of its acreage.

At the same time, Eisner and Wells began to notice that Disney's theme parks were not guaranteed, non-stop money machines. The effects of a recession and the Persian Gulf War pushed park revenues down slightly and profits down drastically in 1991. The parks recovered slowly, but by 1993 were generating less profit than Disney's filmed entertainment for the first time in nearly 30 years. Still, Disney's live action films, which had enjoyed an unbroken string of successes through the late 1980s, were beginning to suffer more misses than hits.

In 1992, Euro Disneyland opened near Paris. The executives considered the park, their first in Europe, a sure thing. They ignored veteran managers' warnings against building too many hotels, overpricing, the chilly climate, and French resistance to American pop culture. The park would spend the next fifteen-plus years losing money and teetering on the edge of bankruptcy.

So, too, in 1993, the company announced plans for a Disney's America historical theme park near colonial Williamsburg, Virginia. Critics were appalled that Disney might desecrate hallowed ground near Civil War battlefields and possibly turn slavery and other sensitive moments of the nation's history into theme park rides. Eisner arrogantly dismissed the criticisms, enflaming the situation. Disney abandoned the project.

Until the icy reception to Euro Disneyland, corporate had avoided interfering too deeply with theme park management. The background of Eisner and Wells' team meshed with what had been ailing Disney: movies and television. So Dick Nunis and top management at Disney World and Disneyland were left comparatively to their own devices, albeit given a lot more attractions and other facilities to market and generate revenue from. And they did.

Burbank wanted more. A change in management had revitalized the studio and particularly the animation department. Outsiders with retail backgrounds had launched the successful chain of Disney Stores. But the old-timers at the theme parks continued clinging to what they called "show," but corporate saw as "fat." Now was the time to inject 21st Century management into the parks.

The first big change came in 1991. Nunis, whose bluntness chafed Eisner and others in corporate, was "promoted" to chairman of Walt Disney Attractions and replaced as president by Judson Green, who would oversee day-to-day operations. A numbers man, Green had joined Disney in 1981 as a senior vice president and chief financial officer, after beginning his career as a CPA with Arthur Young & Co. in Chicago.

Over the next few years, fresh-faced youngsters with Ivy League MBAs started popping up backstage at Disney World. None had any theme park experience. Yet these new executives and consultants were charged with analyzing and advising on how the parks should be run. Managers soon found themselves spending half of each workday recounting and justifying every move they made.

Seniority, once a virtue, suddenly became a black mark. "Most of us stopped wearing our 20-year pins and rings because we had become targets," Spencer Craig said. "They couldn't understand us and didn't think we could or would change. I'd say, 'I'm a buyer. I have to change five times a year!'"

Old-timers who used to pride themselves on remaining current with the "Order of the Red Handkerchief," a club for workers on Disneyland's old Mine Train ride, stopped carrying around their membership cards. Retirees would no longer receive a personalized "Disney Hall of Fame" picture.

To jumpstart the transition, "Old Disney" managers were offered generous retirement packages and threatened that anyone who stayed past June 1994 would receive reduced insurance benefits. Just before the deadline, 45-to-60-year-old veterans retired by the dozens. Operations' primary defenders of show, Bob Mathieson and Bill Sullivan, retired on the same day. Nunis would stay on in his marginalized position another five years, as—he would confide to associates—a thorn in Eisner's backside.

With Mathieson and Sully out of the way, their successors were free to discard expensive elements that added greatly to the Disney show, but not necessarily the bottom line. Within three months of their leaving, the Magic Kingdom pulled the plug on the labor-intensive Davy Crockett's Explorer Canoes and 20,000 Leagues under the Sea attractions. One by one, the remaining show elements on Main Street—the Firehouse, Main Street Cinema, Main Street Bookstore, Penny Arcade, House of Magic—were transformed into generic stores. The West Center Street cul-de-sac, which created a charming courtyard in front of the flower market, was enclosed and swallowed up by the Emporium. The antique and silversmith shops in Liberty Square were replaced by a Christmas ornament outlet. The Contemporary's Top of the World dinner theater was remodeled into a conventional restaurant. Live entertainment was replaced by an animatronic performer at the Tomorrowland Terrace. The Adventureland Veranda closed entirely.

Initially, most guests didn't seem to notice. Yet internally, that common pursuit of show had been the glue that kept every division, in fact every cast member, moving selflessly in the same direction. Every effort, no matter what one's position, had been directed at creating happiness for the guests. As show became increasingly, overtly subservient to the new, executive-mandated goal of generating maximum amounts of cash, divisions lost their incentive to help each other. Teamwork fell by the wayside. Suddenly everyone became consumed with covering their own backs.

The kingdom further splintered in 1994 when Frank Wells was killed in a helicopter crash. Theme park operations had lost a leader who at least tried to understand their idiosyncrasies. Eisner, too proud to accept another executive as equal, assumed sole leadership of the company, both creative and financial. Both sides of the business were to suffer. Eisner became further overextended when, less than two years later, Disney acquired Capital Cities/ABC, which added a broadcast network, ten broadcast television stations, four cable networks, 21 radio stations, two publishing companies, seven daily newspapers, and six international media companies.

Several of the divisions were ailing. The only sure thing seemed to be the fourth theme park at Disney World. The additions of EPCOT Center and then Disney-MGM energized revenues for the resort and the company as a whole. And the next logical target was a wild animal-themed park designed to filter guests from Busch Gardens and Sea World.

Imagineers spent the early 1990s dreaming up park concepts and attractions, under Eisner's preference that they revolve around animals. Designers visited hundreds of zoos and traveled to Africa and Asia. They quickly discovered that displaying wild animals in captivity had become a sensitive topic. So, Disney hired staff from respected zoos and assembled an independent advisory board with leaders from the top environmental organizations.

The company kept word of the project under wraps until the spring of 1994 when small groups of Disney World tourists were pulled aside for a brief marketing study. First, they were shown a confidential video introducing them to the proposed wildlife park. Concept art depicted visitors entering the park through a lush grotto of flowers, streams and waterfalls, tentatively called Genesis Gardens. Imagineers already knew they would be changing the title, since the name sounded "too Biblical," especially considering the first stop was a fourteen-story-tall icon called The Tree of Life.

Crossing Safari River into the central Safari Village, the proposed park branches into five different lands. The first, Beastly Kingdom, land of myths of legends, splits into the realms of Good and Evil. The Evil side features the Dragon's Tower, an inverted roller coaster that weaves through the burned-out castle of a treasure-hoarding dragon. Before the trip, bats hanging upside-down from darkened perches implore riders to help them rob the dragon. The ensuing chase through the castle ends with a fiery confrontation with the dragon. In the Good realm, guests walk through the Quest for the Unicorn, a maze of mythological creatures to "seek a hidden grotto where a unicorn lives," and Fantasia Gardens, a musical boat ride past dancing hippos and other characters from *Fantasia*.

In Africa, guests enjoy nature walks, visit a gorilla preserve, and board Jeeps for a 20-minute safari across the savannah, viewing giraffes, zebras and elephants. During the environmentally correct adventure, poachers slay a mother elephant, but are captured before they can attack its orphaned baby.

At Preservation Station, visitors tour the park's conservation and rare animal breeding facilities.

In Asia, leopards, rhinos, monkeys and other exotic animals populate a faux rainforest with colorful waterfalls and mysterious ruins. The wildlife can be viewed from nature trails or a white-water rafting ride with an anti-logging backstory. Passengers learn that the muddy rapids were caused by deforestation, which threatens the animal habitats. Fortunately, the ride ends at a maharajah's hunting palace that has been converted into the headquarters for Operation Tiger, which rescues tigers and restores rainforests so "man and animal [can] live in harmony."

In Dinoland, guests enjoy the Boneyard Playground sandbox; the Excavator, a rickety roller coaster through a dinosaur dig; and a simulator ride that travels back in time to save prehistoric animals from the comet that ended the age of the dinosaurs.

After viewing the marketing presentation, guests were asked to complete a questionnaire gauging their opinions on each element of the park. They were even asked to pick a name; did they prefer Disney's Animal Kingdom, Disney's Wild World, Disney's Animal Adventure, Disney's Wild Territorium, The Animal Expedition at Disney, or Disney's Animal Encounter? Most importantly, the survey wanted to know, would the park convince them to cancel a side trip to Busch Gardens?

Continuing the frantic hotel expansion was a no-brainer. After Tishman completed the Swan and Dolphin hotels in 1990, Disney built its own Yacht Club and Beach Club resorts nearby, followed by the sprawling mid-level properties Port Orleans and Dixie Landings. Next on tap were a luxury resort near the campground and an Atlantic City boardwalk and hotel across the lake from the Yacht Club.

Disney now offered lodgings in every category except for timeshares and budget motels—markets they had intentionally avoided because of their tawdry reputations. The timeshare industry was known for high-pressure sales, shabby upkeep of properties, inflexibility in vacation times, and difficulty in reselling contracts. Yet they did ensure repeat visitors year after year, and those were visitors who weren't staying on Disney property. The company decided to expand into timeshares, if it could eliminate the primary complaints. Disney would instead stress low-pressure sales and superior accommodations. A flexible point system replaced set weeks. And the company would buy back under-priced resale contracts to protect the timeshare's value. Disney designed the first Key West-style dwellings along a golf course bordering Lake Buena Vista. Sales began in 1991. Within three years, the Disney Vacation Club had built 497 units and sold half the available contracts. They hurried to develop plans for additional properties, but these would be more strategically based at existing Disney hotels to consolidate expenses and improve accessibility.

Similarly, Disney thought it could succeed in the budget motel arena by controlling operating costs per unit. They just had to build a huge number of rooms and compensate for the meager furnishings with over-the-top theming. In 1992, Disney announced it would construct three "All-Star" complexes totaling over 4,500 rooms, plus a water park, in Osceola County. Listing for $69 to $79 a night, the no-frills accommodations would offer about 270 square feet and two double beds, instead of the average 400 square feet with two queen-size beds and a day bed found at Disney's luxury properties. The towels would be an inch shorter, the sheets a lower thread count, the carpeting less plush, and the lamps and tables scaled down as well. The rooms would contain no hand or face cream, sewing kits, scissors or other fancy amenities; just soap and conditioner. The rooms would open to a paved, outside hallway, instead of a thickly carpeted interior hallway. There would be a central food court in place of table service restaurants. And staffing would be drastically lower—0.38 workers per room instead of the 1.1 to 1.5 workers per room at the luxury hotels. Most telling, instead of charming details, the motels would be designed with gigantic, brightly colored icons; the All-Star Sports would feature four-story football helmets and tennis ball cans, the All-Star Music a huge juke box and musical instruments, and the All-Star Movies larger-than-life Dalmatians and a 35-foot-tall Buzz Lightyear.

One challenge of opening the first facilities in Osceola County was their distance from all the action on Disney's Orange County property. As a cross-promotion scheme, when Blizzard Beach opened in 1995, the water park sent its costumed mascot, Ice Gator, to visit the nearby All-Star motels. Children spotted the big blue alligator in the lobby and rushed to greet him, only to stop in their tracks upon realizing they had no idea who this character was. The character's handler then explained that he came from Blizzard Beach, and how it was right next door and loads of fun.

Motel visits were actually more pleasant than the character's normal duty—which was greeting guests near the Lottawatta Lodge as they entered the park in the mornings. "Unfortunately," remembered Josh Edwards, "most guests (a) didn't know the character—although he *is* in the park's logo—and (b) wanted to get the prime locker space so they could quickly get their buns up to the big slides before they got busy. So Ice Gator usually just dodged people as they ran past him."

Ice Gator's costume was made entirely of thick rubber, so the character could frolic with guests in the water. "Airtight," Edwards noted. "Yup. Airtight. In Florida. In the summer. Oops. Unfortunately, this made the suit much less breathable and *much* heavier than a standard rubberhead suit. Also, the gator had a huge tail, again of heavy waterproof material. This made it very difficult to navigate—and not thwack small children with your backside."

Each hotel or water park might consume 50 to 75 acres. So to squeeze a return out of the thousand of undeveloped acres, Eisner concluded he would have to expand beyond traditional amusement-related businesses. He chose two ideas that unintentionally traced back to Walt's desire to build a city that other cities could learn from. Walt's immediate successors, stumped on how to build an actual city, proposed instead creating "a school for cities." Being an entertainment company, Walt Disney Productions envisioned the school primarily as a cultural center, an EPCOT Institute of the Arts, that could teach how to produce ballets and assemble classical orchestras. Its seminars on city planning could be beamed by satellite to countries around the world.

Eisner, inspired by his fondness for the Chautauqua Institute in New York, pictured such an institute as luring a whole new type of clientele to Disney World: adults looking for a cultured vacation. Disney already had in place much of the infrastructure—the underused townhomes, golf course, tennis courts, and swimming pools at Lake Buena Vista. It had become increasingly difficult to lease the townhouses, so Disney had been left to market them to tourists on a nightly basis. The proliferation of on-site hotels and the introduction of spacious Disney Vacation Club rooms made these rooms superfluous. So Disney converted the 58-acre complex into the Disney Institute. Guests custom-designed their own packages, for a minimum three-night stay, that included accommodations and access to more than 80 programs and workshops, such as rock climbing, cooking, golf and animation. Dozens of guest artists and speakers agreed to teach, perform and mingle, including pro athletes, animators, architects, computer experts, financial advisers, chefs, choreographers and conductors the likes of John Williams and Elmer Bernstein. Costumed characters, however, were outlawed, to maintain the more serious atmosphere.

At the same time, Disney broke ground on the second new venture—an actual city on 4,900 acres of its most outlying Osceola property, surrounded by 4,700 acres of greenbelt. Being Disney, the company was not content to build a conventional city. Theirs had to be heavily themed, basically as a revival of Norman Rockwell's America powered by state-of-the-art technology. According to sales brochures for the town of Celebration, "There once was a place where neighbors greeted neighbors in the quiet of summer twilight. Where children chased fireflies... The movie house showed cartoons on Saturday... The grocery store delivered... Remember that place?... It held a magic all its own. The special magic of an American hometown."

The quaint-looking homes appeared as if they had been plucked from Main Street USA. Front porches promoted neighborliness. Garages were hidden in the back, accessed by unseen alleys. All stores were a short walk away, in a central town center, to limit automobile traffic. Beneath the veneer of old-fashioned charm, all homes were equipped with fiber-optic cable for phone and television. The town's health facility, designed to look like a Mediterranean-style hotel, had no waiting rooms; patients would be paged when their doctor was ready to see them and they could leave their car with a valet. The Celebration School employed cutting-edge teaching methods for grades K through 12.

The company wanted Celebration to feel special, but not exclusive. It would not be a gated community. Disney envisioned the town more as a tourist attraction, especially since the downtown merchants would require tourist dollars to keep their upscale specialty shops viable.

The parallels to Walt's EPCOT, down to the projected 20,000 residents, were unmistakable. Both contained technologically tweaked, romanticized small towns of 50 years earlier. Walt's inspiration was turn-of-the-century Marceline. Generations of the 1990s harkened back to the Ozzie and Harriet suburbs of the 1950s.

Eisner later boasted in interviews and in his biography, *Work in Progress*, that Celebration was built in part to make good on Walt's promise of a futuristic city. In truth, at the time Eisner saw the connection to EPCOT as a negative; the public would invariably compare the two, and his real city would likely pale when held up to Walt's more altruistic dream.

Certainly, Celebration planners struggled with the same challenges of how to maintain the perfection. Homeowners received a phone book-sized manual of community standards—regulating everything from the ratio of grass, trees and shrubs on their property to the color of their curtains (white or off-white only). Residents were surveyed regularly. Those who accepted the gift of a free computer and cell phone lived with a "Zeus Box" that tracked every call they made and every website they visited. Roving security guards, backed up by Osceola County sheriff's deputies, constantly patrolled the city, as if it were an extension of the Magic Kingdom. And, to protect its monopoly voting power over its entire property, the company de-annexed Celebration from the Reedy Creek Improvement District, as it had done with Little Lake Bryan when it decided to build apartments at the retreat.

Not everyone was scared off by Celebration's mountain of regulations. On November 18, 1995, a lottery attracted nearly 5,000 hopefuls vying to secure the first 351 houses and 122 apartments. Phase one included six architectural styles priced from $128,000 to $900,000—about one-third more than comparable homes outside of Celebration.

Many of the lottery winners did not consider themselves lucky for long. A construction labor shortage contributed to a large number of construction defects, from crooked walls and leaky roofs to garages being built across property lines. One house was constructed so poorly it had to be torn down and rebuilt from the foundation up. One resident, exasperated at her collapsing home, tried to ward off unsuspecting new homebuyers, but was barred from hanging signs at her home. Instead, she plastered her car with images of lemons. Neighbors called her the Lemon Lady.

Other homeowners tired of the armies of tourists that rolled through town on a daily basis, gawking at the picture-perfect landscape and marveling at how the residents looked so much like real people. Disney eventually removed its name from Celebration road signs, which may have given passersby the impression that the town was another theme park.

Larger problems surfaced at the Celebration School. Although the school was owned and operated by the conservative Osceola County School Board, its instructors used experimental teaching methods, such as multi-age classrooms, progress reports in place of grades, and student-directed study plans. The freeform atmosphere troubled parents accustomed to judging their children's progress by competitive grades and test scores. Parents began rebelling. Teachers began quitting. In time, the school reverted to more conventional classes and techniques.

The new park executives' resentment toward traditions affected not only how the parks were run, but also what type attractions were added. The Magic Kingdom's Tomorrowland, mired in a rosy 1970s view of the

CASTLE OF HORRORS. To celebrate Disney World's 25th anniversay, the Magic Kingdom redecorated Cinderella Castle as a giant birthday cake, repainting it Pepto Bismol pink and adding gigantic lollipops, gum drops, and birthday candles. Guests hoping to glimpse the beautiful castle, particularly those on their honeymoon or enjoying a one-in-a-lifetime visit, were horrified. (October 1, 1996) *Photo by Frank Anzalone, Frank Anzalone Photography, San Jose, Ca.*

future, was long overdue for an extreme makeover. Stark white buildings were repainted in metallic colors with neon accents. The Carousel of Progress was renamed Walt Disney's Carousel of Progress, to warn visitors that the show was a relic from the distant past. As the centerpiece of the overhaul, Mission to Mars was replaced by the edgier Alien Encounter. During previews for the new attraction, some guests were so terrified they fled early. Others screamed so loud, they drowned out parts of the script. Eisner didn't think the show was scary enough. He ordered it shut down to rework the storyline and in-theater effects to make it even more intense. His plan worked. The revised attraction succeeded in upsetting even more guests, who weren't expecting anything so intense at the Magic Kingdom.

EPCOT Center's Future World had found itself in the same dilemma as Tomorrowland—facing waning public interest because it celebrated the future, and the future seemed to have passed it by. Future World had not added a new attraction since the Wonders of Life pavilion five years earlier, and attendance had declined every year since. Most every component of Future World was updated. The Land's animatronic Kitchen Kabaret show was replaced by the louder Food Rocks. The Listen to the Land boat ride lost its exuberant theme song and became Living with the Land. *Captain EO* was replaced by a recent movie tie-in, *Honey, I Shrunk the Audience*. CommuniCore and its futuristic displays were transformed into the flashier Innoventions, highlighting new consumer electronics. Spaceship Earth, which exited past displays of hulking, obsolete computers, received a more up-to-date finale and narration by Jeremy Irons in place of Walter Cronkite. An ill-suited stage show, The Magical World of Barbie, pacified sponsor Mattel. Even the name of the park changed, to Epcot 94, stressing that the place was different and current.

The days were also numbered for the sole whimsical element at Epcot, Journey into Imagination. Year in and year out, the attraction had been the park's number two draw, second only to Spaceship Earth. Visitors typically entered the Imagination pavilion first by riding Journey into Imagination, exited into the ImageWorks play area, and finally ended up in the 3-D theater. With the opening of *Honey, I Shrunk the Audience*, new management realized it now had a weapon to kill off Figment and Dreamfinder. They switched the main queue line in front of the pavilion so that it instead led to the 3-D theater. Immediately, ridership at Journey into Imagination plummeted. Overnight, the ride fell

NEW DIRECTION. Revamped attractions, such as the Enchanted Tiki Room: Under New Management, deride traditional Disney entertainment. (2006) *Photo by Al Lutz, MiceAge.com*

from the park's number two attraction to number eight. Executives could then use charts and graphs to prove to Kodak that the public had lost interest in the ride, since overnight it had fallen from number two to number eight. The ride was closed, and its show building gutted. The replacement, Journey into *Your* Imagination, eliminated Dreamfinder, reduced Figment to a cameo, and replaced the rich imagery, scenery and storytelling of its predecessor with simplistic decorations, cheap optical tricks, and smart aleck humor. By moving the ImageWorks post-show area downstairs, they also made the ride significantly shorter. Audiences hated it. Riders could not figure out what had happened to Figment.

What guests failed to realize was that the theme parks had been taken over by executives who looked down on the Ways of Walt and found classic entertainment quaint, out of step. They preferred their attractions hip and affordable.

Most telling, they attempted to make Walt's animatronic bird revue,

the Tropical Serenade, relevant to modern audiences by reworking it as
The Enchanted Tiki Room: Under New Management. The replacement
begins the same as the old show did, when suddenly Iago, the squawking
sidekick from *Aladdin*, crashes the performance. He proclaims that he
has taken over the theater, ridicules the existing entertainment as dated
and unbearable, and promises to spice things up so he can make lots of
money. The new show mocked not only Walt's landmark creation, but
also the millions of guests who enjoy his innocent, family-friendly offerings—namely, Disney World's primary customer base. And, though
delivered in a light-hearted way, the message is clear: "new management" is motivated entirely by profits and sees its customers as rubes.

Soon after, the company began phasing out its sole customer loyalty
program. For more than 40 years, the Magic Kingdom Club had offered
token discounts on theme park admissions. In its place, Burbank
launched the Disney Club, which offered similarly insignificant savings,
but for an annual fee. The switch angered long-time members. The
Disney Club lasted just three years.

By the time the fourth theme park was officially announced in June
1995, its name had been changed to Disney's Wild Animal Kingdom and
its budget set at more than $760 million. Recognizing the project as
somewhat unconventional, Disney placed it under the creative control of
Joe Rohde, both an artist and an adventurer, who had just designed the
unconventional Adventurer's Club at Pleasure Island and whose free
spirit—and jewelry—had earned him the nickname "the earring at
Imagineering."

As consultants, the company had assembled a who's who of zoo offi-
cials, leaders of wildlife and animal protection groups, and other envi-
ronmental experts, including famed primate researcher Jane Goodall.
The permanent staff included former curators from the San Diego Zoo,
Zoo Atlanta, St. Louis Zoo, Portland Zoo, and the National Zoo in
Washington, D.C.

No matter, moments after the project was announced, environmental-
ists went on the warpath. The outcry further motivated park designers to
ensure the park oozed environmental friendliness. None of the more than
1,000 animals imported into the park would be from the wild; every one
was to be purchased from a zoo or other licensed facility, after having
spent its entire life in captivity.

To prove its greenness, Disney incorporated pro-ecology, anti-development messages into every corner of the park. The park benches, which featured backrests carved as turtles, eagles and crocodiles, were made from recycled materials. Most attractions featured blatant conservationist themes—the safari ride vilified poachers, the *It's Tough to Be a Bug* 3-D movie poked fun at pesticides. Anti-logging graffiti was spray-painted across the construction fences.

The company vowed to follow the guidelines of the "Species Survival Plans" and made a series of well-publicized donations to wildlife foundations and national parks. Disney played up its environmental commitment at every opportunity, often stressing the "Environmentality" program the parks had launched a few years earlier. The company spent $30 million purchasing the Walker Ranch, an 8,500-acre mix of wetlands, prairies and forests, filled with endangered plant and animal species, that state environmental officials had been trying desperately to acquire for 20 years. Disney then donated the site to the Nature Conservancy. In exchange, the site would be renamed the Walt Disney Wilderness Preserve and, more importantly, Disney World would be exempted from creating hundreds of mini-mitigation projects to compensate for loss of wetlands while developing the rest of its property. They even set the fourth gate's grand opening for April 22, 1998—Earth Day.

The park had to present the animals in a natural setting, as if they were roaming freely across the 100-acre savannah. Instead of cages, designers surrounded habitats with hidden barriers that would keep predators away from their prey—and the guests. The lions and lionesses were placed on a "Pride Rock" mesa, separated from the tram by an unseen moat. The wildebeests were surrounded by slats of wood, spaced just far enough apart to trap any wayward hooves between the boards. To dissuade other animals from wandering off, clumps of "hot grass"—low-voltage electrical fencing that looked like chimney brooms—were blended in with the bushes. Feeding stations were hidden in tree bogs, to force animals to graze in view of the audience. At night, the animals would be rounded up and herded into protective enclosures.

Although the conservation focus played well with the press, the company's Marketing department was less enthusiastic. Wildlife preservation lends little sales punch to a vacation brochure. For nearly three years, anyone interviewed about the park spoke primarily about the animals, usually in serious tones. The publicists—backed by Eisner—insisted the park be rebranded as a place for fun and adventure, instead of a homework assignment.

Terms like "biodiversity" and "healthy planet" were permitted on park maps and handouts *inside* the park. But on the outside, advertising and publicity were to emphasize "thrilling attractions" and "close encounters with exotic creatures." Press releases promised "heart-pounding adventure"—despite the park having only one thrill ride. Most importantly, the word "zoo" was taboo. Zoos sounded mundane; every big city had one. Members of the media who used the term were to be corrected.

The promotional tactic left some environmental experts scratching their heads, wondering why Animal Kingdom, after years of unapologetically painting itself green, now seemed to be abandoning the color. The move also gave ammunition to the critics who claimed that Disney had only been pretending to care about the animals; theirs was just another theme park enslaving wildlife for entertainment. "Those animals are going to be living in concrete or steel enclosures during the night," noted a spokesperson for the Humane Society of the United States. "For [Disney] to say this is a natural habitat is really stretching it."

Ironically, Walt was an unabashed nature lover long before anyone dreamed of an animal rights movement. His True-Life Adventure films in the 1950s did more to endear wildlife to wide audiences than a thousand protests could ever hope to. His one major environmental boondoggle, Mineral King, was opposed by the Sierra Club not so much for the ski resort itself, as for the roads that would have to be carved through untouched wilderness to make the attraction accessible. Even after Walt's death, his successors continued fighting to win government and public support, until reluctantly abandoning the project a decade later.

In Florida, Disney immediately set aside 7,500 acres in the southwest corner of its property as a wilderness preserve and holding basin for the stormwater runoff from the canals. The company wanted a native Floridian to manage its environmental issues, someone familiar with the terrain and wildlife. Fred Harden, a local entomologist, initially was hired in 1970 to lead the pre-opening expulsion of the insects. He stayed on as the Improvement District's pollution control director. Harden oversaw a complete property-wide environmental program. He actively managed the conservation area. After construction crews removed logs from a stream, conservationists complained that alligators and turtles had lost a place to dry the fungus out of their feet. At great expense, Disney restored the logs. Harden constantly monitored the quality of the water flowing onto and out of the property. And he protected and catalogued every species of plant, tree, bird and animal on property.

"There were deer, vicious wild hogs, bobcats, alligators, a few snakes," recalled Reedy Creek's Tommy Sparks. "Wild turkeys were common in the wooded areas. I saw a couple of bears, through the Reedy Creek swamp. You dig any size hole in Central Florida, an alligator will find it. They were all over. We had to trap the hogs. People would see them in a ditch and think, 'Isn't that the cutest thing! Hogs on World Drive!' They're dangerous; they'll cut you with their tusks or bite you. We'd use corn to set traps and relocate them to the Disney conservation area."

The hogs would tear up medians and other grassy areas, destroying the landscaping. Worse, the sight of wild pigs distracted motorists' attention and caused numerous traffic accidents. So, whenever the beasts started settling into areas visible to the public, Reedy Creek workers quickly relocated them to the back side of the property.

In the early days, PR man Sandy Quinn invited down to the property Ross Allen, a performer who staged shows with snakes. Disney hoped Allen might find some reptiles to clear away. Snakes, said Bill Hoelscher, "like the palmetto that you see here in Florida, because rodents and little baby rabbits, their food chain, live in there. [Allen] went out and looked all around for snakes and did not find that many. He found some, but the heavy construction equipment, the big Caterpillars and pile drivers, shook the ground and snakes didn't like the vibrations. They got away from that. After we opened, we never found anything inside the Magic Kingdom except a black snake or a garter snake. But out on the campground we used to find some pretty hefty rattlesnakes that we would catch and then turn them over to the snake guy at Gatorland."

Ill-mannered alligators were moved to the conservation area. "That's where we took all the gators who became nuisances out on the golf courses," Hoelscher noted. "Usually alligators are afraid of people, if you don't mess with them. We had guys who would go in and glean golf balls out of the ponds, and the gators wouldn't bother them. They were not on their food list. Before we opened, we had an alligator in the lake behind the Preview Center that we called P.C. We used to feed him— that was wrong. If we had chicken, we'd always give P.C. the bones. We could clap and here would come this battleship. He was our friend. But guests would take dogs out of their cars and go down by the lake, and P.C. began to scan those dogs pretty good. So we called in the Florida Fish & Game Commission. They came out and said, 'Look, alligators are supposed to sleep during the day. They're nocturnal. They eat and hunt at night. You're getting this guy all confused.' So they trapped him and moved him down into the swamp conservation area."

To this day, alligators occasionally float through the resort's interconnected waterways and suddenly appear on the grassy banks behind Space Mountain or in the marshes around Tom Sawyer Island. At the Fort Wilderness campground, a more than seven-foot-long gator pounced on a seven-year-old boy who was kneeling beside a pond feeding the ducks. As the reptile began pulling the lad into the pond, his brother and sister ran over, beat on its head, and wrenched their brother from its jaws. The boy suffered cuts and punctures to his thigh, knee and lower left leg.

A few months before the Magic Kingdom opened, Bob Wacker was leaving Fantasyland at about 3 a.m. when he saw a panther walk out of the queue line for It's a Small World. Wacker speculated, "He saw the light and wanted to know what was going on."

Disney World's first public showcase for nature was the small island in the middle of Bay Lake. The flat, eleven-acre mound of scrub brush and poisonous vines was visible primarily from the campground. WED first envisioned the spot as "Blackbeard's Island," a pirate-themed playground along the lines of Disneyland's Tom Sawyer Island. Two years later, while adding a play area to Disney World's Tom Sawyer Island, Imagineers decided to clear the Bay Lake island, rename it Treasure Island, and play up both adventure and nature themes. Workmen hauled in 15,000 cubic yards of sandy soil for landscaping, more than 500 tons of boulders, and another 500 tons of trees, including 20 varieties of palm, ten species of bamboo, and hundreds of types of plants from around the world. They sculpted the terrain into rolling, grass-covered hills, lined with winding footpaths, cascading streams, and three elevated lagoons. An enormous aviary would hold various types of exotic birds. For atmosphere, the island was dotted with lamp posts made to look as if they were burning oil, plus a shipwreck, Ben Gunn's Cave, Spyglass Hill, and a lookout post with skull and crossbones waving overhead.

Vacationing families lured to Treasure Island by the young explorer's theme soon discovered that the attraction was more suited for bird watchers than rambunctious children. Remote and requiring separate admission, the island was never a big draw, and in 1978 was renamed Discovery Island to focus on the rare plants and animals.

Despite its failure to attract tourists, the sanctuary did succeed in attracting unwelcome locals. Wild vultures started attacking the island and its native wildlife. The vultures stole food from the pelicans and other birds, destroyed stork and pelican nests and eggs, harassed the flamingos, killed a baby swan, and pecked the eyes of the Gallapagos tortoises until they drew blood. The birds tore up the island's furniture and defecated on the boardwalk. Native Florida egrets and white ibises defecated on pathways and were annoyingly loud. Falcons and hawks used the island as a base of operations, waiting for feeding time—the moment stage shows at the Magic Kingdom released a flourish of defenseless pigeons into the air.

Attendants unsuccessfully tried to scare away the birds of prey. They altered the feeding patterns for the island's inhabitants. They strung out special magnetic tape, intended to disorient the birds. The shiny striping was both ineffective and unattractive, making the island look like a used car lot. Workers fared slightly better by installing sprinklers in the vultures' favorite landing spots.

Desperate, attendants began in 1988 to catch the vultures. Now they just had to figure out what to do with them. In May 1989, they legally secured a permit to capture and relocate up to 100 vultures. Workers erected a small, windowless tin shed, large enough to comfortably hold about three birds. They set traps around the island. Once trapped, however, the vultures would not be taken without a fight. The workers used sticks to beat the birds into submission before tossing them into the shed. Emboldened, workers expanded their clean-up operations. They began knocking eggs from the nests of native egrets and ibises. Using a .22-calibre rifle, they fired birdshot at the hawks, falcons and owls.

An anonymous tipster, appalled by the animal cruelty, alerted fish and game authorities. Initially, the island's curator denied the charges. But the ensuing two-month investigation revealed that employees had trapped at least 149 birds and beaten eight to ten of them to death. They crammed as many as 72 into the shed at one time, allowed the dark enclosure to reach hazardous temperatures, and supplied no perches and little food or water, leading to fifteen additional deaths.

Federal and state prosecutors filed seventeen criminal charges against Disney World, the curator, and four other workers. The company had violated the time span, record keeping, notification and body count restrictions of its permit. The employees were accused of animal cruelty. Disney quickly settled the case, pleading guilty to a single charge of violating the Migratory Bird Treaty Act. The company agreed to pay fines of $20,000 and donate $75,000 to promote conservation. It would submit to regular inspections. The state would refrain from pressing charges if the company committed no other wildlife violations for one year.

The five indicted workers were reassigned to new positions in other areas of the resort. Unfortunately, hundreds of vultures continued terrorizing Discovery Island. Attendants turned to gentler scare tactics. They tried to ward off the birds with loud noises and strobe lights. They strung plastic wire over two tortoise ponds. They installed sprinklers and special flashing tape near the pond shores. They gathered the exotic animals into protective cages for feeding time. A licensed consultant attached small radio transmitters to the vultures' legs to discover where they were coming from. Yet progress came slowly. And none of the tricks prevented the hawks and falcons from snatching the show pigeons. In 2002, Disney World discontinued pigeon releases.

Similarly, the opening of the Living Seas pavilion at EPCOT unexpectedly provided Disney with environmentally unfriendly publicity. Leader Kym Murphy's team spent one year on a small island in the Florida Keys collecting tropical fish, sharks and other exotic species. And as careful as they were, some casualties were inevitable. On December 28, 1985, an hour before the first public glimpse at the attraction, one of six prized dolphins, four-year-old Gino, became tangled in the net handlers used to move the mammal through the tank. Panicking, he suffered a fatal heart attack. In 1987, two more dolphins died within three days of each other due to internal injuries—a nine-year-old female of a brain hemorrhage and a six-year-old male of fractured vertebrae. Because dolphins rarely run into objects in their tanks, investigators suspected Bob, the dominant male, was to blame. Less than three years later, Bob roughhoused his remaining female poolmate, twelve-year-old Katie, worsening her lung condition and leading to her death.

Even Murphy had trouble defending his safety record after losing four of six dolphins in six years, conceding it was "pretty cruddy."

The most critical phase of launching an animal park comes in safely transporting the animals to the facility and acclimating them to their new surroundings. Most facilities suffer some casualties in the process, which would generate the negative publicity Disney's Animal Kingdom was so desperate to avoid. Seven months before opening, in September 1997, the park lost a female black rhinoceros. The animal swallowed an eighteen-inch stick, which punctured its intestine and caused infection. Disney insisted the rhino must have eaten the stick before coming to Animal Kingdom, since the animal was not fed woody materials in the park and the stick belonged to a tree species not found in Central Florida.

In late December, four cheetahs died of kidney failure after ingesting ethylene glycol, the main ingredient in antifreeze. Again, Disney claimed the animals must have swallowed the toxic chemical before arriving at Animal Kingdom two weeks earlier.

Soon after, two Asian small-clawed otters died after gorging themselves on seeds of a loquat, a citrus fruit not normally part of their diet. Workers quickly removed the tree.

In February, a female hippopotamus, which had arrived ten days earlier from a zoo in Europe, died of blood poisoning from multiple infections on its back and feet. The hippo had been treated with antibiotics to no avail.

The same month, during testing of the safari ride, a West African crowned crane darted beneath one of the Jeeps and was run over. A few weeks later, another crane suffered the same fate. In response, Disney installed additional mirrors on the Jeeps and relocated the cranes to an area protected from the roadway. Later, they attached bumper guards to the front and sides of the vehicles to keep animals out from under them.

On March 24, a newly arriving white rhinoceros died while anesthetized for a routine medical exam.

U.S. Department of Agriculture inspectors had visited the park five times during the month prior and found it in compliance with all regulations. Yet the rash of deaths—and anonymous tips that the animal handlers were up to no good—convinced the USDA to take another, closer look. If any serious violations turned up, the park could be fined and perhaps lose its license. The day before Animal Kingdom's grand opening, the USDA issued it a clean bill of health.

Although the Wildlife Conservation Society and other mainstream groups backed the project, the deaths stirred up preservationist groups fundamentally opposed to holding animals in captivity. The day before the park's opening, the Animal Rights Foundation ran a full-page ad in the *New York Times* decrying Disney's environmental record. That night, activists attempted to break into the park's animal containment area by pushing down a perimeter fence, but fled before they could be identified.

On opening day, about 20 protesters picketed beneath an Animal Kingdom billboard on U.S. Highway 192 near the entrance to Disney property. They wore T-shirts reading, "Eisner, Are You That Cruel to Your Children?" and carried signs screaming, "Dead Animal Kingdom," "Disney Cartoons Yes, Live Animals No," and "Disney: A Tragic Kingdom for Animals." Police watched over the picketers and kept traffic moving.

Animal Kingdom had held previews through April to work out any kinks. Disney discovered that children were roasting because the 1,000 rental strollers didn't have hoods to shade the tots from the hot sun. The strollers were shaded by opening day.

The company spent an estimated $30 million on inaugural activities and media coverage, though festivities were intentionally less glitzy than the star-studded unveiling of Disney-MGM. For the most part, appearances by Hollywood stars—such as Disney board member Sidney Poitier and ABC television's Drew Carey and Michael J. Fox—were restricted to a series of private events during the days before the grand opening, usually with the ABC television cameras rolling. At Animal Kingdom, Disney explained, "the animals are the celebrities." Even the official dedication ceremony on opening morning was held before any guests were allowed into the park. Fireworks were omitted in favor of a confetti shower of biodegradable rose petals. As a consolation prize, the thousands of guests who were locked out of the dedication received a commemorative poster.

Visitors had begun lining up outside the parking lot before dawn. The park was scheduled to open at 7 a.m., but Disney opened the gates an hour early to reduce congestion. The marquee safari ride opened shortly thereafter, by which time 1,000 people were lined up across Harambe Village. By 7:00, the 6,000-car lot was full. Fifteen minutes later, the park reached its capacity of 28,000 paid guests and ticket takers stopped admitted guests unless they had an annual pass or multi-park ticket.

Overall, operations flowed relatively smoothly. Attraction waits times

fell to comfortable levels as the day wore on. The only significant break-
down was a one-hour closure at the Countdown to Extinction ride, which
duplicated the complicated ride system and track layout of Disneyland's
Indiana Jones Adventure.

Animal Kingdom's slender roster of attractions could ill afford any
downtime. Just as at Disney-MGM, lack of rides was a top complaint. At
more than 500 acres, Animal Kingdom may have been Disney's largest
park, yet it featured two laboratory displays, four shows, a nature trail,
character greeting area, playground, and five attractions, counting the
train that transported guests to the lab. In fact, there was so little to do
that by early afternoon, most guests had seen everything they wanted to
see and left.

Disney blamed the guests themselves. In rushing from ride to ride,
they were missing out on the main attraction: the park itself. Visitors
who complained that there wasn't enough to do just had to work a little
harder to have fun, since at Animal Kingdom, "the script is looser."
Disney began stationing cast members along the quiet pathways to point
out macaws gathering in one tree or a two-toed sloth snoozing in another.

The safari ride received the best reviews, although some guests complained that the vehicles sped too quickly through the savannah or traveled long stretches without coming across any animals. Adults found the
ride's narrative corny, while children were upset by the climactic
encounter with a fake dead elephant "killed by poachers." Imagineers
initially assumed the scene was no different than Bambi losing his mother or *The Lion King's* Simba losing his father. Yet those animated slay-
ings were handled off-screen. Disney removed the carcass from the
safari and toned down the storyline.

Other tweaks were aimed at making the park appear more exciting.
The dinosaurs on Countdown to Extinction were given scarier lighting
and infusions of bad breath. More characters were allowed to roam
beyond the predetermined character greeting areas.

The intense heat was another sore spot, since the park's lush foliage
trapped the humidity. So, too, Animal Kingdom lacked the many air-
conditioned buildings found at other parks, where the doors were often
kept open to help cool the outside. In time, Disney installed dozens of
misting fans.

The biggest disappointment was the Discovery River Boat Tour. The
attraction was supposed to offer two selling points: one, to serve as

transportation to Asia, which come opening day featured nothing more than a bird show, and two, to showcase animatronic dragons and other props from Beastly Kingdom along its riverbanks. Beastly Kingdom, however, had been cut from phase-one construction, and the few water-side props that had been installed were typically left unused. As a result, the boats ended up slowly circling the river to view plants and trees the likes of which could be seen just walking around the park. Visitors felt cheated after being lured into line by fanciful discovery boats reminiscent of the Jungle Cruise's explorer vessels. It didn't help that skippers would walk the boat showing off banana spiders and snakes.

"We just couldn't convince people it wasn't the Jungle Cruise," recalled one opening day worker. "They'd queue up for an hour-and-a-half for a fifteen-minute boat ride. Their expectations were so high, we couldn't meet that."

After six months of complaints that there was nothing to discover, the boats were renamed the Discovery River Taxis, stressing that the vessels were transportation and little else. By the end of the year, Disney devised a more synergistic and hopefully marketable solution: repainting the boats in bright colors and piping in pop music and commentary by Radio Disney disc jockeys. The Radio Disney River Cruises proved equally unappealing. Within six months, the ride closed permanently.

Having to leave the boats tethered to their docks to avoid guest complaints was an awkward decision, considering how desperately Animal Kingdom needed more attractions. "It was sad to see these boats tied up at various places as set pieces," said Imagineer George McGinnis, who designed the vessels. "The experience reminds me of the Swan Boats at the Magic Kingdom that were shut down after a short time. The People-Mover survived for years without much story along with it, but then it was up high with a view of the park. Apparently a boat ride needs more."

Quibbles aside, by the time Animal Kingdom opened, Disney was convinced it had another hit on its hands. The company forecast that the park would draw as many as ten million visitors in its first year. Its opening also provided the perfect excuse to raise ticket prices at all the parks by more than $2 a day—its steepest increase in years. At the same time, the company unveiled a solid quarterly earnings report and plans for a three-for-one stock split, its third under new management. It was as if the good times would never end.

16

The Polite Force

Even as the resort expanded, Disney World contentedly maintained the same low-key security philosophy that Walt had instituted at Disneyland and planned for his city of EPCOT. Signs of heavy-handed law enforcement might disrupt the tranquil atmosphere. He wanted to lull visitors into good behavior.

Reedy Creek's charter allowed the district to form its own police force. Disney instead ceded such powers to the sheriffs' departments of Osceola and Orange counties. Deputies could be called in cases of severe lawbreaking. To keep the peace on a minute-by-minute basis, Disney World assembled a calm, reactionary security department.

When the Magic Kingdom first opened, most of the more than 100 officers were either outfitted in a plain blue uniform or, inside the park, dressed to fit their assigned area—an Old West sheriff in Frontierland or a Keystone Kop on Main Street. About ten plainclothes officers were assigned to the stores, blending in with the crowds, but keeping their eyes open for potential shoplifters. None packed guns, just a two-way radio worn holster-high on the hip. Even those who patrolled the outer reaches of the property were equipped with only a five-gallon gas can, five-gallon water can, and jumper cables.

Unwelcome behavior and emergencies were monitored discreetly. Cast members tuned to dozens of special-frequency radio channels, viewed television screens linked to hidden surveillance cameras, and oversaw computerized alarm systems alerting of burglary, fire or intruders activating infrared sensors or pressure-sensitive mats along the ride tracks.

Guards needed an imposing presence, to discourage resistance from troublemakers who had to be confronted. Security officers were required to stand at least six feet tall and weigh 200 pounds. Most of the full-timers had civilian or military law enforcement experience. The part-timers were often school teachers, who typically had the right authoritarian demeanor and were available to fill in for full-timers on weekends and supplement them during busy holidays and summer.

Those suspected of the most common crime—shoplifting—were usually just kicked out of the park. "We're not here to keep 'law and order,'" said Chuck Cone, Disney World's first director of security. "We maintain 'peace and quiet.'"

Even the employee handbook confirmed: "We don't have 'guards'… they would be out-of-place and out of character. We have courteous security hosts who are concerned for the safety of guests, hosts and hostesses and people's property."

Disney World preferred that guest problems be dealt with by its own officers, Cone explained, "who know more about our company philosophy and situation, than by a complete outsider from a law enforcement agency." For more serious infractions (burglars, uncooperative shoplifters, violent offenders), Security would call the Orange County Sheriff Department. Deputies, however, were required to use the Magic Kingdom's back entrance and keep their sirens off. Disney security could not make an arrest, but Reedy Creek's city codes gave all cast members the right to detain anyone "causing a disturbance" until the sheriff arrived or to eject anyone from the property who refused to leave when asked.

Even speeders had to be handled by the sheriff. "We didn't have authority to make an arrest," officer Henry "Ray" Carter said. "We would radio ahead, stop the driver, and have the officer show up to write a ticket. Orange County couldn't patrol; they had to be called to come on our property. But once they were on our property, they had full authority."

Guards stationed at the Main Gate visually screened guests not for what they might be hiding, but for how they looked. The inspectors were called the "SOAP" crew, for "Standard Operations of Admission Procedures," and because their job was to "clean the guests up before they came into the park." The crew turned away as many as 18,000 guests a year from the Magic Kingdom, for violations from being barefoot to being intoxicated.

Whenever possible, guards wanted to help visitors to meet the requirements. Security asked guests to turn their shirts inside out or put on another shirt if their clothing bore graphic illustrations or text. "We had to learn all the lingo [for drugs]," Carter said. "If women had too brief of a top or too brief of a bottom, we'd make them change. They always tried to give you an argument, but they usually had something else in the car or at their hotel room. We wouldn't allow Hell's Angels jackets, chains, knives. They would try to carry their helmets in, but we made them put them in a locker; they could be used as weapons."

A few slipped through. "One woman got through," recalled officer Sam Holland, "who seemed to be wearing only a men's shirt. Security sent out a call over the radio. Dozens of officers responded. We stopped her near the flower stand. She was in a low-cut bikini under the shirt. We made her go back to the Contemporary and put on a pant suit."

Others might not become offensive until after they entered the park. In the early 1970s, an unstable Vietnam War veteran took off all his clothes while riding the Skyway. He hopped off at the Tomorrowland Station, naked, and ran through Tomorrowland and to Main Street, until Security could arrive to nimbly escort him backstage.

Officers were instructed to make use of the underground tunnels and back roads throughout the property to be seen by as few guests as possible. The preference, explained one officer, was to "extract a problem off the street to the tunnel rather than drag some screaming person down Main Street."

Shoplifting became so widespread that the resort was forced to add more and more undercover officers. Soon, plainclothes personnel made up more than a quarter of the security force.

"Shoplifting was one of the biggest headaches," Carter admitted. "People from South America would take things home to sell at a 100-percent profit margin. We had so many cases of lawyers, teachers, and even law enforcement from other parts of the country, Boy Scouts, one of our own supervisors, even nuns stealing earrings."

Other nabbed shoplifters included a church minister and his family and a sheriff within three months of retirement. One prolific shoplifter was caught in 1980 with $28,000 worth of merchandise.

Security is encouraged to remain firm yet gentle, even to the point of escorting drunk drivers back to their hotel rooms rather than calling the sheriff and ruining their vacation. Still, charges occasionally surfaced of over-aggressive behavior. Not long after the Magic Kingdom opened, ride operators encountered a "disturbance" on the Haunted Mansion and notified Security. Officers apprehended six teenagers and held them at Security headquarters for four hours while trying to locate their parents. One of the boys sought $10,000 in court for the abuse. A jury gave him $500.

In 1986, a brother, sister and friend got into a fight with another party as they were leaving EPCOT's Living Seas pavilion. The friend supposedly knocked another guest unconscious and kicked him in the head, before the threesome fled. Witnesses alerted Security, which forcibly detained the group as they tried to push through the park exit. The trio claimed guards handcuffed their wrists, tied their legs, bloodied the brother's nose in pushing him against a wall, and knocked his sister unconscious by shoving her against a wall. The siblings filed suit over the rough treatment and were awarded $1 million by a jury.

Aggravated by the heat and crowding, small inconveniences have caused guests to become unexpectedly violent. Someone inadvertently stole their "saved" spot to watch the parade. Someone stepped in front of them while they were trying to take a photo. Someone looked at their girlfriend. Someone accidentally cut in front of them in line. In fact, full-scale brawls broke out in 1999 when Disney World first introduced its FastPass ride reservation system. To those who didn't understand the new system, cast members seemed to be authorizing certain guests to cut to the front of the line.

More often, unhappy guests head for City Hall, where Guest Relations' renowned generosity invited complaints, both sincere and outrageous, as well as outright scams. Among the most common objections is rain. Guests evidently think that Disney should be able to control the weather, because whenever a drizzle begins, dozens of guests start screaming for a refund. "We don't want to give money back, so we might offer a comp[limentary] ticket to come back at another time," said host Kyle Madorin. "That's very common."

Visitors also get upset when they are unexpectedly drenched on rides, particularly Splash Mountain. Guest Relations staffers have always been perplexed at this complaint, considering the first word of the ride's name is "Splash" and, while climbing into the boats, passengers can't help but notice the seats are dripping wet. Incredulous, hostesses finally walked through the queue, counted the number of signs warning passengers they would get wet, and posted the figure at the Guest Relations office.

For those who got absolutely soaked, Madorin recalled, "we might give them a free T-shirt. Most of the time they were after free tickets or money. A South American group said they were going to demand their money back through their consulate."

Guests commonly complain of being bombarded by birds. The parks become so littered with stray food, that flocks of seagulls hover overhead, waiting for an opportune feeding time. Unfortunate visitors below are regularly pelted with bird droppings. Several have even been attacked by gulls hoping to snatch a hot dog from their hand.

Some complainers became regular visitors at Guest Relations. As a result, hostesses at the various parks began compiling a database of anyone who came in to complain and what compensation they were given. "The same people would come in ten or twelve times," Madorin said. "They knew how to work the system. They knew the key words. There were hundreds of them. We called them 'gypsies.' They would try to get free meals or rooms comp'ed at hotels. They would hit multiple parks, so we would alert the other parks and their hotel."

The databases were all linked, so hostesses would know if they were being set up. Yet staffers were not allowed to tell off anyone, even suspected scam artists. They still had to use "subtleties" and follow the LAST policy (Listen, Apologize, Solve, Think).

Disney World clerks and ticket sellers must also be vigilant for visitors attempting to use stolen credit cards or counterfeit bills. Over the years, numerous counterfeiters have been nabbed. In 1974, a gang of seven was arrested for passing phony travelers checks at the Magic Kingdom and Disneyland.

Others have tried to forge admission tickets. During the mid-1980s, two brothers spent three years selling thousands of duplicated ducats to tourists along International Drive. They were finally caught trading 5,000 three-day tickets for eleven pounds of cocaine—and sentenced to ten years in prison.

Illegal tickets are even more likely an inside job. In 1988, a cast member headed home for the night with his pockets stuffed with tickets. He was caught and jailed for six months.

Four years later, an employee stole $1.74 million in tickets from a Disney vault and sold them to a middle man for $200,000. Security quickly noticed the tickets were missing and began interviewing workers with access to the vault. The culprit confessed and gave Disney most of the money he had received for the stolen tickets. He was sentenced to two years of community service and 25 years of probation.

The same year, hidden cameras caught a ticket seller at Disney-MGM pocketing partially-used tickets, which guests had traded in to upgrade. The woman pleaded guilty to grand theft and agreed to work undercover spying on co-workers suspected of the same crime. Disney estimated such ticket upgrade schemes had cost the company more than $400,000.

In 1990, Security became aware that money was beginning to disappear from the cash bags that Wells Fargo guards picked up from various points around the resort. A four-month investigation revealed that two armored truck officers had skimmed at least $14,700 from the bags.

Another employee stole a co-worker's car and was caught when he returned to the park to pick up his paycheck—driving the stolen vehicle. A clerk at the Contemporary pilfered computers from the hotel. Security identified the culprit after three weeks of undercover work.

Cast members are occasionally accused of molestation. The company kept most of the charges quiet—until 2004, when a thirteen-year-old girl and her mother claimed that while posing for pictures at Mickey's Toontown Fair, Tigger fondled their breasts. The 36-year-old actor was arrested, then suspended without pay. Within a week of the national media breaking the story, authorities were flooded with 24 more complaints of inappropriate touching by Disney World characters, most of them against Tigger. Four months later, the actor was proved innocent in a jury trial, during which his lawyer put on the Tigger outfit to demonstrate how difficult it was to maneuver and see from inside the costume.

Four months after the Magic Kingdom opened, the switchboard operator began receiving calls from a man who demanded $90,000 in $20 bills or he would "blow up something." As proof, he directed investigators to a utility shed near the "canoe run" in Frontierland, where deputies found a gunpowder device wired to two canisters of neon gas and a clock. The time bomb was real and, if detonated, would have caused considerable damage. Disney attempted to make the payoff. An employee dropped off the money at his requested time in the lobby of an Orlando hotel, but no one came to claim it. By this time, investigators determined that the phone calls originated somewhere on Disney property.

Five weeks later, the park again began receiving bomb threats, this time demanding $250,000. During a series of calls, the man led a park executive from one telephone booth to another for more than four hours. The calls finally stopped. No explosives were found. Police analyzed the voice on the recorded threats to pinpoint a disgruntled 23-year-old man who had recently quit the Magic Kingdom after three months. The charges were later dropped due to insufficient evidence.

In 1982, two cast members spotted a 27-year-old tourist sitting on a bench in Town Square playing with a hand grenade. Security officers confiscated the grenade, covered it with a bomb blanket, and called sheriff's deputies, who arrived to arrest the man. The suspect claimed that the grenade had been deactivated. In truth, it contained sodium chloride tablets and could have exploded by adding a chemical. A search of his belongings revealed he also had a gas mask and an empty first-aid box.

Violent crimes have been rare at Disney World, but considering the resort's size and that hundreds of thousands of people will be on property at any given moment, bad things will happen.

The first victim to make news headlines, back in 1973, was Deborah Jean McCartney, a 20-year-old clerk at the Contemporary, who was last seen leaving the hotel in a Disney limousine. Her lifeless body was found in a ditch, fourteen miles away. Although her killer was later apprehended, investigators never determined whether she was actually murdered on Disney property.

The company could not argue that the incidents occurred elsewhere when, a few years later, people starting jumping off the Contemporary. In 1978, a 27-year-old tourist was arrested at the hotel for shoplifting. After making bail, he returned to the Contemporary, leapt from the twelfth floor's interior balcony, and crashed down through the skylight roof of the fourth-floor clothing store. Three years later, another 27-year-old man jumped from the penthouse observation deck to the parking lot fourteen floors below. Then in 2002, a distraught 28-year-old who worked at the Pecos Bill Cafe in the Magic Kingdom jumped to his death from the observation platform.

Several other purported deaths—a jilted lover leaping to his death from the eighth floor, a busboy on his break falling from the observation deck after being startled by wasps—remain undocumented.

In 1983, a housekeeper at the Contemporary was followed to work by her estranged husband, a 31-year-old former Disney World custodian with a violent criminal record. The man abandoned his car behind the hotel, partially blocking the service entrance to the basement, and began arguing with his wife as she walked toward the lockers. Her husband pulled out a .38-caliber revolver and opened fire, striking his wife in the chest, leg and neck. He then turned the gun on himself, firing a fatal shot into his own chest. His wife survived.

Armed robbery has been attempted on several occasions. In one instance, a man brandishing a toy gun attempted to hold up the cash register at the Top of the World restaurant, but was apprehended when, while trying to make his getaway, he ran into a tree. Another gunman robbed a clerk transporting cash in the Magic Kingdom, but that money also was recovered.

In 1980, a man used a baseball bat to break the window in the back of a River Country ticket booth. He opened the door, hit the cashier over the head with the bat, and grabbed her cash. Two hours later, the batsman confronted another cashier in a hallway who was transporting several bags of money from the Ticket and Transportation Center to the cash control office. She handed over several thousand dollars, and he fled. The following evening, a cashier was taking money from the Plaza Pavilion restaurant to be deposited when a man bumped into her from behind and began hitting her until she fell to the ground and dropped her money bag. He grabbed the bag and disappeared into the crowd. Shortly thereafter, Security apprehended a guest matching the thief's description, although they could not locate the stolen loot.

In 1981, a monorail rider pulled out a pistol as the train approached the Magic Kingdom station. He demanded that two fellow passengers hand over their money and park passes. The gunman warned his victims to remain in the monorail car until he and his accomplice escaped into the station.

The uptick in crime on Disney property in the early 1980s did not go unnoticed by the sheriff's department. With the opening of EPCOT Center about to drastically expand the resort's public areas, authorities asked the company to launch a crime awareness program for its guests and employees. Management ignored the request. "They won't have any part of it," a detective said. "They don't want their guests to know there's a problem."

Although Disney World established the state's first 911 emergency telephone system, all calls went to company switchboard operators, who decided whether to call the sheriff or to handle the emergency internally, by notifying only company security or emergency personnel.

In 1986, a few hours after EPCOT had closed for the night, a gunman took an employee hostage and ordered another cast member to let them into the park's cash control building near the entrance. When the worker inside refused, the man dragged the hostage to a teller window and demanded money from a cashier. As the hostess nervously stacked together a few hundred dollars, the gunman impatiently fired a shot into the cashier's tray. He finally grabbed the money, released the hostage, and fled to his car.

Later that year, a rifle-toting man with a stocking mask over his head entered the back of the Plaza Pavilion restaurant and demanded cash. He was handed $2,000 in five Disney bags and ran off. A nineteen-year-old employee was later arrested and charged with armed robbery.

In 1989, a man wearing a Goofy hat and a Mickey Mouse sweatshirt walked into the Tomorrowland Terrace restroom and pulled a knife on a tourist standing at a urinal. "Don't move or I'll kill you," the man threatened, pressing the knife against his victim's back. The tourist handed over his wallet. He was treated for two puncture wounds to the back.

In 1993, a man, who was waiting with his daughter for a tram in the Magic Kingdom parking lot, was grabbed from behind by a mentally-disturbed woman. She pulled a six-inch paring knife from her sock and slashed his neck. The woman returned the blade to her sock and calmly walked off into the woods. Moments later, as she walked by a second man with a young daughter, she cut him on his hands and arms. The men received stitches, the woman—once apprehended—far more serious treatment.

Late one evening in 2002, three armed suspects ambushed a Virgin Megastore employee in the Downtown Disney parking lot. He was robbed at gunpoint, bound, forced into the trunk of his car, and driven around Orlando for several hours while his assailants used his ATM cards. After they had emptied his bank accounts, the suspects abandoned the vehicle off International Drive. The victim managed to kick out the car's back seat and escape. His abductors, meanwhile, returned to Downtown Disney and confronted four tourists as they were leavin

Pleasure Island. They too were robbed at gunpoint and driven down International Drive, until the drivers turned off into a wooded area and got bogged down in sand. The suspects fled, but were tracked down by police soon after.

In 1990, an assailant brandished a knife at a nineteen-year-old woman near Pleasure Island's main entrance. He forced her into her car and commanded her to drive around for several hours, stopping at ATMs to withdraw money from her account and parking twice in secluded areas so he could rape her. Soon after, a Kissimmee man was arrested for the crimes.

On Halloween 1992, Reedy Creek Fire Department's 911 operator received a frantic call from a guest at the Caribbean Beach Resort. The woman, visiting from Maine, said she and her ten-month-old daughter had returned to their room, unaware that an assailant was hiding inside. She said he covered her eyes and mouth with tape, bound her to a bed, and raped her. The child sat nearby, nibbling a cookie. After the rapist left, the woman freed herself and dialed 911.

Reedy Creek sent an ambulance to the room and alerted Disney Security, whom the operator assumed would notify the sheriff. When, after a half-hour, deputies did not arrive, the dispatcher called the sheriff's station. Deputies arrived and noted the scene looked a tad unusual. In particular, the tape used to bind the woman was not strained or twisted, as should have been the case if she had really struggled with an attacker.

Nonetheless, the Caribbean Beach was in a comparably vulnerable location. Unlike Disney's other, relatively secluded properties, the hotel was right off the highway. The Caribbean Beach immediately began posting security officers at its entrance. Disney drew up plans to add a guard booth and security gate first to the Caribbean Beach and eventually to all of its hotels. The crime scene, room 5515 of the Aruba building, was kept hard-locked indefinitely.

Disney also revised its 911 policy. The company admitted that changes had already been in the works, but were being implemented earlier due to the incident. Dialing 911 would still put callers in touch with a Reedy Creek Fire Department dispatcher, but instead of her having to manually dial the sheriff's office, she could now push a button and calls would be switched over automatically.

Eight months after reporting the rape to police, the victim filed suit against Disney. She sought more than $1 million because of the inadequate 911 system, ineffective security patrols and accounting of room keys, poor screening of employees, and insufficient maintenance of guest room door locks. The company offered her $200,000. She refused.

A few months later, investigators received a tip from one of the victim's disgruntled relatives. Evidently, the woman and her brother were traveling con artists who hoped to win big money in a lawsuit. First, the woman had sex with an acquaintance so investigators would find evidence of recent sexual activity. Then she allowed her brother to tie her to the hotel bed and severely beat her with a stick. The following spring, her brother died of an undisclosed illness. Two months later, the woman pleaded guilty to grand theft and falsely reporting a crime. She was sentenced to three-and-a-half years in prison.

The morning of September 11, 2001, began like any other at Walt Disney World. Thousands of visitors were already inside the resort's four theme parks when news arrived that hijacked planes had hit the World Trade Center towers in New York. Authorities speculated that other high-profile sites — including Disney World — could also be targets. Burbank quickly made the call to evacuate all four parks. Announcements were played over the parks' public address systems announcing that the parks had closed. Cast members herded visitors out of the attractions, shops and restaurants and then, linking hands with co-workers, formed a "human wall" to gently guide the guests to the exits, where they were handed a free ticket for readmission at a later date. To avoid a panic, cast members were not to inform guests exactly why the parks were closing.

Security at Disney World would never be the same. No longer could Disney afford the invisible approach. Security had to be evident, as a deterrent if nothing else. When the parks reopened the next morning, a phalanx of officers lined up in front of the turnstiles to perform mandatory bag checks, inspecting purses, backpacks, fanny packs, strollers and camera cases.

The resort quickly increased the size of its security force to more than 1,000 officers. Guests visiting any of the hotels were now required to provide their name and driver's license number to a guard at the front gate. Backstage tours were temporarily rerouted to prevent guests from actually going backstage.

In time, primary backstage entrances were equipped with hydraulically powered, anti-terrorist barricades—sturdy enough to prevent a ten-ton truck carrying explosives from barreling through at 70 miles per hour. These were the same backstage areas that for 20 years anyone could walk or drive into with nothing more than a friendly wave to the token guard on duty.

In the short-term, anything that might remind anyone of September 11 was altered. On the Jungle Cruise, skippers were instructed to cut out all jokes associated with a downed airplane scene near the hippo pool. The Timekeeper, featuring a CircleVision show that included a brief glimpse of the World Trade Center, was closed indefinitely.

Yet even tougher choices lie ahead. People were suddenly afraid to get on an airplane. Guests by the hundreds began calling in and canceling their Disney World reservations. The resort found itself with 55,000 cast members ready to serve, 22,000 hotel rooms, and capacity for 200,000 guests at its theme parks—and, for the first time, the masses had no interest in buying.

17

Backwards to the Beginning

BUSINESS at Disney World had already been slowing due to recession. But September 11 hit the resort like nothing ever had. Attendance all but evaporated.

Disney stock, which over the previous year had lost 42 percent of its value, dropped eighteen percent the day the stock market reopened—and kept falling as the week wore on.

For the company, the plunge in attendance could not have come at a worse time. The Disney Decade had ended with a whimper. Newer ventures either struggled, like ABC's television lineup, or collapsed entirely, like its billion-dollar Go.com web portal.

Yet even more traditionally based products struggled, primarily due to oversaturation. The Disney Stores retail division, which opened its first shop in Glendale in 1987, spread to 700 stores by the late 1990s. Disney clothing and trinkets, once sold only at Disney theme parks, were now available at every downtown mall. In 2001, Disney began closing and selling locations, finally placing the entire money-losing chain on the sales block in 2003.

Disney animation's fortunes peaked in 1994 with the release of *The Lion King*, inspiring Disney and competing studios to crank up their feature animation output. Successive releases would fare increasingly poorly until ten years later Disney would stop making traditionally animated films altogether. For years, animation had been the most visible sign of

real movie making at Disney-MGM. The park had already sold off much
of its production equipment and its post-production division, and converted two of its three soundstages into an attraction, Who Wants to Be a
Millionaire: Play It. In January 2004, Disney completely shuttered its
Florida animation studio.

Anything superfluous was eliminated. To generate quick cash, Disney
World sold its in-house telephone company, its insurance company, and
the nearby Crossroads shopping center. The company also began planning its escape route from Celebration. In 2002, Disney sold its remaining residential acreage in the town to Arvida, the development company
it had owned in the mid-1980s. A year later, Disney put the town center
and golf course up for sale. Buyers were required to maintain the community's "core ambience," but it would no longer be Disney's town.

In California, Disneyland's performance was dragged down by the
opening of an undistinguished second gate, Disney's California
Adventure. Disney World's bottom line was similarly plagued by the
opening of its fourth gate. During Animal Kingdom's first year, attendance at Disney World's other three parks each slipped by about ten percent, suggesting Animal Kingdom was cannibalizing the other parks'
visitors. Part of the problem came from the new park's condensed operating schedule. Due to its lack of attractions, the limited hours the animals could be kept on display, and resultant lower popularity, Animal
Kingdom usually closed at 5 p.m., hours before its sister parks.

So when September 11 hit, the company had to act fast. Disney World
immediately cut back on park operating hours and entertainment.
Restaurants were temporarily shuttered. Rides were operated at minimal
capacity, with minimal staffing. Several attractions were mothballed
indefinitely, including the Carousel of Progress. Coincidentally, the
parks were just about to launch a "100 Years of Magic—One Man's
Dream" promotion to celebrate Walt's one-hundredth birthday. The closure of Carousel of Progress—the only structure in the entire park that
could be dusted for Walt's fingerprints—verified that the anniversary
tribute was nothing more than a marketing ploy.

The "Surprise Mornings" perk, which permitted on-property hotel
guests to enter the parks an hour before regular guests, was replaced
with a less expensive "Character Caravan," a bus that took a group of
characters to the hotels for a meet and greet in the lobby.

At some hotels, entire floors were closed off to guests. Construction

INTO THE BACKGROUND. Chief executive Michael Eisner *(right)* steps back as Governor Jeb Bush takes the stage. In kicking off the "100 Years of Magic" promotion, the governor echoed the earlier sentiments of his brother, President George W. Bush, in urging Americans to return to pre-9/11 traveling habits. (December 5, 2001) *Photo by Frank Anzalone, Frank Anzalone Photography, San Jose, Ca.*

on the first phase of the 5,760-room Pop Century budget resort, which had already had been slowed by recession, was halted. The Pop Century wouldn't open its first rooms until more than two years later. Next, Disney closed all 1,000 rooms at the mid-priced Port Orleans Resort's French Quarter section. A month later, they began shuttering most of the complex's remaining 2,000 rooms.

One day after the Port Orleans announcement, they decided to shut down the under-performing Disney Institute. Disney had already discovered that most people who vacation at Disney World want a Disney World vacation, filled with magic and Mickey Mouse, not tips on gardening. The most popular classes at the Institute covered animation and Imagineering, but with attendance capped at 35 per session, unhappy visitors often had to settle for cooking or photography instead.

Staffer Dennis Snow found the experiment "very interesting, but from a financial standpoint, it wasn't catching on. So [in 2000] it was merged with Business Seminars, an operation that had existed for a long time in which companies come to Disney World to benchmark against Disney. That way, Business Seminars got a campus that they could operate on, and the Disney Institute got an infusion of money."

But even customized programs for large groups weren't enough to sustain the Disney Institute. Disney calculated it would be more cost effective to hold the seminars in a hotel meeting room and have attendees stay at its hotels. Seven weeks after 9/11, Disney officially gave up on the Disney Institute.

The Disney Vacation Club timeshare division was one bright spot, at least at Disney World. On-property DVC units, at least those a stone's throw away from one of the theme parks, sold out in about a year. DVC resorts farther away, such as at Florida's Vero Beach and South Carolina's Hilton Head Island, remained on the market after more than five years. Disney decided for the time being to scrap all new non-Disney World properties, including units adjacent to Disneyland Paris, and concentrate exclusively on Disney World. After 9/11, plans were also shelved for an Eagle Pines DVC development along one of Disney World's golf courses in favor of retooling the Disney Institute as a Saratoga Springs DVC property.

At the same time, Disney pulled the plug on the aging River Country water park. Guests would instead be funneled to the higher-capacity, more profitable Blizzard Beach or Typhoon Lagoon.

The sudden slump also left Disney in a quandary as to what to do with all of its employees. Thirty years earlier, full-timers comprised the core of the workforce, supplemented by "permanent part-timers" on weekends and by seasonal workers during busier periods. In time, the resort transitioned to a larger percentage of part-time help, who would earn a lower wage and be ineligible for benefits.

To keep the applicants coming, a few months before the opening of Disney-MGM, the resort had opened a $10-million casting center abutting I-4. The old personnel offices, housed in trailers in a remote section of the property off S.R. 535, were so hard to find that prospective employees often got lost and gave up looking. The considerably more visible and accessible offices, resembling a fanciful Venetian castle, allowed Disney to immediately hire 2,300 new employees. The center initially drew about 2,000 applicants a week, vying for Disney's ever-growing supply of near-minimum-wage jobs.

The College and International programs filled the balance. Yet by the late 1980s, the U.S. government began cracking down on companies abusing the J-1 visa system. Disney pre-emptively lobbied for a special visa that would allow companies to hire temporary foreign workers for unskilled positions where they could share the history, culture and traditions of their home country. The Q-1 visa, nicknamed the "Disney visa," passed in 1990. The International Program no longer had to keep up the charade that its motives were educational. Disney was able to double the number of international workers to about 1,500 by hiring hundreds of Africans and Asians to run rides at Animal Kingdom, handle bags at the Animal Kingdom Lodge, and staff booths at Epcot's Millennium Village. As the College and International programs grew larger, individual participants began feeling less special, as if Disney viewed them as numbers to fill a quota rather than as world leaders of tomorrow. And, consequently, the company ended up with a growing number of college-aged workers who took their jobs less seriously.

The influx of unskilled labor also allowed Disney to hold down wages for everyone, causing some old-timers to resent the new hires. "We're seen as too expensive to Disney, due to the high cost of benefits, union representation, paid sick and vacation time, and higher wages—a tempting target, no doubt!" griped one full-timer. "The [College Program kids] are seen as cheap, disposable labor with no union rights, no benefits, low wages, and money being siphoned back into the company coffers via the lucrative housing agreements."

After 9/11, park officials announced they would be forced to lay off several thousand employees. Union representatives exploded. And Disney, for once, was in no mood for a nasty public fight. The company promised not to terminate anyone—except for about 100 show performers. Instead, they stopped hiring and assigned the minimal number of hours to existing cast members. Management had little choice. Full-timers were protected by union contracts. College and International program participants were basically captives on the property. In the coming years, the resort would make its staffing more flexible by outsourcing more positions, starting with highly specialized duties, but eventually expanding to general positions such as custodians, valets and baggage handlers. After decades of being a shining example of how to hire, train and utilize ideal employees, Disney was admitting that an outside company could do the job better—or at least less expensively.

By 2001, the resort had stopped adding E-ticket rides. Management figured it could entice vacationers just as easily with a flashy new parade. Besides, corporate had lost its appetite for building anything unique. Unique meant unproven and risky. They had seen costs spiral out of control on GM's Test Track at Epcot. During testing, the complicated software that controlled the thrill ride sent an empty car hurtling off the track and into a wall. The attraction opened nineteen months late. From then on, any theme park additions were to be modest, "off-the-shelf" attractions that could generate fresh images for the billboards or pad out the number of attractions at Animal Kingdom.

Post-9/11, management for the first time in years needed to give the public a compelling reason to revisit Disney World. The company reluctantly unveiled plans for high-profile new attractions, costing a combined hundreds of millions of dollars, at all four parks.

Attendance at the parks slowly recovered. Disney's stock price did not. Roy E. Disney again resigned from the Disney board and helped lead a second coup, this time culminating in Eisner's resignation. Eisner's hand-picked successor, Bob Iger, shared his mentor's rigid focus on the bottom line. Under Iger, price hikes continued unabated. Outsourcing intensified. Disney World began selling off large chunks of "excess" land on the fringes of its property to home and condominium developers and leasing other borderline acreage to outside hospitality and retail firms.

Unlike Eisner, Iger was a fence mender rather than an egotistical bully. He helped patch up relations with Roy, among others, as well as the company's alienated fan base. Iger's Disney wouldn't dwell on impressing guests with post-modern architecture or hip new types of entertainment; it would make a more concerted effort to better focus on what fans liked best, classic Disney entertainment. Prophetically, four months before Iger's promotion to chief executive was announced, the blood-thirsty animatronic monster at the Magic Kingdom's Alien Encounter was replaced by the lovable cartoon character Stitch.

Walt Disney had dreamed of the day when he could build his own city. In Florida, the Walt Disney Company has created a virtual metropolis. Yet the Florida Project's underlying principles—that daring quest for innovation to better the world, that "spirit of EPCOT"—have all but vanished. The least experimental component of the entire place—the time-worn Magic Kingdom theme park—has become the template for every operation.

Because the Magic Kingdom continues drawing more than fifteen million guests a year, whether or not there's anything new to see, management is less likely to change, improve and at times adequately maintain anything. Its popularity has led the other parks, which once had more distinctive identities, to mimic the Kingdom's fantasy personality, such as inserting Donald Duck into Epcot's Mexico boat ride or plopping a giant Sorcerer's Apprentice hat in front of Disney-MGM's once-iconic Chinese theater. In fact, Disney-MGM has abandoned any pretense of being a real movie studio.

So, too, Animal Kingdom's unabashed fascination with conservation—at times overbearing yet at least distinctive—is increasingly downplayed. One marketing campaign advertised the park as "nahtazu" (pronounced *not a zoo*). More recent, quality additions, such as an Exhibition Everest coaster and a *Finding Nemo* stage show, provide the park with much-needed attractions, but blur the boundaries between the Animal and Magic kingdoms.

The biggest shift has come at EPCOT Center, now known simply as Epcot. World Showcase hasn't received a new country since Norway was added in 1988. Today's Future World, however, illustrates that the park's loss of Center has been more than just a name change.

At the Living Seas, the heavy educational bent has given way to a light-hearted treatment by the cartoon cast of *Finding Nemo*. Except on the busiest of days, the doors to the Wonders of Life pavilion remain locked. Both pavilions are without sponsors, who historically financed a hefty percentage of the park's operation and maintenance. Corporations could no longer justify paying up to $10 million a year with little demonstrable return. As their contracts expired, AT&T abandoned Spaceship Earth, Exxon departed the Universe of Energy, American Express left the American Adventure, and numerous companies pulled out of Innoventions.

Other participants were bad fits to begin with. To originally underwrite the Living Seas, Disney hooked United Technologies Corporation, parent company of such diverse subsidiaries as Otis elevators, Carrier air conditioners, Pratt & Whitney aircraft engines, and Sikorsky helicopters. UTC had no deep sea connections, but Disney World did use its air conditioners and elevators. The conglomerate fantasized of making the name "UTC" as well known as its subsidiaries by stressing that it was "in the forefront of high technology, and the newest frontier we want to conquer is the sea." Price tag: $60 million for twelve years. UTC would not renew.

Metropolitan Life Insurance Co., one of the companies included in Disney's employee benefits package, would pay $72 million to host the Wonders of Life for twelve years. The sponsorship, considered an "ego trip" for MetLife's chairman, lapsed once a new chairman took over.

"Some of those [sponsorships] were pyramids people built in their companies' heyday," said Bob Ziegler, who took over Participant Affairs for Disney World in 1988. "MetLife and UTC were there just for hospitality. We didn't use a lot of UTC products, and [MetLife] didn't sell a lot of insurance at Walt Disney World. Few people saw the sponsorship and said, 'Hey, I need some life insurance!'"

Next door, the Universe of Energy seems more dated than ever, despite a complete overhaul in 1996. Unfortunately, the addition of Ellen Degeneres, Bill Nye the Science Guy, and Willard Scott now ties the attraction to the 1990s.

The sedate World of Motion has given way to the thrill ride Test Track. Its neighbor is even more turbulent. In 2003, Horizons was replaced by Mission: Space. Here, guests are placed in a giant spinning centrifuge that subjects them to twice the force of normal gravity, simulating a flight to Mars. Ironically, its introduction resembled the rough test-and-adjust period of another simulated space attraction, Space Mountain, nearly 30 years earlier.

Mission: Space is so realistic that, from its first day, guests began stumbling out of the attraction, searching for a place to sit down and complaining of dizziness, nausea and chest pains. So many people threw up on the ride that Disney began stocking motion sickness bags in the capsules. In its first two years, nearly 150 passengers sought medical attention after riding Mission: Space. Then, in June 2005, a four-year-old boy with a rare, undiagnosed heart disease passed out during a trip and never recovered. Ten months later, a 49-year-old woman from Germany who suffered from severely high blood pressure became sick on Mission: Space, was rushed to the hospital, and died the next day.

Enough was enough. Three weeks later, Disney announced that guests would be given the option of riding a tamer version of Mission: Space—with the centrifuge turned off.

At The Land, the hosts on the boat ride have been replaced by prerecorded narration. Food Rocks has been bulldozed to create a queue for Soarin', an ultra-widescreen movie viewed as if from a hangglider. To save money, it uses the same California travelogue shown at Disney's California Adventure, an awkward fit in Florida. Yet the attraction is a huge crowd-pleaser, a return to what Disney does best: fully immersing guests in an exotic environment without subjecting them to zero-gravity forces or cheap plywood characters.

Disney has learned it doesn't have to be Universal or Sea World to dominate. Instead, the resort has uncovered more effective methods for holding guests hostage on its property. In 2005, Disney World revamped its entire ticket price structure—forgoing the old maximum seven-day tickets for one-to-ten day tickets that were tremendously front-loaded. A one-day pass cost $59.75 plus tax, but the difference between nine and ten days was only $2. The program was called Magic Your Way, but the intention was to strongarm visitors into doing everything Disney's way. Park hopping privileges cost extra. If tickets were not used within fourteen days, guests had to pay a hefty surcharge to prevent them from expiring. Disney also rolled out a free shuttle service from the airport to its on-property hotels, including free plane-to-hotel room baggage handling, discouraging guests from renting a car to drive off and spend their money elsewhere, and a dining plan that could only be purchased for every day of one's stay. Though expensive for Disney, the programs caused sharp losses of business at competing amusements, as well as for airport baggage handlers, shuttle drivers, and rental car agencies.

At the Imagination pavilion, Epcot begrudgingly shut down the revamped Journey into Your Imagination after two years of rising complaints and declining ridership. Disney spent $8 million reinserting Figment into every scene. The redesigners reworked the storyline and effects, and resurrected the old Sherman Brothers theme song, "One Little Spark." Journey into Your Imagination *with Figment* is a marginal improvement. But the ride's giant turntable had been demolished during the first remodel. There was no longer a mechanism for telling a story and introducing guests to Figment. "You can meet Figment, but you don't know who he is," laments creator Tony Baxter. For new management, that's enough.

Spaceship Earth remains the sole holdover from opening day—at least on the inside. Regrettably, for eight years beginning in 1999, the eighteen-story geosphere was topped with a 25-story-tall cartoon wand, diminishing the scale and cheapening the aesthetics of this once grand icon.

EPCOT the city was the dream of a man hoping to change the world. EPCOT Center was the reality of men desperately trying to make good on that dream. Yet they believed more in the dreamer than the dream itself. And world-changing innovation and creativity rarely flow from obligation. Even the vast technological advances employed by their Reedy Creek Improvement District were only being borrowed. Someone else invented them. Reedy Creek may have given them greater visibility, but even that point is debatable considering Disney's secretive nature. Any spectacular innovations other companies and communities would have eventually discovered without Disney.

Still, Walt's immediate successors remained committed to finding ways for the companies' trademark inventiveness, optimism and altruism to infect the world around them. Instead, the outside world penetrated them. Walt Disney Productions turned into the Walt Disney Company, a dead-ringer for every other global conglomerate. No better, no worse. Some admirers, blinded by the company's high-minded history and endearing products, may contend that Disney is superior to other corporations. Others, who hold Disney to a higher standard because of its benevolent past, may argue that it's worse.

In the end, Disney came to terms with the fact that, at least without Walt, it was an entertainment company—granted, a highly proficient and successful one, but one beholden to millions of shareholders. It could no longer take the risks necessary to change the world by building a futuristic city. Maybe one day another innovator will come along who can pull off a real, live Experimental Prototype Community of Tomorrow. Sadly, this world doesn't produce a whole lot of Walt Disneys.

notes

Abbreviations for Primary Sources

I – Interview by author
AB – *Amusement Business*
Today – *Cocoa Today*
F&E – *Eyes & Ears*
FFF – *Flash from 4500*
LL – *Lakeland Ledger*
LAT - *Los Angeles Times*
MH – *Miami Herald*
NYT – *New York Times*
OCR – *Orange County Register*
OBJ – *Orlando Business Journal*
OS – *Orlando Sentinel*
SS – *Orlando Star-Sentinel*
SPT – *St. Petersburg Times*
TT – *Tampa Tribune*
WSJ – *Wall Street Journal*
Building -- *Building a Company: Roy O. Disney & the Creation of an Entertainment Empire* (Hyperion, 1998) Bob Thomas
Married – *Married to the Mouse: Walt Disney World & Orlando* (Yale University Press, 2001) Richard E. Foglesong
Prizer – *Orlandoland (Orlando) Magazine* (11-70, 10-76, 10-81, 5-83, 10-96) Edward L. Prizer
Risk – *Risk, Ruin & Riches: Inside the World of Big-Time Real Estate* (MacMillan, 1986) Jim Powell
Walt – *Walt Disney: An American Original* (Simon & Schuster, 1976) Bob Thomas

Chapter 1

Page 13. *EPCOT Film:* Film Transcript
13. Conference: *OS* 2-3-67, *TT* 2-3-67

Chapter 2

17. Early history: *Walt, Building*
20. Fighting Wrather: *I* Hoelscher; In 1964, Disney began fighting against Sheraton's plans to build an 18- to 20-story hotel next to Disneyland. In 1966, the Anaheim city council finally turned down Sheraton's initial request, but allowed them to build a smaller hotel. Then, in 1967 the city passed an ordinance restricting building heights within eye-shot of the park.
20. Motel rooms: Hotel bureau estimates, *I* Lindquist, who recalled there being 3,000 motel rooms by 1957.
20. Celebrity Sports Center: *I* Allen, *I* Baker, 1976 brochure; Disney sold Celebrity Sports Center to private investors in 1979, and it closed about 15 years later. The facility was torn down in the late 1990s to

make room for a Home Depot.
21. Small World capacity: Fact sheet 64
22. Land search: *I* DeWolf, *I* Foster, *I* Price, *Prizer*; Roy also made several trips out to Florida in 1964, signing into hotels as "Roy Davis." For the most part, Walt stayed behind, for fear he would be recognized and blow everyone's cover.
23. Monorail: Walt personally pitched a monorail to Las Vegas in 1960; it took the Strip 35 years to take him up on the offer.
29. Live on property: *I* Smith, *Prizer*; The Smiths' bungalow was roughly on the site of where Disney would later build a conference center. The house was then relocated to use as an environmental laboratory. The airplane shed was used for years as a maintenance shed.
32. "Let him win": *I* DeWolf
33. Foster City: *I* Foster

Chapter 3

35. EPCOT the City: *Walt Disney & the Quest for Community* (Steve Mannheim, 2002), *EPCOT Film* Transcript, *SS* 10-10-82
39. Roy changes plans: *Building*
39. Villa Nova: *I* Smith
40. Conference: *OS* 2-3-67, *TT* 2-3-67
42. "No provision for the crown": *I* Foster
42. "Walt's gone": *E-Ticket* Spring 02
44. Hotel designs: *I* Curry, brochures
48. Early construction: *Prizer*; Although initially 19 flood control gates were installed, there are now at least 23 gates on property.
50. Convertible bonds: *I* Foster, *Building*
51. Early marketing: *I* Quinn
54. Jock's Corner: *I* Hoelscher, *I* Sparks; Jock's was also known as Johnny's Corner.
54. Preview Center: *I* Burner, *I* V. Curry, *I* Hoelscher, *I* Lindquist, *I* Quinn

Chapter 4

57. Two Mansions: *I* Baxter
57. Imported parts: *Pensacola Journal* 1-31-71
58. Monorail: *Prizer*
59. Cardone: *Today* 8-17-80; The Central Food Facility worked so well, a few years later it was expanded to 135,000 sq. ft. Still, they did occasionally run out of certain items and, in a pinch, managers would raid the Piggly Wiggly in Kissimmee.
60. Recruitment trips: *I* Hoelscher, *I* Vaughn
61. Tatum barks: *I* Sullivan
64. Potty fire: *I* Penfield
64. J.B. Allen ousted: *I* McDeed, *I* Moss, *I* Raschy, *I* Roland

65. Construction worker problems: *I* Carter, *I* Curry, *I* Roland
66. Western International: *I* Curry, *I* Dice
66. Hilton Inn South: *I* Curry, *I* Rosen, *I* Sullivan, *Married*; Hamilton later considered filing suit against Disney for taking advantage of the situation. In the end, he decided that action against the Big Cheese would do him more harm than good. His hotel ended up doing just fine, and that road he paved to his hotel became International Drive, a popular 15-mile strip of hotels, restaurants, and attractions.
68. Bay Hill cottages: *I* Allen, *I* Curry, *I* Hoelscher, *I* Roland
69. Modular construction: The rooms for the tower were 39'11" long plus balcony, the rooms for the garden annexes were 32'7" long. The factory had 26 separate assembly points within six separate areas—for (1) receiving structural tubular members, (2) two parallel assembly lines for floor and ceiling frames, (3) joining floor, ceiling and wall panels to form a room shell, (4) outfitting mechanical installations, (5) interior finishing, and (6) exterior finishing, waterproofing, inspection and cleanup.
70. Tempo Bay: *I* Curry
72. Nunis: *I* Eno, *I* Hoelscher, *I* Lindquist, *I* Nabbe, *I* Van Dyke, *MH* 9-20-82; Execs uniformly acknowledge that Nunis willed the park completed on time. Said Tom Nabbe: "There's no doubt in my mind that without him—daily out there marching the troops, refusing to take no for an answer, we'd still be waiting for those trams."
73. *Life* shoot: *OS* 4-10-88
74. Patton: The caricature was a gift from Jack Olsen, v.p. of merchandise.
74. Adventureland concrete pour: *I* Burner
74. Pajama party: *I* Allen, *I* Curry, *I* Mathieson
76. Campground delay: *I* Hoelscher, *I* Kambak
76. Castle dinner: *I* Baxter, *I* Burner, *I* Roland
77. H'ard: The co-worker was Hoelscher
77. Roland in charge: *I* Roland
79. Unfinished: *I* Sullivan, *I* Wooten
80. Hench, Labor Day, landscaping: *Prizer*
81. Debugging: *OS* 7-25-71
81. Subs: *I* Gurr
82. Trams: *I* Gurr, *I* Lindberg
83. Justice paint job: *I* Hoelscher
84. Green side up: *Prizer*, *I* Curry, who insists, "It was me, not Nunis, who said it first." Popular legend—and everyone else I spoke with—attribute the line to Nunis.

Chapter 5
85. Opening: *Prizer*
86. First family: *I* Lindquist, *MH* 12-8-82, *OS* 12-9-82 (EPCOT first family lawsuit)
88. Headline: *Mamaroneck Times* 10-2-71
89. *60 Minutes*: *I* Lindquist, *I* Ridgway

89. Sub delays: *I* Baxter, *I* Gurr, *OS* 10-14-71
90. Jungle repaint: *I* Baxter
90. Transportation issues: *I* Baker, *I* Gurr, *I* Hoelscher, *I* Kellogg, *I* Lindberg, *I* Nabbe, *I* Van Dyke
90. Keel boats: *Spotlight WDW* Summer 78
90. Osceola Class steamers: *I* Lindberg
92. New trams: *I* Baker, *I* Gurr, *I* Hoelscher, *I* Lindberg, *I* Van Dyke, *FFF* 3-17-72
93. Topiaries: *I* Baxter; As they began phasing out using the trams to the main gate, the topiary figures were moved to the road that led to the Contemporary and to create the edges of parking spaces.
93. Carousel anthem: *Florida* 12-81
93. Opening ceremonies, lost lunches: *I* Christensen, *ConnChord* 3-72; The "ketchup out of the train station" observation was made by Christensen's wife, Karen, while watching at home on TV.
94. Electrical water pageant: Original script 72
95. Roy sees TV, transfers power: *Building*
95. Golf: *OS* 4-10-88
96. Christmas crowds: *I* Sullivan, *OS* 12-27-71, *LL* 12-28-71
98. Food challenges, crepes: *I* Burner, *I* Pospisil, *I* Ziegler
100. Rush expansion: *Orlandoland* 1-72, *MH* 1-23-72, *Highlander* 1-30-72, *Milwaukee Journal* 1-30-72, *TT* 4-16-72, *LL* 10-22-72
100. Swan Boats: *I* Hoelscher, *I* Mathieson

Chapter 6
102. Runaway modular costs: *NYT Magazine* 10-22-72
103. Hotel buyout: *I* Curry, *I* Roland, *I* Smith, *Playboy* 74, *SPT* 1-11-72, *Building*
104. Off-site parking: *I* Dice
104. Luau: *I* Bloustein, *I* Burner, *I* Dice
105. Wave machine: *I* Curry, *I* Hoelscher, *I* Jones, *I* Pospisil, *I* Rosen, *Columbus Ledger-Enquirer* 7-3-71, *E&E* 11-71, *OS* 1-27-72; Years later, the Grand Floridian wedding chapel would be built on Nunis's Surfrider Beach.
105. Junk: *I* Curry, *I* Roland, *OS* 10-22-71; The Eastern Winds was built in Hong Kong at the Hip Hing Cheung shipyard in 1963. It deteriorated prematurely, however, after maintenance painted its teak decks, preventing the wood from breathing, and eventually had to be retired.
107. Contemporary overwhelmed, unique policies: *I* Curry, *I* Dice, *I* Kahn, *I* Rosen, *I* Ziegler, *Playboy* 74
109. Paint line to hotels: *I* Rosen
109. Ansul in kitchen: *I* Curry
109. Olsen: *I* Kahn, *I* Tangel
110. Toy rifles: *I* Busch
110. Poly shops: *I* Craig
110. Free shoeshine: *I* Tangel
111. Top of the World: The supper club

opened 2-13-72, with singer Gloria Loring, followed by the Four Freshmen, Tex Beneke, and the Modernaires. Headliners would stay up to two weeks.

112. Management changes: *I* Allen, *I* Curry, *I* Degelmann, *I* Dice, *I* Roland, *I* Rosen, *I* Sullivan, *OS* 11-19-72, *New Hampshire Sunday News* 5-16-76, *Playboy* 74

115. Refurb: *I* Degelmann

116. Motor Plaza: *I* Curry, *I* Foster, *I* Rosen

116. Dutch Inn: *MH* 2-14-77

Chapter 7

118. Maintenance: *Painting Contractor* 1-77, *Restaurants & Institutions* 10-1-81

118. Christmas tree: *I* Mathieson

119. Utilidors: *Miami News* 7-6-71, *MH* 11-8-81, *Florida Today* 9-29-81, *Popular Mechanics* 10-71, *Actual Specifying Engineer* 2-73

119. Vacuum tubes: *Popular Mechanics* 10-71

121. DACS: *E&E* 2-1-75

121. Energy: *I* Jones, *Adhesives Age* 9-1-90

122. "That's EPCOT": *Actual Specifying Engineer* 2-73

122. RCID: *OS* 1-12-87, 6-1-89, 2-24-91

123. Residents: *I* Jones, *I* Sparks, *OS* 1-12-87

123. Lake Buena Vista homes: *LL* 1-26-72, *OS* 11-19-72, *Disney News* Winter 73/74, *Bradenton Herald* 4-20-75

125. Arrive Alive: *FFF* 3-28-72, 4-6-72, 5-16-72, 5-31-72, 6-6-72, 6-22-72; *E&E* 5-27-72, 10-27-73; *Playboy* 74

126. STOLport: *I* Kahn, *I* Van Dyke, *FFF* 12-4-71, *E&E* 5-27-72, *OS* 11-19-72

127. Outside hotels: *Florida Trend* 6-77, *Prizer*, *Highlander* 1-16-74; Harris Rosen, terminated by Disney, bought a distressed hotel on International Drive for pennies on the dollar and opened the first of what would be a hotel empire.

128. Layoffs: *SS* 1-10-74, 1-11-74; *Variety* 1-16-74

128. Gas crisis effect: *I* Elrod, *I* Sullivan, *Washington Post* 11-18-73, *NY Sunday News* 12-23-73, *AB* 1-26-74, *SS* 2-12-74, *NYT* 2-24-74, *Osceola Sun* 4-24-74, *Prizer*

128. Rehire: *Wa. Post* 2-16-74

128. Slow recovery: *Today* 2-7-74

128. Gas reserves: *I* Roland

129. Solar building: *I* Jones, *Florida* 8-20-78

129. Nuclear plant: *I* Jones

130. Marketing: *I* Elrod, *I* Pontius, *Prizer*

130. Chase program: *I* Healy

131. Slow rebound: *Prizer*

Chapter 8

133. Safety: *National Safety News* 7-72

133. Disneyland accidents: *Mouse Tales*

134. Space Mt. history: *I* Hoelscher

134. Space Mt. loop: *I* McGinnis

135. Edna's test ride: *I* Baxter

136. Space troubles: *SPT* 3-6-75, 3-7-75; *OS* 4-25-75, 1-28-79, 6-23-84; *MH* 6-17-79

137. Raymond quotes: *Sarasota Herald-Tribune* 5-11-75

138. Falling objects: *SS* 1-5-81, *I* Madorin

139. Mansion conveyor: *OS* 5-11-83, 5-27-83

140. Boat dock bumps: *OS* 10-13-75, 12-29-02

140. Moulding: I Lee, *OS* 2-8-90

140. Splash death: *OCR* 11-6-00, *LAT* 11-6-00

140. Lawsuits: *American Lawyer* 3-83, *SPT* 3-22-87, *MH* (Hiassen article), *OS* 7-488

140. Bus vs. trash truck: *OS* 8-29-87, 2-7-90

140. Paralyzed: *OS* 10-23-82, 5-10-83; *MH* 5-11-83, *Oregonian* 5-11-83

141. Fall into canal: *SS* 7-30-81

142. Fall off tram: *OS* 7-20-90

142. Lady hit by tram: *OS* 8-30-85

142. Grand Prix suit: *OS* 1-26-87, *LAT* 2-3-00

142. Swimmer injury: *SS* 6-30-81, *OS* 2-10-83

142. Moat death: Goode suit, *OS* 12-23-82, 7-12-84, 3-8-85, 4-14-85, 12-5-86, 2-2-88

143. River Country drownings: *OS* 8-10-82, 8-11-82, 9-1-82, 12-19-84, 7-11-89, 8-3-89

144. Boat blast: *LL* 11-5-74, *OS* 11-5-74

145. Electrocution: Johnson death certificate

145. Falling beam death: *SS* 12-23-81

145. Anderson fatal fall: *OS* 6-8-82, 6-9-82

145. Typhoon burst pipe: *OS* 4-26-88

145. Dolphin fall: *OS* 8-15-89

146. MGM fall: *OS* 2-9-90

146. Miranda Skyway: *OS* 5-25-82, *I* Szulc

146. Barlow Skyway: *OCR* 2-15-99

146. Parade death: *OCR* 8-12-04

148. Monorail safety devices: *OS* 3-14-71, *Huntington Herald-Dispatch* 12-27-89

148. First monorail crash: *I* Gurr

148. Second monorail crash: *SS* 2-13-74, 2-14-74, 2-15-74, 3-5-74

149. Monorail rig crash: *Reuters* 8-30-91

149. Falling sign: *SS* 4-7-82, 4-8-82

150. Baby falls off tram: *OS* 7-14-82

150. Canal car crash: *OS* 1-15-86, 1-16-88

150. Sprite crash: *OS* 10-10-89, 2-25-90

150. Car crash: *OS* 7-15-90

150. Parking lot plane crash: *OS* 11-22-84, 11-23-84, 11-24-84, 11-28-84, 12-1-84

151. Plane crash: *Ultralight Flying* 9-87, 10-87

151. RCFD: *E&E* 10-13-73, *Fire News* 1-30-76, *I* Sparks

151. Pennington: Press release 8-31-72

152. Monorail fire: *I* Cullity, *I* Halpin, *OS* 6-27-85, 6-28-85, 7-4-85, 11-14-87, 6-23-89; *LaSalle News Tribune* 8-1-85

154. PeopleMover fire: *OS* 1-9-87, 1-10-87

154. Workshop fires: *OS* 12-21-89, 6-14-90

155. Deaths: (Space) *SS* 8-14-80, 8-15-80, 8-16-80, 8-19-80; *OS* 6-18-84, 6-20-84, 6-21-84, 6-22-84, 6-27-84; (Body Wars) *OCR* 5-18-95; (Mission: Space) *OCR* 6-18-05, *AP* 7-12-05; (MGM) *OCR* 6-30-06

155. Dorothy O'Connor: *I* Van Voorhis

Chapter 9
157. Haunted by painting: *Prizer*
157. Playboy controversy: *Playboy* 74
159. EPCOT announced: *Osceola Sun* 5-16-74, *Advertising News* 6-15-74
159. Early EPCOT plans: *SS* 6-17-74, 7-17-75; *Chicago Tribune* 5-16-74, *Plain Dealer* 7-16-75, *TT* 1-11-76, *Disney News* Spring 76, *AB* 3-77
160. Presentation: *Prizer*
162. Disneyland sponsors, national ad buys, Smucker's, Sara Lee, Roy's help: *I* Clark
164. Citrus board: *I* Clark, *TT* 3-6-83
165. Coke: *I* Clark, *I* Roland
166. International trips: *I* Baker, *I* Clark, *I* Lindquist, *I* Smith, *Prizer*
167. Trouble finding sponsors: *SS* 6-5-77
168. New York office, Washburn: *I* Clark
168. Cooper: *I* Gurr, *TT* 1-11-76
169. GM: *I* Clark, *I* Gurr, *SS* 1-29-78
170. Exxon signs: *SS* 1-27-78
171. Late 1970s plans: EPCOT Center booklets, *LL* 11-16-80; American Adventure was eventually trimmed back to two primary hosts to streamline the presentation and because of fears that too many guests wouldn't know who Will Rogers was.

Chapter 10
176. Stock: On 12-16-74, Disney's share price fell to $17.63, its lowest point since 1958.
177. Promotion, Tatum, Walker: *I* Roland
178. Gerstman, Wynn, Tishman, Poly expands: *I* Roland, *Risk*
179. Open at 9:02: *OS* 10-24-82
179. *USA Today* pulls out: *SS* 12-12-81
179. Costa Rica: *SS* 5-23-79
179. Proposed pavilions: EPCOT Center promotional booklets 78-82
179. Venezuela: *Sun-Tattler* 11-4-81
180. Prep package, timber: *I* Roland, *Risk*
181. Sinkholes: *Industry Week* 5-26-80, *Risk*
181. Dredge lagoon: *OS* 10-24-82, *Risk*
182. Imagination: *I* Baxter
183. Astuter, Horizons: *I* McGinnis
184. VIP lounges: *I* Baker, *I* Clark, *I* Pritchett
185. Germany boat ride: As a nod to the boat ride past miniature structures, Disney instead set up a miniature train outside, winding through a German countryside.
188. Tokyo: *I* Jones, *I* McCoy
190. Cough drop quote: *I* Degelmann
190. Bricks quote, Zovich: *Risk*
191. Monorail contract: *I* Roland, *Seattle Journal of Commerce* 5-24-80, *Risk*
191. Thrust blocks: *I* Roland, *Risk*
192. Prototypes difficult: *Industry* 5-26-80
192. Energy turntable: *Risk*
192. Revisions: *I* Roland, *OS* 10-24-82, *Risk*
193. Year out, emperor, curbs, concrete: *Risk*
194. Weather reports: *Risk*
194. Contractors, competitions: *I* Roland, *Risk*

195. Hench, landscaping: *Risk*
196. No Mickey: *I* Lindquist
197. Figment stuff: *Business Monday* 9-28-81
197. Norway glass vendor: *I* Busch
198. Be authentic: *I* Bloustein, *I* Busch, *I* Pritchett; The original open-air American Gardens stage featured acts from many countries not represented elsewhere in EPCOT, such as Greece and Spain.
200. Mexico maypole: *I* Busch, *I* Sullivan

Chapter 11
201. Recruiter quote: *OS* 6-13-71
202. Set costume sizes: *I* Hawk
203. U of D platitudes: "Destination... WDW" 72, "Your Role in the WDW Show" 75
203. Casting criteria: *SS* 5-3-69, 3-30-71, 6-13-71, 7-1-71; *Charlotte News* 1-20-72
204. Hire friendliness: *SPT* 5-5-86
204. Disney Look: *Today* 4-23-72, *Palm Beach Daily News* 4-29-73, *OS* 12-25-90, 6-29-94
206. Promote from within: *E&E* 5-27-72
206. Hall of Fame: *I* Jacobs
206. Working conditions: *Fort Lauderdale News* 6-1-80
207. Say What?: *Main Street/Adventureland News* 6-72, *Spotlight WDW* Summer 78
208. Space Mt. prank: *I* Kraftchick
210. Nose & Throat: *OS* 12-27-89
212. Characters: *Today* 11-2-75, 6-13-79; *Ottawa Citizen* 6-19-90
213. Drunk Mickey: *Hackensack Record* 6-20-85, *OS* 7-23-85, 9-25-86, 6-29-89
213. America on Parade: *Newsday* 11-16-75
214. Character controversy: *OS* 10-1-81, *TT* (*NYT* article) 10-2-81, *Virginian Pilot* (*Chicago Tribune* article) 10-18-81, *People* 10-25-81, *Sojourners* 11-81
216. Characters unionize: *OS* 8-19-82
217. Unions formed: *I* Passilla, *I* Vaughn
218. Union negotiations: *OS* 5-1-83, 5-2-83, 11-16-88, 12-18-88, 8-27-89; *Typographical Journal* 1-74; *Reuters* 11-12-88; *OCR* 11-17-88, 6-15-01
218. Musicians strike: *OS* 10-22-80, 10-28-80
219. Turnover: *Today* 4-25-72
220. Employee gas station: I Vaughn; The backstage gas station was closed after the energy crisis subsided, and later became the Vista Credit Union building.
221. College Program: *I* Wacker, Birnbaum Travel column 2-10-90, *Exploring* 3-89, www.wdwcollegeprogram.com
222. International Program: *I* Schwartz, *I* Wacker, *SS* 4-23-82, 9-2-82; *OS* 7-29-89, *Ottawa Citizen* 2-8-86, *Chronicles of Higher Education* 2-19-86; For Chinese students, Disney worked with the Chinese Embassy in Washington, D.C.

Chapter 12
229. Rush to finish: *OS* 9-26-82

229. Previews: *MH* 10-1-82
229. Projected operating hours: *E&E* 5-7-82; In announcing these hours, Disney stipulated that they were subject to change and, while World Showcase regularly opened two to three hours after Future World, it's unlikely that it ever opened as late as 2 p.m., since that would kill lunch business at the international restaurants.
230. Ride troubles: *Orlando Magazine* 1-83
230. EPCOT films: *I* Eades
232. Journey into Imagination: *I* Baxter, *Disney News* Winter 82/83
232. Ceremony: *E&E* 5-7-82, 10-1-82, *Prizer*
233. Day 1: *I* Baker, *OS* 10-2-82, *MH* 10-2-82, *TT* 1-2-82, *Fort Lauderdale News* 10-2-82
233. Mexico's electricity: *OS* 10-24-82
234. Feeder: *I* Hoelscher, *I* Sullivan, *I* Ziegler
234. First week: *OS* 10-3-82, 10-6-82, 10-10-82; *Stuart News* 10-6-82
237. Mine: *San Francisco Chronicle* 10-16-82
239. Crowd reaction: *MH* 10-3-82, *Prizer*
239. Cultural critics, minorities: *Next* 7-80
240. Land complaints: *OS* 11-10-82
241. "Where's Mickey?": *I* Eades
242. Astuter revue: *I* Eades, *I* McGinnis
242. ORI: *Colorado Springs Gazette Telegraph* 2-26-83
245. Construction claims: *I* Roland; Disney and Tishman quickly settled all construction suits, except for one filed by Morrison-Knudsen. Four years later, when Wells became president, he demanded that all loose ends be tied up. Morrison-Knudsen ended up agreeing to the deal Disney proposed four years earlier, plus interest.

Chapter 13
246. Local incentives: *OS* 10-83
247. Reorganization: *I* Baker, *I* Vaughan, *I* Ziegler, *OS* 1-28-84, Internal Memo
247. Changes: *Time* 4-25-88, *Storming the Magic Kingdom* (John Taylor, 1987)
252. Tishman hotel deal: *I* Roland
253. Bob Small: *I* Hamilton, *Hotel & Resort Industry* 6-89
253. Caribbean Beach: *I* Hamilton
254. Nov. restructuring: All departments were grouped under three v.p.s, Bob Mathieson for the two parks, Ed Moriarty for resorts, and Phil Smith for administration.
254. Tinker Bell: *I* Lindberg, *I* Sullivan, *Today* 8-2-85; Flying Tinker Bell didn't remain a "bootleg job" for long. Disney quickly legitimized the position.
255. 15th party: *I* Elrod, *I* Lindquist, *OS* 9-17-86, *Wa. Post* 10-6-86, *News-Sun* 10-16-86
256. Charette: *I* Price, *OBJ* 9-28-86
256. EPCOT is complete: *OBJ* 9-28-86

Chapter 14
259. Sea World: *I* M. Jacobs, *I* Mathieson

261. MGM creation: *Orlando Magazine* 5-89
261. MGM early plans: *Orlando Magazine* 8-85, *Montreal Gazette* 10-31-87
263. MGM vs. Universal: *Los Angeles Magazine* 8-88, *Chicago Tribune* 4-26-89, *WSJ* 4-27-89, *Wa. Post* 5-89, *Forbes* 9-18-89, *Variety* 12-19-88, *AB* 5-20-89, *Insight* 10-30-89; In early 1989, Cineplex-Odeon sold its 50% stake in Universal Studios Florida to Britain's Rank Organization for $150 million—a $58-million profit above what it had paid two years earlier.
263. Woody at the gate: *OS* 5-20-87, 5-22-87
264. Burbank fight: *Married, Los Angeles Magazine* 8-88
267. Pleasure Island plans: *Orlando Magazine* 9-86, *Calendar* 6-4-89
268. PI stabbing: *OS* 7-23-89
268. PI changes: *OS* 3-14-90, 4-13-90, 5-10-92, 7-16-90; *Newark Star Ledger* 3-18-90
270. Typhoon Lagoon: *OS* 6-12-89, *Surfing* 10-89, *Body Boarding* 10/11-89; Surfing and bodyboarding would be allowed for competitions and clinics.
270. MGM opening: *E&E* 4-27-89, *Pitt. Post Gazette* 5-3-89, *Sioux City Journal* 5-7-89
271. MGM flaws: *I* Halpin, *I* Moore, *Houston Post* 5-1-89, *OS* 7-20-89
271. Eastwood, Footlight Parade: *I* Halpin
272. VW fire: *I* Miller; Herbie, charred to its shell, was "repurposed" as a parade float.
273. Rush expansion: *OS* 8-1-89
274. Indy injuries: *OS* 7-8-89, 7-10-89, 9-17-89, 10-18-89, 12-14-89, 12-17-89, 3-1-90, 4-4-90; An even more serious accident occurred 2-15-03, when actor Kyle McDuffie playing Indiana Jones fell about 30 feet from a zipline and didn't move after hitting the pavement below. Crewmembers rushed to his side and set up a barrier so the audience couldn't see him. He was rushed to a local hospital by helicopter and treated for critical head and shoulder injuries.
275. Muppets deal: *OS* 8-29-89, 5-17-90, *Travel Agent* 6-11-90
275. Cease fire: *Travel Weekly* 6-28-90
275. USF final touches: *WSJ* 5-9-90
275. USF opening: *Chicago Sun-Times* 7-23-90, *OS* 7-1-90, *Birnbaum Travel* 7-13-90; When Universal Studios Florida opened 6-7-90, admission cost $29 per adult, as promised $2 less than Disney's $31.
276. Tower of Terror: *OS* 6-12-94

Chapter 15
278. Disney Decade: *OS* 1-15-90
279. Community involvement: *I* Morgan, "Good Neighbors" booklet 83
279. Mag-Lev: *Married, SPT* 5-1-89, *OS* 5-14-89, *Kissimmee News-Gazette* 10-5-89
280. Fight for impact fees: *Married, OS* 2-9-86
281. Nunis, Green: *OBJ* 4-14-95, *E&E* 10-1-91

281. Consultants: *I* Baker, *I* Craig, *I* Roland
281. Red Handkerchief: *I* Van Dyke
281. Hall of Fame: *I* G. Jacobs
283. AK early plans: *OS* 3-26-94, 3-29-94
284. Timeshare: *Rocky Mountain News* 1-1-95
285. All Stars: *OS* 8-16-93
285. Ice Gator: *I* Edwards; Disney had limited success with waterproof costumes in the summer of 1973 for a water skiing show on the Seven Seas Lagoon. In addition to stunt skiers and parasailers, the Wonderful World of Water's cast of 23 included Goofy and hippos in tutus. In 2002, WDW celebrated the "dog days of summer" with appearances by Pluto at Typhoon Lagoon and Goofy, in "patriotic swimwear," at Blizzard Beach. The characters interacted with guests at attractions, posed for photos, and occasionally jumped in the water.
286. Institute: *I* Korkis, *I* Snow
288. Celebration troubles: *NYT* 9-19-99
290. Magic Kingdom changes: *OS* 1-17-95, *Sioux City Journal* 4-16-95
290. Epcot changes: *OS* 1-3-94, 4-20-95, *WSJ* 3-14-94, *OCR* 6-24-94
293. Walker Ranch: *E&E* 1-7-93; Florida developers who built on wetlands were required to create miniature preserves near their projects to make up for what they were destroying. Disney argued that the requirement resulted in countless miniature wetlands too small to support any wildlife.
293. AK design: *Parade* 2-22-98, *Time* 4-20-98
294. Harden: *Cast Magazine* Summer 73
294. Conservation area: Tourists were kept out of the conservation area. "Serious students of nature," however, could arrange to take electric boats 1.5 miles down a creek that bordered the swamp for a closer look.
295. Wild pigs: *OS* 5-12-86, 7-25-86
296. Gator bite: *OS* 10-12-86, 1-22-88
296. Treasure Island: *Disney News* Spring 74
297. Discovery Island: *E&E* 11-13-81
297. Vultures: *OS* 9-21-89, 9-24-89, 1-6-90, 4-6-90, 7-11-90; *USA Today* 9-26-89, *WSJ* 1-8-90
298. Dolphin deaths: *Florida Trend* 5-86, *OS* 8-22-90
299. AK animal deaths: *OS* 4-12-98: Deaths became rarer once the animals became acclimated. During one thunderstorm that came upon the resort before animal handlers had a chance to move the animals indoors, lightning struck and killed a giraffe on the safari attraction.
299. USDA probe: *OS* 4-8-98, *LAT* 4-12-98
300. AK opens: *OS* 4-23-98; Opening day's final tally would be closer to 33,000. On the same day, one-day/one-park admissions rose to $42 for adults, $34 for kids, plus tax.
301. AK reviews: *OCR* 4-22-98

301. Countdown to Extinction: The ride was later renamed Dinosaur, to tie in with an animated movie of the same title.

Chapter 16
303. Low-key security: *OS* 5-7-73, *E&E* 4-20-74, *TT* 1-28-79
304. SOAP: *I* Carter, *I* Holland, *E&E* 10-24-91
306. Boys sue: *SS* 7-27-72, *TT* 1-28-79
306. Brawlers sue: *OS* 2-21-86, 1-29-90
307. Counterfeit ring: *SS* 9-14-74
307. Ticket frauds: *OS* 9-12-93
307. Stolen tickets: *OS* 3-13-85
308. Wells Fargo robbers: *OS* 3-24-90; The The guards were caught by linking $2,000 missing from the WDW Shopping Village to cash found in one suspect's vehicle.
308. Bomb: *Chicago Daily News* 2-4-72, *TT* 2-6-72, *MH* 5-5-72, *Miami News* 6-28-72, *Denver Post* 1-31-73
308. Bomb threats: *OS* 12-22-74, *Today* 12-22-74, 12-24-74
309. Grenade: *OS* 10-19-82, *Jacksonville Journal* 10-20-82
309. McCartney, first suicide: *TT* 1-28-79
309. Contemporary fall: *SS* 4-5-81; The 2002 suicide occurred the same night that the drunk Grand Floridian guest drowned in the Seven Seas Lagoon.
310. Shooting/suicide: *OS* 1-5-83
310. Bat man: *SS* 7-13-80
310. Robberies: *SS* 7-16-80, 1-3-81
310. Monorail robbery: *SS* 3-11-81
311. Armed robberies: *OS* 6-20-86, 6-24-86
311. Goofy hat robber: *OS* 12-6-89
311. Crazy stabber lady: *OS* 8-14-93
311. Abductions: *OS* 3-14-02
312. Rape: *OS* 6-21-90, 6-23-90
312. Scam: *OS* 11-17-92, 6-24-93, 10-6-93
314. Barricades: Installed in spring 2004, the $30,000 barricades were the same model used in front of the U.S. Embassy in Iraq.
314. Jungle plane: The airplane wreckage had been installed near the hippo pool when, in preparation for the opening of Animal Kingdom, management stopped skippers from shooting at hippos. The joke backstage became that hippos were responsible for downing a plane from the sky. The back half of the plane had been lying around since the opening of Disney-MGM, where its front half was used in the Great Movie Ride's *Casablanca* scene.

Chapter 17
316. MGM moves away from production: *I* Allen, *OS* 1-24-96, 9-29-96, 6-6-97
316. Feature Animation closes: *OS* 1-17-04
316. Disney sells Celebration: *OCR* 1-17-04
318. Hiring for MGM: *OS* 3-27-89
319. College Program complaints: *AP* 7-4-05
322. Ego trips: *I* Clark, *I* Ziegler

Index

Order Form

Quantity   Amount

_____   **Realityland: True-Life Adventures at Walt**
             Disney World (hardcover) @ $27.95   _____

_____   **Mouse Tales: A Behind-the-Ears Look at**
             Disneyland (softcover) @ $15.95   _____

             GOLDEN ANNIVERSARY SPECIAL EDITION:
             Mouse Tales: A Behind-the-Ears Look at
             Disneyland (Limited Edition hardcover with audio
             CD "A Walk in the Park: A Guided Tour of
_____   Disneyland in 1955") @ $35.95   _____

_____   **Mouse Under Glass: Secrets of Disney Anima-**
_____   **tion & Theme Parks** (hardcover) @ $23.95   _____
             (softcover) @ $15.95   _____

_____   **More Mouse Tales: A Closer Peek Backstage at**
_____   **Disneyland** (hardcover) @ $24.95   _____
             (softcover) @ $15.95   _____

                                   Total for book(s)   _____
     Postage: Add $2 for first book, $1 for each additional   _____
     Sales Tax: **California residents** add 7.75% tax   _____

                       Amount enclosed (U.S. funds)   _____

Ship Book(s) to:

_____

_____

_____

_____

IF THIS IS A LIBRARY COPY,
PLEASE PHOTOCOPY THIS PAGE

BONAVENTURE PRESS

P.O. Box 51961
Irvine, Ca. 92619-1961
www.bonaventurepress.com